Teaching God's Sons and Daughters

Essays in Honor of
Allen Black

GlossaHouse Festschrift Series 5
GFS 5

Teaching God's Sons and Daughters

Essays in Honor of Allen Black

Editors
Garrett E. Best
Lance R. Hawley

Teaching God's Sons and Daughters
Essays in Honor of Allen Black

© GlossaHouse, LLC 2025

All rights reserved. No part of this book may be reproduced or transmitted in any form or by any means, electronic or mechanical, including photocopying or recording, or by means of any information storage or retrieval system, except as may be expressly permitted by the 1976 Copyright Act or in writing from the publisher. Requests for permission should be addressed in writing to the following:

GlossaHouse, LLC
110 Callis Circle
Wilmore, KY 40309
www.GlossaHouse.com

Teaching God's Sons and Daughters
Essays in Honor of Allen Black
Edited by Garrett E. Best and Lance R. Hawley

    5 — (GlossaHouse Festschrift Series; Ref.)
    Includes bibliographical references.

    ISBN: 978-1-63663-129-5 (pb)
                  978-1-63663-130-1 (hb)

1. Bible. Old Testament—Criticism, interpretation, etc. 2. Bible. New Testament—Criticism, interpretation, etc. 3. Allen Black.

The fonts used to create this work are available from: www.linguistsoftware.com/lgku.htm

Cover design by T. Michael Halcomb

Text layout and interior book design by Andrew J. Coutras

Indices prepared by Andrew J. Coutras

GLOSSAHOUSE FESTSCHRIFT SERIES

The purpose of the *GLOSSAHOUSE FESTSCHRIFT SERIES* is to honor mentors, colleagues, friends, and leading experts in the scholarly community while advancing research in the areas of ancient and modern languages, contexts, texts, and hermeneutics.

SERIES EDITORS
Fredrick J. Long

T. Michael W. Halcomb

VOLUME EDITOR
Andrew J. Coutras

Contents

Contributors ix

Abbreviations x

Introduction
Garrett Best and Lance Hawley 1

The Gospel Before the Gospels
D. Clint Burnett 9

Meaningfully Misunderstanding the Markan Messiah: Ironic Intercalations in the Second Gospel
Kevin B. Burr 27

"We Know You Are True and Teach the Way of God Truthfully" (Matt 22:16): Reading the Hebrew Bible with Jesus in Matthew 22
Paavo N. Tucker 41

The Gospel of Luke and His Portrayal of Women
Alicia Williamson and Carl Williamson 53

"Not even in Israel": The Centurion's Servant and the Dynamics of Faith in the Gospel of Luke
Gregory Stevenson 65

"We Gave Up All Hope of Being Saved" (Acts 27:20): What Does Luke's Shipwreck Narrative Teach about God's Providence?
George Goldman II 79

The Restoration of Israel, the Kingdom of God, and the Church in Luke-Acts
Mark C. Black 89

Here Is Your King! The Characterization of Jesus in John 18–19
Jesse Robertson 107

An Exegesis of 1 Peter 5:8–9 with an African Reading and Application
Ananias Moses 121

Living as an Exile with an Unbelieving Husband (1 Peter 3:1–7)
John Mark Hicks 135

Adornment in Context: Illuminating the Passages on Womanhood in 1 Timothy
Anessa Westbrook 149

Justification by Faith (and Works)?
Barry Blackburn 163

"As Long as the Heavens are Above the Earth": Children in Deuteronomy
Harold Shank 181

Genesis 1 as Pedagogy
Nathan Bills 193

The Imagery of Níkē (Victory), Animal Sacrifice, and Incense Offering on an Ephesian Altar: An Ephesian Altar with Two Níkai at Sacrifice
Richard E. Oster, Jr. 203

Bibliography and Indices 223

    Bibliography 225

    Author Index 247

    Subject Index 254

CONTRIBUTORS

Garrett Best, Ph.D., is Chair of the Department of Bible and Ministry at York University in York, NE.

Nathan Bills, Th.D., is Dean of the School of Humanities and Social Sciences at Heritage Christian University in Accra, Ghana.

Mark Black, Ph.D., is retired Professor of New Testament at Hazelip School of Theology, Lipscomb University, in Nashville, TN.

Barry Blackburn, Ph.D., is Emeritus Professor of New Testament at Point University in West Point, GA.

D. Clint Burnett, Ph.D., is a Visiting Scholar at Boston College in Chestnut Hill, MA.

Kevin B. Burr, Ph.D., is Assistant Professor of Bible and Ministry at Harding University in Searcy, AR.

George Goldman II, Ph.D., is Professor of New Testament and Greek at Lipscomb University in Nashville, TN.

Lance Hawley, Ph.D., is Associate Professor of Old Testament at Harding School of Theology in Searcy, AR.

John Mark Hicks, Ph.D., is retired Professor of Theology from the Hazelip School of Theology at Lipscomb University in Nashville, TN.

Ananias Moses, MDiv, is a minister at Oodi Church of Christ in Oodi, Botswana.

Richard Oster, Ph.D., is Professor of New Testament, Emeritus, at Harding University in Searcy, AR.

Jesse Robertson, Ph.D., is Associate Dean of the College of Bible and Ministry at Harding University in Searcy, AR.

Harold Shank, Ph.D., is the Executive Director of Global Christian Studies and National Spokesperson for Network 1:27.

Gregory Stevenson, Ph.D., is Professor of Bible and Ministry at York University in York, NE.

Paavo Tucker, Ph.D., is an adjunct instructor for Lipscomb Hazelip School of Theology, ACU Graduate School of Theology, and Global Awakening Theological Seminary

Anessa Westbrook, D.Min., is Co-Executive Director of the Center for Ministry at York University in York, NE.

Alicia Williamson, MA, MACM, is an Instructor for the College of Bible and Ministry at Harding University in Searcy, AR.

Carl Williamson, DMin, is the Andy T. Richie Jr. Distinguished Chair for Discipleship and Church Planting at Harding University in Searcy, AR.

ABBREVIATIONS

AB	Anchor Bible
ABD	*Anchor Bible Dictionary*. Edited by David Noel Freedman. 6 vols. New York: Doubleday, 1992
ABRL	Anchor Bible Reference Library
AUSS	*Andrews University Seminary Studies*
AYB	Anchor Yale Bible
BDAG	Danker, Frederick W. Walter Bauer, William F. Arndt, and F. Wilbur Gingrich. *Greek-English Lexicon of the New Testament and Other Early Christian Literature*. 3rd ed. Chicago: University of Chicago Press, 2000 (Danker-Bauer-Arndt-Gingrich)
BECNT	Baker Exegetical Commentary on the New Testament
BHGNT	Baylor Handbook on the Greek New Testament
BNP	Brill's New Pauly
BNTC	Black's New Testament Commentaries
BTB	*Biblical Theology Bulletin*
BZNW	Beihefte zur Zeitschrift für die neutestamentliche Wissenschaft
CBQ	*Catholic Biblical Quarterly*
CurBR	*Currents in Biblical Research*
DJG	*Dictionary of Jesus and the Gospels*. Edited by Joel B. Green, Jeannine K. Brown, and Nicholas Perrin. 2nd ed. Downers Grove: Intervarsity, 2013
DNTB	*Dictionary of New Testament Background*. Edited by Craig A. Evans and Stanley E. Porter. Downers Grove: Intervarsity Press, 2000
DPL	*Dictionary of Paul and His Letters*. Edited by Gerald F. Hawthorne and Ralph P. Martin. Downers Grove: InterVarsity, 1993
HvTSt	*Hervormde teologiese studies*
HTR	Harvard Theological Review
IBC	Interpretation: A Bible Commentary for Teaching and Preaching
ICC	International Critical Commentary
IG	*Inscriptiones Graecae. Editio Minor*. Berlin: de Gruyter, 1924-
IRT	Issues in Religion and Theology
JBL	*Journal of Biblical Literature*
JETS	*Journal of Evangelical Theological Society*
JRS	*Journal of Roman Studies*
JSNT	*Journal for the Study of the New Testament*
JSOT	*Journal for the Study of the Old Testament*
LCL	Loeb Classic Library

LIMC	*Lexicon Iconographicum Mythologiae Classicae.* Zürich: Artemis Verlag, 1992.
LNTS	Library of New Testament Studies
Neot	*Neotestamentica*
New Docs	*New Documents Illustrating Early Christianity.* Edited by Greg H. R. Horsley and Stephen Llewelyn. North Ryde, NSW: The Ancient History Documentary Research Centre, Macquarie University, 1981-
NIB	*New Interpreters Bible*
NICGT	New International Commentary on the Greek Testament
NICNT	New International Commentary on the New Testament
NICOT	New International Commentary on the Old Testament
NIGTC	New International Greek Testament Commentary
NovT	*Novum Testamentum*
NovTSup	Supplements to Novum Testamentum
NTL	New Testament Library
NTS	*New Testament Studies*
OCM	Oxford Classical Monographs
OGIS	*Orientis Graeci Inscriptiones Selectae.* Edited by Wilhelm Dittenberger. 2 vols. Leipzig: Hirzel, 1903-1905
ResQ	*Restoration Quarterly*
SBLMS	Society of Biblical Literature Monograph Series
SEG	Supplementum epigraphicum graecum
SHBC	Smyth & Helwys Bible Commentary
SIG	*Sylloge Inscriptionum Graecarum.* Edited by Wilhelm Dittenberger. 4 vols. 3rd ed. Leipzig: Hirzel, 1915–24
SJOT	*Scandinavian Journal of the Old Testament*
SNTSMS	Society for New Testament Studies Monograph Series
SP	Sacra Pagina
TDNT	*Theological Dictionary of the New Testament.* Edited by Gerhard Kittel and Gerhard Friedrich. Translated by Geoffrey W. Bromiley. 10 vols. Grand Rapids: Eerdmans, 1964–1976
ThTo	*Theology Today*
TynBul	*Tyndale Bulletin*
UF	*Ugarit-Forschungen*
VT	*Vetus Testamentum*
WAW	Writings from the Ancient World
WBC	Word Biblical Commentary
WUNT	Wissenschaftliche Untersuchungen zum Neuen Testament

Introduction

Garrett Best and Lance Hawley

"A disciple is not above the teacher, but every disciple who is fully qualified will be like the teacher."
Luke 6:40

"Let us then adapt ourselves to our pupils with a love which is at once the love of a brother or a sister or a father or a mother. When once we are linked to them in heart, the old familiar things will seem new to us. So great is the influence of the sympathetic mind that, when our students are affected by us as we speak and we by them as they learn, we dwell in each other and then thus both they, as it were, speak within us what they hear, while we after a fashion learn in them what we teach."
Augustine, *On Catechizing the Uninstructed* 12,17

THE LIFE OF ALLEN BLACK

Personal Life

Robert Allen Black, Jr. was born on September 23, 1951, in Summerville, GA. Allen is the son of Robert Allen and Peggy Black. He is the oldest of two other siblings, Mark and Ginny (Black) Hornsby. Until 1963, the family lived in Rossville, Columbus, and Rome, GA. In 1963, they moved to Birmingham, AL, where Allen graduated from Berry High School in 1969. That same year, his family moved to Atlanta, GA.

Allen attended Freed-Hardeman College in 1969. Although it was a two-year school, Allen stayed a third year to participate in a new three-year program for Bible majors and graduated in 1972. While at Freed-Hardeman, he helped start the social club Theta Tau, but more importantly, he met Nancy Owens during those years. Because Freed-Hardeman was a junior college at the time, they both transferred to Harding College in 1972. Allen married Nancy on December 28, 1973. During their more than 50 years of marriage, they have lived in Searcy, AR, Missouri, Atlanta, GA, Memphis, TN, and currently reside in Smyrna, TN. They have two daughters, Stacey Stewart (Cameron) and Amy Thomas (Eric). Between the two daughters, Allen and Nancy have four grandchildren (Greysyn, Hayden, Kinely, and Ava). His family celebrates him as a loving husband, father, and grandfather.

Allen is also known for having several hobbies. He has always enjoyed music, and when he was around 16 years old, he was the keyboardist in a rock band. His love of music has extended into the rest of his life and one of his favorite things is attending concerts. His love of travel has taken him (and sometimes Nancy) to France, England, Italy, Hawaii, Honduras, Israel, Turkey, and Greece. He enjoys watching documentaries, reading books, and writing. Much of his life is spent with family, going on vacations, attending events for his grandkids, spending time with friends, and supporting the Auburn Tigers.

Education and Academic Life

Allen graduated with a B.A. in Bible and English Literature in 1974 from Harding College. He went on to earn his M.Th. at the Harding University Graduate School of Religion (now Harding School of Theology) in 1980. From 1980–1985, Allen pursued his PhD in New Testament at Emory University where he worked with Carl Holladay and completed his dissertation entitled, "The Conversion Stories in the Acts of the Apostles: A Study of their Forms and Functions."

Allen taught the New Testament and Greek at Harding University Graduate School of Religion (renamed Harding School of Theology in 2011) from 1983–2024. He served as dean from July 2015 to July 2021. As a teacher, it is difficult to sum up the immense influence that Allen had on the theological formation of his students and their ministries. He bridged the gap between biblical scholarship and holy living (1 Peter) so well. He became known among his students and colleagues as "everyone's favorite professor," because of his outstanding pedagogical skill, his approachableness, and his interest in student success. Students knew for certain that he cared for them and their spiritual health. One of Allen's strengths was keeping up with the field of New Testament studies and integrating it into his courses. He stayed current, which is a significant factor in him remaining a student favorite to the conclusion of his teaching career. Allen's interest in contemporary social trends and ability to bridge the gap between ancient and modern contexts was on display in all of his classes. His courses ranged from Greek, Advanced Introduction to the New Testament, Exegesis, Gospels, and Family Issues in the New Testament. His care for the church charted the course for the focus of his teaching.

In his role as dean of HST, Allen led the faculty through consensus building and prayerful discernment. He shepherded the school in a time of rapid technological change. For a little while, HST was on the cutting edge, implementing live streaming into the classroom through Zoom. Allen led the faculty in expanding hybrid learning (HST LIVE, 2017) to almost all of the curriculum. Without this change, it is hard to imagine that the school would have endured the age of online learning. The paradigm change precipitated the massive expansion of HST's reach throughout the globe, a feature that Allen celebrated and promoted throughout his tenure as dean.

Allen was a regular participant at the Society of Biblical Literature meetings. Most notably, he organized and led the Church of Christ Professors worship gathering at SBL 2015–2021, a group that Allen thought of as his second church. Allen wrote two commentaries in the College Press series. The first was on the Gospel of Mark, and the second was co-authored with Mark Black on 1–2 Peter. He also wrote several articles and published lectures, most of which focus on the Gospels and ecclesiological concerns. His curriculum vitae lists an impressive number of presentations made for gatherings of church leaders all over the world. His influence among Churches of Christ and work with churches navigating contemporary social issues is especially noteworthy. It is largely on account of his reputation for outstanding and influential teaching and service to the church that he was awarded the Distinguished Teacher Award from Harding University in 2000 and the Distinguished Christian Service Award from Pepperdine University in 2009.

Ministry

While at Freed-Hardeman, Allen preached for the Church of Christ in Wildersville, TN. While living in Memphis from 1975–1977, Allen and Nancy were members of the Park Avenue Church of Christ. From 1977–1983, Allen preached for the Moreland Avenue Church of Christ in Atlanta. From 1987–2024, Allen was on staff at the Highland Church of Christ in Memphis, TN, as education minister. In 1991, Allen and his friend Jay Shappley, began a Sunday morning Bible class called the Hope class, which met every Sunday morning until January 2025, when the Blacks moved to Smyrna, TN.

Through the years, Allen has gone overseas to teach and preach in Kenya, Japan, Germany (8 times), Switzerland, Argentina, Honduras, Canada, Mexico, and the Netherlands. He is not afraid to help churches address difficult topics. He has been and still is a go-to resource and invited speaker among church leaders for navigating pressing issues of gender and sexual ethics.

FROM THE EDITORS

I (Garrett) was an MDiv student at Harding School of Theology from 2010–14, where I was blessed to have Allen for multiple classes. I still have trouble referring to him as "Allen" because he has always been the respected "Dr. Black" to me. I attribute much of my passion for exegesis, Greek, and the Gospels to his influence. In all his courses, he combined a mastery of the scholarly literature and biblical text with pastoral sensitivity and love for students. He was kind, patient, and humble, and he exhibited a passion for studying Scripture. Truly, he was a master teacher.

My time at HST was a major transition period in my life and faith, and as I discerned the kind of life that God was calling me to pursue, Allen provided a model for me to imitate. I recently taught a course at York University introducing the New Testament to Bible and Ministry majors. Teaching a course covering the same material that he taught me was a reminder of the influence he has had on my understanding of Scripture. As a professor, he was always honest with the data in his interpretations, but he modeled how to interpret Scripture to deepen one's faith and serve the church.

In the years after graduating from HST, Allen became a mentor and, even more importantly, a friend, supporting me throughout my PhD program and serving as a trusted voice for me as an early-career scholar. I cannot overstate the impact that Allen has had on my life, ministry, and scholarship. I am honored to participate in this volume to honor him. I join the many alumni who owe a great deal of gratitude for the ways he invested in us inside and outside the classroom.

I (Lance) studied at HST 1999–2003 and had Allen for courses in Greek, Exegesis, Hebrews, and Synoptic Gospels. He was a model teacher, exhibiting thorough command of the subject matter, maintaining high standards for his students, and creating a learning environment that invited participation and collaboration. He always showed such respect for students and had an unpretentious demeanor that put students at ease. His pastoral sensibilities went well beyond the classroom. For example, when I had my first child, he visited my wife and I in the hospital. I was shocked and so honored, but this kind of care was normal for Allen.

Not long after arriving on HST's campus in Memphis, I was offered the opportunity to work as Allen's graduate assistant, a position I was blessed to have for all four years of my MDiv studies. Allen quickly became my mentor in scholarship and faith. I have fond memories of sitting with him in his office discussing our work together, which in hindsight was more for my benefit than his. He gave me early opportunities to help teach Greek and run research projects. One of the projects was to find and make a list of all of the biblical prayers, which took me down some life-shaping paths. Allen was a mentor in prayer when we met in his office and in the classroom. He is a person of deep moral conviction and character. What a blessing to have had Allen as my teacher!

Twelve years later, I found myself as Allen's colleague, taking a teaching position at the same time that Allen became dean of HST. He led HST with the same skill and care with which he taught, including navigating the move into the world of online education and shepherding the school through the COVID-19 pandemic. Allen is a consensus builder and fostered unity among the faculty. I attribute much of my own approach to teaching and the work of HST to his leadership. He is an encourager and a wise counselor. Allen would say that graduation day was his favorite day of the academic calendar, not so much because it was the end of the semester, but because he enjoyed rejoicing with our graduates. He loved his students sincerely. To have witnessed his career with HST is to have seen the faithful work of God among us, and Allen's influence will no doubt endure by the grace of God through his students and their ministries. I am blessed to take part in this project to honor Allen, my teacher and friend.

ABOUT THIS VOLUME

One of Allen's most important scholarly contributions was an essay entitled, "'Your Sons and Your Daughters Will Prophesy . . .' Pairings of Men and Women in Luke-

Acts."[1] There, Allen persuasively demonstrated that Luke was profoundly influenced by passages in Isaiah (for example, 43:6–7; 49:22; 60:4) that Israel's future blessings would flow to both sons and daughters. This emphasis motivated the author to include male-female pairings throughout the two-volume work to illustrate the fulfillment of God's blessings to Israel, which had indeed occurred through the life, death, and resurrection of Jesus Christ, which were poured out on Pentecost. Following this theme in Allen's academic work, the volume is entitled *Teaching God's Sons and Daughters: Essays in Honor of Allen Black*. Many of Allen's friends, colleagues, former students, and his brother Mark were invited to contribute essays in honor of Allen. The essays in the volume honor Allen's legacy by making scholarly contributions in these essays while also demonstrating pastoral sensitivity. We are also grateful to Allen's daughters and family members for sharing biographical information about Allen's life.

In chapter one, D. Clint Burnett examines Paul's letters to reconstruct the earliest proclaimed gospel of Jesus the Messiah, highlighting its divine origin, apocalyptic nature, fulfillment of God's promises to Israel, and Paul's special role as herald to the Gentiles. Burnett contrasts Paul's gospel presentation with shallow forms in modern evangelical preaching. In chapter two, Kevin Burr shows how in the Gospel of Mark, irony plays a key role in revealing deeper theological meanings, particularly through the technique of intercalation, where two stories are interwoven to emphasize themes like the nature of God's family, Jesus's power over death and disease, and the disciples' need for vigilance in their faith. In chapter three, Paavo Tucker explores how Jesus's interpretation of the Hebrew Scriptures in Matthew 22 challenges the contemporary church to read the Bible with an enchanted, Trinitarian worldview with the Great Tradition which leads to loving God and neighbor. Tucker argues that Jesus provides a hermeneutical model for interpreting Scripture today that integrates theology, emotion, and action. In chapter four, Alicia and Carl Williamson highlight the significant role of women in Luke's Gospel as active disciples who follow Jesus, are transformed by Him, and engage in spreading the gospel. The authors argue that women today can draw inspiration from their example to actively participate in evangelism and ministry while embodying faithful discipleship. In chapter five, Greg Stevenson analyzes Luke 7:1–10 through the lens of civic benefaction to show that the centurion's actions demonstrate the upside-down nature of the kingdom of God, the last shall be first and the first shall be last. The centurion embodies the kingdom's values of humility and selflessness, and he becomes the exemplar over religious insiders.

In chapter six, George Goldman studies how God's providence, human decisions, divine guidance, and natural events interact together in Paul's travel narrative in Acts 27 to fulfill God's purposes. Goldman emphasizes that God's purposes in the world are not always found in the spectacular but often unfold through natural processes and

---

[1] *Scripture and Traditions: Essays on Early Judaism and Christianity in Honour of Carl R. Holladay*, ed. Patrick Gray and Gail R. O'Day (Leiden: Brill, 2008), 193–206.

human decisions. In chapter seven, Mark Black argues that Luke and Acts demonstrate that Jesus, the Davidic Messiah, came to restore ethnic Israel to its promised identity. The early church understood itself to be the faithful remnant of Israel, into which gentiles entered through the Messiah. Black traces several eschatological expectations that appear in the Hebrew Scriptures and are embodied in the ministry of Jesus and the early church in Luke-Acts. In chapter eight, Jesse Robertson uses rhetorical analysis of the Fourth Gospel to demonstrate how Jesus's crucifixion, though outwardly a symbol of shame and suffering, is reframed as the ultimate display of his divine kingship and glory. He shows that the author draws on the audience's familiarity with passages from the Hebrew Bible, especially the figure of David, to depict Jesus as the King who loves, suffers, dies, and is resurrected for the salvation of all. In chapter nine, Ananias Moses presents an exegesis of 1 Peter 5:8–9, which encourages believers to rely on God's grace and the Christian community to withstand persecution and spiritual dangers. Throughout the essay, Moses applies the insights gained from the text to his African context. In chapter ten, John Mark Hicks posits that the recipients of 1 Peter were socially marginalized, and the author advocates for a missional, peaceful engagement with oppressive social structures, urging wives, slaves, and imperial subjects, to submit in a way that witnesses to Christ without endorsing or promoting injustice. The exhortations of the book avoid the extremes of rebellion and compliance with patriarchy.

In chapter eleven, Anessa Westbrook explores Paul's instructions to women in 1 Timothy 2 within the cultural, religious, and social context of Ephesus, arguing that Paul's directives on adornment, childbearing, submission, and teaching were targeted responses to false teachings and cultural confusion in the Ephesian church. In chapter twelve, Barry Blackburn argues that both faith and works are essential for final salvation and demonstrates how the Stone-Campbell Movement rightly resisted the "faith alone" doctrine in favor of a fuller biblical approach to justification. In chapter thirteen, Harold Shank shows how the book of Deuteronomy emphasizes the importance of children in the faith community, highlighting their teachability, spiritual capacity, and vulnerability. Shank argues that Deuteronomy presents a vision of a just society where children are protected through God's law, grace, and care for the vulnerable, including orphans and the oppressed. In chapter fourteen, Nathan Bills illustrates how Genesis 1 can serve as a model for Christian pedagogy by envisioning God's act of creation as a form of "homemaking." Focusing on the divine characters of God in the creation narrative, Bills recommends that educators reflect these qualities–delegating authority, fostering community, and promoting beauty and rest–in their teaching practices. In the final chapter, Richard Oster explores the symbolic role that the goddess of victory Níkē played in ancient Greco-Roman art and religion as the representation of divine assurance of success in both military and religious endeavors. Oster shows how this symbolism is taken up in the New Testament, where concepts like wreaths and palm fronds, often associated with Níkē, were part of the iconographic world of the audiences. The essay recommends that scholars in biblical studies make use of Greco-Roman visual materials to enhance our understanding of the New Testament.

1
The Gospel Before the Gospels

D. Clint Burnett

INTRODUCTION

One of the most informative courses of my graduate work was Prof. Allen Black's "Seminar in the Synoptic Gospels." This class convinced me of the validity of the so-called Two Source Hypothesis, which is a theory that explains the literary relationship among the Gospels of Matthew, Mark, and Luke by positing that the authors of Matthew and Luke used Mark and a no-longer-extant written collection of sayings of Jesus known as Q—the abbreviation of the German word *Quelle*, which means "source"—independently of each other to compose their respective works.[2] Moreover, Prof. Black demonstrated the benefits of redaction criticism—how the authors of Matthew and Luke used, edited, and redacted Mark—for illuminating the background, theology, and various themes of each of these so-called Synoptic Gospels.[3] For Prof. Black's years of teaching the Gospels in the academy and proclaiming the gospel in word and deed in his life and ministry, I wish to honor him in this essay by examining the earliest re-constructable gospel of the Christian movement. In the process, I shall divide this essay into three parts. The first, "Locating the Earliest Re-constructable Gospel," discusses methodological issues associated with this inquiry and the most appropriate sources for the task at hand, Paul's letters. The second part, "The Components of the Earliest Re-constructable Gospel," unpacks the various components of this gospel, which consists of: (1) its divine origin, (2) its apocalyptic nature, (3) a concise narrative of the Messiah event, (4) its eschatological focus, (5) its fulfilling of God's promises to Israel in Scripture, and (6) the proclamation of the gospel to the gentiles. Finally, in the "Conclusion," I summarize my findings.

LOCATING THE EARLIEST RE-CONSTRUCTABLE GOSPEL

Because our modern NT begins with the Gospels—Matthew, Mark, Luke, and John—and a theological history of the earliest church, the Acts of the Apostles, this essay's inquiry seems easy to answer. We can read these aforementioned works closely and

---

[2] Throughout this essay, gospel with a lowercase "g" refers to a proclamation, while Gospel with a capital "G" refers to the written, canonical Gospels, Matthew, Mark, Luke, and John, to which I refer by their traditional names.

[3] The first article I published on NT studies began as a term paper for Prof. Black's course: D. Clint Burnett, "Eschatological Prophet of Restoration: Luke's Theological Portrait of John the Baptist in Luke 3:1–6," *Neot* 47 (2013): 1–24.

reconstruct the gospel that Jesus and the earliest Christians proclaimed. There are, however, three difficulties with such a straightforward use of the Gospels and Acts. First, the authors of these documents composed them sometime after the Messiah event, that is, the incarnation, life, death, resurrection/ascension of Jesus, and his commissioning of his disciples to herald the gospel to the ends of the earth.[4] Today, scholars debate how much time elapsed between Jesus's earthly ministry and the composition of the Gospels and Acts. Even if one grants the earliest possible dating of Matthew through Acts (between AD 42 and 70), almost a decade stands between the Messiah event and the composition of the first canonical Gospel, Mark.[5] If one follows the scholarly consensus about the dating of Mark and places its composition in the late AD 60s to early 70s, then more than three decades elapsed between Jesus's earthly ministry and the Gospel in question.[6] During this ten to thirty-year period, the continued preaching of the gospel probably resulted in its refinement and development, which may have included the addition of content or, at least, a better grasp of the significance of Jesus's earthly (and heavenly) ministry for the Church and the world.[7]

Second, it is unclear if the Gospels were known as such in the first century AD. Matthew and Luke, who probably used Mark to compose their works, call their Gospels a "book" (βίβλος; Matt 1:1) and "narrative" (διήγησις; Luke 1:1), respectively.[8] If Luke considered Mark one of "the many" narratives that existed when he composed his Gospel (Luke 1:1–4), then it seems that for the author of the third Gospel, Mark is not a Gospel but a διήγησις. It is true that Mark begins his Gospel with the phrase "the

---

[4] Matt 28:18–20; Luke 24:44–53; Acts 1:8.

[5] Most scholars agree that Mark is our first canonical Gospel because it appears that Matthew and Luke used Mark to compose their works. For a recent, thoughtful redating of the NT documents, which places the composition of the Gospels and Acts between AD 42 and 70, see Jonathan Bernier, *Rethinking the Dates of the New Testament: The Evidence for Early Composition* (Grand Rapids: Baker Academic, 2022), 35–84. For an older, but still important early dating of the Gospels and Acts, which places their composition between AD 45 and 65, see John A. T. Robinson, *Redating the New Testament* (Philadelphia: Westminster, 1976), 86–117.

[6] For more widely accepted dating of the NT documents, see Raymond E. Brown, *An Introduction to the New Testament*, The Abridged Edition (New Haven: Yale University, 2016), 44–57; Mark Allan Powell, *Introducing the New Testament: A Historical, Literary, and Theological Survey*, 2nd ed. (Grand Rapids: Baker Academic, 2018), 140–60.

[7] For the idea that the passing of time increases one's understanding of the significance of a historical event, see John Lukacs, *A Student's Guide to the Study of History* (Wilmington: ISI Books, 2000). This development is certainly evident in the history of Christianity with the formation of the classical doctrine of the Trinity and Chalcedonian Christology, which occurred only after much reflection and heated debate on the meaning of the Messiah event and the interpretation of Scripture. For more information, see Justo L. Gonzalez, *A History of Christian Thought in One Volume* (Nashville: Abingdon, 2014).

[8] All translations are my own unless otherwise noted and my translations of the NT are based on *Novum Testamentum Graecae*, 28th Rev. ed., ed. Barbara and Kurt Aland et al. (Stuttgart: Deutsche Bibelgesellschaft, 2012).

beginning of the gospel" (Ἀρχὴ τοῦ εὐαγγελίου; Mark 1:1). This could mean that he thought of his work as a Gospel. The difficulty with this conclusion is that in every other Marcan occurrence of "gospel" (εὐαγγέλιον), the noun carries the meaning of a proclamation, not a written document. Therefore, Mark's use of "gospel" (εὐαγγέλιον) appears to argue against the proposal that he regarded his Gospel as a Gospel.[9] Similarly, the use or lack thereof of "gospel" (εὐαγγέλιον) and its verbal cognate "to proclaim the gospel" (εὐαγγελίζω) in Matthew, Luke, and John suggests that they did not view their works as Gospels either. In Matthew, "gospel" (εὐαγγέλιον) and "to proclaim the gospel" (εὐαγγελίζω) signify a proclamation of the gospel.[10] Εὐαγγέλιον does not appear in Luke or John, and while εὐαγγελίζω is found in Luke, it does not appear in John. Moreover, like Matthew, Luke's use of εὐαγγελίζω carries the meaning of a proclamation, not a literary work.[11] In short, for the authors of the canonical Gospels, the gospel appears to have been an oral message, not a written publication. How and why Christians in the second century AD came to call these works Gospels remains a mystery.[12]

The third difficulty in a straightforward use of the Gospels and Acts to reconstruct the earliest re-constructable gospel relates only to Acts. Luke's second volume contains several evangelical speeches of various early Christian leaders.[13] While Luke incorporated tradition dating from the earliest days of the Christian movement in these orations, they are his compositions in that they resemble each other in style, vocabulary, and theology.[14] Moreover, these homilies are in keeping with Greek and Roman historiographic conventions, which means that they are not word-for-word transcriptions but summarizations that capture the "sense" of the sermons.[15] This does not mean that some

---

[9] This is clear as one "proclaims" (κηρύσσω) the gospel, one "has faith in" (πιστεύω ἐν) the gospel, or one performs an action "for the sake of" (ἕνεκα) the gospel: Mark 1:14, 15; 8:35; 10:29; 13:10; 14:9; see also 16:15.

[10] Each time Matthew uses εὐαγγέλιον he says that someone "heralds" (κηρύσσω) it: Matt 4:23; 9:35; 24:14; 26:13. For his one use of εὐαγγελίζω, see Matt 11:5.

[11] Luke 1:19; 2:10; 3:18; 4:18, 43; 7:22; 8:1; 9:6; 16:16; 20:1.

[12] For more on the titles of the Gospels, see Martin Hengel, *The Four Gospels and the One Gospel of Jesus Christ: An Investigation of the Collection and Origin of the Canonical Gospels*, trans. John Bowden (Harrisburg: Trinity Press International, 2000), 48–56.

[13] For discussion of speeches in Acts, see C. H. Dodd, *The Apostolic Preaching* (London: Harper & Brothers, 1954), 17–35; Joseph A. Fitzmyer, *The Acts of the Apostles: A New Translation with Introduction and Commentary*, AB 31 (New York: Doubleday, 1998), 103–8.

[14] See Fitzmyer, *Acts*, 105–7.

[15] This was famously articulated by Thucydides in his *History of the Peloponnesian War*: "As to the speeches that were made by different men, either when they were about to begin the war or when they were already engaged therein, it has been difficult to recall with strict accuracy the words actually spoken, both for me as regards that which I myself heard, and for those who from various other sources have brought me reports. Therefore the speeches are given in the language in which, as it seemed to me, the

scholars have not attempted to sift these speeches to discover the earliest proclaimed gospel. This process, however, is difficult, somewhat arbitrary, and historians disagree about their conclusions.[16]

The most methodologically appropriate source for locating the earliest re-constructable gospel is our oldest agreed-upon Christian texts, Paul's letters, which date between the late AD 40s and the mid-60s.[17] As with the Gospels and Acts, the use of these sources for this purpose is not without difficulty, which are two in number. The first is that we must decide which letters attributed to Paul to use for reconstructing the earliest gospel. Due to differences in language, style, and theology among some Pauline epistles, many scholars conclude that the apostle is not responsible for, that is, he did not dictate, all thirteen letters in the corpus. Consequently, historians tend to classify Paul's letters into three types: (1) the undisputed letters, Romans, 1–2 Corinthians, Galatians, Philippians, 1 Thessalonians, and Philemon, which all scholars agree the apostle composed; (2) the disputed letters, Ephesians, Colossians, and 2 Thessalonians, which some exegetes contend Paul did not compose; and (3) the Pastoral epistles, 1–2 Timothy and Titus, which many (but not all) historians propose that disciples or most often a single disciple of Paul wrote in his name after his death.[18] The more we learn about ancient scribal culture, the composition of Greco-Roman letters, the concept of an author in antiquity, and the theological agendas of those who first questioned Pauline authorship, the more I am convinced that all letters in the Pauline corpus are Pauline in some sense and that the modern discussions of authorship are methodologically flawed.[19]

---

several speakers would express, on the subjects under consideration, the sentiments most befitting the occasion, though at the same time I have adhered as closely as possible to the general sense of what was actually said" (Thucydides, *History* 1.22.1 [C. F. Smith]).

[16] Dodd contends that primitive Christian sources stand behind Luke's speeches (*Apostolic Preaching*, 17–35), while Hans Conzelmann considers them Lucan "literary creations" (*Acts of the Apostles: A Commentary on the Acts of the Apostles*, trans. James Limburg, A. Thomas Kraabel, and Donald H. Juel, Hermeneia [Philadelphia: Fortress, 1987], xliii–xliv).

[17] It is probable that the epistle of James predates Paul's letters. However, neither εὐαγγέλιον nor the verb εὐαγγελίζω is found in it.

[18] For discussions of introductory matters of Paul's letters, see the standard NT introductions: Brown, *Introduction*, 163–251; D. A. Carson and Douglas J. Moo, *An Introduction to the New Testament*, 2nd ed. (Grand Rapids: Zondervan, 2005), 331–595; Powell, *Introducing the New Testament*, 271–442. For a recent discussion of Paul and pseudepigraphy, see Stanley E. Porter and Gregory P. Fewster, eds., *Paul and Pseudepigraphy*, Pauline Studies 8 (Leiden: Brill, 2013).

[19] For an excellent discussion of the concept of an author in the ancient Near East that is good "to think with" the concept of authorship in the Greco-Roman world, see Karel van der Toorn, "Authorship in Antiquity: Practice and Perception," in *Scribal Culture and the Making of the Hebrew Bible* (Cambridge: Harvard University, 2007), 27–50. For a discussion of Greco-Roman scribes and letter writing, see E. Randolph Richards, *Paul and First-Century Letter Writing: Secretaries, Composition and Collection* (Downers Grove: InterVaristy, 2004). For a discussion of the history of the question of Pauline authorship and the Pastorals, see Luke Timothy Johnson, *The First and Second Letters to Timothy: A New Translation with Introduction and Commentary*, AYB 35A (New Haven: Yale University, 2001),

Therefore, in this essay, I draw freely upon the thirteen Pauline letters. However, as we shall see, most of my data come from the so-called undisputed Pauline missives.

The second difficulty in using the apostle's letters to reconstruct the earliest proclaimed gospel is that his epistles are contextual documents written to churches and individual Christians. This means that they are missives composed for specific purposes, at specific times, to specific addressees, to achieve specific theological ends.[20] Thus, Paul's letters do not contain a systematic presentation of the gospel that he proclaimed. This contextual difficulty is compounded by the fact that the apostle composed these epistles to groups of people and individuals who had already obeyed the gospel. For this reason, we should not expect him to recount in detail something to which his addressees had already assented.[21] This difficulty notwithstanding, there are four instances in the Pauline corpus when the apostle discusses and even summarizes the gospel that he heralded: Rom 1:1–5; 1 Cor 15:1–7; Gal 1:11–16; and 1 Thess 1:9–10.[22] None of these passages contain the full scope of the gospel as Paul preached it, which means that any reconstruction will be fragmentary. However, because one of these summaries is addressed to the Roman Church (Rom 1:1–5), a church that the apostle did not found, Paul probably elaborates on the gospel more so than in the other passages. Therefore, I shall rely heavily on Rom 1:1–5 and supplement it with the other three texts as well as data from the Pauline corpus. To this end, we can arrive at a rough

---

55–90. For an ancient discussion of authorship of Revelation that resembles discussions in modern NT introductions, see Eusebius, *History* 7:25. For more on the theological presuppositions of Enlightenment and Post-Enlightenment scholars, see Alister E. McGrath, *Historical Theology: An Introduction to the History of Christian Thought*, 3rd ed. (Hoboken: Wiley Blackwell, 2023), 196–299.

[20] For an excellent treatment of the contextual nature of Paul's letters, see Michael J. Gorman, *Apostle of the Crucified: A Theological Introduction to Paul and His Letters*, 2nd ed. (Grand Rapids: Eerdmans, 2016).

[21] The term gospel is almost an exclusively Pauline word in the NT. Almost all its appearances, sixty of the seventy-six occurrences (roughly 79%), are in Paul's letters. Scholars generally agree that Paul most often uses εὐαγγέλιον as a technical term for the content of his preaching, but that sometimes he uses the noun to describe the process of evangelizing (Gal 2:7; Phil 4:3, 15; 1 Cor 9:14b, 18b; 2 Cor 2:12; 8:18). Εὐαγγελίζω is found fifty-four times in the NT, twenty-one of which are in Paul's letters. Unlike the noun in his epistles, this verb does not have the exclusive technical connotation of preaching the gospel (1 Thess 3:6). For more on the gospel in Paul's letters, see Adolf von Harnack, *Constitution & Law of the Church in the First Two Centuries*, ed. H.D.A. Major; trans. F.L. Pogson (New York: Williams & Norgate, 1910), 292–303; Dodd, *Apostolic Preaching*, 4–28; Peter Stuhlmacher, "The Pauline Gospel," in *The Gospel and the Gospels*, ed. Peter Stuhlmacher (Grand Rapids: Eerdmans, 1991), 149–72; Joseph A. Fitzmyer, "The Gospel in the Theology of Paul," in *To Advance the Gospel: New Testament Studies*, 2nd ed. (Grand Rapids: Eerdmans, 1998), 149–61; Michael Wolter, *Paul: An Outline of His Theology*, trans. Robert L. Brawley (Waco: Baylor University, 2015), 51–69.

[22] In 1 Cor 15:1; Gal 1:11, Paul acknowledges that he is providing a summary of "the gospel that I gospeled" in Corinth and Galatia (probably southern Galatia); in Rom 1:1–5, he expounds on the content of the gospel (Rom 1:1–5); and in 1 Thess 1:9–10, he rearticulates the main points of his proclamation in Thessalonica.

outline of the gospel that Paul proclaimed, which consisted of six main components: (1) the gospel's divine origin, (2) its apocalyptic nature, (3) a concise narrative of the Messiah event, (4) the gospel's eschatological focus, (5) the gospel as the fulfillment of God's promises in Scripture to Israel, and (6) Paul's special role in the gospel, as herald of the gentiles (see Table).

Table: The Earliest Re-constructable Gospel

Components of the gospel Paul heralded	Rom 1:1–5	1 Cor 15:1–7	Gal 1:11–18	1 Thess 1:9–10
(1) Divine origin	"God's gospel"		"The gospel . . . is not from humans; neither did I receive it from a human nor was I taught it, but it is through an apocalypse of Jesus the Messiah"	
(2) Apocalyptic nature			"The gospel is . . . through an apocalypse of Jesus the Messiah . . . But when God . . . was pleased to apocalyptically reveal his Son to me"	
(3) The Messiah Event	"Born from the seed of David according to the flesh . . . declared God's Son in power by the Spirit of holiness in the resurrection from the dead"	"That the Messiah died on behalf of our sins . . . that he was buried and that he was raised on the third day"	"His Son whom he raised from the dead"	
(4) Eschatological Focus	"his Son . . . who was declared God's Son in power by the Spirit of holiness at the resurrection from the dead"	"The Messiah . . . was raised on the third day"		"to wait for his Son from heaven, whom he raised from the dead, Jesus who rescues us from the coming wrath"

(5) Grounded in and the fulfillment of Scripture, i.e., the OT	"God's gospel, which he proclaimed before through his prophets in the Holy Scriptures about his Son . . . Jesus the Messiah our Lord"	"The Messiah died on behalf of our sins according to the Scriptures, that he was buried and that he rose on the third day according to the Scriptures"		
(6) Paul's special role in the gospel	"Paul, slave of the Messiah Jesus, called apostle set apart for God's gospel . . . Jesus the Messiah our Lord, through whom we received grace and an apostolate for the obedience of faith among all the gentiles on behalf of his name"		"God . . . was pleased to reveal his Son to me so that I might herald him among the gentiles"	

The first component of the gospel that Paul heralded is its divine origin. According to him, the gospel begins with the God of Israel because he is its source. Thus, when the apostle composes the letter to the church in Rome and begins to explicate the gospel to them, he calls it "God's gospel" (Rom 1:1).[23] This type of genitive construction, εὐαγγέλιον θεοῦ, is known as a genitive of origin, which highlights that God is the gospel's fountainhead.[24] The content of the gospel, however, is God's work in the world through his divine Son, the Messiah Jesus. Consequently, in Romans, Paul goes on to note that God's gospel is "about his Son" (περὶ τοῦ υἱοῦ αὐτοῦ; Rom 1:3).[25] To stress that God's work through Jesus is the content of the gospel elsewhere in his letters, Paul

---

[23] See also Rom 15:16; 2 Cor 11:7; 1 Thess 2:2, 8, 9; 1 Tim 1:11.

[24] C. E. B. Cranfield, *The Epistle to the Romans*, ICC, 2 vols (Edinburgh: T&T Clark, 1975) 1:55; Joseph A. Fitzmyer, *Romans: A New Translation with Introduction and Commentary*, AB 33 (New York: Doubleday, 1993), 232; Robert Jewett, *Romans: A Commentary*, Hermeneia (Minneapolis: Fortress, 2006), 102; Richard N. Longenecker, *The Epistle to the Romans*, NIGTC (Grand Rapids: Eerdmans, 2016), 60.

[25] Fitzmyer, *Romans*, 233; Longenecker, *Romans*, 63. See also 2 Cor 5:19.

uses three genitival phrases: God's Son's gospel, the Messiah's gospel, and the Lord Jesus's gospel.[26] Thus, for Paul, the gospel's divine origin has a distinctive binitarian shape: it stems from Israel's God and is about his work through his Son, Israel's Messiah.[27]

The reason why the apostle's proclamation of the gospel underscores its divine origin relates to the way in which God revealed it to him, which brings us to our second observation, the gospel's apocalyptic nature.[28] Paul stresses that he is in the Messiah because God apocalyptically revealed, ἀποκαλύπτω, the identity of his divine Son to him on the Damascus Road, which forever altered and changed his life.[29] He notes that while in the midst of persecuting Jews who professed Jesus as the Messiah (Gal 1:13–14), God "was pleased to apocalyptically reveal (ἀποκαλύπτω) his Son to me" (Gal 1:16).[30] It was at this time that the apostle says, "the gospel (came to him) through an apocalypse (ἀποκάλυψις) of Jesus the Messiah" (Gal 1:11–12).[31] Therefore, God's

---

[26] For "God's Son's gospel," see Rom 1:9. For "the Messiah's gospel," see Rom 15:19; 1 Cor 9:12; 2 Cor 2:12; 9:13; 10:14; Gal 1:7; 1 Thess 3:2; see also 2 Cor 4:4. For "the Lord Jesus's gospel," see 2 Thess 1:8. Oftentimes, Paul drops any modifier and refers to the message that he preaches as "the gospel" (Rom 1:16; 11:28; 1 Cor 4:15; 9:14, 18, 23; 15:1; 2 Cor 8:18; Gal 1:11; 2:2, 5, 14; Eph 3:6; 6:19; Phil 1:5, 7, 12, 16, 27; 2:22; 4:3, 15; Col 1:5, 23; 1 Thess 2:4; 1 Tim 1:11; 2 Tim 1:8, 10; Phlm 13). Sometimes he calls it "my gospel" (Rom 2:16; 16:25; 2 Tim 2:8) or "our gospel" (2 Cor 4:3; 1 Thess 1:5; 2 Thess 2:14). In one case, the apostle differentiates between the gospel preached to the circumcision and the gentiles (Gal 2:7) and in another, he calls it "the gospel of our salvation" (Eph 1:13) and "the gospel of peace" (Eph 6:15).

[27] In Paul's economy of salvation, he does not connect the Spirit with the gospel in any genitive construction. However, the Spirit appears in his summary of the gospel in Rom 1:4. I am grateful to Garrett Best for this reminder.

[28] Scholars continue to debate the concept of apocalyptic and the extent to which Paul was an apocalypticist. For more information, see J. Christiaan Beker, *Paul the Apostle: The Triumph of God in Life and Thought* (Philadelphia: Fortress, 1980), 135–81; J. Louis Martyn, "Epistemology at the Turn of the Ages," in *Theological Issues in the Letters of Paul* (Nashville: Abingdon, 1997), 89–110; J. Louis Martyn, *Galatians: A New Translation with Introduction and Commentary*, AYB 33 (New Haven: Yale University, 1997), 97–105; Beverly Gaventa, *Our Mother Saint Paul* (Louisville: Westminster John Knox, 2007); John K. Goodrich, Jason Maston, and Ben Blackwell, eds., *Paul and the Apocalyptic Imagination* (Minneapolis: Fortress, 2016); Martinus C. de Boer, *Paul, Theologian of God's Apocalypse* (Eugene: Cascade, 2020); Jamie Davies, *The Apocalyptic Paul: Retrospect and Prospect* (Eugene: Cascade, 2022).

[29] 1 Cor 9:1; 15:8–9.

[30] "God" may not appear explicitly in the Greek text of Gal 1:15, but Hans Dieter Betz and James D. G. Dunn conclude that it was God is the implied subject of the verb "was pleased" (εὐδόκησεν) (Hans Dieter Betz, *Galatians: A Commentary on Paul's Letter to the Churches in Galatia*, Hermeneia [Philadelphia: Fortress, 1979], 69; James D. G. Dunn, *The Epistle to the Galatians*, BNTC [Peabody: Hendrickson, 1993], 62).

[31] This genitive construction is probably an objective genitive because, according to Gal 1:16, God apocalyptically revealed his Son to Paul. See F. F. Bruce, *The Epistle to the Galatians: A Commentary on the Greek Text*, NIGTC (Grand Rapids: Eerdmans, 1982), 89; Marytn, *Galatians*, 144.

transfer of Paul into the realm, sphere, or domain of the Messiah, which used to be called Christ mysticism but is now referred to as participation in Christ, comes neither from his study of Scripture nor some reasoned position (Gal 2:20) but is the result of his belief in an otherworldly message that God apocalyptically revealed to him. The acceptance of this message through faith and baptism resulted in a new ontological existence for the apostle (and for his converts, too), the invasion of new creation (Gal 6:15) into the enemy-occupied territory of the present evil age (Gal 1:4).[32]

The third component of the gospel that Paul heralded narrated concisely the main points of the Messiah event, Jesus's Davidic descent, death, burial, and resurrection. Paul begins his summary of the gospel in Romans by noting Jesus's genealogical descent from King David, "he was descended from the seed of David according to the flesh" (Rom 1:3; see also 2 Tim 2:8).[33] Among the "first principles" (πρῶτοι) of the tradition that the apostle received and passed onto the Corinthian Christians was that the Messiah died "on behalf of" (ὑπὲρ) humanity's sins "according to the Scriptures" (1 Cor 15:3).[34] The sacrificial (ὑπὲρ) and atoning nature of Jesus's death that released Christians from the bondage of the cosmic power of Sin must have held prominence for Paul in his proclamation. He ensures that the Roman Christians know that all, Jews and Greeks, are under the cosmic power of Sin and that "while we were still weak, at the proper time, the Messiah died on behalf of (ὑπὲρ) of the ungodly ones."[35] The apostle points out to the Galatian Christians that Jesus "gave himself on behalf of (ὑπὲρ) our sins so that he might rescue us from the present evil age" (Gal 1:4). And, in another letter he composed to the Corinthian Christians, he informs them that God "made the one who did not know sin on behalf of (ὑπὲρ) us so that we might become the righteousness of God in him" (2 Cor 5:21).

The next parts of the Messiah event that Paul's gospel underscored were Jesus's burial and resurrection. Thus, two more first principles of the gospel that the Corinthian Christians received were that "the Messiah ... was buried (ἐτάφη) and was raised on the third day according to the Scriptures" (1 Cor 15:4). While this is the only place in Paul's summaries of the gospel that he focuses on the burial of Jesus, the empty tomb must have been a part of his proclamation, for it appears to have been a component of

---

[32] 2 Cor 5:17; Gal 6:15. According to Paul, God predetermined him to be a herald of new creation before his birth when "he set me apart (ἀφορίζω) in his mother's womb" for this divine purpose (Gal 1:15). He probably refers to this election in Romans when he says that he "was set apart" (ἀφωρισμένος) for God's gospel (Rom 1:1). The passive form of the verb, ἀφορίζω, is what is known as a divine passive.

[33] Gal 4:4. See Matthew V. Novenson and the preceptive comment, "despite a robust tradition of anti-Christian polemic from the second century onward, we find no genealogical challenge to the Davidic ancestry of Jesus" (*The Grammar of Messianism: An Ancient Jewish Political Idiom and Its Users* [Oxford: Oxford University, 2017], 82–91, quote from 89).

[34] Rom 14:15; 1 Cor 11:24; 2 Cor 5:14–15, 21; 1 Tim 2:6; Titus 2:4.

[35] Rom 5:6–7; see also Rom 3:9; 5:12, 20–21; see also Gal 3:22.

the early Christian baptismal liturgy.³⁶ Both in Romans and Colossians the apostle notes that believers have been "co-buried with him (the Messiah) (συνετάφημεν οὖν αὐτῷ; συνταφέντες αὐτῷ)" in baptism (Rom 6:4; Col 2:12).³⁷ The emphasis on Jesus's resurrection appears in the gospel-summaries of Romans and 1 Thessalonians. In the former, the apostle relays that our Lord Jesus the Messiah "was decreed God's Son in power by the Spirit of holiness at the resurrection from the dead" (Rom 1:4). In 1 Thessalonians, Paul reminds his audience that he encouraged them "to wait for his (God's) Son, whom he raised from the dead, from heaven" (1:10).³⁸ Therefore, the resurrection must have held a prominent place in Paul's preaching, which is supported by his discussion of the message (ῥῆμα) he heralds (κηρύσσω) in Romans (Rom 10:8), for one's confession of Jesus's lordship and of God's raising of him from the dead results in deliverance (Rom 10:9).³⁹ Finally, Paul's description of the Messiah event in 1 Corinthians included references to witnesses of the resurrection. Paul notes that after this event, the resurrected Jesus appeared to Cephas/Peter, the Twelve, over five hundred, James, and then to all the apostles (1 Cor 15:3–7), which must include him (1 Cor 15:8–11). What is more, the apostle highlights that, like him, some of the five hundred witnesses to the resurrection are alive and thus can give evidence of their experience (1 Cor 15:6).⁴⁰

The fourth component of the gospel that Paul heralded is its eschatological focus, which centered on the already completed work of Jesus's first coming and the soon-to-be-finished work of his second. The former consisted of the launching of the invasion of new creation into the present evil and enemy-occupied age with the Messiah's birth (Rom 1:3), death, burial, and resurrection on the third day (1 Cor 15:3–4; Rom 1:4; 1 Thess 1:10). While a direct reference to God's enthronement of Jesus at his right hand, which occurred after the resurrection, is lacking in the Pauline summaries of the gospel, the connection between Jesus's lordship and his resurrection/enthronement suggests

---

³⁶ Some scholars conclude that because Paul omits any reference to the tomb, he knew nothing of the empty tomb tradition found in the Gospels. See Hans Conzelmann, *1 Corinthians: A Commentary on the First Epistle to the Corinthians*, ed. George W. MacRae, trans. James W. Leitch, Hermeneia (Philadelphia: Fortress, 1975), 255. However, given that Jesus is interned, his burial in a tomb is probably presupposed.

³⁷ It is important to note that burial under the ground was not the commonest burial practice in the Greco-Roman world. Rather, most people were placed above ground in tombs and in holes hewn into the rock, as in the case of Jesus (Matt 27:60; Mark 15:46; Luke 23:53; John 19:41).

³⁸ See also 1 Cor 15:12–58; Phil 3:10.

³⁹ See also Rom 10:1–21; 1 Cor 15:14.

⁴⁰ See Gordon D. Fee, *The First Epistle to the Corinthians*, NICNT, rev. ed. (Grand Rapids: Eerdmans, 2014), 810. Although Conzelmann argues that the stress is on those witnesses who have died, which anticipates Paul's discussion of the resurrection body in the rest of the chapter and that those who died between the Messiah's first and second comings "attain to life" (*Corinthians*, 257–58).

that the former presupposes the latter.[41] The Messiah's not-yet-completed work focused on the events that will transpire at his second coming, which will bring new creation to its fullness.[42] Thus, Paul encourages the Thessalonian Christians to wait for this event, which will result in their deliverance from God's wrath (1 Thess 1:10). This escape from divine anger must be why the apostle informs the Corinthian Christians that it is by holding to the gospel that they received that they "are *being* saved" (by God) (σώζεσθε). This fulfillment of salvation is the completion of the resurrection event, which began with the Messiah, the resurrection's "first fruit" (ἀπαρχή; 1 Cor 15:20), and will end with the raising of all to God's final assize. For this reason, Paul refers to Jesus's resurrection in his gospel with a plural partitive genitive, the resurrection "*from the dead ones* (νεκρῶν)" (Rom 1:4; 1 Thess 1:10).[43] This phrase acknowledges the Messiah as the first one whom God resurrected while stressing that the rest of deceased humanity is to follow. In short, Paul's gospel underscored that believers live between the two comings of Jesus in the overlap of the ages (1 Cor 10:11) and in the era in which the resurrection is in progress. I must stress, however, that this is not an intellectual ascent for Paul, but the already-but-not-yet-completed nature of the gospel means that his proclamation is infused with God's new creative power and results in an ontological transformation and the ethical formation of those who are in the Messiah. At baptism, believers are incorporated into the crucified, resurrected, and reigning Lord, at which time they are given the Holy Spirit by whose power they are to live out the resurrection of the Messiah amid the beginning of the end of the present evil age (Rom 13:11–12). Therefore, they are to use the power by which God raised the Messiah to walk in newness of the eschatological life, the full benefit of which they will soon experience (Rom 6:4).[44]

The fifth component of the gospel Paul heralded is the surprising fulfillment of God's promises to Israel found in Scripture, what the Church calls the OT. Since the Reformation, many Protestant scholars have stressed the discontinuity between OT in general and the Torah in particular and the gospel. Martin Luther preached a famous

---

[41] Rom 1:4; 8:34; 1 Cor 15:25; see also Acts 2:29–36. For more on Jesus's enthronement, see D. Clint Burnett, *Christ's Enthronement at God's Right Hand and Its Greco-Roman Cultural Context*, BZNW 242 (Berlin: de Gruyter, 2021).

[42] According to Paul, Jesus must reign as Lord King until God places every enemy under his feet, the last of which is death (1 Cor 15:24). The defeat of this cosmic power will occur at Jesus's second coming when believers will receive an imperishable, immortal, and incorruptible body (1 Cor 15:50–55).

[43] See also Rom 4:24; 6:4, 9; 8:11; 10:7, 9; 1 Cor 15:12, 20; Gal 1:1; Eph 1:20; Col 1:18; 2:12; 2 Tim 2:8.

[44] Life (ζωή) in Paul's letters almost always has the connotation of everlasting life or life infused with divine power (Rom 2:7; 5:10, 17, 18, 21; 6:4, 22, 23; 7:10; 8:2, 6, 10; 11:15; 2 Cor 2:16; 4:10, 11, 12; 5:4; Gal 6:8; Eph 4:18; Phil 2:16; 4:3; Col 3:4; 1 Tim 1:16; 4:8; 6:12, 19; 2 Tim 1:1, 10; Titus 1:2; 3:7), the exceptions being Rom 8:38; 1 Cor 3:22; 15:19; Phil 1:20; Col 3:3.

homily entitled "The Distinction Between the Law and the Gospel," in which he argued that "the doctrine of the Law should ... be kept apart from the Gospel."[45] While there are sound theological and contextual reasons for Luther's stress on this supposed dichotomy in Christianity in the sixteenth century, there is not a single place in Paul's letters or in his summaries of the gospel in which he contrasts Torah/OT with gospel.[46] To the contrary, he anchored his proclamation in the OT. The first thing Paul informs the Roman Christians about the gospel is that "it was proclaimed previously through his prophets in the Holy Scriptures" (Rom 1:2). He notes that among the "first principles" (πρῶτοι) of the gospel he inherited and handed down to the Corinthian Christians was that "the Messiah died on behalf of our sins according to the Scriptures, that he was buried, and that he was raised on the third day according to the Scriptures" (1 Cor 15:3–4).[47] Thus, Jesus's death and resurrection occurred according to God's predetermined plan set forth in the OT.

Paul's use of three titles for Jesus in his summaries of the gospel underscores this prediction/fulfillment scheme. In Romans, he points out that the content of the gospel is "about God's Son" (υἱός θεοῦ), who is "the Messiah" (Χριστός) and our "Lord" (κύριος). The first title, υἱός θεοῦ, comes directly from the OT and stresses that Jesus is the royal, Davidic king (Rom 1:3–4; Gal 1:16; 1 Thess 1:10).[48] In 2 Sam 7 Old Greek, the prophet Nathan tells King David that God decreed that after the monarch passes God will raise up "seed" (σπέρμα) "from your loins" (ἐκ τῆς κοιλίας σου; 2 Sam 7:12) who will be God's Son: "I will be his father and he will be my Son" (ἐγὼ ἔσομαι αὐτῷ εἰς πατέρα, καὶ αὐτὸς ἔσται μοι εἰς υἱόν; 2 Sam 7:14). For this new king, God "will prepare his kingdom" (ἑτοιμάσω τὴν βασιλείαν αὐτοῦ) and "raise up his throne into the age" (ἀνορθώσω τὸν θρόνον αὐτοῦ ἕως εἰς τὸν αἰῶνα; 2 Sam 7:12–13). In return, this progeny of David will build a house for God's name (2 Sam 7:13).

---

[45] Martin Luther, "The Distinction Between the Law and the Gospel," trans. Willard L. Bruce, *Concordia* (1992): 153–63, quote from 154. Paul's testimony from Romans contradicts this view, for he notes that the message that he preaches is found in Deut 30:11–14 (Rom 10:5–9) and that his gospel upholds the Torah (Rom 3:31).

[46] The Lutheran scholar of early Christianity von Harnack first pointed out this observation in the early twentieth century. He, however, agreed with Luther that "the whole" of Paul's "own conviction" was the opposition between Torah and gospel (*Constitution*, 301).

[47] It is unclear to which "Scriptures" Paul refers. For the possibilities that Jesus's death refers to Isaiah 53 and his resurrection Hos 6:2, see Joseph A. Fitzmyer, *First Corinthians: A New Translation with Introduction and Commentary*, AYB 32 (New Haven: Yale University, 2008), 546–8. Elsewhere, Paul notes that "Scripture" foresaw God's justification of the gentiles by faith and not by works of Torah and "proclaimed the gospel beforehand to Abraham that 'All the gentiles will be blessed by you'" (Gal 3:8).

[48] See also Rom 1:9; 5:10; 8:3, 29, 32; 1 Cor 1:9; 15:58; 2 Cor 1:19; Gal 2:20; 4:4, 6; Eph 4:13; Col 1:13. For an informed discussion of God's Son and Messiah in the OT, Second Temple Judaism, and NT, see Adela Yarbro Collins and John J. Collins, *King and Messiah as Son of God: Divine, Human, and Angelic Messianic Figures in Biblical and Related Literature* (Grand Rapids: Eerdmans, 2008).

The divine adoption of the newly crowned king of Israel became part of the Israelite/Judahite coronation ceremony, at which time God decreed the new sovereign was his "begotten ... son" (בני אתה אני היום ילדתיך/Υἱός μου εἶ σύ, ἐγὼ σήμερον γεγέννηκά σε; Ps 2:7). Some Second Temple Jews interpreted these texts as prophecies about the coming Davidic king. One of the sectarian works in Hebrew from the Dead Sea Scrolls, 4Q174, explains that 2 Sam 7:12–14's reference to David's "seed" (זרע) as God's "son" (בן) refers to "the branch of David" (הואה צמח דויד), which is another royal, Davidic title (Jer 23:5; 33:15), who will appear "in Zion in the last days" (בצי]ון בא[חרית הימים; 4Q174 11–12). Paul's understanding of Jesus's sonship resembles the interpretation of 2 Sam 7:12–14 from 4Q174 and his proclamation of the gospel must have applied the title to Jesus. In support, after acknowledging that the gospel is about God's Son in Romans, the apostle notes Jesus's Davidic genealogy, stressing the verbal connection with 2 Sam 7 Old Greek with the use of σπέρμα: he "is descended from the seed of David according to the flesh" (τοῦ γενομένου ἐκ σπέρματος Δαυὶδ κατὰ σάρκα; Rom 1:3).[49]

The second title, "the Messiah" (χριστός), is the Greek translation of the Hebrew term מָשִׁיחַ, meaning "anointed one" (Rom 1:1, 4; 1 Cor 15:3; Gal 1:12). This epithet was not used exclusively for kings in the OT, for priests, the high priest, God's old covenant people in general, and Cyrus the Great are all called "anointed."[50] Notwithstanding this varied use of משיח/χριστός, the title in the OT most often refers to Israelite and Judahite kings who were anointed with oil at their coronation.[51] Some Second Temple Jews interpreted OT passages about royal messiahs as prophecies about a coming future king whom God would use to rescue his people from foreign oppression.[52] Of particular importance are two sectarian documents from the Dead Sea Scrolls written in Hebrew. The first makes an enigmatic reference to God "begetting the messiah" (יוליד [אל] א[ת] המשיח), which is an allusion to Ps 2:7 and 2 Sam 7:12–14 (1 QSa 2:11–12). The second work calls the "Branch of David" (צמח דויד), a figure that we have already seen was called God's Son, "the righteous messiah" (משיח הצדק) in 4Q252 5:3–5. That Paul applied the title to Jesus and anchored his understanding of Jesus's messiahship in the Scriptures (Rom 1:2; 1 Cor 15:3) means that when he heralded Jesus as the Messiah,

---

[49] The only other place in the Pauline corpus that connects King David to Jesus is 2 Tim 2:8. However, the connection is evident in the Apostolic Fathers: Ig. *Eph.* 18:2; 20:2; Ig. *Tralles* 9:1; Ig. *Rom.* 7:3; Ig. *Smyr.* 1:1; Did. 9:2; 10:8. The latter two texts evince that Jesus's Davidic lineage was part of the Eucharistic liturgy of the church or churches connected to the Didache.

[50] For priests, Exod 28:41; 30:30; etc. For the high priest, Exod 40:13; Lev 4:3, 5, 16; 16:32; etc. Lev 4:3, 5, 16; etc. For Israel in general, Ps 105:15; Hab 3:13. For Cyrus, Isa 45:1.

[51] Judg 9:8, 15; 1 Sam 9:16; 10:1; Pss 2:2; 18:50; 20:6; etc.

[52] Pss Sol 17:32; 18:0, 5, 7; CD 12:23–13:1; 14:19; 19:10–11; 1QS 9:11; 1QSa 2:11–12, 14, 20.

he must have had the OT prophecies about the coming future king of the world in mind (Pss 2; 21; 72; 110).[53]

The last OT title that Paul calls Jesus in his proclamation of the gospel in Romans is κύριος, which is the most used epithet for Jesus in his letters.[54] For Paul, there is a direct connection between Jesus's lordship and his resurrection. Thus, he tells the Roman Christians that Jesus "was decreed God's Son in power according to the Spirit of holiness by the resurrection from the dead, Jesus the Messiah our κύριος" (Rom 1:4).[55] Most scholars interpret Jesus's lordship as in some way articulating his divinity. Some conclude that the epithet reflects the covenant name of God revealed to Moses at the burning bush on Mount Sinai (Exod 3:14) and argue that the title identifies Jesus as participating somehow in God's identity. Other scholars propose that κύριος identifies Jesus as YHWH in some sense.[56] There is no doubt that the title in question has divine connotations for Paul (1 Cor 8:5–6). However, I propose that Jesus's lordship is *also* royal, Davidic, and messianic. The most quoted OT text in the New, Ps 110:1, calls the ancient Davidic king of Israel/Judah "lord" (אדון; κύριος) and notes that he is God's coregent, ruling at his right hand.[57] It is evident from his letters that Paul interpreted Jesus's resurrection as the literal fulfillment of this text (Rom 8:34; 1 Cor 15:25), which means that his use of the epithet reflects Jesus's status as the exalted Lord who reigns as the coregent Messiah at God's right hand (Rom 1:3–4; see also Acts 2:34–36).[58]

One final note about the anchoring of the gospel in the OT is that some scholars suggest that a tension exists between this and the gospel's apocalyptic nature.[59] Such a tension, however, is modern and is not one that affected apocalyptically minded Second Temple Jews. For example, the author of the commentary on Habakkuk found among the Dead Sea Scrolls and written in Hebrew illustrates how ancient Jews could believe

---

[53] For most of the last century, many scholars doubted that Paul's use of χριστός for Jesus was royal. Instead, they concluded that for Paul the title was akin to Jesus's last name. Matthew V. Novenson, surveying the use of what he calls "honorifics" in the Greco-Roman world including Second Temple Judaism, has shown that χριστός in Paul's letters is a royal "honorific" like Augustus, Epiphanes, etc., but one shaped by OT messianic texts (*Christ among the Messiahs: Christ Language in Paul and Messiah Language in Ancient Judaism* [Oxford: Oxford University Press, 2012]; Novenson, *Grammar of Messianism*).

[54] See Larry W. Hurtado, "Lord," in *Dictionary of Paul and his Letters*, ed. Gerald F. Hawthrone, Ralph P. Martin, and Daniel G. Reid (Downers Grove: InterVarsity Press, 1993), 560–69.

[55] See also Phil 2:9–11.

[56] For a concise discussion, see D. Clint Burnett, *Studying the New Testament Through Inscriptions: An Introduction* (Peabody: Hendrickson, 2020), 58–67.

[57] For a discussion of the evidence supporting this view, see Burnett, *Studying*, 67–76.

[58] See Burnett, *Christ's Enthronement*.

[59] See, for example, Douglas J. Moo, *A Theology of Paul and His Letters* (Grand Rapids: Zondervan, 2018), 1–42; N. T. Wright and J. Christiaan Beker, *Paul: Narrative or Apocalyptic* (Minneapolis: Fortress, 2023).

on the one hand that the fulfillment of God's promises to Israel were predetermined in Scripture and on the other that God's fulfillment of them would be unexpected and revealed only through apocalyptic knowledge. According to the passage in question, God communicated to Habakkuk what to write about the end of the age, but he did not disclose to the prophet when that time would come. However, God did reveal that information in the form of a mystery to the leader of the sectarian group, the Teacher of Righteousness:

> God told (דבר) Habakkuk to write the things coming upon the last generation (הדור האחרון). However, he did not make known (to Habakkuk) the end of the age (גמר הק). And he (Habakkuk) says, "so that the one who reads it may run" (Hab 2:2).[60] Its interpretation is about the Teacher of Righteousness to whom God made known all the mysteries of the words of his servants, the prophets (הודיעו אל את כול רזי דברי עבדיו הנבאים). "For still the vision is for the appointed time. It testifies to the end (לקץ) and it is not deceptive" (Hab 2:3). Its interpretation is that the end of the last (days) (הקץ האחרון) will be long and (it will be) more than all that the prophets have spoken, for the mysteries of God (רזי אל) are extraordinary (1QpHab 7:1–5a).

Consequently, for the author of this commentary, God provided the prophets in general and Habakkuk in particular with prophecies to the extent that he "told" (דבר) the latter what to say, but not with the "how" and "when" of the fulfillment of his divine communications with them.[61] That information God provided only to the Teacher of Righteousness, to whom he "made known all the mysteries of the words" of the prophets. The term that the commentator uses for "mystery" (רז) is found only in one OT book, the apocalyptic work of Daniel, where it means divinely revealed, apocalyptic information.[62] The commentator picks up this meaning of רז, and, as Timothy Lim

---

[60] Habakkuk 2:2 is an enigmatic verse whose translation is debated: "so that a runner may read it" (NRSV); "so he may run who reads it" (RSV, ESV); "so that a herald may run with it" (NIV). For discussions, see Francis Andersen, *Habakkuk: A New Translation with Introduction and Commentary*, AYB 25 (New Haven: Yale University, 2001), 198–204; J. J. M. Roberts, *Nahum, Habakkuk, and Zephaniah: A Commentary*, NTL (Louisville: Westminster John Knox, 1991), 108–10.

[61] Timothy H. Lim concludes, "The pesherist [or the author of the work] seems to have other prophets and their predictions in mind, beyond Habakkuk and his oracles" (*Earliest Commentary on the Prophecy of Habakkuk* [Oxford: Oxford University Press, 2020], 103).

[62] Dan 2:18, 19, 30, 47. John J. Collins notes, "The Hebrew form of the word 'mystery' (רז), a Persian loanword, occurs often in the Dead Sea Scrolls to denote cosmological (1QH 1:11–12) or eschatological (1QM 14:14; 1QS 11:3–4; 1QpHab 7:8) mysteries or even the 'mysteries of the words of his servants the prophets' (1QpHab 7:4). Initially, here [in Dan 2:18], the connotation seems to be simply

observes, he uses it to explain the difference between "the perceived delay" of the words of the prophets and their unexpected apocalyptic fulfillment, according to the Teacher of Righteousness.[63] Similarly, I submit that Paul believed much the same about the gospel in his proclamation of it. God had foretold of its coming in Scripture (Rom 1:2; 1 Cor 15:3), but he did not reveal its "when" and "how" to the OT saints.[64] God disclosed these mysteries to Paul in Jesus and the Church "through an apocalypse of Jesus the Messiah" (δι' ἀποκαλύψεως Ἰησοῦ Χριστοῦ; Gal 1:12) that God "apocalyptically revealed" (ἀποκαλύπτω) to him (Gal 1:15–16). For this reason, the apostle, using the Greek translation of the Hebrew term רז, μυστήριον, calls the Messiah event a "mystery." Thus, Paul refers to his preaching of the gospel in Corinth as "the mystery of God" (τὸ μυστήριον τοῦ θεοῦ; 1 Cor 2:1). In this mystery, God has hidden his wisdom, "which he predetermined before the ages" (ἣν προώρισεν ὁ θεὸς πρὸ τῶν αἰώνων; 1 Cor 2:7; see also 2:8–9). However, for Christians, "God has revealed" this mystery "through the Spirit" (ἡμῖν δὲ ἀπεκάλυψεν ὁ θεὸς διὰ τοῦ πνεύματος; 1 Cor 2:10; see also Col 1:26). Therefore, for Paul, while God foretold the gospel in the OT, its startling fulfillment was only revealed apocalyptically in the Messiah and the Church.

The sixth and final component of the earliest reconstructable gospel was Paul's special place in it as herald to the gentiles. This component of the gospel is evident not only in that Paul composed numerous letters (some of which are no longer extant) to churches that were made up mostly of gentile converts to Christianity but also in that he stresses his role as herald of the gentiles in the texts we are considering. He tells the Roman Christians that the resurrected Lord is responsible for the grace and the apostolate that he has received, defining the latter as "an apostolate for the obedience of faith among all the gentiles on behalf of his (the Messiah's) name" (δι' οὗ ἐλάβομεν χάριν καὶ ἀποστολὴν εἰς ὑπακοὴν πίστεως ἐν πᾶσιν τοῖς ἔθνεσιν ὑπὲρ τοῦ ὀνόματος αὐτοῦ; Rom 1:5).[65] The apostle testifies to the Galatian Christians that the purpose of God apocalyptically revealing his Son to him was so that he could fill his predetermined divine commission of proclaiming the gospel "among the gentiles" (ἐν τοῖς ἔθνεσιν; Gal 1:15–16). In 1 Thessalonians, he relates the effects of the obedience of the Thessalonian Christians to the gospel: "how they turned from idols to God to serve the living and true God" (1 Thess 1:9). Finally, although direct references to Paul's apostolate for the gentiles is missing in his summary of the gospel in 1 Corinthians 15, his use of second person plural verbs and pronouns highlights his original proclamation of the gospel among the Corinthian Christians, most of whom were former pagans (1 Cor

---

the puzzle of the dream, but the dream itself is found to disclose an eschatological mystery" (*Daniel: A Commentary on the Book of Daniel*, Hermeneia [Minneapolis: Fortress, 1993], 159).

[63] Lim, *Earliest Commentary*, 104.

[64] Rom 4:1–25; Gal 3:8.

[65] See also Rom 15:18, 26.

12:2): "Now I made known *to you*, brothers and sisters, the gospel that I gospeled *to you*, which *you received*, in which also *you stand*, through which also *you are being saved*, if *you hold* to the certain message that I gospeled *to you*, unless *you had faith* in vain. For I passed down *to you* among the first principles of what I received." (Γνωρίζω δὲ ὑμῖν, ἀδελφοί, τὸ εὐαγγέλιον ὃ εὐηγγελισάμην ὑμῖν, ὃ καὶ παρελάβετε, ἐν ᾧ καὶ ἑστήκατε, δι' οὗ καὶ σῴζεσθε, τίνι λόγῳ εὐηγγελισάμην ὑμῖν εἰ κατέχετε, ἐκτὸς εἰ μὴ εἰκῇ ἐπιστεύσατε. παρέδωκα γὰρ ὑμῖν ἐν πρώτοις, ὃ καὶ παρέλαβον; 1 Cor 15:1–3a).

CONCLUSION

To summarize this essay, the most methodologically appropriate source to discover the earliest re-constructable gospel in the Christian movement is our earliest agreed upon Christian texts, Paul's letters. In four of these epistles, Rom 1:1–5; 1 Cor 15:1–7; Gal 1:11–16; and 1 Thess 1:9–10, the apostle summarizes the gospel that he proclaimed in his evangelization of Jews and Greeks, Greeks and barbarians, and slaves and freepersons in the eastern and probably western Mediterranean world.[66] From these summaries, we can arrive at a partial reconstruction of this gospel, which consisted of six components: (1) the gospel's divine origin, (2) its apocalyptic nature, (3) the concise presentation of the Messiah event in it, (4) the gospel's eschatological focus, (5) the gospel as the fulfillment of God's promises to Israel in Scripture, and (6) Paul's special place in the gospel as the herald of it to the gentiles. As I conclude this essay, I reflect upon how Paul's proclamation of the gospel differs from much preaching in our modern-day American context, especially among the supposedly more evangelical Christians, the group known as evangelicals. It seems that many would find the apostle's emphasis on the apocalyptic nature of the gospel, its eschatological focus, the gospel as the fulfillment of God's promises to Israel in Scripture, and the concise presentation of the Messiah event in it, especially Jesus's Davidic descent and ascension to God's right hand, at best odd and at worst too much information in their attempt to make converts. I suggest that one reason for this situation is that many American Christians have accommodated and acculturated the gospel to our present cultural situation to the extent that they have forgotten the first thing that Paul affirmed about the gospel: its divine origin. The gospel is from God and relates his work through his divine Son Jesus and his life-giving Spirit. For this reason, it is and must always be otherworldly, odd, and even strange because it does not consist of any wisdom of, from, or by this present evil age. In short, it is, as Paul notes, a mystery, which those who are not being saved consider foolishness. My prayer is that the American Church can rediscover the supernatural nature of the gospel and thus find a way to faithfully conform her proclamation of

---

[66] For the early tradition that Paul preached the gospel in Spain, see the apostle's desire to go there in Rom 15:24, 28 and 1 Clem 5:5.

it to that of the earliest Christians in our own context. If this occurs, God only knows what miracles he will work in the Church and in the world.

2
Meaningfully Misunderstanding the Markan Messiah: Ironic Intercalations in the Second Gospel

Kevin B. Burr

I want to share a personal note before beginning the present article. I first met Allen Black in the spring of 2010 during a night class he was teaching on the Gospel of Mark. In a packed room, I sat enthralled as I watched him masterfully handle questions about the interpretation of various passages, the meanings of certain Greek words, and the import of quotes and allusions to the OT and other points of contact with the Synoptic tradition. As Allen taught, it became clear to me that I should take as many classes with him as I could. But what was not clear to me then was just how much Allen would become a mentor and later a friend. His guidance has extended far beyond the classroom, for perhaps more than any other professor at HST, he has shaped me to become the student, author, scholar, and professor I am today. It is in memory of our first meeting that I have chosen to write on the Gospel of Mark to honor a διδάσκαλος ἀγαπητός.

IRONY: AN INVITATION TO SEE BEYOND

"Irony occurs when the elements of the story line provoke the reader to see beneath the surface of the text to a deeper significance."[67]

A long time ago in a galaxy far, far away, the most evil villain devised by George Lucas was a career politician who happened to be a Sith Lord. Sheev Palpatine was Supreme Chancellor of the Galactic Republic who, under his alias Darth Sidious, surreptitiously orchestrated both sides of the seemingly endless, galaxy-wide Clone Wars, which led to the gradual thinning and degradation of the Jedi Order. He did this while slowly manipulating the young, impressionable, and emotionally vulnerable "Chosen One," Anakin Skywalker, isolating him from and poisoning him against the Jedi. When Palpatine was ready to reveal his true nature to Skywalker, he relayed the story of one Darth Plagueis who sought to use the Force to create and sustain life; unexpectedly, however, he was killed by his apprentice, whom the audience comes to discover was Darth Sidious/Palpatine all along. At the opportune moment, Palpatine hauntingly

---

[67] Jerry Camery-Hoggart, *Irony in Mark's Gospel: Text and Subtext*, SNTSMS 72 (Cambridge: Cambridge University Press, 1992), 1.

declares to Skywalker that Plagueis's death was "... ironic. He could save others from death, but not himself."[68]

Lucas's use of irony in Star Wars is multi-layered: characters consistently do and say things imbued with more meaning than other characters realize while, at the same time, the audience understands the characters' actions more fully than the characters themselves. For example, not only does Palpatine let the Jedi train Anakin Skywalker/Darth Vader, who is instrumental in bringing about the Jedi's downfall, but Palpatine has also groomed the very one who will kill him in *Return of the Jedi*. D. C. Muecke describes the presentation of irony as a dual-layered narrative structure where characters in ironic situations exist in a lower level, whereas the audience/readers (or the ironist) are situated in an upper level.[69] This ironic structuring is interwoven throughout Star Wars and in other famous tragedies like Sophocles's *Oedipus Rex* or Shakespeare's *Romeo and Juliet*. The audience is aware of Oedipus's true lineage and knows he hunts himself; Thebes suffers by the actions of their patricidal and incestuous king. The audience grieves as Romeo rashly commits suicide because we are privy to Juliet's plan to fake her death. The characters who are victims of irony—the titular characters in the aforementioned plays—have insufficient understanding of their actions and/or the consequences thereof, and the narrator/author takes advantage of the victim's insufficient awareness.

Equally ironic is the downfall of such a powerful Sith Lord in *Episode III* who "could save others from death but not himself." But for George Lucas, the irony does not stop there: with this grave pronouncement, the antagonist delivers a pointed and villainous line of irony to the story's Chosen One concerning salvation from death with words that are historically associated with grievous betrayal—and with these words, the audience is invited to see beyond what Palpatine says. Readers of the Gospels will surely see in Palpatine's statement language similar to (if not an intentional echo of[70]) the Passover crowd which called for Jesus's death: while the Gospels' protagonist—also a "Chosen One"—hangs on the cross, the chief priests and scribes deride him, saying "He saved others; he cannot save himself" (Mark 15:31b).[71]

While it is evident that George Lucas has carefully built irony into his tales of a galaxy far, far away, he is nevertheless an apprentice when compared with irony master Mark the Evangelist whose Gospel is deeply embedded with subtle and sophisticated

---

[68] Ian McDiarmid, "Tragedy of Darth Plagueis the Wise," *Star Wars: Episode III – Revenge of the Sith*, directed by George Lucas (Los Angeles: 20th Century Fox, 2005).

[69] D. C. Muecke, *The Compass of Irony* (London: Methuen, 1969), 19, quoted in James L. Resseguie, *Narrative Criticism of the New Testament: An Introduction* (Grand Rapids: Baker Academic, 2005), 67.

[70] See the seven tests for echoes from the late Richard B. Hays, *Echoes of Scripture in the Letters of Paul* (New Haven: Yale University Press, 1989), 29–33.

[71] All Scripture citations are NRSV unless otherwise noted.

irony.[72] According to James Resseguie, irony mainly occurs in two modes: verbal and situational.[73] Verbal irony can be found when characters do not mean what they say; that is, characters often say things that carry greater meaning than they intend. For example, in the eyes of the people, it is ridiculous for the Messiah to suffer and die, so the crowd mockingly implores Jesus to save himself (Mark 15:30). The irony is that Jesus viewed his suffering and death as key components to his messianic mission (see also 8:31; 9:31; 10:33-34). Situational irony occurs when events mean more than they seem to the characters involved. For example, Jesus's crucifixion is the "central irony" of the Gospels as it "turns out to be his elevation to kingship."[74]

Particularly in biblical narratives, irony has three primary functions: 1) to persuade the audience to the narrator's viewpoint; 2) to foster a community of believers; and 3) to emphasize claims beyond what can be conveyed plainly.[75] Using the examples above, Mark uses irony to deepen his audience's understanding of Jesus, particularly his need to suffer and die. By deepening their understanding, the audience can move from the lower level (where the characters exist) to the upper level with other initiated believers. Perhaps readers will see more clearly God's work in the world or see themselves in the characters such as the religious elite, the oft witless disciples, or the marginalized and disenfranchised. Lastly, irony is a powerful literary tool that dramatically reveals its meaning in unexpected ways. It invites the reader to see beyond what has been said, as when Pilate unwittingly labels Jesus "king of the Jews" (Mark 15:2), the first time Jesus is associated with this title in Mark. With only these few examples, it is clear that by means of irony, Mark has highlighted meaningful misunderstanding throughout his gospel.

Mark opens his account with a simple, bold, and politically-charged proclamation: "The beginning of the good news of Jesus Christ, the Son of God,"[76] and then, with breathless pacing, narrative vividness, and careful literary structuring, the evangelist capably guides the audience/reader on a tour de force of Jesus's ministry from his

---

[72] C. Clifton Black, *A Three-Dimensional Jesus: An Introduction to the Synoptic Gospels* (Louisville: Westminster John Knox, 2023), 66.

[73] See also Resseguie, *Narrative Criticism*, 69–73.

[74] Joel Marcus, "Crucifixion as Parodic Exaltation," *JBL* 125.1 (2006): 73–87, at 73.

[75] Resseguie, *Narrative Criticism*, 73.

[76] Mark uses the words εὐαγγέλιον and υἱὸς θεοῦ in his opening line, which appear (or allude to, so υἱὸς θεοῦ) in an inscription from Priene, dated 9 CE. See the discussion in Everett Ferguson, *Backgrounds of Early Christianity*, 3rd ed. (Grand Rapids: Eerdmans, 2003), 46–47. While there is some debate regarding the textual authenticity of υἱὸς θεοῦ in Mark 1:1, it may be original due to its representation in codices B and D, so Bruce M. Metzger, *A Textual Commentary on the Greek New Testament: A Companion Volume to the United Bible Societies' Greek New Testament*, 3rd corrected ed. (London: United Bible Societies, 1975), 73.

baptism to the climactic crucifixion.[77] For Mark, his readers must understand that Jesus's ministry, death, and resurrection are the ultimate revelation of God's decisive work in the world. The setting of the Gospel of Mark is the created order and realm of human activity,[78] but things have gone terribly amiss due to the presence of evil. Jesus thus arrives and, in surprising ways, begins to usher in the reign and rule of God into a world that lies under the curse of sin (see also Gen 3). The true nature of Jesus's work is revealed to some and hidden from others (see also 4:10–12). It is revealed to those who suffer disease (for example, 1:30–31), demons (1:23–26), and death (5:35–43), but hidden from those who reject Jesus's ministry (3:6) or take offense at his teaching and power (3:22–30; 6:1–6). The revelation of God's work in overturning evil and establishing his kingdom in unexpected ways (see also the parables in Mark 4:1–34) and the choice to accept or reject God's Messiah are thus dominant themes in the Gospel of Mark. It is therefore appropriate to label Mark's Gospel "apocalyptic," in the sense this Gospel "is where mysteries are propounded and revealed, where secrets unavailable elsewhere find their paradoxical elaboration," according to N. T. Wright.[79] In other words, apocalyptic reveals what was once hidden and can occur at the macro-level (for example Dan 7–12; Rev 4–22) or the micro-level (Mark 13). How apocalyptic serves this unveiling function is to manifest the theological significance of events in real time and space and, as importantly, to unequivocally reject the notion that evil has the final say.[80]

IRONIC INTERCALATIONS IN MARK

Irony functions, as noted earlier, to lead the audience/reader to see something more significant or meaningful than what is apparent. As a literary device, then, irony is perfectly suited for the Gospel of Mark given the thematic importance of hiddenness and revelation, and the apocalyptic quality of this Gospel; modern readers and scholars of the Second Gospel should expect to find irony throughout his account. One way in which Mark highlights dramatic or verbal irony in his narrative is through his masterful

---

[77] See, for example, the comments of Donald Guthrie, *New Testament Introduction*, 3rd rev. (Downers Grove: InterVarsity Press, 1970), 53.

[78] Described as the "cosmic setting" by David Rhoads, Joanna Dewey, and Donald Michie, *Mark as Story: An Introduction to the Narrative of a Gospel*, 2nd ed. (Minneapolis: Fortress, 1999), 64–65.

[79] N. T. Wright, *The New Testament and the People of God* (Minneapolis: Fortress, 1992), 392. See also the discussion of apocalyptic in 280–338 and specifically how the Gospel of Mark is apocalyptic in 390–96. To summarize Wright, he views Mark's Gospel as a Christian narrative apocalypse. Along similar lines as Wright, Richard Hays's own brief summary of the Gospel of Mark is exceedingly apocalyptic: "Mark re-narrates the story of Israel by seeking to show that, in the events of Jesus' life and death, God has a last torn open the heavens and come down and that in Jesus the Christ both judgment and restoration have come upon Israel in a way prefigured in Scripture" (*Echoes of Scripture in the Gospels* [Waco: Baylor University Press, 2016], 19).

[80] Wright, *People of God*, 392.

employment of intercalation, that is, the interweaving of two stories by sandwiching one within another or within an A-B-A pattern.[81] The purpose of this sandwich technique is to demonstrate that two events which at first seem disconnected are, in fact, mutually illuminating.[82] As Mark, therefore, joins these together, the reader is drawn to perceive a more significant meaning than what is apparent. Intercalation thus functions as a sophisticated mode of ironic presentation. There are possibly nine intercalations in Mark's Gospel, though some find fewer.[83] For this study, I will analyze Mark's sandwiching of the Beelzebul controversy story (3:20–35), a double healing (5:21–43), and the fulfillment of the prediction concerning Peter's denial of Jesus (14:53–72). By the technique of intercalation in each of these sections, Mark has carefully drawn his readers' attention to certain key themes which will be highlighted below.

Out of His Mind to Outsiders: Mark 3:20–35

In Mark 3:20, such a great crowd gathers around Jesus that he is unable to eat.[84] His extraordinary reputation, we come to find out, has captured the attention not only of

---

[81] For a brief definition of intercalation/sandwich structure, see Rhoads et al, *Mark as Story*, 50–52. Robert H. Stein, argues a true intercalation combines "clearly separate stories" (*Mark*, BECNT [Grand Rapids: Baker Academic, 2008], 115); of the same opinion is Helen K. Bond, *The First Biography of Jesus: Genre and Meaning in Mark's Gospel* (Grand Rapids: Eerdmans, 2020), who argues Mark has joined "completely independent stories," 172.

[82] See the discussion in Francis J. Moloney, *The Gospel of Mark: A Commentary* (Peabody: Hendrickson, 2002), 107.

[83] See C. Black, *Three-Dimensional Jesus*, 59–60, who lists 2:1–12 (*pace* Stein, *Mark*, who believes 2:1–12 is a single unit [115]); 3:1–6; 3:19b–35; 5:21–43; 6:6b–30; 11:12–25; 14:1–11; 14:53–72; and 15:6–32. See also James R. Edwards, "Markan Sandwiches: The Significance of Interpolations in Markan Narratives," *NovT* 31.3 (1989): 193–216, at 193; and Mary Ann Beavis, *Mark*, Paideia: Commentaries on the New Testament (Grand Rapids: Baker Academic, 2011), 19. Tom Shepherd, "The Narrative Function of Markan Intercalation," *NTS* 41.4 (1995): 522–40, and Bond, *First Biography*, 171–72, (see especially notes 11–12) believe there are only six intercalated pericopae in Mark. In his introductory textbook on the Gospels, Joshua W. Jipp suggests the entire Gospel of Mark can be viewed as a Markan sandwich (*Reading the Gospels as Christian Scripture: A Literary, Canonical, and Theological Introduction* [Grand Rapids: Baker Academic, 2024], 168), but intercalation is typically understood as the sandwiching of two, maybe three (so Bond) pericopae, not an entire Gospel's worth.

[84] Although Joel Marcus sees pre-Markan tradition in this section, he believes it "seem[s] fairly certain ... that Mark himself is responsible for framing the whole complex about scribal opposition ... between the stories that imply Jesus's alienation from his own family" (*Mark 1–8: A New Translation with Introduction and Commentary*, AB [New York: Doubleday, 2000], 278). Marcus's work focuses more on source-critical perspectives to the Gospel of Mark, and while there is value in determining what underlies Mark's narrative, narrative criticism enables readers to discern the evangelists' purposes more clearly than source criticism. For a brief description of the rise of narrative criticism, including some critiques, see Jeannine K. Brown, "Narrative Criticism," *DJG* 619–24.

the people in general but of his family in particular, who go out to "grab"[85] him because they believe he "is out of his mind" (3:21b, NET, ESV). At this point in the narrative, it is appropriate to ask, what has led Jesus's family to think he is mentally unwell? Have they heard he is garnering a reputation as a popular teacher and healer (1:14–15 and passim)? Have they heard he is causing trouble with religious leaders and potentially bringing disrepute and shame to himself and to them (see also 2:1–12, 23–28; 3:1–6)? Precisely who is responsible for the belief that Jesus is unwell is unclear,[86] but whatever Jesus's family believes about him in 3:20, Mark indicates it is not especially positive.[87] Immediately after this point in the narrative, scribes from Jerusalem arrive on the scene with a more serious and explicit accusation that Jesus is empowered by Beelzebul and casts out demons with demonic power (3:22).

Upon the scribes' arrival, Mark begins the compositional sandwich, part B of the A-B-A pattern. The result is that the "juxtaposition [of the two accounts] encourages the audience to look for comparisons and contrasts, and in so doing to appreciate greater complexities of meaning than might otherwise be thought present, both in connection with the characters and the situations in which they find themselves."[88] How has Mark

---

[85] Mark 3:21b (ἐξῆλθον κρατῆσαι αὐτόν), my translation. BDAG s.v. κρατέω (564.3), "of taking hold of forcibly and also without the use of force"; the lexicon glosses this verb in Mark 3:21 with "take hold of," "grasp," or "seize," with the implication that they would try to physically remove Jesus from the crowd or the premises, or both. Elsewhere in the Gospel of Mark, the verb κρατέω (usually translated "arrest," or "seize") has an exclusively negative connotation when, as in 3:21, Jesus is the intended or actual object: the authorities seek to *arrest* Jesus in 12:12; the chief priests continue to plot how they can *arrest* Jesus in 14:1; Judas conspires with the guards to *seize* the one he kisses in 14:44, and see also 14:46; Jesus tells the authorities they could have *arrested* him publicly in 14:49; likewise, John the Baptizer is *seized* in 7:3. Along similar (negative) lines, Jesus criticizes the Pharisees who "having abandoned the commandment of God, cling [κρατέω] to the tradition of men" (7:8, my translation). In stark contrast, Jesus himself is the subject of κρατέω three times in Mark, and in all three cases Jesus takes hold of (κρατέω) someone's hand in order to raise or lift up (ἐγείρω) the person he has just healed: Peter's mother-in-law in 1:31; Jairus's daughter in 5:41; and a boy cured of demonization in 9:27. It appears the combination of κρατεώ and ἐγείρω (with ἀνίστημι in 9:27) is a Markan trope that depicts Jesus as the one who takes hold of and raises the sick, the dead, and the possessed and (proleptically) raises them to new life. Coincidentally, illness, possession, and death are the three categories of healing Jesus performs in the intercalations analyzed in this study.

[86] Allen Black sees some ambiguity in the origin of the accusation that Jesus is out of his mind (*Mark*, The College Press NIV Commentary [Joplin: College Press, 1995], 83), but Beavis (*Mark*, 68), following Marcus (*Mark*, 271), believes the accusation originates with the family and possibly suggests demonic activity (see also John 10:20).

[87] In light of the rest of the story, Pheme Perkins argues that "Juxtaposing the tradition about breaking with one's birth family to join those around Jesus and the accusation that Jesus is a magician adds dark tones to the family episode" (*Introduction to the Synoptic Gospels* [Grand Rapids: Eerdmans, 2007], 141).

[88] Bond, *First Biography*, 172. Bond (172) and Stein (*Mark*, 177–78) both assert the two units of 3:20–35 were originally distinct narratives. While it is, in my estimation, entirely possible that the scribes arrived at the same time as Jesus's family was attempting to retrieve him (perhaps covering for Jesus

done this? By slowly uncovering the striking similarities shared by the ones who should be most invested in Jesus—his family[89]—and by those who should perceive God's power most clearly—the scribes.

Upon hearing the accusation against him, Jesus "called them to him" (3:23a) to respond. Precisely whom Jesus calls is not stated, but it is reasonable to expect some combination of those present as he begins to teach them with the parable of the divided kingdom.[90] Jesus's response is split into two parts: a defensive counterargument (3:23b–26) and a retort, including a counter-accusation (3:27–29). He first highlights the absurdity of his working with Satan by pointing out that Satan would not work against himself, for doing so would bring about his own end. Jesus then offers a parabolic, if not also apocalyptic, description of his ministry in which a thief foils a "strong man" by "binding" him and plundering his goods; for the reader, the story of the strong man addresses the accusation, but it is reasonable to suspect Jesus's audience is largely unaware that he himself is the thief, the one who breaks into the strong man's house to plunder his goods.[91]

---

with the claim that he is mentally unwell which might save him from legal trouble [so Craig S. Keener, *The IVP Bible Background Commentary: New Testament*, 2nd ed. (Downers Grove: InterVarsity Press, 2014), 136]), Stein argues the "agreement of the Matthean and Lukan parallels against Mark in 3:22–27 ... suggests that this tradition was also found in Q" (*Mark*, 178). Q, however, is falling somewhat out of favor in current Jesus research (see, for example, Mark Goodacre, *The Case Against Q: Studies in Markan Priority and the Synoptic Problem* [Harrisburg: Trinity Press International, 2002]; and John C. Poirier and Jeffrey Peterson, *Marcan Priority Without Q: Explorations in the Farrer Hypothesis*, LNTS 455 [London: Bloomsbury, 2015].); it may be more plausible, therefore, to think that Matthew has followed Mark in retaining the setting—an accusation against Jesus—while simply omitting the reference to Jesus's family, so R. T. France, *The Gospel of Matthew*, NICNT (Grand Rapids: Eerdmans, 2007), 47; *pace* R. Alan Culpepper, *Matthew: A Commentary*, NTL (Louisville: Westminster John Knox, 2021), 239, who also believes Matthew follows Q.

[89] Family cohesion and issues of honor, shame, and the importance of safeguarding family reputation and, therefore, community safety underlie this narrative. See also David A. deSilva, *Honor, Patronage, Kinship & Purity: Unlocking New Testament Culture*, 2nd ed. (Downers Grove: InterVarsity Press, 2022), 191–92.

[90] Although Mark's description in 3:23 of Jesus's teaching as "parables" may seem odd to modern readers, Allen Black helpfully indicates that the evangelists employed the term "parable" to refer to a variety of anecdotes or sayings, rather than the narrower, modern understanding of "parable" to refer exclusively to metaphorical stories (*Mark*, 84).

[91] Adela Yarbro Collins states, "In this saying, Jesus' argument returns to figurative language and reaches its climax. Here, however, he does not use a comparison in the classic rhetorical sense. This brief saying is more like a fable in that it veils a claim that the Markan Jesus does not want to make explicit" (*Mark: A Commentary*, ed. Harold W. Attridge, Hermeneia [Minneapolis: Fortress, 2007], 233). If Yarbro Collins is correct, Jesus's obtuse parable in 3:27 coheres neatly with what he says later in Mark 4:11–12 regarding the function of parables to conceal.

Immediately after these short parables, Jesus warns that those who blaspheme against the Holy Spirit will never be forgiven. What precisely this means is debated,[92] but in context, it clearly refers to the scribes' accusation in which they obstinately attribute to Satan what should clearly be perceived as God's work.[93] Robert Stein astutely observes an additional literary twist in this passage: "It is ironic that those (the scribes) so adept in defining what sin is and who debated what sins are unforgivable ... were themselves guilty of the one unpardonable sin. In rejecting what the Spirit was doing in the ministry of Jesus, the scribes were rejecting God."[94]

Following this troubling teaching, Mark reintroduces Jesus's family, who finally make their way through the crowd to get Jesus's attention (3:31). Family cohesion, not to mention the honor and shame intertwined in proper family behavior, is a significant socio-cultural factor in Jesus's day; for his family to come out to get him and for him to rebuff their efforts is a serious breach of cultural mores and possibly an affront to his own mother given her presence.[95] Cultural issues being what they are, Mark has subtly included another point of irony by contrasting how he refers to Jesus's family with how Jesus refers to his spiritual family. In 3:21 Mark describes Jesus's "family" as οἱ παρ' αὐτοῦ, or more literally "those beside him."[96] Wherever the location of Jesus's family in 3:21 (which is not actually beside Jesus given the size of the crowd), by the time Mark reintroduces them in 3:31, they are physically *outside* the house, unlike the ones *inside* with Jesus. When he hears his family is outside, he responds and "[t]he people upon whom he fixes his gaze, *those around him* (περὶ αὐτόν) listening to Jesus' words, are to be his new family, replacing his blood family, described in v. 21 as *those beside him* (οἱ παρ' αὐτοῦ)."[97]

With this intercalation in Mark 3, the evangelist has subtly hinted that family or professional status, lineage, birthright, or other cultural markers are insufficient to make one a member of God's family. Rather, doing God's will makes one truly a member of God's family (see also John 1:13; 8:39–47). By weaving these stories together and drawing out the similarities in two seemingly unrelated events, Mark has intentionally highlighted an insight of which the characters themselves are unaware but which the audience/reader can discern all the more clearly.

---

[92] See, for example, Beavis's excursus in which she summarizes various church leaders' positions on blasphemy of the Holy Spirit (*Mark*, 70–71).

[93] In 3:30 Mark connects Jesus's warning with the scribes' accusation with a causal ὅτι: see the discussion in Rodney J. Decker, *Mark 1–8: A Handbook on the Greek Text* (Waco: Baylor University Press, 2014), 86.

[94] Stein, *Mark*, 186.

[95] Especially considering the importance of the fifth commandment in Judaism; see, for example, Keener's comments on Luke 9:59–60 in *IVP Bible Background Commentary: NT*, 205.

[96] Major translations consistently render οἱ παρ' αὐτοῦ as "family" (NRSV/UE, ESV, NET, NIV).

[97] Moloney, *Gospel of Mark*, 84 (original emphasis).

The ultimate pay-off for the first intercalation we have considered is the resurrection: this act of divine intervention decisively demonstrates Jesus's empowerment by God (contra the perspective of certain scribes, Pharisees, and Jewish authorities) as well as Jesus's anointing as God's eschatological agent, that is, the Christ (see also Mark 14:61–62). Perhaps the chief irony of the Gospel of Mark is that the one chosen by God was rejected by God's people, yet the chosen, righteous sufferer was vindicated in the end (see also Jesus's appeal to Ps 22). But the ironic juxtaposition of Jesus against others who represent diabolic opposition to God is found throughout Mark's account. The narrative threads Mark began in 3:20 run through another famous passage, the exorcism of Legion from the Gerasene demoniac. The context in 3:22–27 relates to Jesus's miraculous power, and in 3:27, Jesus parabolically presents himself as the one who can enter the strong man's house, bind him, and plunder his goods. The Greek word for "bind" here (see also ESV; "tie up," NRSV) is δέω, "to confine a pers[on] or thing by various kinds of restraints" (BDAG, 221.1). Surely it is no accident, then, that in Mark 5, Jesus encounters a demonically strong man whom no one was able to bind (δέω, 5:3) with shackles or chains (5:3–4). After a brief exchange, Jesus subdues this strong man—empowered by Satan, who himself is the "strong man" of 3:27—by sending away the demonic hoard into a nearby herd of pigs.[98] Although this particular action of Jesus may seem peculiar to modern readers, Joy Vaughan indicates that ancient exorcisms sometimes included "stories that situate the banishment of demons to a new dwelling place as part of the cure. Further, concession requests by a demon are not uncommon in antiquity. The demons want to avoid their eschatological fate since the ἄβυσσος is a place of punishment."[99] The demons plead with Jesus not to be sent out of the region, but the demons' removal from this man could enable them to harass others; ironically, what the demons did to the man (5:5), they beg Jesus not to do to them (5:7). As the demons spot the nearby herd of pigs they petition Jesus to send them into them. Jesus consents, perhaps signaling that the demons have indeed left the man.[100] The pigs, however, prove to be uncooperative hosts, and instead of remaining in the area (per the demons' wishes), they rush into the lake and drown. Herein lies

---

[98] Yarbro Collins notes that "binding" language in the OT and other Jewish literature demonstrates God's power over evil forces (for example, Leviathan in Job and Azazel in 1 Enoch) and here in Mark 3 it "evokes connotations of the divine warrior and his (royal) messiah or other agent in battle" (*Mark*, 233).

[99] Joy L. Vaughan, *Phenomenal Phenomena: Biblical and Multicultural Accounts of Spirits and Exorcism* (Waco: Baylor University Press, 2023), 145. Regarding the language of "binding" in exorcism, Keener observes "Magical texts sometimes speak of 'binding' demons by incantations (to manipulate them), but this is not the idea here (nor does Jesus ever say, 'I bind you' to a demon)" (*IVP Bible Background Commentary: NT*, 137).

[100] See Craig S. Keener, *Miracles: The Credibility of the New Testament Accounts*, 2 vols. (Grand Rapids: Baker Academic, 2011), 784, who observes that in some Jewish exorcism accounts, "[a]s in paganism, the visible proof of [a demon's] departure by some outward act often remained important."

another point of irony: the ἄβυσσος (into which Satan will be temporarily "bound," δέω; see also Rev 20:2) is sometimes connected to the watery depths into which spirits are imprisoned.[101] Immediately prior to Jesus's encounter with the Gerasene demoniac, he dramatically calmed an intense storm on the Sea of Galilee (Mark 4:35–41). With that extraordinary nature miracle still in the background of Mark 5, the demonized herd charges into the very place where Jesus has just powerfully demonstrated his mastery of creation. The Lord over all creation is also the Lord over all creatures.

THE FRAMING OF FEAR AND FAITH: MARK 5:21–43

Immediately following this extraordinary series of interwoven, miraculous events, Mark introduces another set of sandwiched stories in 5:21, the raising of Jairus's daughter and the healing of the woman with the flow of blood. When Jesus crosses back to the other side of the sea, a local synagogue ruler named Jairus approaches him humbly[102] and pleads with Jesus to heal his little daughter.[103] Jesus has become no less famous since 3:20, so once again, a large crowd follows him *en route* to Jairus's house. From this crowd, emerges another "daughter" (see also 5:34), who has suffered terribly with a flow of blood for twelve years.[104] Mark poignantly stresses her faith as she weaves her way through the throng, no doubt coming in contact with numerous people who could contract her ritual uncleanness (see also Lev 15:28).[105] In a moment of desperation and against cultural propriety, she reaches out and touches the edge of Jesus's clothes. The power that goes out of Jesus (5:30) immediately stops what had gone out of the woman (5:29). Jesus at once recognizes what has happened, and asks who has touched him. While the disciples are surprised Jesus would ask this given the encroaching crowd, Jesus's question is certainly not for his sake but for the woman's[106]; at a

---

[101] I. Howard Marshall, *The Gospel of Luke: A Commentary on the Greek Text*, NICGT (Grand Rapids: Eerdmans, 1978), 339.

[102] John Donahue and Daniel Harrington argue Jairus's humble posture of falling at Jesus's feet is "startling since the last time Jesus appeared in a synagogue the narrative ended with a plan to kill him (3:6)" (John R. Donahue and Daniel J. Harrington, *The Gospel of Mark*, SP 2 [Collegeville: Liturgical Press, 2002], 179).

[103] Mark uses the diminutive θυγάτριον rather than θυγάτηρ in Matt 9:18//Luke 8:42.

[104] Yarbro Collins notes the "large crowd that was introduced in v. 21 is mentioned again in v. 24, and the additional comment is added that the crowd was pressing upon him. This detail has a double function. On the one hand, it begins to heighten the suspense about whether Jesus will arrive in time to heal the dying girl. On the other, it prepares for the secret approach of the woman with the flow of blood" (*Mark*, 279–80).

[105] For another view, Lynn H. Cohick argues the woman herself was considered unclean, but she may not have caused the uncleanness of others (*Women in the World of the Earliest Christians: Illuminating Ancient Ways of Life* [Grand Rapids: Baker Academic, 2009], 208).

[106] Mark plainly indicates Jesus is aware of others' thoughts (see also 2:8). Elsewhere, God asks questions that are intended to provoke certain responses—particularly confession—from those whom he

rhetorical level, the disciples' question may actually highlight the woman's faith.[107] With "fear and trembling" (5:33), she confesses her deed, admitting her faith in Jesus's ability to heal, and he, in turn, rewards her faith. In the last, tender moment between Jesus and this unnamed woman, he affirms her status before God by calling her "daughter"—a subtle yet powerful reminder of two important points: that "whoever does the will of God" (3:35) is in God's family, and that another daughter's plight initiated this scenario in the first place.

No sooner than Jesus has comforted the woman, associates of Jairus bring the tragic news that his daughter is now dead (5:35). Jesus tells him, "Do not fear, only believe" (5:36), echoing the same note of fear the woman faced earlier (5:33). When they arrive the place is a din of weeping and wailing, and Jesus orders everyone outside except Jairus, Peter, James, and John. Quietly and without fanfare, Jesus enters the daughter's room, takes her by the hand,[108] and raises her back to life. The girl, we are told after she lives again, was also twelve years old (5:42; see also 5:25).

How, then, are these stories mutually illuminating? Bond sees several meaningful connections emerge in this unit.[109] The initial comparison focuses on Jairus and the woman: he is named, male, and in a position of religious authority, whereas his narrative counterpart is unnamed, female, and in a position of religious uncleanness. Jairus approaches Jesus publicly and humbly, while the woman approaches Jesus humbly but hidden. In the end of their respective stories, both are rewarded for their faithfulness to Jesus. Yet, as the story progresses, the narrative slowly yet surely shifts its primary focus from Jairus onto his daughter, at which point "new themes begin to emerge."[110] John Donahue and Daniel Harrington observe several significant comparisons between the two female characters. They are specifically referred to as daughters who face life-and-death situations from which they need salvation, that is, deliverance (see also σῴζω in 5:23, 28). Mark indicates the importance of faith in both accounts; although Jairus's faith is highlighted, his faith is nonetheless important for his daughter's restoration. Lastly, "[i]n these two narratives Jesus not only rescues the two women from death but also restores to them their life-giving capacity,"[111] both of whom are connected by the number twelve (5:25; 42).

---

questions. God's first questions in Gen 3 provide a useful comparison: see the discussion in Bill T. Arnold, *Genesis*, New Cambridge Bible Commentary (New York: Cambridge University Press, 2009), 67; and John Goldingay, *Genesis*, Baker Commentary on the Old Testament (Grand Rapids: Baker Academic, 2020), 77.

[107] So Donahue and Harrington, *Mark*, 180.

[108] Mark 5:41, καὶ κρατήσας τῆς χειρὸς .... See the discussion above in footnote 19.

[109] See Bond, *First Biography*, 172.

[110] Bond, *First Biography*, 172.

[111] Donahue and Harrington, *Mark*, 181.

Mark envisions Jesus's ministry as initiating the kingdom of God (see also Mark 1:14–15), which is both here in some (albeit limited) capacity but will be experienced fully at Jesus's return. These stories provide further proof that the hidden kingdom of God is slowly yet relentlessly breaking into the world, shattering the bonds of demons, disease, and even death itself. God's people must therefore have faith, that is, be faithful to Jesus, God's anointed king.[112]

DENIAL AND DETERMINATION: MARK 14:53–72

By sandwiching the account of Peter's failure within the story of Jesus's trial,[113] Mark develops certain themes and invites his audience to see beyond the individual events. After the tense scene in the Garden of Gethsemane where Peter, James, and John cannot remain awake to pray, one disciple (Judas) arrives while the rest scatter (Mark 14:43–50). Jesus is arrested and led before the chief priests, while only Peter follows at a distance (14:54). Having earlier pledged his faithfulness to Jesus (14:29), Peter appears to be a man of his word.

Once Peter is situated in the courtyard, Mark cuts to Jesus, who stands before the chief priests. The proceedings are fraught with difficulty, for none of the witnesses can muster any claims that come remotely close to justifying the death penalty, let alone can anyone present true testimony against Jesus. Mark specifically mentions a claim that Jesus would destroy the temple and raise it with one not made by hands (14:58; see also John 2:19), but not even this accusation could suffice. The high priest, therefore, took matters into his own hands and asked Jesus directly if he was the Messiah, to which Jesus responded affirmatively (14:60–62).

Falsehood pervaded Jesus's initial trial before the high priest, and now falsehood pervades Peter's part of the story. As he warms himself by the fire, a servant girl interrogates Peter, asking if he is an associate of Jesus, the first of three accusations against him. Peter denies this and distances himself further from the others and, ironically, further from Jesus (Mark 14:68). The servant girl, now with bystanders (14:69), encounters Peter and accuses him again, but he denies it a second time. Finally, other bystanders accuse Peter the Galilean (14:70) of knowing Jesus (from Nazareth, see also 14:67). This is too much for Peter, and given his penchant for hyperbole (see also 14:29 where he assures Jesus that even if "all others" desert him, he will not), Peter curses and swears an oath that he does not know Jesus. As the rooster crows a second time, Peter realizes what he has done and weeps bitterly (14:72).

---

[112] See also Donahue and Harrington, *Mark*, 182; and Bond, *First Biography*, 173. For the importance of understanding "faith" as faithfulness or allegiance, see Matthew W. Bates, *Salvation by Allegiance Alone: Rethinking Faith, Works, and the Gospel of Jesus the King* (Grand Rapids: Baker Academic, 2017), 77–100.

[113] The "trial" of Jesus before the Sanhedrin is better understood as a hearing or inquiry, so Craig S. Keener, *The Historical Jesus of the Gospels* (Grand Rapids: Eerdmans, 2009), 313–17.

Black observes an important contrast in this intercalation in which Mark has juxtaposed "Jesus and his brave confession before the high priest with the testing of Peter and his cowardly denials before a servant girl who worked for the high priest."[114] This scene is also rich with allusions to Jesus's teaching in Caesarea Philippi: in Mark 8, Jesus is the questioner; in Mark 14, Jesus is interrogated; in Caesarea, Peter is rebuked (8:33), while in Jerusalem, Jesus is accused.[115] In yet another ironic twist, Peter's distancing from Jesus represents the leadership of Israel: from 3:6 onward, the Jewish leadership should have been among the first to recognize God's work in Jesus, but their faithless distancing from God and toward Rome, whose power they court in 15:1–15, is fully manifest as they, ironically, charge Jesus with blasphemy for telling the truth.

While Mark has clearly not shied away from a "cowardly and even pathetic" portrayal of Peter,[116] his failure provides a cautionary tale: believers in Jesus must remain vigilant, for even those who followed him most closely could fall short (or misunderstand him altogether, see also 3:20–21). Jesus, on the other hand, is forever faithful and embodies the steadfast love of the LORD (see also Lam 3:22). Nevertheless, later Christians would surely know of Peter's apostleship and long work with the fledgling church. As tragic as Peter's denial is, the rest of the story demonstrates there is forgiveness available for the repentant.

CONCLUSION

Although Mark's Greek style may lack the eloquence and sophistication of the other Synoptic evangelists,[117] he admirably makes up for it by skillfully crafting a powerful, nuanced, and theologically profound narrative presentation of Jesus's ministry, death, and resurrection. Throughout the Second Gospel, the evangelist employs irony to emphasize major themes and to encourage his audience to investigate further who Jesus is (Christology) and what that means for them (discipleship). Moments of verbal or situational irony throughout the Gospel subtly highlight the people's meaningful misunderstandings of the Messiah. One noteworthy way Mark does this is by the intercalation, or sandwiching, of two distinct narratives in order to lead his readers to see a deeper meaning or more substantial connection between the two stories. In the three intercalations I analyzed above, Mark consistently highlighted the true natures of Jesus

---

[114] Allen Black, *Mark*, 256–57.

[115] Mary Ann Beavis, "The Trial before the Sanhedrin (Mark 14:53–65): Reader Response and Greco-Roman Readers," *CBQ* 49 (1987): 581–96, at 586, quoted in Beavis, *Mark*, 223.

[116] Donahue and Harrington, *Mark*, 428.

[117] See Beavis, who believes Mark's Greek "resembles the language of a Hellenistic popular novel" (*Mark*, 17). David A. deSilva's comments are representative of scholarly opinion on the quality of Mark's Greek style: "The Greek style of Mark is less refined, giving the narrative a more straightforward and forceful tone than the more ornate Luke" (*An Introduction to the New Testament: Contexts, Methods & Ministry Formation*, 2nd ed. [Downers Grove: InterVarsity Press, 2018], 180).

and discipleship. In the first sandwich (3:20–35), Mark demonstrates that Jesus is worthy of one's total allegiance over family responsibility or cultural propriety and that neither earned status (like that of the scribes) nor inherited standing (like that of Jesus's family, that is, those born into the covenant) suffice to qualify one to be God's family—rather, doing God's will is required. Through the second sandwich (5:21–43), Mark highlighted Jesus's extraordinary power in the face of the most hopeless situations, chronic illness and death. The importance of faith was fully displayed as Mark deftly drew faithfulness through the crowd right alongside the nameless woman who modeled the kind of faith Jairus needed. In the end, both were rewarded for their faithfulness. Finally, in the third intercalation (14:53–72), Mark tragically juxtaposed Peter's faithlessness with Jesus's faithfulness. While Peter, stand-in for the disciples and the Jewish leadership, rejects God's chosen one time and again, Jesus remains resolute and steadfast in his devotion to God and, consequently, in his devotion to those he came to save.

3
"We Know You Are True and Teach the Way of God Truthfully" (Matt 22:16): Reading the Hebrew Bible with Jesus in Matthew 22

Paavo N. Tucker

I had the privilege of serving as a teaching assistant to Dr. Allen Black from 2009–2011 while I was a student at Harding University Graduate School of Religion. My initial academic interests were in the New Testament. Halfway through my M.Div, I came to the realization that the New Testament cannot be understood apart from a grasp of the Hebrew Scriptures, and so I took a detour into Old Testament studies for several of my elective courses, fully intending to return to a focus on the New Testament. The now fifteen-year "detour" has taken me to a Ph.D. in Old Testament and a decade of research and teaching Hebrew and Old Testament to seminary students. Back in the day, Dr. Black graciously suffered my wanderings into the territory of Old Testament studies, and I am delighted now to return to continue the conversations about New Testament interpretation that Allen and I shared during our time of working together. In this spirit, I offer the following reflections on what we can learn about interpreting the Hebrew Bible from Jesus in Matt 22:15–46. The following overview of this chapter will focus on salient features of the text that help us reflect on Jesus's hermeneutical approach to the Hebrew Scriptures, before drawing some conclusions on what it means to read the Hebrew Bible as disciples of Jesus today.

MATTHEW 22:15–22: TRADITIONS AT ODDS

Matthew 22 describes a range of hermeneutical disputations between Jesus and his opponents that take place in the final week of our Lord's life.[1] In Matt 22:15–46, Jesus is challenged by questions from the Herodians (vv. 15–22), the Sadducees (vv. 23–33), and the Pharisees (vv. 34–40). Though little is known of these groups outside the references to them in the New Testament, based on their challenges in Matthew 22, we

---

[1] These disputations are the main focus of Matt 21–23. On the theme of Jesus as a teacher of the Hebrew Scriptures, see particularly Daniel M. Gurtner, "Jesus as Teacher of Israel's Scriptures in His Judaic Context," in *Jesus as Teacher in the Gospel of Matthew*, ed. Charles L. Quarles and Charles Nathan Ridlehoover (London: Bloomsbury/T&T Clark, 2023), 32–48.

may propose that the concerns of the Herodians were political,[2] the Sadducees were notoriously anti-supernaturalists, and the Pharisees could be considered legalists in their interpretations of the Scriptures. Jesus had earlier warned his disciples of the dangers of the "leaven" of the interpretive traditions of the Pharisees and Sadducees (Matt 16:6–12), whose teachings and presuppositions hindered them from perceiving the work of God that Jesus was embodying. The ripostes of Jesus to the challenges of these groups offer definitive indictments of the limitations of the interpretive traditions reflected by the Herodians, Sadducees, and Pharisees, whose vantages hindered them from learning from Jesus.

After Jesus entered Jerusalem and cleansed the temple (21:1–23), he was challenged by the religious authorities to declare the authority by which he was acting (21:23–27). In response, Jesus tells three parables that identify the leaders of Israel as unfit for their roles due to their hypocrisy (21:28–22:14).[3] The leaders then re-engage the controversy with the question by "disciples of the Pharisees and the Herodians" (vv. 15–16), which sets the stage for the following debates to ensue. The inquirers, who are plotting how to entangle Jesus in his words (v. 15),[4] appear disingenuous: "Teacher, we know that you are true and teach the way of God truthfully, and you do not care about anyone's opinion, for you are not swayed by appearances." This flattering statement will turn out to be an accurate assessment of the Lord as the true "Rabbi" who is not influenced by peer pressure or human traditions in his interpretation of the Scriptures, as Jesus is the one who "teaches the way of God truthfully" and silences his opponents. The initial inquiry, "is it lawful to pay taxes to Caesar?" is asking Jesus his opinion regarding what is "right, authorized, permitted, proper" (ἔξεστιν) regarding the political debates raging at the time. Though the inquiry as it is phrased is not explicitly about interpreting the Scriptures, the standard that determines what is right, authorized, permitted, and proper is, of course, the Hebrew Bible. In other words, they are wanting to know which political approach did Jesus's reading of the Hebrew Bible support? Politics at the time was a blood sport, and the question is intended to force Jesus to choose a side in the debate on taxation—the litmus test for how to respond to the Roman occupation. They are hoping his response would result in alienating the crowds—either undermining his popular support as a Messianic contender or getting him killed by the Romans for instigating revolt through refusing the tax. The response of Jesus brilliantly side-steps the trap, while posing a more pressing question back to the inquirers: "render to Caesar the things that are Caesar's, and to God the things that

---

[2] The Herodians were supporters of the Herodian dynasty, who had been granted rule by Roman favor (Everett Ferguson, *Backgrounds of Early Christianity*, 3rd ed. [Grand Rapids: Eerdmans, 2003], 533).

[3] Mark Allan Powell, *Matthew*, IBC (Louisville: Westminster John Knox, 2023), 329.

[4] On the tests paralleling the challenges of the devil to Jesus in Matt 4:1–11, see Powell, *Matthew*, 329.

are God's" (v. 21; ESV). The statement conveys a comprehensive political theology that is as expansive as it is enigmatic; from the preceding context, it is apparent that the Roman denarius, with the image of Caesar on it, belongs to Caesar. But what is it that is to be rendered to God? Nothing less, it appears, than "the surrender [to God] of all one was and possessed,"[5] in accordance, of course, with the teachings of the Torah. Given the discussion of the *Shema* that follows in vv. 34–40, what Jesus has in mind is presumably the giving of the entire self, in loving devotion to God, as for example Deut 10:12–13 articulates this commitment with the expansive, "what it is that the Lord requires of you," that is, "fearing the Lord, to walk in his ways, to love him, to serve him with all your heart."[6]

MATTHEW 22:23–33 THE SADDUCEES: YOU DO NOT KNOW THE SCRIPTURES, NOR THE POWER OF GOD

The next group that steps forth to challenge Jesus is the Sadducees. What we know of them outside the Scriptures emerges as significant in this encounter with Jesus.[7] As wealthy aristocrats who collaborated with Rome to maintain control of the elite religious establishment in Jerusalem, they were responsible for the elaborate rituals of the temple cult. They believed only in the authority of the Torah from the Hebrew Scriptures, and their religious-political focus coincided with anti-supernatural tendencies that denied the "resurrection, angels,[8] and spirit" (Acts 23:8). Perhaps, having lost a sense of transcendence, they are throwing themselves fully into building the earthly kingdom of God through pragmatic social activism that is married to the power-structures of empire. They are, of course, theists, but we may wonder what kind of this-worldly, non-spirit worldview they inhabited. The question they pose to Jesus reflects their lack of belief in the resurrection, as they raise an interpretive crux regarding the possibility of resurrection (vv. 24–28): a woman without offspring is left widowed and subsequently is married in turn to six brothers of the deceased, each of which dies without leaving children. In the resurrection, which of the seven brothers will the widow be espoused to? The question, which is based on the law of Levirate marriage in Deut 25:5–10 that requires a man to marry the widow of a deceased brother in order to secure care for the woman and the family inheritance, is perfectly reasonable and points to an interpretive conundrum that would have many a theologian scratching their heads. The

---

[5] Craig S. Keener, *The Gospel of Matthew: A Socio-Rhetorical Commentary* (Grand Rapids: Eerdmans, 2009), *kindle*.

[6] See, for example, Powell, *Matthew*, 331.

[7] Ferguson, *Backgrounds*, 519–20;

[8] "Angels" here may refer to human spirits, as Jesus will go on to make his response to the Sadducees based on the condition of angels, which would be problematic if the Sadducees denied the reality of angels (W. D. Davies & D. C. Allison, *Matthew 19–28*, vol. 3, ICC [London: T&T Clark, 2004], 227).

response of Jesus serves as a challenge to all of us who struggle to wrap our minds around the resurrection to beware of the leaven of the Sadducees. The Lord reprimands the Sadducees for being "wrong" in their presuppositions and starting points to the question, in that they do not know the Scriptures nor the power of God (v. 29). Jesus proceeds to make an important point about "resurrection" life[9] and the realm of Heaven, which applies not only to the question of resurrection, but to all of our theological perceptions about the kingdom of God and ministry of Jesus. When it comes to understanding the "resurrection life" (v. 30), our traditions and categories of interpretation that we bring to Scripture, based on our limited experiences of earthly life—here pertaining to matters of marriage, but extendable to all matters of theology as related to material existence–are limited and inadequate to grasp the inbreaking reality of the resurrection life and the kingdom of God that is taking place in the ministry of Jesus. The resurrection life, in other words, is not like something that we already know and can fathom (v. 30). It is something greater and more wonderful than anything we can imagine (see also 1 Cor 2:9).[10] The traditions of the Sadducees and their disenchanted theological imaginations[11]—the "leaven" that Jesus warned the disciples about (Matt 16:11–12)—kept them from perceiving the inbreaking of the supernatural, resurrection-life kingdom of Heaven that Jesus was bringing. Their imaginations were stunted by an Enlightenment-like reading of Scripture and unfamiliarity with the reality of the power of God.

Jesus challenges their hermeneutic based on a familiar passage from the Torah, Exod 3:1–8, where Yahweh speaks to Moses from the burning bush and commissions him to deliver Israel out of Egypt. The theological foundation of this deliverance is the promise of God to Abraham, Isaac, and Jacob to bring their descendants out of Egypt and give them the promised land (see also Gen 15). Jesus emphasizes this commitment of Yahweh by referencing the statement "I (am) the God of your fathers" (אנכי אלהי אביך), where the Greek Translation makes the null-copula explicit, Ἐγώ εἰμι ὁ θεὸς τοῦ πατρός σου, translated as "I am the God of your father." Because of this covenant relationship, Yahweh is committed to be faithful to the patriarchs and bring their descendants out of Egypt. According to Jesus, this affirmation in Exod 3:6 was not just spoken to Moses, but the Sadducees, as readers of the text of Exodus, are expected to read in it "what was said to *you* by God" (Matt 22:31)—thus making the Scriptural address immediate and personal. The significance of Jesus's quotation and explanation of the Scripture as a response to the Sadducees, "'I am the God of Abraham, and the God of Isaac, and the God of Jacob.' He is not the God of the dead, but of the living"

---

[9] As Davies and Allison note, "in the resurrection" (v. 30) means "in the resurrected condition" (*Matthew 19–28*, 227).

[10] See also Powell, *Matthew*, 332, 334.

[11] So Davies and Allison, they "deny the resurrection because they imagine the eschatological future others profess to be mundane and terrestrial" (*Matthew 19–28*, 226).

(v. 32), can be taken in various ways. Of the various expositions of this statement, I will mention only a few details as the most poignant.[12] First, the significance may hinge on the present tense of the verb "I am (εἰμι) the God"[13] as implying the continuing existence of the long-dead patriarchs at the time of the pronouncement.[14] This would suggest that God's faithfulness to the patriarchs, solidified through covenant, surely extends beyond the grave and includes continuing provision and relationship in the world to come. That is, Yahweh is "not the God of the dead, but of the (currently) living (patriarchs)." The implications of this statement are vast. Abraham, Isaac, and Jacob are living, reclining at the banquet table and awaiting those who will join them (Matt 8:11). Other saints who are long-deceased, such as Moses and Elijah, are at large and available for appearances (Matt 17:3). At the death of Jesus, the power of God was released into the cosmos, causing an earthquake, tearing the veil of the temple, and raising many from the dead (Matt 27:51–52). The resurrection life that the living God brings through the life, death, and resurrection of Jesus, envisions "the eschatological future not as an earthly paradise but as something transcendent, as a time and place in which the boundaries between heaven and earth will become indistinct."[15] The presence of this kingdom is "already;" it is near, at hand, and among you, while it is also deferred, coming, "not yet." The enchanted world of the Gospels, the worldview of Jesus, is a lot stranger than our modern Enlightenment assumptions presume. It is populated by angels and demons, appearances of deceased saints, and regular encounters with the post-resurrection Jesus himself, while the universe allows for miraculous healings, walking on water, multiplication of food, passing through walls, and teleportation. These supernatural events continue persistently beyond the Gospels, through the book of Acts, and seamlessly into the post-biblical history of the Church.

Yahweh is the God of the living, whose faithfulness and power unite creation and eschatology, and whose promises assure his people of participation in his life.[16] As Jesus repeatedly warns, however, our worldviews and traditions—our "leavens"—can keep us from seeing what is right in front of us and from participating in the supernatural life of God.[17] Hence, the invitation of the kingdom is repeatedly to "repent," to

---

[12] For a more extensive list of possibilities, see Davies and Allison, *Matthew 19–28*, 231–32.

[13] Matthew adds this verb explicitly (see also the LXX Exod 3:6), which is not found in the parallel in Mark 12:26 (the MT of Exod 3:6 is a null copula clause without a "be" verb).

[14] So most commentators, Robert H. Gundry, *Matthew* (Grand Rapids: Eerdmans, 1994), 446; though not necessarily so.

[15] Davies and Allison, *Matthew 19–28*, 233.

[16] Reinhard Feldmeier and Hermann Spieckermann, *The God of the Living: A Biblical Theology* (Waco: Baylor University Press, 2011), 1.

[17] As C. Leonard Allen and Danny Swick note in their book *Participating in God's Life*, this is particularly a challenge for those raised in Protestant traditions that are deeply rooted in Enlightenment rationalism (Abilene: ACU Press, 2001).

change the way we think (μετανοεῖτε), and "know the Scriptures." This involves accepting the perspective on reality that the Gospels convey and surrendering to the "power of God" that transcends our limited perspectives. Jesus challenges the Sadducees—and all would-be readers of the Hebrew Scriptures—to see themselves as directly and personally addressed by Yahweh at the burning bush, to know that the promises and faithfulness of God apply to them, and to read the supernatural aspects of the Scriptures quite literally—no demythologizing here! In other words, Jesus espouses an enchanted reading of Scripture, wherein we rediscover the Bible as a sacred, dangerous, mysterious, and supernatural presence-filled wonderland; this kind of reading is required to counteract the biblical illiteracy of both liberalism and fundamentalism in an increasingly post-Christian landscape in the Western world.[18]

MATTHEW 22:34–40 LOVING GOD AND NEIGHBOR

The last challenge emerges from the Pharisees, who, having seen Jesus silence the Sadducees, send forth a lawyer to challenge Jesus. The question appears simple enough, but the engagement is described as a "test" (πειράζων), thus presumably to ensnare Jesus in controversy on a complicated topic on which his earlier pronouncements had proved controversial. The question regarding the "great commandment of the law" (v. 36) was commonly debated among rabbis of the time.[19] The answer of Jesus unifies the two great themes of the Torah, love of God as articulated in the *Shema* of Deut 6:4–5, and love of neighbor from Lev 19:18, which Rabbi Akiba had considered the "greatest principle in the law."[20] The meaning of the *Shema*, to love God with all your "heart, soul, and mind," is initially clear enough, involving the entire person. But what kind of love is this that can be commanded? A common conclusion on this question is represented by the commentary by W. D. Davies and Dale Allison, and similar sentiments can be multiplied in the literature: "Love of God, like love of neighbour, is not firstly an attitude or affection but—as the example of Jesus shows—a way of life, the sweat of labour for Another, 'the free service of our wills' (Calvin). This is why, unlike an emotion, it can be commanded."[21]

The same sentiment that separates attitudes, affections, and emotions from action is often reflected in studies of the *Shema* and commands to love God in Deuteronomy and the command to love one's neighbor in Lev 19:18. The phrasing "love the Lord your God with all your heart" is paralleled to Assyrian royal propaganda and rhetoric from the Vassal Treaty of Esarhaddon, in which the subjugated nations are commanded

---

[18] See for example the proposal of Cheryl Bridges Johns, *Re-Enchanting the Text: Discovering the Bible as Sacred, Dangerous, and Mysterious* (Grand Rapids: Baker, 2023).

[19] See also Davies and Allison, *Matthew 19–28*, 239–42.

[20] *Sipre Lev* 19:18.

[21] Davies and Allison, *Matthew 19–28*, 241.

to "love Assurbanipal, son of your Lord Esarhaddon, king of Assyria, as you do your own lives" and to swear loyalty to him "with your entire heart" (*VTE* 266–267, 386), and of course it would be difficult for a subjugated people to conjure up emotional love for their overlord Assurbanipal. Based on these parallels, scholars have usually concluded that "love" means something like "faithful obedience" to the covenant with Yahweh in Deuteronomy.[22]

The bifurcation of emotions from action, however, has been recently called into question, as the emotive actions of obedience cannot be ignored.[23] The philosopher Martha Nussbaum, for example, has argued in her *Political Emotions: Why Love Matters for Justice* that emotions, and especially love, are an integral part of political and moral life. Loving actions do not consistently happen without a sincere and growing emotional commitment of love.[24] A society must secure the emotional commitments of its citizens towards its central aspirations and values for the society to succeed in establishing its vision of justice. How, then, can emotional commitments be developed? According to Nussbaum, emotions "have a narrative structure. The understanding of any single emotion is incomplete unless its narrative history is grasped and studied for the light it sheds on the present response."[25] Thus, narratives can have an impact on emotions, and the way narratives are told has an important function in inculcating emotions. Deuteronomy inculcates an emotive love for God that persuades obedience through a sophisticated narrative rhetorical strategy. As we know from human experience, it is possible to "fall" in love through coming to know and experience life with another person. The narrative framework of Deuteronomy shapes how love is conceived, as the relationship between God and Israel undergirds the formalized expressions of that relationship in covenant language. In this relationship, God's love and care for Israel is born out of a feeling, an emotional attachment to Israel as the children of God. By analogy to Yahweh's love for Israel, Israel's response to the gracious provision of Yahweh should be reciprocated by "falling in love," with an emotional love that is inextricably linked with obedience as faithful response to God that is fundamental to Israel's covenant relationship with God in Deuteronomy.

---

[22] William L. Moran, "The Ancient Near Eastern Background of the Love of God in Deuteronomy," *CBQ* 25 (1963): 77–87; Moshe Weinfeld, "The Loyalty Oath in the Ancient Near East," *UF* 8 (1976): 383–85.

[23] As argued, for example, by Jacqueline E. Lapsley, "Feeling Our Way: Love for God in Deuteronomy," *CBQ* 65 (2003): 350–69, and Bill T. Arnold, "The Love-Fear Antinomy in Deuteronomy 5–11," *VT* 61 (2011): 551–69.

[24] Martha C. Nussbaum, *Political Emotions: Why Love Matters for Justice* (Cambridge: Belknap, 2013).

[25] Martha C. Nussbaum, *Upheavals of Thought: The Intelligence of Emotions* (Cambridge: Cambridge University Press, 2003), 236.

The Torah as rooted in the narratives of God's salvation of Israel intend to inculcate emotional commitments to the ideals of the laws. This love is not just external loving actions but also encompasses internal motivations that lead to proper loving actions within the context of a relationship of commitment. In Deuteronomy, we see the key dynamic of interweaving law and narrative: Law is a gift of God, and it is Israel's response to story. Law is shaped by the actions of God and is given to those who are already redeemed: grace comes before law and obedience. Obedience to the laws does not flow from an abstract, universal moral code, philosophical proposition, or process of nature, but from a particular, and very personal, relationship with a loving God.[26]

The command to "love one's neighbor as oneself" from Lev 19:18 likewise encompasses emotions and actions.[27] Narratives that draw on the history and experiences of a nation are a particularly effective means of motivating love for the ideals and common good of the society. In Lev 19:18, the command to "love your neighbor" is best understood to encompass the emotions of love, as well as the actions of a loving response. The narrative context of placing the laws of the Torah in Israel's liberation from Egypt forms the narrative environment in which Israel learns obedience from the heart. Obedience is given in response to God showing His love for Israel, and showing Israel the value of human life, thus teaching Israel to love their neighbors with emotional commitments that lead to obedience as a crucial part of imitating Yahweh and being holy as Yahweh is holy (Lev 19:2).

Within this context, Jesus's reference to the command to love God and love neighbor likewise integrates emotion and action into a comprehensive way of life that involves loving obedience to God and care for neighbor. This is not an "all you need is love" antinomianism, nor a legalism without affections. The narrative context of the Gospels invites the disciples to know God as their loving *Abba* who cares and provides for their needs, and through coming to know the Father, to love God in a way that leads to obedient response and care also for the neighbor whom God loves. Jesus concludes by summarizing that "on these two commandments depend ($\kappa\rho\acute{\epsilon}\mu\alpha\tau\alpha\iota$) all the Law and the Prophets" (v. 40). The "hanging" of the Law and Prophets from these two principles indicates the true end of the Hebrew Scriptures: "love the Lord your God and love your neighbor: all the rest is commentary."[28] Love functions as a coherent,

---

[26] Jon D. Levenson, *The Love of God: Divine Gift, Human Gratitude, and Mutual Faithfulness in Judaism* (Princeton: Princeton University Press, 2015), 59.

[27] See Paavo N. Tucker, "Why Love Matters for Justice: Political Emotions Between Narrative and Law in the Holiness Code," in *Biblical Ethics: Tensions Between Justice and Mercy, Law and Love*, ed. Markus Zehnder and Peter Wick, Gorgias Biblical Studies 70 (Piscataway: Gorgias, 2019), 83–104.

[28] Davies and Allison, *Matthew 19–28*, 246.

unifying hermeneutic for reading the entire Hebrew Bible.[29] Loving God and neighbor thus becomes a kind of "rule of faith" that guides the interpretation of the Hebrew Bible: the reading of any section of Scripture is intended to lead to a life of loving God and loving neighbor.[30] As James K. A. Smith has elucidated recently, "we are what we love," and it is our loves that carry us forward, either towards God or towards something else through cultural liturgies that intend to shape our desires.[31] Though the commands to love God and neighbor are the most familiar texts in the Hebrew Bible, they are also the most difficult to live out. Jesus challenges us to remember that the reading of Scripture should be a liturgy that shapes our hearts and actions towards love for God and neighbor, and if it is not, then we are to return to the beginning and reconsider how and why we are reading.

MATTHEW 22:41–46 TRINITARIAN

Having silenced the Herodians, Sadducees, and Pharisees through his profound responses to their questions, Jesus poses his own interpretive riddle regarding the identity of the Messiah (vv. 42–45):

> "What do you think about the Christ? Whose son is he?"
> They said to him, "The son of David."

---

[29] R. T. France, *The Gospel of* Matthew, NICOT (Grand Rapids: Eerdmans, 2007), 847; see also Carol J. Dempsey, "Love: The Fulfillment of the Law and the Prophets," in *Biblical Ethics: Tensions Between Justice and Mercy, Law and Love*, ed. Markus Zehnder and Peter Wick, Gorgias Biblical Studies 70 (Piscataway: Gorgias, 2019), 67–82.

[30] See, for example, Powell, *Matthew*, 335–36, on the hermeneutical function of the commands, whose comprehensive nature suggests that their application extends to all matters of Scriptural interpretation. See also, Augustine's guidelines on reading Scripture in *On Christian Doctrine*. This approach has potential for helping us understand difficult and troubling aspects of the Hebrew Scriptures. We see Israel wrestling with these principles, for example, in the Deuteronomic tradition, where right after the command to love God in Deut 6:4–5, Israel is commanded to obliterate their neighboring Canaanites (Deut 7:1–5). The destruction of temptations to idolatry—whether idols or people who may entice Israel astray—is an important feature of exclusively "loving God" in Deuteronomic theology. However, upon Israel's entry into the promised land and their first encounter with the natives, Rahab turns out to be a more devoted Yahwist than many of the Israelites, and the command to obliterate the natives is not applied literally in her case, nor in many other circumstances in the book of Joshua. The overriding concern is devotion to Yahweh, which is balanced with a love for neighbor. Joshua is presented as an ideal Torah Scribe who applies the principles of the law of Moses with wisdom to Israel's circumstances, seeking to be fully devoted to Yahweh, while showing compassion to the natives and not applying the commandments literally. See the discussion in Walter Moberly, *Old Testament Theology: Reading the Hebrew Bible as Christian Scripture* (Grand Rapids: Baker, 2015), 41–74. See also Matthew Lynch, *The Flood and the Fury: Old Testament Violence and the Shalom of God* (Downers Grove: InterVarsity Academic, 2023), 97, for discussion of the interpretation of the Torah in Joshua.

[31] James K. A. Smith, *You Are What You Love: The Spiritual Power of Habit* (Grand Rapids: Brazos, 2016).

> He said to them, "How is it then that David, in the Spirit, calls him Lord, saying,
> 'The Lord (יהוה in the MT, κύριος in the LXX/GNT)
> said to my Lord (אדני in MT, τῷ κυρίῳ μου in LXX/GNT),
> "Sit at my right hand, until I put your enemies under your feet"'?
> If then David calls him Lord, how is he his son?"

The text cited is from Psalm 110, which is the most frequently cited text from the Hebrew Bible in the New Testament. The text of the Psalm is difficult, and we will focus here only on a few details from verse 1. The song, which is introduced as a Davidic Psalm (לדוד, to/for/of David), describes what is known in the Hebrew Bible as a divine council (or heavenly council) type-scene (see also 1 Kgs 22:19–23; Isa 6; Job 1–2; Ps 82, Zech 3, and Dan 7). In this type-scene, a human is granted access to the divine council, where the person overhears or participates in a conversation between God and other spiritual beings.[32] In his exposition of this type-scene from Ps 110:1, Jesus describes four characters: king David (#1), inspired by the Spirit (#2), composes the Psalm, wherein he hears Yahweh (#3 יהוה) in the divine council addressing the "Lord" of David (אדני #4). In context, the "Lord" of David is understood to be the Messiah who is seated at the right hand of Yahweh in the divine council. The point Jesus makes is that the Messiah is not just the son of David, but is indeed the "Lord" of David, a divine being who is seated in a privileged position in the council of Yahweh.[33]

The point that I would like to make from this text regarding reading the Hebrew Bible, however, is not Christological but Pneumatological and Trinitarian, which is rarely noted in secondary literature on the passage. The divine council type-scene of Psalm 110, as understood by Jesus, describes a scene in which the Trinity is engaged in a dialogue: The roles of Yahweh God speaking to the Lord Jesus are clear enough, but an additional point that Jesus makes is the role of the Spirit in the speech of David. David, the author of the Psalm, is inspired by the Holy Spirit (see also 2 Sam 23:2; Acts 1:16–20) to enter into the realm of the divine council and overhear the discussion between Yahweh and the Messiah.[34] As throughout the New Testament, the Spirit is present to identify the Christ, the one anointed by the Spirit, and to point to the work of

---

[32] See, for example, Min Suc Kee, "The Heavenly Council and its Type-scene," *JSOT* 31 (2007): 259–73; and Michael S. Heiser, *Unseen Realm: Recovering the Supernatural Worldview of the Bible* (Bellingham: Lexham, 2015), 29–123.

[33] Keener, *Matthew*, 386; Davies and Allison, *Matthew 19–28*, 254.

[34] On this Trinitarian reading of Psalm 110, see particularly Matthew Bates, *The Birth of the Trinity* (Oxford: Oxford University Press, 2015), 41–84; Christopher R. Seitz, "The Trinity in the Old Testament," in *The Oxford Handbook on the Trinity*, ed. Gilles Emery and Matthew Levering (Oxford: Oxford University Press, 2011), 28–40; Christopher R. Seitz, *The Elder Testament: Canon, Theology, Trinity* (Waco: Baylor University Press, 2018), 193–98, on Luther's Trinitarian reading of Psalm 110.

Christ. According to Jesus, this is not a typological or allegorical reading of Psalm 110, but rather is the literal, historical-grammatical meaning of the text. This suggests that Christological texts of the Hebrew Scriptures, inspired as they are by the Holy Spirit as in Psalm 110, are not just "Christological" texts but also Pneumatological and hence Trinitarian. As Old Testament scholar Brent Strawn points out in his critique of contemporary Christological readings of the Old Testament, many Christological readings are theologically reductionistic and neglect the first, and particularly the third members of the Trinity.[35] A Trinitarian perspective of God which accepts the perichoresis of the Trinity (the interpenetration and inseparable operations of the Three Persons of the Trinity) necessarily involves a revisioning of most Christological interpretations of the Old Testament, if indeed the God of the New Testament revealed as Father, Son, and Spirit, is the God of Abraham, Isaac, and Jacob as revealed in the Hebrew Scriptures.[36] If this is the case, as Nicene theology affirms, then any theological statement about God in the Hebrew Scriptures involves a statement about the Trinity.[37] The divine council type-scenes, such as that described in Psalm 110, thus involve the Trinity. This is not to collapse the economic Trinity into the immanent Trinity, as there is still room to

---

[35] Brent A. Strawn, "And These Three are One: A Trinitarian Critique of Christological Approaches to the Old Testament," in *The Incomparable God: Readings in Biblical Theology*, ed. Collin Cornell and M. Justin Walker (Grand Rapids: Eerdmans, 2023), 167–88.

[36] As Christopher Seitz has made the case from a Trinitarian perspective, the Hebrew Scriptures bear witness to God revealed in the Trinity working in the life of Israel, and then among the people of God in the New Testament (*The Elder Testament*, 48). This is not a matter of reading the Trinity back into the Elder (Old) Testament, but rather, the "ontology of the Old Testament, that is, how the depiction at the center of the Elder Scripture—the divine life of the One Lord God YHWH—opens onto and indeed pressures a specifically Christian reading of the triune God as arising from this first scriptural witness" (*The Elder Testament*, 35).

[37] This is not to dismiss the original sense and context of the Hebrew Scriptures, in which the ancient Israelites who encountered Yahweh did not, of course, know God as Trinity (C. Kavin Rowe, "Biblical Pressure and Trinitarian Hermeneutics," *Pro Ecclesia* 9 [2002]: 295–312). As the Jewish scholar Benjamin D. Sommer has argued, however, ancient Israelites were strict monotheists, whose experience of God nevertheless is described as encompassing a divine fluidity, which accounts for a "single God whose manifestations take action on their own without becoming sufficiently independent to impugn the oneness of that God," such as in the encounter of Abraham and the three visitors in Genesis 18 who are described variously as "the men/the angels/the Lord" (*The Bodies of God and the World of Ancient Israel* [Cambridge: Cambridge University Press, 2010], 126). As noted by Sommer, this model of divine fluidity in the theology of the Hebrew Bible is not often recognized, though texts like Genesis 18 were perceived for example by Augustine and Luther, who did not see the three men as the Trinity, but nevertheless read the chapter as intimating that where God is concerned, three can be one (Sommer, *Bodies*, 132–33). As Rowe argues, it is the ontological pressure of Israelite monotheism, when integrated with theologies of divine fluidity in the Hebrew Bible and then in the New Testament with the divine sonship of the Messiah and the divine identity also of the Holy Spirit (see particularly the personal theology of the Spirit in Luke-Acts), that drives the eventual articulation of the doctrine of the Trinity in an integration of monotheism with divine fluidity.

maintain the distinctive operations of the Persons of the Trinity in both Testaments. Nevertheless, there cannot be a Christological reading of the Hebrew Scriptures that is not also a Pneumatological and, thus, Trinitarian reading. It is the Holy Spirit who reveals the Messiah in both the Hebrew Bible and New Testament, and invites glimpses into the divine council and the inner-Trinitarian dialogue as we see in Jesus's reading of Psalm 110.

CONCLUSION

I am honored to offer this contribution on how Jesus's interpretation of the Hebrew Bible as delineated in Matt 22:15–46 challenges us today to resist the cultural pressures of "being swayed by appearances" (Matt 22:16) in our reading of Scripture. The pericopes of Matt 22:23–33, 34–40, and 41–46 offer us three hermeneutical debates as models of particular lenses for interpreting the Hebrew Scriptures. These vignettes of Scriptural interpretation show how Jesus read the Scriptures with an enchanted, Trinitarian worldview, with an aim of a fully-embodied and emotive response of loving God and neighbor. The interpretive models of Jesus challenged and offended the Bible scholars of his day, and if today we are hearing Jesus accurately beyond the confines of the lenses bequeathed to us from our traditions, we will likely be challenged as well. We are challenged in Matt 22:15–46 to follow Jesus in interpreting the Scriptures with the lenses of an enchanted worldview, with an aim of loving God and loving our neighbor, and from the vantage point of the theological doctrine of the Trinity that is bequeathed to us by the Great Tradition of the church.

4
The Gospel of Luke and His Portrayal of Women

Alicia Williamson and Carl Williamson

INTRODUCTION

The Gospel of Luke distinguishes itself from other gospels by challenging the social norms widely accepted in the first-century church.[1] Luke gives a voice to the needy and reverses the place of who is most important in the kingdom of God. Luke's emphasis on women stands as one of the greatest examples of reversal. Namely, Luke has forty-two passages about women, twenty-three of which are unique to his gospel.[2] Furthermore, Luke mentions thirteen women who are not found in any other place in the New Testament.[3] In Luke, the presence of women often presents itself alongside a male parallel. According to Mary Rose D'Angelo, the male/female parallels "are the most notable feature of the centrality of gender in Luke."[4] In this way, Luke presents a unique

---

[1] This chapter began as a paper written for Dr. Black's Advanced Introduction to the New Testament course at Harding School of Theology. Although I (Alicia) was hesitant to write about females as I felt it would pigeonhole me as a theologian, Dr. Black's encouragement to investigate the women in Luke's gospel intrigued me. Also, how do you say no to someone as kind as Allen Black? As I dove into the research for the paper, my eyes were opened to so many women in the New Testament that had often gone ignored in my Sunday school and Bible classes. Women were everywhere, actively serving in the ministry of Jesus. This paper revolutionized my perspective of the valuable role women played in the first-century church. With every new character came a new way through which God revealed ways women have and continue to serve in his kingdom. I am forever grateful for Dr. Black's gentle nudge to write about this important topic and thankful that my husband, Carl, contributes his perspective on discipleship for the makings of this chapter. We hope the chapter opens the eyes of the readers to the active women in the Gospel of Luke who follow the footsteps of their Savior. Their faithful example teaches the church what discipleship entails.

[2] Jane Schaberg, "Luke," in *Women's Bible Commentary,* ed. Carol A. Newsom and Sharon H. Ringe, expanded ed. (Louisville: Westminster John Knox, 1998), 367–68, and Lora Angeline B. Embudo, "Women Vis-À-Vis Prophecy in Luke-Acts 2," *Asian Journal of Pentecostal Studies* 20 (2017): 112.

[3] The thirteen women are: Elizabeth (1), Anna (2:36–38), the widow of Zarephath (4:25, 26), the widow of Nain (7:11–17), the woman who was a sinner (7:36–50), Joanna and Susanna (8:2, 3), the woman in the crowd who blesses Mary's womb (11:27, 28), the woman who bowed down with infirmity (13:10–17), the woman with the lost coins (15:8–10), Lot's wife (17:32), the pleading widow (18:1–8), and the daughters of Jerusalem (23:28). See Embudo, "Women Vis-À-Vis Prophecy in Luke-Acts 2," 112.

[4] Mary Rose D'Angelo, "(Re)Presentations of Women in the Gospel of Matthew and Luke-Acts," in *Women & Christian Origins,* ed. Mary Rose D'Angelo and Ross Shepard Kraemer (New York: Oxford University Press, 1999), 181.

perspective of the significance of women in the ministry of Jesus and in the life of the first-century church.

There are two types of parallels in Luke. The first type is functional, where two stories are joined together which share a similar point.[5] Oftentimes, the male portion of the story can be found in Mark or Q, while the female portion is unique to Luke and gives insight into Luke's characterization of women. The second type is "architectural," where two similar stories are told in different contexts, which serves to bring the narrative together.[6] Turid Seim describes the Lukan parallels as more than just a literary device. She explains that a true parallel is where there is "a similarity between two examples or episodes with regards to contents, language, form, structure, or quite simply the theme."[7] This criterion helps to determine the significant parallels in Luke's gospel as charted below.[8]

Zechariah (1:5–23, 67–79	Mary (1:26–28, 46–56)
Simeon (2:25–35)	Anna (2:36–38)
Naaman (4:27)	Widow in Zarephath (4:25–26)
Widow's Son (7:11–17)	Jairus's daughter (8:40–42, 49–56)
Jairus (8:40–41)	Woman with the issue of blood (8:42–48)
Men of Nineveh (11:32)	Queen of the South (11:31)
Men healed on the Sabbath (14:1–6)	Woman healed on Sabbath (13:10–17)
Abraham's son (19:9)	Abraham's daughter (13:16)
Man sowed a seed (13:18–19)	Woman hid yeast (13:20–21)
Shepherd with a sheep (15:3–7)	Woman with coins (15:8–10)
Men sleeping (17:34)	Women grinding (17:35)
Peter at tomb (24:12)	Women at tomb (24:1–11)

---

[5] For example, the man with 100 sheep and the woman with 10 coins (Luke 15:1–7 and Luke 14:8–10) and Zechariah and Mary (Luke 1:5–38). See D'Angelo, "(Re)Presentations of Women in the Gospel of Matthew and Luke-Acts," 181–82.

[6] For example, the list of the twelve disciples prior to the sermon on the plain (Luke 6:12–19) parallels the list of women disciples prior to the parables sermon (Luke 8:1–3). See D'Angelo, "(Re)Presentations of Women in the Gospel of Matthew and Luke-Acts," 181–82.

[7] Turid Karlsen Seim, *The Double Message* (Nashville: Abingdon Press, 1994), 13.

[8] Seim, *The Double Message*, 15. Allen Black adds the women who accompany Jesus/The Twelve (Luke 8:1–3; 6:12–16). See Allen Black, "'Your Sons and Your Daughters Will Prophesy...': Pairings of Men and Women in Luke-Acts," in *Scripture and Traditions: Essays on Early Judaism and Christianity in Honor of Carl R. Holladay*, ed. Patrick Gray and Gail R. O'Day (Leiden: Brill, 2008), 196.

Scholars seek to understand how Luke characterizes women based upon these parallels and the large presence women play in the Gospel. There are three perspectives that give insight into Luke's purpose: rhetorical, theological, and literary.[9] This chapter introduces these three possible interpretations of Luke's emphasis on women. Additionally, the chapter defines and describes discipleship in the context of the women in Luke. Finally, the chapter concludes by applying these findings to the ministry of women in the modern church. Luke's emphasis highlights the essential contribution women make in the kingdom of God.

RHETORICAL PERSPECTIVE—A SUPPRESSION OF WOMEN

The rhetorical perspective is largely held by the feminist camp. It suggests that Luke's portrayal of women demonstrates one of silence rather than importance. D'Angelo believes that "Luke is concerned not with changing the status of women, but with the appropriate deployment of gender."[10] She outlines three areas where Luke suppresses the role of women: public character of work, desire to tame and limit prophecy, and his interest in asceticism.[11] This suppression is largely due to the diminishing speaking roles women play throughout Luke-Acts.[12] Therefore, the rhetorical perspective sees Luke failing to honestly reflect the significant role women played in the New Testament church. Barbara Reid argues the only way to clearly see the importance of women is to "dismantle the patriarchal structure itself and replace it with an alternate vision."[13] This alternate vision requires reading the Pauline teachings on women alongside Luke. An example of this perspective shows women as heads of the house churches, which they hosted in their homes, and disciples alongside Jesus, supporting him by their own

---

[9] Black, "'Your Sons and Your Daughters Will Prophesy...': Pairings of Men and Women in Luke-Acts," 195.

[10] D'Angelo, "(Re)Presentations of Women in the Gospel of Matthew and Luke-Acts," 187.

[11] D'Angelo, "(Re)Presentations of Women in the Gospel of Matthew and Luke-Acts," 187. See also Schaberg, "Luke," 369, and Ivoni Richter Reimer, *Women in the Acts of the Apostles: A Feminist Liberation Perspective* (Minneapolis: Fortress, 1995), 252.

[12] The Gospel of Luke contains fifteen occurrences of women speaking while Acts only records five. Furthermore, Luke only records the words of women ten times in the Gospel and three times in Acts. According to Schaberg, the diminishing presence of female dialogue demonstrates Luke's suppression of women. See Schaberg, "Luke," 368.

[13] Barbara E. Reid, *Choosing the Better Part? Women in the Gospel of Luke* (Collegeville: Liturgical Press, 1996), 8. Fiorenza also blames the patriarchal structure for tainting the view of women in Luke. See Elisabeth Schüssler Fiorenza, *In Memory of Her: A Feminist Theological Reconstruction of Christian Origins* (New York: Crossroad, 1987), 52.

means (Luke 8:1–3).[14] Instead, Luke's women appear weak and play the dominant role of nurturers to Jesus without the title of "disciples."[15]

In light of the findings from the rhetorical perspective, Luke's Gospel does not accurately reflect God's view of women and their place of equality with men. Women should be hesitant to serve, like the three women in Luke 8:1–3, where they are forced to support male leadership without having decision-making power themselves.[16] Accordingly, the rhetorical feminist perspective argues that churches must move past the restrictions of the patriarchal world that linger and embrace the spirit of equality for men and women in leadership and service.

THEOLOGICAL PERSPECTIVE—A PLACE FOR WOMEN IN THE KINGDOM OF GOD

The second perspective is centered on a theological emphasis on the fulfillment of prophecy and the kingdom of God. Luke's gospel begins with three prophetic statements by women.[17] Jacob Jervell connects these prophetic examples to the fulfillment of Joel 2:28, "Your sons and daughters will prophesy."[18] The prophecy is further fulfilled on the day of Pentecost when men and women receive the Spirit and salvation (Acts 2:4). The Holy Spirit, characterized by the gift of prophecy, is poured out across all boundary lines to men and women, young and old.[19] The pairings in Acts 2 reveal

---

[14] Reimer, *Women in the Acts of the Apostles: A Feminist Liberation Perspective*, 252. Koperski disagrees that women were the leaders of the house churches since Luke never gives a direct parallel of a male/female leader of a house church. Their role was more one of hospitality, not leadership. See Veronica Koperski, "Luke 10,38–42 and Acts 6,1–7: Women and Discipleship in the Literary Context of Luke-Acts," in *The Unity of Luke-Acts*, ed. J. Verheyden (Leuven: Leuven University Press, 1999): 526, and Ben Witherington, *Women in the Earliest Churches*, SNTSMS 59 (New York: Cambridge University Press, 1988), 148.

[15] Schaberg, "Luke," 369.

[16] Reid, *Choosing the Better Part? Women in the Gospel of Luke*, 133.

[17] Mary (1:46–56), Elizabeth (1:42–45), and Anna (2:38).

[18] Jacob Jervell, *The Unknown Paul: Essays on Luke-Acts and Early Christian History* (Minneapolis: Augsburg, 1984), 154. Black also supports this idea and sees the pairings in Luke1 pointing to the fulfillment of OT prophecy. See Black, "'Your Sons and Your Daughters Will Prophesy...': Pairings of Men and Women in Luke-Acts," 199. Furthermore, Embudo and Seim see the prophetic activity in the beginning of Luke as a "significant eschatological act." See Embudo, "Women Vis-À-Vis Prophecy in Luke-Acts 2," 117, and Seim, *The Double Message*, 183. D'Angelo negates this idea and points out that while Mary and Elizabeth are given long prophetic sayings, they are not portrayed as prophesying. They do not represent prophets nor are a fulfillment of Joel 2. D'Angelo, "(Re)Presentations of Women in the Gospel of Matthew and Luke-Acts," 186.

[19] Seim, *The Double Message*, 164; Embudo, "Women Vis-À-Vis Prophecy in Luke-Acts 2," 125, 132; and Black, "'Your Sons and Your Daughters Will Prophesy...': Pairings of Men and Women in Luke-Acts," 201.

Luke's theological intention. They are a positive portrayal of women who share equally their value in the kingdom of God and their gifts and responsibilities.[20]

Along with the fulfillment of Joel 2:28, Luke also emphasizes the theme of restoration through women. The pairings of physical and spiritual healing for men and women further this theme.[21] Jervell sees the women mentioned in Luke as the daughters of Abraham and, therefore, more significant than the women in Acts because they are heirs to God's promise.[22] These women represent the true Israel that accepts Jesus as Messiah and receives the promised gift of the Holy Spirit. According to Jervell, Luke is less interested in women and more interested in the role the daughters of Abraham play in restoring Israel to God's promise.[23] This leads to his conclusion that women are a part of the church but remain subordinate to men in the role of leadership.[24] In opposition, Embudo sees Luke's inclusion of women to be characterized by a status reversal where women equally participate in the ministry of prophecy (teaching and preaching) and leadership.[25] The theological perspective focuses on God and how he fulfills prophecy through the women in Luke, giving them a place of significance and purpose in his kingdom. Women today continue to find this significance and purpose by utilizing their spiritual gifts and abilities to serve God.

LITERARY PERSPECTIVE—A BALANCED ROLE FOR WOMEN

Seim's *The Double Message* plays a large part in shaping the third perspective on Luke's literary intention of balance. She sees Luke as neither friendly nor hostile towards women but rather seeking to strike a balanced perspective within the context of tradition and social controls that silence women.[26] Luke's use of parallels helps illuminate the women in the text and gives further evidence of segregation that was present

---

[20] Eben Scheffler, "Caring for the Needy in the Acts of the Apostles," *Neot* 50 (2016): 153.

[21] Black, "'Your Sons and Your Daughters Will Prophesy...': Pairings of Men and Women in Luke-Acts," 201–2. Examples include: Widow's Son (7:11–17)/Jairus' daughter (8:40–42, 49–56), Jairus (8:40–41)/Woman with issue of blood (8:42–28), Men healed on Sabbath (14:1–6)/Woman healed on Sabbath (13:10–17).

[22] Jervell, *The Unknown Paul*, 147, 149–50. Jervell states that all women in Luke's gospel are Israelites. This theme continues into the book of Acts where the women are Jews or proselytes. Black questions Jervell's conclusion that all women in Acts are Jews but supports his idea on a theme of restoration in regard to the women in Luke. See Black, "'Your Sons and Your Daughters Will Prophesy...': Pairings of Men and Women in Luke-Acts," 200.

[23] Jervell, *The Unknown Paul*, 157.

[24] Jervell, *The Unknown Paul*, 152, 154, 157. Jervell gives the examples of women serving in Acts 6 under the leadership of men as well as Priscilla mentioned alongside her husband, Aquila, in Acts 18. He does not see Luke as entitling women or emancipating women.

[25] See Embudo, "Women Vis-À-Vis Prophecy in Luke-Acts 2," 138.

[26] Seim, *The Double Message*, 249. Reid supports this idea of a mixed message. See Barbara E. Reid, "The Gospel of Luke: Friend or Foe of Women Proclaimers of the Word?" *CBQ* 78 (2016): 23.

in the first century. While women play an important role in the ministry of Jesus, there is no evidence of surprise in the text that he seeks to violate the social norms of his day.²⁷

The roles women play in Luke-Acts give insight into Luke's literary intention for women. Women are present at the beginning and end of Luke's Gospel. As an illustration, Moyra Dale sees the presence of women shaped around the "rites of passage" when women take a more central role in any culture.²⁸ Jesus invites Mary and Martha to take on the role of disciples by sitting at his feet alongside the men (10:38–42). He helps free Martha of the cultural expectations and shows her what is the true, proper work for a woman, following him.²⁹ Mary Magdalene, Joanna, and Susana support the ministry of Jesus out of their own means (8:1–3). The verb Luke uses here is διηκόνουν and can mean a variety of roles, including serving the poor, ministering to others, and distributing the funds of the church.³⁰ These three women are examples of "proto-deaconesses" in their service and loyalty to Jesus.³¹

While there are many active roles women play, they rarely speak in Luke's Gospel and are almost silent in the book of Acts. Luis Menéndez Antuña explains their limited role as a necessary part of the male-centered bonding that must take place among the

---

²⁷ Black, "'Your Sons and Your Daughters Will Prophesy...': Pairings of Men and Women in Luke-Acts," 197. Black mentions that there is a stronger reaction to the break of the Jew/Gentile barrier than the gender barrier. Witherington supports this idea and states that Jesus was seeking to reform, not reject the patriarchal framework. Ben Witherington, *Women in the Ministry of Jesus: A Study of Jesus' Attitudes to Women and Their Roles as Reflected in His Earthly Life*, SNTSMS 51 (New York: Cambridge University Press, 1984), 129. See also F. Scott Spencer, *Salty Wives, Spirited Mothers, and Savvy Widows: Capable Women of Purpose and Persistence in Luke's Gospel* (Grand Rapids: Eerdmans, 2012), 101.

²⁸ Moyra Dale, "Dismantling Socio-Sacred Hierarchy: Gender and Gentiles in Luke-Acts," *Priscilla Papers* 31, no. 2 (2017): 19; Reid, "The Gospel of Luke: Friend or Foe of Women Proclaimers of the Word?" 18.

²⁹ David Arthur DeSilva, *An Introduction to the New Testament: Contexts, Methods & Ministry Formation*, 2nd ed. (Downers Grove: InterVarsity Press, 2018), 292. See also Koperski, "Luke 10,38–42 and Acts 6,1–7: Women and Discipleship in the Literary Context of Luke-Acts," 521.

³⁰ Karris sees διηκόνουν as a literary tool Luke uses to positively portray women as a "go between" on their mission for Christ. See Robert J. Karris, "Women and Discipleship in Luke," *CBQ* 56 (1994): 8–9. Another view sees διηκόνουν to go beyond the traditional meaning of domestic duty and extend to the ministry of the word and teaching. See Amanda C. Miller, "Cut from the Same Cloth: A Study of Female Patrons in Luke-Acts and the Roman Empire," *Review & Expositor* 114 (2017):112–13, 208, and E. Jane Via, "Women, the Discipleship of Service, and the Early Christian Ritual Meal in the Gospel of Luke," *Saint Luke's Journal of Theology* 29 (1985): 38.

³¹ Sr. Philsy, "Diakonia of Women in the New Testament," *The Indian Journal of Theology* 32 (1983): 112. Spencer additionally adds that these women play the role of master-disciples as well as patron-clients to Jesus. See Spencer, *Salty Wives, Spirited Mothers, and Savvy Widows: Capable Women of Purpose and Persistence in Luke's Gospel*, 102.

disciples.[32] Scott Spencer points out that other than Jesus, men also remain mostly silent in Luke's Gospel as they are not yet prepared to teach.[33] The women's silence is not portrayed as a weakness but a necessary part of learning to be a disciple. Perhaps, Luke shares a missional purpose by silencing the women in order to build the respect of his readers who live in a culture where women play more of a silent role. Dale calls this motive a "high missionary principle" where one lives under the traditions to reach those living in that culture.[34]

While Luke is not violating social norms, he does gently push against cultural traditions. In the Roman world, women, like men, can obtain power through wealth and social connection.[35] This gives insight into the three named women in chapter 8. Women also play a role in the patron-client relationship. Luke, however, erases these boundaries in presenting women who give to and receive from Jesus. For example, Joanna is both a recipient (of Jesus's healing in 8:1) and a benefactor (gives to Jesus of her own means in 8:3).[36] While the push is gentle, it remains clear that Luke presents a Gospel where the teachings of Jesus take precedence over tradition.

The literary perspective of silent yet active women in Luke paints the picture of faithful female disciples serving their Savior within their own cultural context. In today's world, women who are a part of a male-led church can still fulfill their role as faithful disciples in teaching, mentoring, and serving the church. Churches must continue to seek out Jesus's teachings and be willing to change tradition based upon Scripture. Women can find encouragement from the examples of female disciples in Luke's Gospel and, like Martha, recognize their greatest role is found at the feet of Jesus.

---

[32] Luis Menéndez Antuña, "Male-Bonding, Female Vanishing: Representing Gendered Authority in Luke 23:26–24:53," *Early Christianity* 4 (2013): 499.

[33] Spencer, *Salty Wives, Spirited Mothers, and Savvy Widows: Capable Women of Purpose and Persistence in Luke's Gospel*, 119.

[34] Dale, "Dismantling Socio-Sacred Hierarchy: Gender and Gentiles in Luke-Acts," 22. Witherington agrees and sees Luke's parallels as a necessary part of balancing the presence of men with women in a culture that would be hesitant to accept a female-saturated message. Witherington, *Women in the Ministry of Jesus: A Study of Jesus' Attitudes to Women and Their Roles as Reflected in His Earthly Life*, 52, and Ben Witherington and Ann Witherington, *Women and the Genesis of Christianity* (New York: Cambridge University Press, 1990), 202.

[35] Miller, "Cut from the Same Cloth: A Study of Female Patrons in Luke-Acts and the Roman Empire," 205, Spencer, *Salty Wives, Spirited Mothers, and Savvy Widows: Capable Women of Purpose and Persistence in Luke's Gospel*, 104, and Ben Witherington, *The Acts of the Apostles: A Socio-Rhetorical Commentary* (Grand Rapids: Eerdmans, 1998), 334–35.

[36] See Spencer, *Salty Wives, Spirited Mothers, and Savvy Widows: Capable Women of Purpose and Persistence in Luke's Gospel*, 208, and Miller, "Cut from the Same Cloth: A Study of Female Patrons in Luke-Acts and the Roman Empire," 208, for further discussion on the female patron/client relationships representative in Luke.

ACTIVE DISCIPLESHIP IN LUKE'S GOSPEL

Luke 8:1–3 highlights three significant women who exemplify active discipleship: Mary, Joanna, and Susanna. These three women, along with the twelve disciples, are depicted as being "with him [Jesus]" (σὺν αὐτῷ, 8:1). Together, they accompany Jesus as he "proclaims and brings the good news of the kingdom of God" to cities and villages. Holly Carey interprets the phrase "with Jesus" as "shorthand for discipleship and attributed to those who have made sacrifices to follow Jesus and formed a 'willing attachment' to him."[37] Furthermore, Luke's use of parallelism between the Apostles, alongside the term "certain" (τινες, 8:2) women is unique to his Gospel.[38] These are three specific women among many who are following Jesus. To understand the biblical evidence that these women were disciples commissioned to proclaim the gospel, we must first define what it means to be a disciple of Jesus.

A clear and biblical definition of a disciple is found in Matt 4:19: "He [Jesus] said to them, 'Follow me, and I will make you fishers of men.'" This is a simple way to define a disciple without being overly simplistic. From this passage, Jim Putman, Bobby Harrington, and Robert Coleman define a disciple as someone who is following Jesus, being changed by Jesus, and committed to the mission of Jesus.[39] The textual details that describe these women are profound as they reveal women who faithfully follow Jesus, undergo transformation through Jesus, and actively engage in the mission of Jesus.

As has been noted, the women are "with Him," which denotes they actively followed Jesus. Furthermore, the crucifixion narrative describes the women as those "who had followed him from Galilee" (23:49). Additionally, "the women…followed and saw the tomb and how his body was laid," (23:55) they prepared spices and returned to the tomb (23:56–24:1), and they later find the tomb empty at dawn on the first day of the week (24:1). As Carey's analysis points out, "Luke highlights their actions, while the Twelve are simply 'there' with Jesus."[40] In this way, the women embody faithfulness as disciples of Jesus.

Additionally, the women are changed by Jesus as they are "healed of evil spirits and other infirmities" (8:2). Namely, Jesus casts out seven demons from Mary

---

[37] Holly J. Carey, *Women Who Do: Female Disciples in the Gospels* (Grand Rapids: Eerdmans, 2023), 117.

[38] John Nolland, *Luke 1:1–9:20*, Word 35A (Dallas: Word Books, 1989), 365.

[39] Jim Putman, Bobby Harrington, and Robert E. Coleman, *Discipleshift: Five Steps That Help Your Church to Make Disciples Who Make Disciples* (Grand Rapids: Zondervan, 2013), 45–51. See also, Bobby Harrington, Carl Williamson, and Alicia Williamson, *Trust and Follow Jesus: Conversations to Fuel Discipleship*, 2nd ed. (Nashville: Renew.org, 2023), 90.

[40] Carey, *Women Who Do*, 115. The argument stems from Luke's description of women as being active in discipleship, while the Twelve are described with inaction or poor action, seen in such examples as not following Jesus till the end, not quick to believe in the resurrection, etc.

Magdalene who transforms into a faithful follower. Joanna is described as the wife of Chuza, "Herod's household manager," (8:2) but is now known to be the manager of the funds for Jesus. Joanna's managerial role shows evidence of a life that has been transformed by encountering Jesus. The one whose life centered around managing Herod's household now embraces her role of service to Jesus. Transformation found in Christ compels the women to walk in the way of Jesus.

Finally, Luke portrays the women as committed to Jesus. Mary, Joanna, and Susanna "provide for them [him] out of their means," (8:3) demonstrating their commitment to the ministry of Jesus. During the resurrection narrative, the women "remembered his words" (24:8) indicating that they are participants in the resurrected Jesus through their listening and remembering what this means. This leads the women to go and proclaim to the eleven and to all the rest of the resurrected Jesus (24:9). The women are in fact active participants in witnessing the resurrected Christ.

Having now established the women as disciples of Jesus, the next step is to show their overall proclamation of the gospel. Carey argues:

> the immediate context—both in the summary [Luke 8:1–3] and later in Luke 10:1–20—is that of proclaiming the good news of the kingdom of God throughout Galilee. Since we have already been told that women are actively involved in following Jesus, there is no reason to assume that they are absent from the seventy-two who are sent out by him shortly thereafter.[41]

In Luke 8, the women are with Jesus as he proclaims, while Luke 10 invites an unspecified group of people to participate in the witnessing and proclamation of the gospel. Regardless of whether or not women were part of the seventy-two commissioned, it is clear from Luke 8 to the end of the resurrection narrative that women are proclaiming the gospel.

Acts continues Luke's positive portrayal of women as active disciples and proclaimers of the gospel. To illustrate, Acts 8:3–4 describes Saul throwing both men and women into prison, as all those who scatter "went about preaching the word." Likewise, Acts 9:1–2, mentions men and women belonging to the Way being thrown into prison. While the context of the early church lacks clarity on the manner of proclamation of the gospel in the book of Acts, Luke describes women who are "engaged in the spread of the gospel as it moves out of Jerusalem."[42] The bold actions of these early female disciples evoke Saul to later imprison them, revealing the disruptive power of their

---

[41] Carey, *Women Who Do*, 117. See, Robert H. Stein, *Luke*, in *The New American Commentary: An Exegetical and Theological Exposition of Holy Scripture* (Nashville, TN: Broadman Press, 1992), 304, who argues that Luke uses this account to point forward to the church's universal mission after the resurrection.

[42] Carey, *Women Who Do*, 141.

witness to the established order of the day. As these women stand before authorities, the Holy Spirit empowers them with words to speak.[43] As such, the women in Luke and Acts model active disciples of Jesus.

THE SIGNIFICANCE OF ACTIVE DISCIPLESHIP ON WOMEN TODAY

While this chapter does not seek to delineate women's roles in the church, it does hope to serve as a reminder of the vital role women play in the kingdom of God. The women of Luke demonstrate those who actively follow Jesus, are transformed by the Holy Spirit, and engage in the mission of God. As Judith Paulsen affirms, "God is the primary Evangelist, and the church joins in God's work out of joyful gratitude for their own transformation."[44] It is the transformed heart that gratefully goes and spreads the gospel of Jesus Christ.

Just as the women in Luke's gospel actively engaged in discipleship, women today are called to participate in proclaiming the good news of Jesus to their friends and neighbors. The ministry of the disciples "was ministry at its most relational, and it was ministry that resulted in people finding freedom, healing, truth, wholeness, and new life."[45] The women in Luke's Gospel exemplify the selflessness of being disciples of Jesus. Their lives align with Priscilla Pope-Levison's five practices for effective evangelism: practicing hospitality, forming relationships, living with integrity, bearing the Christian message, and rooting oneself in a Christian church.[46] These five practices remain relevant for women today as they engage in the evangelistic proclamation of the gospel. The women of Luke serve as models of evangelism who embrace their commission to be disciples of Jesus who actively share the good news of the gospel to all they meet.

CONCLUSION

This chapter introduced three possible perspectives of Luke's emphasis on women: rhetorical, theological, and literary Furthermore, the chapter sought to apply these findings to the ministry of women in the context of discipleship. While the theological perspective holds many compelling arguments, we believe Luke's intentions are best presented in the literary perspective of a balanced role for women. Luke appears to be less concerned with elevating or demoting the role of women and more concerned with presenting them as examples of faithful followers of Jesus. The women in Luke's

---

[43] Steve Addison, *Acts and the Movement of God: From Jerusalem to the Ends of the Earth* (100 Movements Publishing, 2023), 69. See also, Luke 12:4–12.

[44] Judith Paulsen, *A New and Ancient Evangelism: Rediscovering the Ways God Calls and Sends* (Grand Rapids: Baker Academic, 2024), 165.

[45] Paulsen, *A New and Ancient Evangelism*, 179.

[46] Priscilla Pope-Levison, *Models of Evangelism* (Grand Rapids: Baker Academic, 2020), 182.

gospel, at times, push against culture and, at other times, live within its restrictions. They serve as examples to every Christian woman in using their gifts and abilities to further the kingdom of God.

Robert Karris gives an important reminder that the text does not change over the years, but the reader continues to change and must, therefore, bring fresh eyes in studying the text.[47] The reader must work towards taking off the cultural lenses through which they read scripture and seek to understand the meaning of a text in the world in which it was written. In our best effort to take off our own cultural glasses and read Luke's Gospel, we see a Savior who loves regardless of one's gender, race, or socio-economic status. Luke describes the heart of God as Jesus speaks to the outcasts and loves the unlovable. The kingdom of God is a place where roles are reversed and the least becomes the greatest. It is less about acquiring a position of authority here on earth and more about understanding one's status as a child of God. Kyle Fedler expresses this same idea:

> Jesus did not overturn all of the religious and social customs concerning women. But what he did do was love them as fellow human beings and children of God who were loved by their Father. Jesus saw no moral distinctions between the sexes in the kingdom of God. In his own ministry he seemed oblivious to such distinctions, calling both men and women to repentance and discipleship.[48]

The women of Luke seem less concerned about their position or status and more centered on living as disciples. May God teach all of us to have this same heart.

---

[47] Karris, "Women and Discipleship in Luke," 20.

[48] Kyle D. Fedler, *Exploring Christian Ethics: Biblical Foundations for Morality* (Louisville: Westminster John Knox, 2006), 181.

5
"Not even in Israel": The Centurion's Servant and the Dynamics of Faith in the Gospel of Luke

Gregory Stevenson[1]

As Jesus was on his way to heal a centurion's servant in Luke 7, the centurion sent word for Jesus to cease his journey and instead merely command the healing of his servant (7:6–7). In response Jesus declares, "I tell you, not even in Israel have I found such faith" (7:9).[2] This story of the centurion's servant appears in both Matt 8:7–13 and Luke 7:1–10. The general framework of the story remains the same in both accounts (a centurion's servant is sick, a request is made for Jesus to heal him, the servant is healed, Jesus praises the centurion's faith), but notable differences in the accounts give each a unique emphasis. In Matthew's version, the centurion makes the request of Jesus in person, and Jesus's response to him highlights the rejection of Jewish leaders and the inclusion of Gentiles with the assertion that "many will come from east and west" to dine in the kingdom of heaven "while the heirs of the kingdom" will be cast out (Matt 8:11–12). In Matthew, the centurion's faith is a display of trust in the power and authority of Jesus to heal from a distance and at a word, leading to Jesus declaring, "let it be done for you according to your faith" (Matt 8:13).

Most commentators assign a similar interpretation to Jesus's praise of the centurion's faith in the Gospel of Luke; that is, that it is primarily an acknowledgment of the centurion's belief in Jesus's power and authority.[3] While not denying this element, I argue that Luke's unique shaping of this story holds significant implications for evaluating the centurion's "faith." Matthew's emphasis on the personal interaction between the centurion and Jesus and his theme of Gentile inclusion are not found in Luke's account. Rather, Luke's emphasis on distance between the centurion and Jesus with all

---

[1] I am pleased to contribute to this volume honoring Dr. Allen Black. Dr. Black's excellence in and out of the classroom, his kind and encouraging nature, and his scholarly acumen have been an inspiration to me along with many others. Dr. Black helped to make my experience at the (then) Harding Graduate School of Religion a time of great academic and spiritual growth. I hope that this essay stands as a testament to that influence.

[2] All Bible quotations, unless otherwise noted, are from the NRSV.

[3] Darrell L. Bock, *Luke* (Downers Grove: InterVarsity Press, 1994), 133; Frederick W. Danker, *Jesus and the New Age: According to St. Luke* (St. Louis: Clayton, 1980), 92; Barbara E. Reid and Shelly Matthews, *Luke 1–9* (Collegeville: Liturgical Press, 2021), 227; I. Howard Marshall, *The Gospel of Luke: A Commentary on the Greek Text*, NIGTC (Grand Rapids: Eerdmans, 1978), 278; Robert H. Stein, *Luke* (Nashville: Boardman, 1992), 220; Leon Morris, *The Gospel According to St. Luke: An Introduction and Commentary* (Grand Rapids: Eerdmans, 1974), 138.

of their interactions coming through intermediaries, his description of the actions and words of the Jewish elders, his reference to the centurion's "friends," and the repetitive use of the word "worthy" (7:4, 6, 7) situate his account firmly within the context of civic benefaction, a system of social exchange that was governed by notions of honor, reciprocity, competition, and ambition.[4] Examining Luke's version of this story both within the social context of benefaction and within the literary context of related themes in the Gospel lends insight into character motivations and provides for a nuanced assessment of the centurion's faith.

THE LOGIC OF CIVIC BENEFACTION

Civic benefaction was a system of social exchange that had its origins in the Hellenistic world and was prevalent from the fourth century BCE up through the later Roman Empire. It involved an individual providing a contribution or service to a city or group and in return receiving honorary awards in a public fashion. Both the contributions and services of the benefactor and his or her honorary awards were recorded in a decree that was publicly proclaimed and then set up in a public space. The honors granted to benefactors varied but were drawn from a standard set of options, including statues, wreaths, seats of honor, exemption from taxation, etc.[5]

Unlike the Roman practice of patronage, which was generally a more individualized practice involving an enduring personal relationship between a patron and a client, Hellenistic civic benefaction was a corporate activity involving a public gift or service that benefitted a community as a whole.[6] That the primary act identified in Luke 7 is of the centurion donating a synagogue building for the *collective* benefit of the whole community places his act more firmly within the context of civic benefaction rather than Roman patronage.

Like with many institutions, the realities of civic benefaction often stood in stark contrast with the ideal. Seneca refers to the providing of public benefits as "the chief bond of human society," and asserts that the practice should ideally be motivated by generosity, with the benefactor expecting nothing in return.[7] Although there were no doubt some benefactors who lived up to this ideal, in its typical implementation civic

---

[4] This is a tendency of Luke's that is not solely confined to this story. Frederick W. Danker demonstrates that terminology and concepts central to benefaction can be found throughout Luke and Acts, *Benefactor: Epigraphic Study of a Graeco-Roman and New Testament Semantic Field* (St. Louis: Clayton, 1982), 319–24, 406.

[5] For a detailed listing of possible awards, see Danker, *Benefactor*, 467–68.

[6] Holland Hendrix, "Benefactor/Patron Networks in the Urban Environment: Evidence from Thessalonica," *Semeia* 56 (1991): 40; Stephan J. Joubert, "One Form of Social Exchange or Two? 'Euergetism,' Patronage, and Testament Studies," *BTB* 31 (2001): 23.

[7] Seneca, *Ben.*, 1.1, 4.

benefaction was not public charity.[8] Rather, it was a system that depended for its proper functioning on the exploitation of wealth, the maintenance of social hierarchies, the expectation of reciprocity, and competition.

The maintenance of a social hierarchy defined by the concept of *worthiness* drove much civic benefaction. Paul Veyne notes that benefaction "was the act of a class, the notables, who gave because they felt they were superior to the mass of the people."[9] This class-based superiority enjoyed by benefactors was typically viewed as a virtue within Greco-Roman society and one that was essential for the proper functioning of the system. Aristotle describes two different types of individuals who engaged in benefaction. The first he calls the "magnificent person" (ὁ μεγαλοπρεπής). "Magnificence," according to Aristotle, is "a virtue concerned with wealth" and one that refers not to small acts of charity but to civic benefactions "since these are the greatest forms of expenditure and the ones most honoured."[10] It is not possible, according to Aristotle, for a poor person to be magnificent since they lack the financial means for such public gifts. Thus, the status of benefactor belongs only to those who are "high-born and famous" and who, therefore, possess the essential element of "worthiness" (ἀξίωμα).[11] The second type of benefactor that Aristotle defines is the "great-souled" (μεγαλόψυχος) person.[12] This individual seeks honor because honor is something that all great persons are "worthy" (ἀξίαν) of receiving. After all, the truly great-souled person is "justified in despising other people" because he or she is correct in their estimation of their own superiority. For Aristotle, this quality of being great-souled is, therefore, the privilege of the high-born, the powerful, and the wealthy since these individuals "are esteemed worthy of honour (ἀξιοῦνται τιμῆς), because they are superior to their fellows." Thus, the great-souled person loves to act as benefactor as "a mark of superiority."

The most important sources for understanding civic benefaction are the honorary decrees, which, despite local and temporal variations, maintain a remarkable degree of uniformity and stereotypical phraseology.[13] The elevation of benefactors finds

---

[8] Stephan J. Joubert, *Paul as Benefactor: Reciprocity, Strategy and Theological Reflection in Paul's Collection*, WUNT 124 (Tübingen: Mohr Siebeck, 2000), 53. Paul Veyne argues that it was largely the early Christian community that replaced public benefaction with charity by removing the elements of social stratification and self-gratification that undergirded the system, *Bread and Circuses: Historical Sociology and Political Pluralism* (New York: Penguin, 1990), 19–34.

[9] Veyne, *Bread and Circuses*, 104.

[10] Aristotle, *Eth. Nic.*, 4.2.1, 3, 15.

[11] Aristotle, *Eth. Nic.*, 4.2.13–14.

[12] Aristotle, *Eth. Nic.*, 4.3.10–24.

[13] Joubert, *Paul as Benefactor*, 51; Tessa Rajak, *The Jewish Dialogue with Greece and Rome: Studies in Cultural and Social Interaction*, AGJU (Leiden: Brill, 2000), 377; Veyne, *Bread and Circuses*, 107.

expression in these decrees in several ways, a couple of which are worth mentioning here. First is the common identification of benefactors as "good men" (ἀγαθοὺς ἄνδρας)[14] or "noble and good men" (καλοὺς καὶ ἀγαθοὺς ἄνδρας).[15] These descriptors are more of a social evaluation than a moral one. They identify individuals who are praised as "good" or "noble" precisely because they possess resources, power, or authority and use them to benefit the citizenry. In short, they are "good" because they are benefactors. Second is the prominent role of *worthiness*. The honorary decrees are replete with the language of worthiness, particularly in their use of the term ἄξιος and its cognates. Benefactors, through their actions or donations, are deemed "worthy" of praise and honors,[16] while beneficiaries take pains to ensure their benefactors "will be honored in a manner worthy of their benefactions."[17]

The honoring of benefactors was serious business as those honors confirmed their elevated status and reinforced class distinctions.[18] Civic benefactors were near the top of the social hierarchy, and providing benefits was a means of staying there. Honor was thus a commodity and there was fierce competition for it. Two terms that appear frequently in honorary decrees, both as virtues that benefactors possess and as motivation for their benefactions, are φιλοτιμία ("love of honor") and φιλοδοξία ("love of glory").[19] These terms capture the competitive spirit that drove the desire for public acclaim. Accordingly, Aristotle refers to such acts of civic benefaction as "objects of ambition."[20] The competitive drive for honor and public notoriety fed a system that defined worthiness in terms of wealth and power and delineated class distinctions. As Veyne points out, the honors awarded to benefactors would have become devalued over time if they did not mark off a separate class because too many people would have possessed them. Rather, benefactors "belonged to a respected order which, by awarding these distinctions to itself, merely expressed before everyone its acknowledged superiority."[21]

At the heart of the system of benefaction was the notion of reciprocity. The granting of a benefit created a debt that must be repaid, typically in the form of various public honors. Honorary decrees employ the language of *repayment* (ἀποδίδωμι) when

---

[14] *SEG* 1.366, l. 53; 39.1244, Col. III, ll. 16–17; *OGIS* 339, l. 61; *SIG* 2.569, ll. 40–41.

[15] *IIasos* 153, l. 30; *IG* 12.7.388, ll. 16–17; *IPriene* 50, l.11; 53, l. 16; 99, l. 22.

[16] *IPriene* 53, l.15; *SIG* 2.630, l. 17; *IG* 11.4.1061, ll. 4.

[17] *IG* 2.1227, ll. 21–22. See also *SIG* 1.374, ll.51–52; *IG* 5.1.1432, ll.34–35; *IEph* 4.1443, l. 9.

[18] Joubert, "Social Exchange," 18; "Paul as Benefactor," 22, 52; Veyne, *Bread and Circuses*, 104, 123.

[19] A good example is *IG* 2.360, a late fourth century BCE decree from Attica that utilizes both the noun (φιλοτιμία) and verb form (φιλοτιμέομαι) no less than 6 times in its praise of benefactors, ll. 6–7, 16, 33–34, 64–65, 77.

[20] Aristotle, *Eth. Nic.*, 4.2.11.

[21] Veyne, *Bread and Circuses*, 130.

describing the granting of honors, most commonly with variations on the phrase "repaying favors" (χάριτας ἀποδιδούς). A third-century BCE decree from Athens offers a representative example. While honoring a benefactor named Philippides, the civic leaders introduced the list of honors awarded him by stating, "Therefore, so that it may be clear to all that the People know how to repay favors (χάριτας ἀποδιδόναι) to its benefactors...."[22] The "repayment" of civic benefits with honors, however, only fed the competitive spirit. Receiving a civic benefit placed the beneficiary in the inferior position of owing a debt. By repaying that debt with excessive and public honors, it placed an obligation on the original benefactor to respond in kind. Seneca says that the person "whose duty it is to repay, can never do so unless he out-does his benefactor." This, of course, places an obligation on the original benefactor to respond in such a way as to maintain his or her status and honor, leading to a competition "to outdo benefits by benefits."[23]

The public repayment of civic benefits with honors and the competition this created between benefactor and beneficiary to outdo each other meant that these actions of giving and reciprocating were often motivated more by greed and ambition than by charity or "humanitarian concerns."[24] It became a means of greasing the wheel to the benefit of the city or group by creating pressure on benefactors to persist in their giving and as a means of recruiting potential new benefactors. The primary means by which this was accomplished was *visibility*. Many of the most common honorary awards (statues, crowns, seats of honor) have a visible component that enhanced the honor of the benefactor. These awards were proclaimed in public assemblies and the honorary decree itself was set up in public space to serve as a kind of monument.[25] *Proedria*, or the right to sit in the front seat, enhanced the honor of the benefactor solely through visibility. Being seen sitting in this front seat or "seat of honor" in the theater or at other public events was a clear identification of that individual's importance. One means by which honorary decrees emphasize the visibility of the honors is by declaring that the decree itself and/or statues of the benefactor are to be installed in the "most visible" or "most prominent" place in the city, usually the theater, gymnasium, sanctuaries, or marketplace.[26]

Visibility not only enhanced the honor of the benefactor, but also enhanced the honor and reputation of the beneficiaries. It was important for the beneficiaries to display their gratitude and repayment of favors publicly, both to enhance their own

---

[22] *SIG* 1.374, ll. 50–52. For similar examples, see *OGIS* 248, ll. 22–24; *IPriene* 53, ll. 13–14; 61, ll. 12–14; *SEG* 27.513, ll. 10–13; *IG* 2.505, ll. 41–43.

[23] Seneca, *Ben.*, 1.4.

[24] Joubert, "Paul as Benefactor," 58.

[25] Essentially the decree itself functioned as another one of the honors, Rajak, *Jewish Dialogue*, 376; Veyne, *Bread and Circuses*, 127–28.

[26] *SIG* 2.762, ll. 48–49; *OGIS* 339, ll. 103–105; Danker, *Benefactor*, 77–78, No. 12.

reputation and to encourage further benefaction. The decrees witness to this through their use of the language of sight. Being *seen* honoring benefactors was vital and was a standard part of the honorary formula contained in the decrees, as the following examples illustrate:[27]

> Therefore, so that the people *may be seen* [φαίνηται] to be foremost in repaying gratitude and *may be seen* [φανερὸς εἶ] to be honouring those who confer benefits on itself. (*OGIS* 248, ll. 22–25; italics added).[28]

> Therefore, so that also the People *may be seen* [φαίνηται)] returning appropriate gratitude to its benefactors. (*SIG* 2.709, ll. 47–48; italics added).

> Therefore so that it may be *visible to all* [ἅπασιν ἦι φανερόν] that the Council and the Athenian People know how to repay gratitude. (*IG* 2.505, ll. 41–43; italics added).

This emphasis on visibility also reveals a motive underlying these awards. Here again we see the reality of the practice at odds with the philosophical ideal, which was that benefactors should give and beneficiaries should display gratitude without either expecting any form of reciprocation. In reality, the purpose of reciprocating with honorary rewards and doing so with high visibility was both to encourage the benefactor to continue providing benefits and to recruit new benefactors.[29] A decree from Samos, dated after 243 BCE, makes this motive clear when it states that the honors granted Boulagoras are given so that "we may be seen honoring good men and encouraging many citizens to choose the same course of action."[30] A second century BCE decree from Magnesia authorizes the setting up of a statue of Apollophanes for his role in building the theater. The decree then identifies who they hope to impress by this action: "Therefore so that the magnanimity and gratitude of the People may be visible to all *noble and good* (καλοῖς καὶ ἀγαθοῖς) men and to those choosing *to seek glory* (φιλοδοξεῖν)."[31] As noted earlier, the phrases "noble and good men" and "those seeking glory" identify benefactors, indicating that the Magnesians are specifically targeting potential donors to their city.

---

[27] These examples range in date from about 300–100 BCE and come from Attica and Pergamum.

[28] Translation from Michel Austin, *The Hellenistic World from Alexander to the Roman Conquest: A Selection of Ancient Sources in Translation*, 2nd ed. (Cambridge: Cambridge University Press, 2006), 370–71.

[29] Danker calls this "One of the most common reasons cited for bestowal of honors," *Benefactor*, 437. See also Rajak, *Jewish Dialogue*, 375, 377–78.

[30] *SEG* 1.366, ll. 52–54.

[31] *IMagnesia* 92b, ll. 7–8; italics added.

The system of civic benefaction only thrived and endured as long as it did because it benefited both those who gave and those who received. Aristotle claims the system serves both benefactors, as "lovers of honor," and beneficiaries, as "lovers of money," by granting both what they desire.[32] The competitive aspect inherent in reciprocal exchange ensured that benefactors would seek to outdo both their previous contributions as well as those of other benefactors and that the city/group would labor to provide public rewards that would keep the cycle in motion.

This Hellenistic system of benefaction was widespread and influential, even within Jewish communities. Although several Jewish sources are critical of the practice, viewing the desire for public honors as a mark of false ambition and pride,[33] these sources represent only one reaction on a broad spectrum that ranged from outright rejection to full acceptance.[34] In reality, many Jewish communities embraced the Hellenistic system of benefaction, while adapting it to their sensibilities.[35] One notable difference is that the Jews offered a more restrictive set of honors. They adopted certain standard Hellenistic honors, such as crowns and *proedria* (the seat of honor), while eschewing others (images and statues), likely due to the prohibitions of the second commandment.[36] A second notable difference is that Jewish honorary decrees are far more succinct than their Hellenistic counterparts and more modest in their praise. The necessity of repaying civic benefits with public honors, however, was retained. The following Jewish decree in honor of a (likely Gentile) woman named Tation is representative.

> Tation daughter of Straton, son of Empedon, having built (*or* furnished) the meeting room and the precinct of the *hypaithros* at her own expense, bestowed a favour on the Jews. The synagogue of the Jews honored Tation daughter of Straton, son of Empedon, with a gold crown and seat of honour [προεδρίᾳ].[37]

This public decree and the granting of the seat of honor demonstrate a concern for the visibility of reciprocation as does also a likely first century CE decree from Berenice

---

[32] Aristotle, *Rh.*, 1.5.9. Translation is from Aristotle, *The Art of Rhetoric*, trans. John Henry Freese (Cambridge: Harvard University Press, repr. 2000).

[33] Philo, *Decal.*, 1.4; *Mut.*, 93; Josephus, *Ap.*, 2.217–18; 1 Macc 8:14.

[34] Gregg Gardner, "Jewish Leadership and Hellenistic Civic Benefaction in the Second Century B.C.E.," *JBL* 126 (2007): 329.

[35] Gardner, "Jewish Leadership and Hellenistic Civic Benefaction," 343; Rajak, *Jewish Dialogue*, 373–91. For examples, see Josephus, *AJ*, 14.149–155; 1 Macc 14:25–49; B. Lifshitz, *Donateurs et Fondateurs dans les Synagogues Juives* (Paris: J. Gabalda, 1967); Tessa Rajak and David Noy, "Archisynagogoi: Office, Title and Social Status in the Greco-Jewish Synagogue," *JRS* 83 (1993): 87–91.

[36] Rajak, *Jewish Dialogue*, 374; Gardner, "Jewish Leadership," 328.

[37] Translation from S. R. Llewelyn, *NewDocs* 1:111. See also Lifshitz, *Donateurs et Fondateurs*, no. 13, 21–22.

in which the Jewish community honors a Roman citizen for his renovation of their amphitheatre and includes instructions to set the decree "in the most visible place in the amphitheatre."[38] Although Jewish communities adapted civic benefaction to function within their sensitivities, they generally maintained the essence of the practice—reciprocation—by honoring and encouraging benefactors, including Gentiles, through the granting of honorary awards and public displays of commendation.

THE LOGIC OF THE KINGDOM OF GOD IN LUKE

Greco-Roman society was socially stratified with the elite, the wealthy, and the powerful on top. Hellenistic civic benefaction, although ideally designed as a means for those on top to share benefits with cities and groups, became codified into a system that reinforced the exalted position of the "worthy" elite and facilitated greed on the part of the cities/groups who urged competition among benefactors in order to keep the cycle of benefits flowing. In this context, the Gospel of Luke's teachings on the kingdom of God challenge the very fabric of the system of civic benefaction as commonly practiced. The kingdom of God in Luke upends established social stratification and reverses expectations of who is worthy to participate in the kingdom by asserting that those at the top of the social hierarchy will be brought low while those on the bottom will be lifted up. Luke lays a foundation for this concept in his birth narrative when Mary declares, "He has brought down rulers from their thrones but has lifted up the humble. He has filled the hungry with good things but has sent the rich away empty" (1:52–53).

Luke presents numerous stories where the rich, the proud, and those in power are passed over for divine favor which instead goes to those on the lower end of the Jewish social hierarchy: sinners, Samaritans, the sick, and the poor (5:30–31; 7:36–50; 10:29–37; 16:19–31; 18:9–14). Jesus reinforces the point of these stories with three similar declarations that express the theme of reversal: "Indeed, some are last who will be first, and some are first who will be last" (13:30), "the least among all of you is the greatest" (9:48), and "all who exalt themselves will be humbled, and those who humble themselves will be exalted" (14:11; 18:14). It is not wealth or power itself that is disqualifying for the kingdom of God, according to Luke, but whether a person is seeking a reward now versus a reward in heaven (6:23). For those who are invested in a system that rewards them with wealth, honor, and power, they will seek to protect that investment or, as Jesus states, "For where your treasure is, there your heart will be also" (12:34). So when the Pharisees, who Luke describes as "lovers of money" (16:14), ridicule Jesus's teachings on the value of treasure in heaven over treasure on earth, Jesus responds by declaring that "what is prized by humans is an abomination in the sight of God" (16:15).

---

[38] S. R. Llewelyn, *NewDocs* 4:202–3; Rajak, *Jewish Dialogue*, 382–83.

Jesus's teaching that in the kingdom of God the poor, the hungry, and the hated are blessed rather than the rich, the well-fed, and the respected (6:20–26) represents a value system that runs counter to the value system of civic benefaction. Whereas Jesus counsels, "Be on your guard against all kinds of greed" (12:15), civic benefaction was a system powered by greed, whether greed for honor or greed for acquisition. Jesus takes aim at those who desire the seats of honor in the synagogue (11:43) or at banquets (14:7–8), viewing it as a form of self-exaltation (14:11). He challenges the notion of reciprocation when advising those who would throw a banquet to avoid inviting those who could repay the favor as that would be their reward. Instead, they are to invite those who cannot reciprocate and thus secure treasure in heaven (14:12–14). In Luke 22, when the apostles argue over which of them is the greatest, Jesus calls them out for buying into a worldly value system that is contrary to the kingdom of God when he says, "The kings of the Gentiles lord it over them, and those in authority over them are called *benefactors*. But not so with you; rather, the greatest among you must become like the youngest and the leader like one who serves" (22:25–26; italics added).[39] According to Luke, the kingdom of God represents a different way of being in the world, a way that turns social expectations upside-down and that identifies the last, the least, and the humble as recipients of divine favor over against those who would be first, those who desire greatness, and those who exalt themselves.

JESUS AND THE CENTURION (LUKE 7:1–10)

Luke's version of the healing of the centurion's servant follows immediately after his sermon on the plain (6:17–49). In this sermon Jesus lays out the theme of reversal through a contrasting series of blessings and woes which pronounce blessing on the poor, the hungry, and the hated, while pronouncing woe on the rich, the well fed, and the respected (6:20–26). These pronouncements challenge a societal system that exalts the wealthy and prominent with "a vision of the kingdom of God that dramatically reverses life as it is usually experienced."[40] He then upends the logic of civic benefaction—in which one group receives honor for benefits granted and another seeks benefits through honor granted—by declaring that it is no credit to do good to those who are good to you and that instead one should give without expecting any reciprocation or repayment (6:33–35). Jesus then concludes this sermon by announcing, "I will show you what someone is like who comes to me, hears my words, and acts on them" (6:47). That the conclusion of this sermon leads directly into the story of the centurion suggests

---

[39] For a different interpretation of this text, see David J. Lull, "The Servant-Benefactor as a Model of Greatness (Luke 22:24–30)," *NovT* 28 (1986): 289–305.

[40] Carl R. Holladay, *A Critical Introduction to the New Testament* (Nashville: Abingdon, 2005), 1.254.

that the centurion functions as a concrete example of one who puts the words of Jesus into action.

Immediately following the sermon, Jesus enters Capernaum where he meets a delegation of local Jewish elders sent by a Gentile centurion who desires that Jesus heal his beloved servant. Luke has adapted this story in a way that highlights the centurion's role as a civic benefactor to the local Jewish community by reporting that the elders implore Jesus with the words, "He is worthy (ἄξιος) to have you do this for him, for he loves our people, and it is he who built our synagogue for us" (7:4–5). The phrases "he loves our people" and "built our synagogue for us" are synonymous. In other words, the centurion's love for the Jewish people is less a statement of affection than it is of benefaction. His donation of a synagogue demonstrates his love for the people and so identifies him as worthy of honor and reciprocation. There is a well-established history of Gentiles acting as benefactors to the Jewish community and even funding the construction of synagogues.[41]

Luke's situating of this story in the context of civic benefaction does two things. First, it provides insight into the centurion, establishing him as someone who is wealthy and influential—a benefactor. Luke does not relay the centurion's motivation for building the synagogue. As mentioned, the reference to him loving the Jewish people is a statement from the Jewish elders about his *action* in benefitting the community and not necessarily a statement of his emotional attachment. Did he donate out of virtue, from a genuine affinity with the Jewish populace, or to put the Jewish population in his debt and to acquire public honor for himself?[42] He certainly recognizes a debt owed to him by the Jewish leadership when he calls upon them to serve as his intermediaries.[43] From a narrative standpoint, this introduction of the centurion presents him as one of the rich and exalted individuals that Jesus pronounced woe upon in the preceding sermon. Given the expectation of reversal already established in the Gospel, this leads the reader to suspect that the centurion is set up for a fall.

Second, the inclusion of civic benefaction in this text provides insight into the motivation of the Jewish elders. It is noteworthy that the elders express no interest in the welfare of the centurion's servant. Their eager pleading for Jesus to acquiesce to the centurion's request is not out of concern for the health of the servant but out of concern

---

[41] For more on this and for examples, see Rajak, *Jewish Dialogue*, 380, 383–84; "Archisynagogoi," 88, 90–91; *OGIS* 96, 129.

[42] Joel B. Green calls the centurion's benefaction a "calculated maneuver to win favor among the local Jewish leadership," *Gospel of Luke*, NICOT (Grand Rapids: Eerdmans, 1997), 286.

[43] It is often claimed that the centurion sends a delegation to avoid the cultural insensitivity of Jesus having to come to a Gentile's house (Bock, *Luke*, 132; Nolland, *Luke*, 318; Morris, *St. Luke*, 137). Though possible, this is, as Levine and Witherington note, merely one possible assumption among many, Amy-Jill Levine and Ben Witherington III, *The Gospel of Luke*, New Cambridge Bible Commentary (Cambridge: Cambridge University Press, 2018), 199. Reid and Matthews state that communicating with Jesus through intermediaries "is fitting for someone of his status," *Luke 1–9*, 221.

for the *worthiness* of the centurion. Their actions are motivated by the obligations of reciprocity.⁴⁴ Getting Jesus to do this is a form of repayment for the favors granted to the community by the centurion. Furthermore, given the magnitude of the action they request of Jesus (healing a person from certain death), it is a repayment that would then place the centurion in *their* debt, thus ensuring future benefactions to come. The elders are acting in ways fully consistent with the logic of civic benefaction while fully contrary to the logic of the kingdom of God laid out in the sermon on the plain. They seek to do good to those who have done good to them and give out of a desire to receive something in return. They are enslaved to a "world system whose basis and practices run counter" to the values of the kingdom of God.⁴⁵

Luke's simple statement, "And Jesus went with them (7:6)," is noteworthy for its brevity, offering no insight into Jesus's motivation for doing so. This is particularly striking in that by accepting the elder's recommendation that this man is worthy to have this done for him, Jesus appears to operate within the very system of gift and obligation that he just undermined in the preceding sermon. However, though unstated in the text, what likely drives Jesus's movement here is not a desire to validate the rewarding of benefactors but genuine concern for the dying servant. In this sense, Jesus's actions stand in direct contrast to those of the Jewish elders whose only concern is maintaining the goodwill of their benefactor.

When Jesus draws near to the centurion's house, the centurion sends out a second delegation of "friends"—a term often used to identify the relationship between benefactor and beneficiary—suggesting that these "friends," like the Jewish elders, may be acting out of obligation to their benefactor.⁴⁶ The message from the centurion, delivered through these associates, requests that Jesus cease traveling, "for I am not worthy (ἱκανός) that you should come under my roof; therefore, I did not consider myself worthy (ἠξίωσα) to come to you" (7:6–7; my translation). The centurion's initial declaration of unworthiness, utilizing ἱκανός, is found also in Matthew's version of this story (8:8). The term ἱκανός does appear in honorary decrees but is relatively rare. What is noteworthy, however, is that Luke adds two additional references to worthiness to his account and both of those employ the terminology of worthiness found most commonly in the decrees: ἄξιος and ἀξιόω. These additional references set up a contrast between the declaration of the elders and the centurion's self-declaration:

---

⁴⁴ Halvor Moxnes, "Patron-Client Relations and the New Community in Luke-Acts," in *The Social World of Luke-Acts: Models for Interpretation*, ed. Jerome Neyrey (Peabody: Hendrickson, 1991), 252; Green, *Gospel of Luke*, 285–86.

⁴⁵ Green, *Gospel of Luke*, 287.

⁴⁶ On the use of friendship language in relation to benefaction and patronage, see Alicia Batten, "God in the Letter of James: Patron or Benefactor?" *NTS* 50 (2004): 262; Hendrix, "Benefactor/Patron Networks," 41; Z. A. Crook, "Fictive-Friendship and the Fourth Gospel," *HvTSt* 67 (2011): 1–5.

> The elders: "He is worthy (ἄξιος) to have you do this for him." (7:4)
> The centurion: "I did not consider myself worthy (ἠξίωσα)." (7:7)

Within civic benefaction, the declaration of someone as "worthy" identifies them as a benefactor, an elite, a person of influence. They are worthy of honor, worthy of public adoration, worthy of having their benefits reciprocated. The Jewish elders, accordingly, acknowledge this man's *superiority* with their declaration of his worthiness and seek to reciprocate his largesse in order to remain in his favor. The centurion, in stark contrast, humbles himself and repudiates any notion of worthiness. It is often claimed that the centurion is acknowledging Jesus as his own superior benefactor.[47] This is true but primarily by implication. In other words, it is significant that the centurion does not directly declare *Jesus* to be worthy; rather, he declares *himself* to be unworthy. In Luke's rendering of this story, the focus is less on the centurion exalting Jesus than it is on the centurion humbling himself. This focus has profound implications for understanding the response Jesus gives in verse 9.

Scholars have long recognized that Luke situates this story in a context of benefaction through the additions and adaptations he gives it, yet when it comes to Jesus's declaration on the centurion's faith, this is rarely taken into account. Instead, the declaration gets interpreted as amazement that the centurion believes in the power and authority of Jesus to heal at just a word and from a distance.[48] Although these elements may play a role, they do not satisfy a full accounting of the particular way Luke has shaped his version of the story.

The term "faith" in the Gospel of Luke often identifies a trust in the power and provision of God (5:20; 8:25, 48; 12:28; 18:42), yet it also finds usage in the sense of one's understanding of or orientation towards the kingdom of God. Jesus tells a sinful woman that her "faith" has saved her, a faith that was exhibited through the love she showed in pouring perfume on his feet (7:47, 50). The disciples ask Jesus to increase their "faith" after he tells them to forgive graciously, suggesting the faith they need more of involves a deeper understanding of the demands of the kingdom (17:3–5).

Luke includes several stories in his Gospel that establish a pattern in which Jesus praises the faith of individuals for actions that exhibit an intuitive understanding of his

---

[47] Green, *Gospel of Luke*, 282; Moxnes, "Patron-Client Relations," 253; Luke Timothy Johnson, *The Gospel of Luke*, SP (Collegeville: Liturgical Press, 1991), 118; Levine and Witherington, *Gospel of Luke*, 200.

[48] Reid and Matthews, *Luke 1–9*, 221, 227; François Bovon, *A Commentary on the Gospel of Luke 1:1–9:50*, trans. Christine M. Thomas, Hermeneia (Minneapolis: Fortress, 2002), 263; Danker, *Jesus and the New Age*, 92; Norval Geldenhuys, *Commentary on the Gospel of Luke*, NICOT (Grand Rapids: Eerdmans, 1988), 221; Stein, *Luke*, 220; Bock, *Luke*, 131; Marshall *Gospel of Luke*, 278. Even Green, who otherwise bases his analysis of the story in the social dynamics of benefaction and patronage, ultimately identifies the centurion's "faith" in terms of a recognition of Jesus's authority and his willingness to use that authority on a gentile, *Gospel of Luke*, 288.

teachings. The pattern involves an outsider to mainstream Jewish society whose faithful actions are often contrasted with that of religious leaders or with the Jewish people generally. In 7:36–50, Jesus chastises Simon the Pharisee for how his treatment of Jesus paled in comparison to that of a sinful woman whose faith Jesus praises for demonstrating her love for him through her actions. In 17:11–19, Jesus praises the gratitude shown by a Samaritan leper by contrasting it with the ingratitude shown by nine Jewish lepers. When Jesus then declares that "your faith has made you well," it implies that the Samaritan leper's "faith" involved the fact that he alone understood something about the kingdom that the other nine lacked. In Luke 19, a chief tax collector named Zacchaeus is excoriated by the Jewish crowd as a "sinner" (19:7), but praised by Jesus (19:9). In the preceding chapter Jesus had told a rich ruler to sell everything and give it to the poor, a request the ruler refused. Yet here, this sinful tax-collector freely offered to give up half of his possessions to the poor, thus doing *without being asked* the very thing Jesus requested of the ruler. Zacchaeus received praise for embodying the teachings of Jesus on wealth and possessions. Similarly, Jesus later praised a poor widow for her meager donation of a few small coins in contrast to the wealthy Jews who donate huge sums because she truly enacted Jesus's teachings on self-sacrificial giving. In each of these stories, we see individuals with outsider or marginalized status in some way embodying the teachings of Jesus on the kingdom of God and receiving praise in return. Their "faith" is not simply believing in the power of Jesus, but *practicing* the essence of his teachings. The story of the centurion's servant not only represents this pattern as well, but is actually the first such example and the one that establishes the pattern.

Throughout the Gospel, Luke portrays Jesus as expressing a theme of reversal whereby the first will be last and those who exalt themselves will be humbled. In the sermon on the plain, Jesus incorporates this theme as well and then immediately follows it with the story of the centurion. Within the story itself, Luke adds material that identifies the centurion as a wealthy benefactor—one who in that culture would have been among the "first" and the "exalted." This creates an assumption that the centurion is playing the game, utilizing his high position as benefactor to exact a return on his investment: the healing of his servant. The Jewish elders, who appear fully invested in this system, implore Jesus to do his civic duty by helping them repay their "worthy" benefactor. Yet, the twist in the story comes when the centurion reveals himself to not be playing the game at all when he repudiates the praise of the elders by declaring himself "not worthy."

What the centurion does is humble rather than exalt himself, put himself last rather than first. In contrast to the Jewish elders, the centurion rejects the value system of competition whereby one gives in order to accrue honor and status for oneself and to advertise one's worthiness. He puts into practice the very teachings that Jesus just expressed in the sermon on the plain and, presumably, does so without having heard the sermon. In fact, the text suggests that the centurion has had no prior contact with Jesus (7:3). Thus, when Jesus announces in 7:9, "I tell you, not even in Israel have I found such faith," he acknowledges that this *Gentile* centurion displays an innate insight into the nature of God's kingdom and the teachings of Jesus that the leaders of the Jews have failed to comprehend.[49] The "faith" of the centurion is more than just a trusting in the power of God; it is the centurion's embodiment of the value system of humility that is central to Jesus's teachings in the Gospel of Luke. In the sermon that precedes this story, Jesus praised the one "who comes to me, hears my words, and acts on them" (6:47). This Gentile centurion, however, has not come to Jesus (in fact declares himself unworthy to do so), has not heard his words, and yet despite this, he acts on them. He stands as an example of faith because he, an outsider, grasps the truth of Jesus's teaching that "all who exalt themselves will be humbled, and those who humble themselves will be exalted" (14:11; 18:14). The centurion no doubt believes in the power of Jesus to heal his servant, yet what generates the excessive praise by Jesus is the centurion's intuitive understanding of the kingdom virtue of humility. The story thus establishes a pattern that continues throughout the Gospel of individuals with outsider status being singled out for praise of their faith for exhibiting through their actions an understanding of the logic of the kingdom of God.

---

[49] The extent to which this story represents a criticism of Israel is debated; see Marshall, *Gospel of Luke*, 277, and Nolland, *Luke*, 318. However, given the clear contrast established between the attitudes of the elders and that of the centurion, I believe Green is correct that the text makes explicit the "disjunction" between the elders who are "captive to a world system that has been nullified by the dawning of salvation" and the centurion who displays greater insight into Jesus's mission, *Gospel of Luke*, 285, 288.

6
"We Gave Up All Hope of Being Saved" (Acts 27:20): What Does Luke's Shipwreck Narrative Teach about God's Providence?

George Goldman II

INTRODUCTION

The broad narrative movement of the book of Acts is clear.[1] The Spirit-filled witness to Jesus that began in Jerusalem will eventually go to the "end of the earth" (Acts 1:8). The book ends with Paul in Rome, proclaiming the kingdom of God and teaching about the Lord Jesus Christ boldly and unhindered, though under house arrest (Acts 28:30–31).[2] So, once Paul becomes a major character in Acts, Luke's theological agenda is to portray "Paul as God's chosen instrument destined to reach Rome under God's providential care."[3] Despite this "providential care," Paul's journey to Rome happens in varied and unexpected ways. At a key point the whole journey is put into danger when a storm wipes out Paul's ship, as described in detail in Acts 27. After discussing the overall purpose of the shipwreck story in Acts 27, this essay will examine a few of the details of the narrative with a view toward the lessons one may draw from it about "God's providential care."[4]

THE OVERALL PURPOSE OF THE SHIPWRECK NARRATIVE

The shipwreck narrative in Acts 27 is an engrossing and exciting adventure story, and entertainment is likely part of Luke's purpose for including it.[5] This does not mean that

---

[1] I am grateful for Dr. Allen Black's teaching and mentorship. I not only remember the exegetical tools I learned from him, but also try to put them into practice, and am glad to participate in this volume dedicated to his honor.

[2] Though Rome is not the end of the earth itself, a common interpretation is that Paul's being in Rome signifies that from there the gospel will spread to the end of the earth. See, for example, Patrick Schreiner, *Acts*, Christian Standard Commentary (Nashville: Holman Reference, 2021), 90.

[3] Carl R. Holladay, *Acts: A Commentary*, NTL (Louisville: Westminster John Knox, 2016), 488.

[4] Johnson rightly points out two questions interpreters face: "Why does [Luke] spend so much time and care on what was after all only a voyage?" And of all the details that he could have provided, why might he have chosen these details in particular? (*The Acts of the Apostles*, SP [Collegeville: Liturgical, 1992], 450, 456–57).

[5] Writers were trained to compose sea storm narratives in the Roman imperial period. See Charles H. Talbert and J. H. Hayes, "A Theology of Sea Storms in Acts," in *Luke's Narrative Claim upon Israel's Legacy*, vol. 1 of *Jesus and the Heritage of Israel*, ed. David Moessner (Harrisburg: Trinity Press

Luke invented the narrative. The route and nautical details of Luke's account are realistic.[6] In addition, shipwrecks were fairly common for travelers like Paul, and writing about such an actual event could entail using common literary motifs. Although the role of these types of narratives in ancient literature included entertainment, they also carried other functions, such as teaching moral lessons about peace in crisis or the beauty of friendship.[7] It is possible for the narrative to have historical plausibility and for the author to communicate lessons for his readers at the same time.[8]

Several interpreters propose that Luke's purpose in the shipwreck scene is to illustrate God's verdict that Paul is innocent of wrongdoing. The chapters preceding the shipwreck show human authorities declaring Paul not guilty.[9] By means of the shipwreck and snakebite scenes in Acts 27:1–28:6, God declares Paul not guilty as well.[10] On the other hand, even if surviving a shipwreck may have increased Paul's credibility with an ancient pagan audience that attached divine retribution to storms and snakebites, Luke's readers are not in doubt about Paul's innocence.[11] In addition, a defense of Paul would not require a narrative of this length and detail "since the mere fact of his survival is adequate defense."[12]

International, 1999), 269. Kenneth L. Cukrowski shows how Luke's narrative may mimic Homer's *Odyssey*, which was influential in ancient literature ("Paul as Odysseus: An Exegetical Note on Luke's Depiction of Paul in Acts 27:1–28:10," *ResQ* 55 [2013]: 24–34). Keener notes such influence would not necessarily mean that Acts has left the genre of theological history (*Acts: An Exegetical Commentary*, 4 vols. [Grand Rapids: Baker Academic, 2012–2015], 4:3555).

[6] Eckhard J. Schnabel, "Fads and Common Sense: Reading Acts in the First Century and Reading Acts Today," *JETS* 54 (2011): 255.

[7] Johnson, *Acts*, 451–52.

[8] Schnabel, "Fads," 255. As Warren Carter says about Luke's narrative, "It depicts a literal sea storm and shipwreck which also carry symbolic (though not allegorical) significance" ("Aquatic Display: Navigating the Roman Imperial World in Acts 27," *NTS* 62 [2016]: 81).

[9] Claudius Lysias in 23:29; Festus in 25:25, and Agrippa in 26:31.

[10] Talbert and Hayes, "Theology," 275; Keener, *Acts* (2015), 4:3551. If Luke's goal was to show Paul's innocence, it becomes even less likely that Luke invented this story. As Susan Marie Praeder notes, "Divine favor is demonstrated by calm seas, not by a storm and shipwreck" ("Acts 27:1-28:16: Sea Voyages in Ancient Literature and the Theology of Luke-Acts," *CBQ* 46 [1984]: 704). It is possible that Luke intended a contrast to Jonah. Whereas Jonah's disobedience led to a storm, Paul is obedient, and his survival shows that he is innocent.

[11] See Brian M. Rapske, "Acts, Travel, and Shipwreck," in *The Book of Acts in its Graeco-Roman Setting*, vol. 2 of *The Book of Acts in Its First Century Setting*, ed. David W. J. Gill and Conrad Gempf (Grand Rapids: Eerdmans, 1994), 44, and Joshua W. Jipp, *Divine Visitations and Hospitality to Strangers in Luke-Acts: An Interpretation of the Malta Episode in Acts 28:1–10*, NovTSup 153 (Leiden: Brill, 2013), 11.

[12] Richard I. Pervo, *Acts: A Commentary*, Hermeneia (Minneapolis: Fortress, 2009), 648.

The purpose of the shipwreck narrative in Acts is best seen when it is put into the context of Luke-Acts as a whole. The chart below shows several parallels between what happens to Jesus at the end of Luke and what happens to Paul at the end of Acts.[13]

	Jesus	Paul
Journey to Jerusalem knowing that suffering awaits	Luke 9:31, 51; 13:33; 18:31–33	Acts 20:22–24; 21:13–14
Friends fail to understand	Luke 9:45; 18:34	Acts 21:4, 10–12
Arrest and four trials	Luke 22:66–23:13	Acts 23–26
Declared innocent three times	Luke 23:4, 14, 22	Acts 23:9; 25:25; 26:31
Meal with parallel language of taking bread, giving thanks, and breaking (the bread)	Luke 22:19 (λαβὼν ἄρτον εὐχαριστήσας ἔκλασεν)	Acts 27:35 (λαβὼν ἄρτον εὐχαρίστησεν ... καὶ κλάσας)

These parallels cause some to go so far as to relate Paul's survival of the shipwreck and snakebite to Jesus's death and resurrection. Patrick Schreiner, for example, states, "In the Hebrew Bible, 'plunging into the waters' figuratively meant 'going to one's death.' Being saved out of them is resurrection."[14] Although this last parallel is not exact because Paul does not actually die or resurrect, there is a common theme visible here. "Even through the very forms of suffering that appear to destroy the gospel—such as Jesus's crucifixion or Paul's imprisonment—the living God is at work to accomplish his purposes."[15] Paul's determination to go to Jerusalem seems tied to his belief that the Jews remain part of God's purpose. As Willie James Jennings notes, this is not "the story of a lone man destined for tribulation. ... Just as with Jesus, the Spirit leads an obedient one who will do the will of God into Jerusalem."[16] Paul's further desire to see Rome (Acts 19:21) is tied to his mission to the Gentiles. Jerusalem and Rome are the

---

[13] For these parallels and several others, see Charles H. Talbert, *Literary Patterns, Theological Themes, and the Genre of Luke-Acts*, SBLMS (Missoula: Scholars, 1974), 17–23, and Schreiner, *Acts*, 567–69.

[14] Schreiner, *Acts*, 644.

[15] Craig S. Keener, *Acts*, New Cambridge Bible Commentary (Cambridge: Cambridge University Press, 2020), 635.

[16] Willie James Jennings, *Acts*, Belief: A Theological Commentary on the Bible (Louisville: Westminster John Knox, 2017), 197.

respective centers of power.[17] Paul's trip to Rome is bound up with the broader purposes of God in Luke-Acts, and the shipwreck takes on greater significance within this framework. With this background in place, the remainder of this essay will focus on what lessons the shipwreck narrative may teach about God's providence.

LESSONS IN PROVIDENCE

Providence Works Through Human Decision Making, Whether Good or Bad

In Acts 27:10, Paul advises the group not to leave Fair Havens on Crete: "I see (θεωρῶ) that the voyage will happen with damage and much loss, not only of the cargo and the boat, but also our lives (ψυχῶν)."[18] Some interpreters think Paul's advice here is only the human judgment of a frequent traveler.[19] The text mentions that it was a dangerous time to sail (27:9), and divine revelation is not required to know this. Other interpreters, given how specific Paul's forecast is, think Paul was given divine guidance about the travel plan. "God can provide nautical wisdom that even experts lack."[20] This interpretive difference provides an interesting lesson regarding decision making and divine providence. The book of Acts shows that God works both through decisions based on common sense and decisions based on divine guidance.[21] Indeed, in Acts 21:1–16, Paul's decision to go to Jerusalem despite prophetic warnings shows that it is sometimes hard "to separate divine revelation from human interpretation."[22]

---

[17] Robert C. Tannehill, *The Acts of the Apostles*, vol. 2 in *The Narrative Unity of Luke-Acts: A Literary Interpretation* (Minneapolis: Fortress, 1990), 266.

[18] All translations are those of the author.

[19] For example, see Rapske, "Acts," 29. Rapske points to Paul's prediction of loss of life that did not happen. However, divine prediction can be conditional.

[20] Keener, *Acts* (2020), 599. Haenchen believes Luke portrays it as a "prophetic alliance with God." Ernst Haenchen, *The Acts of the Apostles: A Commentary*, trans. Bernard Noble and Gerald Shinn (Philadelphia: Westminster, 1971), 709. So also Jipp, *Divine Visitation*, 31–32.

[21] Sometimes divine guidance is explicitly mentioned, such as the decision to go on the first missionary journey from Antioch and to go to Macedonia on the second journey (13:1–3; 16:10). Also see the divine guidance in 18:9–10 and 23:11 which both have themes of keeping Paul from fear associated with his following of God's call on his life. At other times, the means of the divine guidance is not stipulated. In 16:6–7 the narrator says that the Holy Spirit prevented them from speaking the word in Asia, and the Spirit of Jesus did not allow them to go to Bithynia. Was this discerned through divine prophecy or more natural causes? At other times Paul makes decisions based on "natural" events. In 20:3, Paul changes his plan from sailing back to Syria to taking an overland route through Macedonia because of a plot by Jews against him. Paul appeals to Caesar in 25:9 because Festus had asked him to go to Jerusalem for trial.

[22] Tannehill, *Acts*, 263. It could be that Paul's friends knew Paul would face hardship in Jerusalem and misguided him because of their concern for Paul's safety. The text of 21:4, though, does say that they told Paul "through the Spirit" (διὰ τοῦ πνεύματος) not to go to Jerusalem. Tannehill ends his discussion of Acts 21:1–16 with: "Appeal to divine guidance is not an easy escape from the ambiguities of human life" (*Acts*, 263).

Paul's view while in Fair Havens was that everyone should stay there for the winter, but that plan was foiled by the decision of the majority, possibly based on greed: the desire to get as close to Rome as possible in order to sell the grain sooner. It is not clear whether Paul's advice in 27:9–12 rises to the level of divine prediction, but even if it does, such guidance requires human discernment, and this passage shows that regardless of the decision made, God can still work.[23]

Providence Does Not Eliminate Times of Doubting

Another detail relevant to the issue of providence is the narrator's statement in 27:20 that after going many days without seeing the sun or stars, "finally, all hope of our being saved was being given up."[24] Statements about losing hope in the midst of a storm are a frequent part of shipwreck scenes in ancient literature.[25] Some interpreters think the "we" who lose hope cannot include Paul since he soon reports an angelic vision that promises all will be saved (27:21–26). Ernst Haenchen criticizes what he sees as Luke's unrealistic image of Paul as someone who never despairs: "[Luke] knows only the strong, unshaken favourite of God who strides from triumph to triumph."[26] However, the narrative does not say exactly what day Paul got this vision of the angel. Paul says he received the vision on "this night," but Luke does not indicate on which day of the storm Paul gives the speech.[27] This leaves open the possibility that the storm was so bad that even Paul thought God's plan for him to see Rome had changed, and this idea is supported by the angel's admonition to Paul not to be afraid.[28]

It is encouraging to see that Paul persisted even when hope was lacking. This narrative shows that God can bring deliverance in hopeless times, even if that deliverance comes not by dramatic interventions but in more subtle ways.[29] Jennings's optimistic application is: "The prophetic word always comes at the times when hope is drained, because God will not allow hope to die in this world."[30]

---

[23] When Paul's friends are unable to keep Paul from going to Jerusalem they say, "May the Lord's will be done" (Acts 21:14). This echoes Jesus's prayer in the garden in Luke 22:42.

[24] λοιπὸν περιῃρεῖτο ἐλπὶς πᾶσα τοῦ σῴζεσθαι ἡμᾶς. The imperfect tense περιῃρεῖτο could be inceptive with the meaning of "we began to lose all hope of being saved."

[25] Praeder provides a sampling of these ("Acts 27–28," 692).

[26] Haenchen, *Acts*, 711. For Paul as not part of the "we," also see Stanley E. Porter, *Paul in Acts*, Library of Pauline Studies (Peabody: Hendrickson, 2001), 54, and Keener, *Acts*, (2015), 4:3620.

[27] Eckhard J. Schnabel, *Acts*, Zondervan Exegetical Commentary on the New Testament (Grand Rapids: Zondervan, 2012), 1041.

[28] Richard N. Longenecker, "The Acts of the Apostles," in *Expositor's Bible Commentary*, vol. 9, ed. Frank E. Gaebelein and J. D. Douglas (Grand Rapids: Zondervan, 1981), 561.

[29] David R. Bauer, *The Book of Acts as Story: A Narrative-Critical Study* (Grand Rapids: Baker Academic, 2021), 241–42.

[30] Jennings, *Acts*, 237.

Even though all on board were in danger of losing hope, the hope in God that is possible for believers plays an important role for everyone on the boat. Craig Keener notes that when Christians experience suffering along with non-Christians, they have an opportunity for spiritual leadership. "When Christians and non-Christians are suffering, they share in their common humanity, but Christians' hope for God's purpose in the midst of their suffering can help provide others with meaning and courage."[31]

Providence Impacts "All"

Why does Luke emphasize that all 276 people on the ship were rescued (27:22, 24, 44)?[32] Tannehill takes the salvation of all on the ship as a theological detail that implies universalism.[33] However, unless one sees universalism as the teaching of Scripture as a whole, it is unlikely to be Luke's intention here. Acts elsewhere puts emphasis on faith in Jesus and the need for sinners to repent (for example, Acts 2:38; 13:48). "If we read Acts and its author, as well as the main characters of Acts, in the historical and theological context of the missionaries and theologians in the first century, a universalist interpretation becomes quickly untenable."[34] Rather, because the majority of those saved are pagans who do not worship God, the salvation of all on the ship points to Paul's mission to Gentiles, who are now included in the kingdom.[35] Joshua Jipp highlights the Isaianic quotations that frame Luke's entire narrative. In Luke 3:6, John the Baptist quotes Isa 40:5 that "all flesh will see the salvation of God," and in Acts 28:28, Paul follows up a quote from Isa 6:9–10 with "this salvation has been sent to the Gentiles." Jipp concludes, "This framing technique suggests that the reader may read everything in between as related to the process whereby God's salvation goes to all peoples."[36] The salvation of all on the ship emphasizes the scope of God's mission.[37]

This lesson is a good place to discuss the meal that Paul has on the boat. The sharing of meals together is not found in other ancient shipwreck narratives and comes rather from Luke's use of meals in Luke-Acts.[38] Many think the context of this meal in the

---

[31] Keener, *Acts* (2015), 4:3569.

[32] The angel says that in addition to saving Paul's life, God has also "granted" (κεχάρισται) to Paul all those who are sailing with him (27:24). The language of "granting" likely means that Paul had prayed for the safety of all on the boat as well as for himself. See Schnabel, *Acts*, 1043. Tannehill notes that the sailors were doing their thing (tending to the boat), and Paul was doing his (praying) (*Acts*, 332).

[33] Tannehill, *Acts*, 337–38.

[34] Schnabel, "Fads," 264–65.

[35] J. Bradley Chance, *Acts*, SHBC (Macon: Smyth and Helwys, 2007), 510.

[36] Jipp, *Divine Visitation*, 34.

[37] Note that God protects all the people, but not the ship or its cargo. Carter believes this shows that Paul can benefit from the Roman system and its transportation, but God's priorities are not co-opted when the empire places profit over people (Carter, "Aquatic Display," 93).

[38] Praeder, "Acts 27–28," 696–97.

middle of a storm with a crowd that includes mostly non-Christians rules it out as being the eucharist. However, several point out that though the actions of taking bread, breaking it, and giving thanks are typical of what Jews did at every meal, "the coincidence in language with that the Last Supper can hardly be accidental."[39]

Paul's entreaty for all to eat in 27:33 mentions food three times, emphasizing that the purpose was eating for physical survival (πρὸς τῆς ὑμετέρας σωτηρίας, in 27:24).[40] They need food to have the strength to survive getting to shore since they have not eaten for a long time. Despite the emphasis on eating for physical strength, the sharing of bread in the context of the table of Jesus is also a witness that God's power is present and at work.[41] As at Emmaus (Luke 24:13–35), "Christians could never be sure when a meal might turn out to have a eucharistic, sacramental character."[42] To the Christians who saw deeper significance, the meal would communicate the presence of Jesus. To the others, it would be just a meal to strengthen them physically. Regardless of whether the meal is the eucharist, the wording echoes the meals of Jesus and indicates the Lord's presence with all.[43] This meal is a sign that a greater power can be at work in the midst of the storm.

---

[39] C. K. Barrett, "Paul Shipwrecked," in *Scripture: Meaning and Method: Essays Presented to Anthony Tyrell Hanson for his Seventieth Birthday*, ed. Barry P. Thompson (North Yorkshire: Hull University Press, 1987), 60. See also John Mark Hicks, who notes that the Western text's addition of "giving also to us" creates the fourfold eucharistic formula of take, break, give thanks, and give ("Breaking Bread in Luke-Acts V: Acts 27," *John Mark Hicks* [blog], March 26, 2009, https://johnmarkhicks.com/2009/03/26/ breaking-bread-in-luke-acts-v-acts-27/). And, though the context of this meal on the boat includes non-Christians, we can't assume that outsiders were excluded from the first century eucharist.

[40] Schnabel, *Acts*, 1045. Praeder notes that the word "salvation" (σῴζειν) is common in the ancient sea voyage literature referring to physical rescue ("Acts 27–28," 692). Many, including Praeder, think Luke's use of that wording in the wider narrative of Acts to refer to spiritual salvation indicates a spiritual sense to the word in the shipwreck narrative as well. Although words can have more than one meaning, one cannot assume both meanings are present when the context indicates one of those, and in a shipwreck narrative the meaning is physical salvation. Salvation from a shipwreck and salvation from sin, which requires faith in Jesus, are two very different things. See Schnabel, "Fads," 264–65.

[41] Johnson, *Acts*, 459.

[42] Barrett, "Paul Shipwrecked," 61–62.

[43] Chance, *Acts*, 510. Chance also notes the concern for all also shows up when the centurion forbids the soldiers to kill the prisoners in 27:42–43. He could have just protected Paul, but the providence that underlies this whole narrative is concerned not just with Paul or even only the Christians, but with all (*Acts*, 507).

Providence Works in Concert with Human Activity

Various details show that God's work to save Paul requires human activity and expertise.[44] Paul's closing comment in 27:26, "Nevertheless, we must run aground on some island," is brought to fulfillment only with the nautical maneuvers described later in the narrative. People needed to eat in order to survive. Paul's good behavior while a prisoner is also a factor in God's salvation. The centurion, who likes Paul, saves his life and those of the other prisoners as well (27:43). The narrative throughout shows a relationship between God's sovereignty and human activity.[45] "It is striking that Luke has none of the dramatic reversals of fortune at sea that could be attributed to a direct intervention by the deity."[46]

In 27:31, the sailors needed to stay on the ship rather than escape in the smaller lifeboat. Paul tells the centurion and soldiers, "If these men do not remain in the boat, you cannot be saved." Keener suggests this means for the sailors not to trust their human means of salvation, which would have only saved a few, but rather to trust God to save all.[47] Robert Wall thinks that the point is the need for proximity to Paul due to his being the agent of God's saving grace. Therefore, that there will be no loss of life is "due to God's provident care and not the efforts of a skilled crew (see v. 23)."[48] However, Robert Tannehill rightly notes that the efforts of the sailors and soldiers "are not simply the foil for divine rescue. They do not simply demonstrate the uselessness of human action."[49] The salvation of God is accomplished not by "tinkering with natural and human processes by arbitrary interventions" but takes place in concert with human decisions.[50] A balance is required here. Providence is not a matter of just letting go and letting God, but neither is it worked out merely by human activity without the hope that comes from God's living and rescuing presence.[51]

---

[44] Pervo mentions an interesting anecdote in this regard: "The late Dieter Georgi once challenged the students in a Harvard New Testament seminar by asking, 'When does Acts 27 become a miracle story?'" (*Acts*, 652).

[45] Keener, *Acts* (2020), 608.

[46] Johnson, *Acts*, 458.

[47] Keener, *Acts* (2020), 607. But Keener does go on to say that the skill of the sailors will help all make it to shore.

[48] Robert W. Wall, "The Acts of the Apostles: Introduction, Commentary, and Reflections," in *NIB*, vol. 10, ed. Leander E. Keck et al. (Nashville: Abingdon, 2002), 351–52.

[49] Tannehill, *Acts*, 330.

[50] Johnson, *Acts*, 458.

[51] N. T. Wright, *Acts for Everyone: Part 2, Chapters 13–28* (London: SPCK, 2008), 233.

Providence Cannot Be Discerned by Negative Events

There are some times in Acts when disciples are rescued from prison, but more often, trials just have to be endured.[52] God can show his power by stilling a storm, as Jesus did (Luke 8:22–25), but also by bringing his followers through the storm and allowing them to save others as well.[53] The narrative of the snake bite on the island and how the islanders react (28:1–6) has an explicit contradiction of the idea that retributive divine providence can be attached to negative events. Paul was not bitten by a snake because he was a sinner. He was neither being punished by a god nor a god himself.[54] Sometimes, events are just events. Storms and snakebites are not the way that God brings justice. Even though Paul is saved in this case, suffering no harm is still the exception rather than the rule for Paul and Christian disciples in general.[55]

Providence Occurs in the Journey, Not Just the Destination

The narrative in Acts of Paul's journey to Rome shows that despite threats and uncertainty, Paul does not stop witnessing to the gospel. Though the narrative has mentioned that the final goal is Paul's testifying in Rome, the openness and uncertainty of the journey provide unexpected opportunities for witness and God's saving activity. This teaches an important point about witness: "It is not limited to sacred moments or particular audiences but instead takes place freely among strangers, at all times, and in the most foreign places."[56] The lives of the soldiers and sailors became caught up in the mission of God. They thought it was their journey, their work, and their risk. "They are in God's history and the Spirit's journey with Paul. Paul is their prisoner, but they are captive inside his mission."[57] There is a certain hubris here. Believers have hope in moments of despair because they see their lives as part of a grander story. This means that wherever the journey goes, other people along the path become participants as well. As Jennings beautifully notes, "It is a hubris that dares to speak at the site of despair and chaos, saying God lives and so too we will live."[58] A belief in God's providence in moments of crisis causes one to notice the unexpected people encountered along the way.

---

[52] Chance, *Acts*, 508.

[53] Keener, *Acts* (2015), 4:3567.

[54] Keener, *Acts* (2020), 614.

[55] William J. Larkin, Jr., *Acts* (Downers Grove: InterVarsity Press, 1995), 380.

[56] Troy M. Troftgruben, "Slow Sailing in Acts: Suspense in the Final Sea Journey (Acts 27:1–28:15)," *JBL* 136 (2017): 967–68.

[57] Jennings, *Acts*, 237.

[58] Jennings, *Acts*, 237.

CONCLUSION

God didn't still the storm, but he did protect all the people on the boat. Jesus had calmed a storm in Luke 8:22–25, showing his divine power, but the message is different here.[59] In this narrative, we sense Luke's belief that God has acted in history, but in more subtle ways: speaking prophecies, giving Paul a vision that he shares with his fellow travelers, and in human decisions. When decisions are made which turn out to be bad, the consequences still happen. God's activity in the world is not always spectacular and clear but can happen through natural and human processes. Luke, Paul, and their fellow travelers may have spent time on the beach recounting the storm, the foiled escape of the sailors, and the soldiers' wanting to kill the prisoners, and despite all this, everyone was saved. The eyes of faith are able to perceive these processes as "revealing the purposes and call of God."[60]

When our lives are shaped by the gospel, our own survival serves the needs of the kingdom and is taken up into a broader purpose. In Paul's speech to the Ephesian elders in Acts 20:24, he says that for him, suffering in the short term was worth the future benefit to the kingdom.[61] Believers have faith that their lives are intended for a greater purpose. Though the path to that goal is uncertain and fraught with various perils, we believe that God's broader purpose will happen as God has said (Acts 27:25; see also Luke 1:38). Even though the narrative of Acts ends with Paul in Rome, it frustratingly does not report what ultimately happens to him. That provides insight into the ultimate goal of God's providence:

> The narrative is not ultimately about Paul, nor for that matter any other human, but rather the focus is upon the power of the exalted Christ, who through the Spirit causes the proclamation of the gospel—the word of God—to move exponentially from Jerusalem to the end of the earth, overcoming all challenges and hindrances.[62]

---

[59] Talbert and Hayes, "Theology," 277.

[60] Johnson, *Acts*, 458.

[61] Keener, *Acts*, (2015), 1:447.

[62] Bauer, *Acts as Story*, 248.

7

The Restoration of Israel, the Kingdom of God, and the Church in Luke-Acts

Mark C. Black[1]

INTRODUCTION

In the first chapter of Acts, Jesus's apostles ask him, "Lord, is this the time when you will restore the kingdom to Israel?" (Acts 1:6) Many interpreters think the apostles asked a foolish question, still expecting a literal rather than a spiritual kingdom. In recent decades, however, Jacob Jervell and others have argued that the author considered the apostles' question entirely appropriate.[2] These interpreters believe that Luke was teaching his readers that Jesus, the Davidic Messiah, would indeed restore the kingdom to Israel.[3]

What *did* Jesus's disciples mean when they asked about the restoration of Israel? What did Jesus mean by his response? Did Luke think that Jesus and the church *spiritualized* the prophetic promises that Israel would be restored and given victory over her enemies? Did Luke believe that God had abandoned his former plans? Did Luke

---

[1] I cannot overstate my indebtedness to and love for my brother Allen. He introduced me several decades ago to the thinking of Jacob Jervell on the restoration of Israel. Much more importantly, no one has had more influence than he in my life, including faith, career, family, morality, and service to the church and to others.

[2] Jacob Jervell, *Luke and the People of God: A New Look at Luke-Acts* (Minneapolis: Augsburg, 1972); Jacob Jervell, *The Theology of the Acts of the Apostles* (Cambridge: University Press, 1996). Among many others who have made important contributions to this discussion, see N.T. Wright, *The New Testament and the People of God* (Minneapolis: Fortress, 1992); N.T. Wright, *Jesus and the Victory of God* (Minneapolis: Fortress, 1996); Isaac W. Oliver, *Luke's Jewish Eschatology: The Restoration of Israel in Luke-Acts* (Oxford: Oxford University Press, 2021); and James D. G. Dunn, *Baptism in the Holy Spirit: A Re-examination of the New Testament Teaching on the Gift of the Spirit in Relation to Pentecostalism Today*, 2nd ed. (London: SCM, 2010). Richard Bauckham, "The Restoration of Israel in Luke-Acts," 435–87 in Restoration: Old Testament, Jewish, and Christian Perspectives, JSJSup 72, ed. James Scott (Leiden: Brill, 2001); Michael E. Fuller, *The Restoration of Israel: Israel's Re-gathering and the Fate of the Nations in Early Jewish Literature and Luke-Acts*, BZNW 138 (Berlin: de Gruyter, 2006); Craig S. Keener, *Acts: An Exegetical Commentary* 4 vols. (Grand Rapids: Baker Academic, 2012–2015); David P. Moessner, *Jesus and the Heritage of Israel: Luke's Narrative Claim upon Israel's Legacy,* vol. 1 of *Luke the Interpreter of Israel.* LNTS 452 (Harrisburg: Trinity Press International, 1999); David Rudolph and Joel Willitts, eds., *Introduction to Messianic Judaism: Its Ecclesial Context and Biblical Foundations* (Grand Rapids: Zondervan, 2013).

[3] My view is that Luke, the physician who traveled with Paul, most likely wrote Luke-Acts.

understand the church to be God's *replacement* for Israel? What were Luke's teachings about Israel, the kingdom of God, and the church in Luke-Acts?

My thesis is that, according to Luke, Jesus came to restore ethnic Israel; Jesus and the church did not spiritualize the words of the prophets; the previously–hidden kingdom of God welcomed its first citizens on Pentecost; and the entrance of gentiles into restored Israel was accomplished just as the prophets had foretold. The early church understood itself to be the faithful remnant of Israel in the new age inaugurated by Messiah Jesus.

To support this thesis, I will briefly summarize certain traditional beliefs, structures, and practices of first-century Judaism.[4] I will also summarize numerous eschatological expectations of Israel's prophets and in what sense Luke saw them as being fulfilled. I will then compare these with the same topics in Luke's portrayal of the early church.

TERMINOLOGY

Two Greek terms that have been translated poorly in the English New Testament have furthered misunderstanding of important themes in the present study. The first is Χριστός (Christos), which should be translated *Messiah*.[5] In Luke's first-century Jewish world, the word *Messiah* referred to God's eschatological king who was to reign over restored Israel. The English translation *Christ* does not convey that meaning.

A second mistranslated Greek term is ἐκκλησία (ekklesia), the word translated "church" in English translations. The early Christians understood ἐκκλησία (ekklesia) in light of its repeated usage in the Greek translation of the Old Testament, the Scriptures read most often by first-century Jews. There it refers to the nation of Israel assembled for worship, teaching, or the like.[6] Regrettably, the word "church" fails to convey the early Christians' claim to be the eschatological *assembly of Israel*. If the terms ἐκκλησία (ekklesia) and Χριστός (Christos) were translated accurately, readers would understand that the early church claimed to be the *assembly of Israel* that followed *the Messiah of Israel* and worshipped *the God of Israel*.

SYNAGOGUES, BELIEFS, AND PRACTICES

General

Throughout the Roman world, Jews were united by their ancestry, beliefs,

---

[4] This is not a claim that all ancient Jews thought and behaved in the same ways. However, Jewish second-temple writings and especially the NT offer evidence that a majority of first-century Jews shared the fundamental beliefs and practices discussed herein.

[5] Fortunately, the recent editions of the NIV and NRSV translate Χριστός (Christos) as "Messiah."

[6] Greek translators of the OT used ἐκκλησία (ekklesia) to translate the original Hebrew term קהל "the assembly (of Israel)." Since most Jews and Christians in the first-century were unable to read Hebrew, they read Scripture in a Greek translation (called the Septuagint).

practices, and leadership structures. Most important was their common view that the Old Testament, or better, "First Testament,"[7] was their authority in faith and life. They maintained a strong synagogue network that allowed them to stay connected with other Jews. Diaspora Jews often traveled to Jerusalem to celebrate Passover and other festivals, to visit friends and family, and to offer sacrifices. There was great unity among the synagogues in the Mediterranean world.[8]

Adherents

Only ethnic Jews attended the synagogues, with two exceptions. First, there were sometimes *proselytes* in their gatherings. Proselytes were gentiles by birth, but they were fully Jewish in their beliefs, religious practices, and lifestyles. They observed the whole Law of Moses, including those laws that functioned to identify them as Jews, such as Sabbath observance, avoidance of unclean food, and circumcision. The ethnic Jews, especially those in the Diaspora, were glad to have proselytes as full members of their synagogues.

Synagogues also welcomed a second group of gentiles called "God-fearers." These gentiles revered Jewish monotheistic beliefs and Jewish moral standards, but they saw no reason to observe the ritual laws that signified Jewish identity. God-fearers were considered friends of the synagogue, but they were not full members. God-fearers are prominent in the Book of Acts because they were among the most receptive hearers of the gospel message.

Worship

Some ancient synagogues met in dedicated buildings, while others met in homes. They met on the Sabbath for worship, which included prayer, Scripture reading, instruction, chanting of psalms, and recitation of Scriptures and creedal statements. Their meeting places were used for various purposes other than worship, such as education, legal assemblies, distribution centers for food, refuge for travelers, and other community gatherings.

Baptism

First-century Jews practiced baptism for several purposes. Before entering the temple area, for example, Jews immersed themselves in water to remove ritual impurity.

---

[7] The phrase "Old Testament" is an unfortunate description, suggesting that it has been *replaced* by the "New" Testament. I will use the term "First Testament" hereafter.

[8] For more information regarding synagogues and their functions, see Anders Runesson, *The Origin of the Synagogue: A Socio–Historical Study* (Schweden: Almqvist & Wilksell, 2001); Lee Levine, *The Ancient Synagogue: The First Thousand Years*, 2nd ed., (New Haven: Yale University Press, 2005); and Bruce Chilton and Edwin Yamauchi, "Synagogues," *DNTB* 1145–53.

Some had baptismal pools in their homes, where they dipped their utensils, other objects, and sometimes themselves. Proselytes were baptized to cleanse them from the moral impurity of their former gentile lives. Proselyte baptism also served as the initiation ritual for their full acceptance as Jews.

Leadership

Each synagogue had a "ruler of the synagogue" who looked after the Torah scrolls, organized and presided over meetings, and tended to administrative needs. There were also assistants to the synagogue leader who took care of lesser tasks.

All of the synagogues within a city or region were overseen by a single group of "elders," older men who dealt with matters regarding religious instruction, relationships with local officials, threats to fellow Jews, disciplinary actions, and the like. The council of elders in a city or region was a smaller version of the Sanhedrin in Jerusalem, the council of elders who had great influence over all Jews.

The Jerusalem Sanhedrin, a group of seventy men, were allowed by the Romans to rule over most Jewish religious, legal, administrative, and political matters. It was led by the High Priest, whose role was far more political than religious in the first century. The High Priest and Sanhedrin had authority over some Jews even outside Judea, as demonstrated in Acts 7:1–2, in which the High Priest sent Saul of Tarsus to Damascus to arrest Christian Jews.

Church and Synagogue

Like the non-Christian Jews of their day, the Scriptures of the first Christians were the writings of the First Testament. However, unlike their fellow Jews, the church believed that the Scriptures pointed broadly and deeply to Messiah Jesus. The earliest churches were Jewish synagogues who believed Jesus was the Messiah. They most likely referred to themselves as the ἐκκλησία (ekklesia) in order to distinguish themselves from the non-Christian synagogues. The worship, structures, and other practices of the early church remained very much like those of traditional synagogues.

Church Worship

Jewish Christians continued to meet for worship on the Sabbath, either gathering with traditional Jewish synagogues or in homes of Christians. Church worship was like synagogue worship, including prayer, Scripture reading, teaching, chanting of psalms, and recitation of Scripture and creeds (for example, Phil 2:5–11; Col 1:15–20). However, these Christian Jews prayed in the name of Jesus, wrote songs and creedal statements about Jesus, taught about what it meant to be Jesus's disciples, and so on.

Lord's Supper

In addition to Sabbath worship, the church met regularly and shared communal meals (Acts 2:42, 46). On the first day of the week, they worshipped and ate a meal that was based on the Passover supper shared by Jesus and his disciples on the night before his death. This meal celebrated the death of Jesus as the ultimate sacrificial Passover lamb. It came to be known as the "Lord's Supper" or "Eucharist," a time of communal thanksgiving and anticipation of the future messianic banquet (Isa 25:6). In other words, early Christians gave new meaning to the Jewish Passover meal.

Baptism

The early church maintained the Jewish practice of baptism, adapting its meaning to the new reality created by Messiah Jesus. As was true of John's baptism and proselyte baptism, Christians were baptized for forgiveness of moral rather than ritual impurity. However, this new form of Jewish baptism was adapted to the eschatological age of the Messiah. Peter's words on Pentecost provide the essence of Luke's teaching: "Repent and be baptized every one of you in the name of Jesus Christ so that your sins may be forgiven, and you will receive the gift of the Holy Spirit" (Acts 2:38).

Leadership

The early churches largely maintained Jewish leadership and organizational structures. It is likely that the hosts of house churches were equivalent to the leaders of the traditional Jewish synagogues. The deacons in the early church were probably the same as the assistants in the synagogues.

Like the Jewish synagogues, Christian churches had a council of elders that had authority over all the congregations (house churches) in each area. The elders functioned as pastors, administrators, judges, liaisons to city officials, and the like. Luke mentions that Paul appointed elders in each of the towns where he planted churches (Acts 14:23).

Luke tells his readers that the *apostles* were the authoritative leaders of the renewed Israel, as Jesus had promised (Luke 22:28–30). In Acts 3–5, Luke narrates a series of episodes in which the Sanhedrin attempted to discredit and destroy the church. Instead, the apostles preached boldly, performed miracles, and defeated the efforts of the Sanhedrin. Luke thus demonstrated that the apostles, not the Sanhedrin, were the true leaders of Israel.

The apostles had the responsibility to authenticate and teach the new beliefs of Christians (Acts 2:42–43), administer discipline (Acts 5:1–11), receive and distribute financial gifts (Acts 4:34–35; 6:1–5), approve new missions (Acts 8:14–17), and make authoritative decisions for the churches (Acts 15). Luke emphasizes Peter's role as the primary leader of the apostles for the first decade or so (Acts 1:12–5:42; 10:1–11:18;

12:1-19) until he left Jerusalem to travel among the churches. After Peter, James, the brother of Jesus apparently became the "first-among-equals" (Acts 12:17; 15:13–21; 21:17–25).

Eschatology

The eschatological beliefs of the early church were very similar to those of first-century Jews, anticipating the time when God would keep his promises to Israel.[9] After preaching against the sins of Israel and their dire consequences, the prophets promised that, in the last days, God would send Israel a righteous king, the Messiah, who would defeat their gentile enemies and establish justice and peace for Israel.

Eschatological Promises

God's promises through the prophets included many events in Israel's future. The reader of Luke-Acts might even imagine that Luke made a list of God's eschatological promises and then made certain to narrate the fulfillment of each of them in his narrative.

1. God promised Abraham that his descendants would become a great and prosperous kingdom and that they would become a blessing for all of humanity (Gen 12:1–3 et al.). Luke reflects this promise throughout Acts, most clearly in Acts 3:20–21: "You are the descendants of the prophets and of the covenant that God gave to your ancestors, saying to Abraham, 'And in your descendants all the families of the earth shall be blessed.'"
2. Moses told Israel, "The Lord your God will raise up for you a prophet like me from among the people; you shall heed such a prophet" (Deut 18:15). Luke repeats Moses's promise and its fulfillment subtly in Luke 9:35 ("Listen to him!") and clearly in Acts 3:22–24.
3. God promised David that he would bless his son and "establish the throne of his kingdom forever" (2 Sam 7:13). Luke makes many references to Jesus being the promised son of David (Luke 1:32; 3:31; 18:38–39; Acts 13:22) and enthroned at the right hand of God (Acts 1:9–11; 2:29–35).
4. Malachi prophesied that God would send Elijah to call Israel to repentance before "the day of the Lord" (Mal 4:5–6). Luke identifies Elijah with John the Baptist, who called Israel to repentance just before the coming of Jesus (Luke 1:17).

---

[9] As noted above, not all Jews had the same beliefs. However, "there was a dominant notion of a Davidic Messiah, as the king who would restore the kingdom of Israel, which was part of the common Judaism at the turn of the era." John J. Collins, *The Scepter and the Star* (New York: Doubleday, 1995), 209.

5. Many prophets promised that God would forgive Israel of her sins that led to her punishment (Isa 1:18; 44:22; Jer 31:31–34; Ezek 36:25–28). Luke repeatedly writes that God forgave her sins in the sacrifice of Messiah Jesus (Luke 1:76–79; 24:47; Acts 2:38–39; 5:31).
6. Several prophets predicted that God would gather his scattered people from all across the earth (Isa 11:11; Ezek 37:21; Jer 29:14). When Luke writes about those who heard Peter speak on Pentecost, he lists fifteen regions across the world from which Jews had come to live in Jerusalem (Acts 2:5–12).
7. Several prophets said that God would reunite Israel and Judah (Isa 11:2; Ezek 37:21; Hos 1:10–11). Luke stresses that Jesus will reunite Israel and Judah in the restored Israel. He chooses twelve apostles to represent the twelve tribes. The church welcomes the Samaritans (from the tribes of Ephraim and Manasseh) as part of ethnic Israel (Luke 10:2–4; 9:51–56; Acts 1:21–26; 8:8–25).
8. Numerous prophets promised that God would save only a remnant from ethnic Israel (Isa 10:20–23; 11:11; Jer 31:7; Mic 4:6–7). Luke stresses that most Jews rejected Jesus, so that God saved only a remnant. The remnant was a small minority of the Jews, but their numbers were not insignificant: three thousand, then five thousand, then myriads (Acts 2:41; 4:4; 21:20).
9. Many prophets promised that God, on the day he restored Israel, would pour out the Holy Spirit upon all of his people (Joel 2:28–32; Ezek 36:25–27; Isa 32:15). Luke highlights that God poured out his Spirit on responsive Jews at Pentecost, and Peter promises that this gift is for all of Jesus's followers (Acts 2:1–6; 2:38–39).
10. God promised that he would rid Israel of her corrupt and oppressive leaders (Isa 9:6–7; 56:10–12; Jer 23:1–6; Ezek 34:1–16). In Luke and Acts, Luke portrays the Sanhedrin as corrupt. He narrates the apostles taking over as the leaders of true Israel, and he records Jesus's prophecy that Jerusalem and its leaders would be destroyed (Luke 9:22; 19:47; 21:20–24; 22:66; Acts 3–5; 23:14–15; 26:10–12).
11. God promised the prophets that he would restore the kingdom to Israel under a faithful Davidic ruler (Amos 9:11–15; Ezek 37:15–28; Jer 30:3; 33:7; Mic 4:6–8; see also 2 Sam 7:10–16). Luke emphasizes that God is restoring the kingdom by sending the Messiah and gathering the faithful remnant (Luke 22:28–30; Acts 1:6; 15:16).
12. Almost all of the prophets spoke of the future in which God would judge the nations, the enemies of Israel. They taught that the detestable sins of the gentiles would lead to their final destruction. They foretold God's future world in which evil would be wiped out and in which righteousness and peace would prevail (Isa 11:14; 17:12–14; 29:8; 60:12; Mic 4:1–13). Luke reminds his readers of the

coming judgment on Israel's enemies and all who reject God's offer of salvation (Luke 1:71–74; 17:26–30; Acts 17:30).
13. Prophets promised that in the future God would provide abundance for the poor and justice for the oppressed (Isa 42:7; 61:1–3; Mic 6:8). According to Luke, the early church provides for her poor and comforts her oppressed and looks forward to the day when the Messiah will establish justice throughout the world (Luke 1:52, 71; 4:16–30; Acts 2:44–45; 4:32–35).
14. Isaiah and Jeremiah prophesied that God would heal the disabled and the diseased (Isa 29:18; 35:5–6; Jer 31:8). Jesus and the early church heal many, demonstrating the future blessings for all God's people in the eschatological age (Luke 4–7; Acts 2:43; 3:1–10; 8:7; 9:33).
15. The prophets told Israel that God would welcome the nations/gentiles into his kingdom. Despite their regular condemnation of the sinful nations, the prophets also spoke about God's love for all people and his future blessings on the many pious gentiles who would seek him (Isa 2:2–4; 11:10; 49:6; 56:6–7; 66:18–21; Amos 9:11–12). In Luke-Acts, Jesus tells the apostles that they are to preach to all nations (Luke 24:47–48; Acts 1:8). The plot of Acts follows the expansion of the church from Jews in Judea to gentiles in Rome (Acts 4:25–30; 10–11; 13:46; 15:3–21).
16. Isaiah foretold that God would release all the earth from its bondage to sin and establish righteousness, peace, and prosperity in "the new heavens and the new earth" (Isa 2:4; 11:6–9; 35:5–7; 65:16–25; 66:22). Luke teaches that God has begun the new creation through his community and his Spirit, and he will complete it at the second coming, "the time of universal restoration that God announced long ago through his holy prophets" (Acts 3:20–21).
17. Isaiah and Daniel prophesied that God would resurrect his people from the dead (Isa 26:19; Dan 12:2). Luke teaches in his Gospel that God raised Jesus and will resurrect all of his people at the second coming. In Acts, the central teachings of Peter and Paul include the resurrection of Jesus and the future resurrection of God's people (2:22–26; 13:32–37; 17:18, 32; 23:6, 8; 24:15, 21).

The Apostles and the Restoration of Israel

Having surveyed these eschatological promises and their fulfillment in Acts, we are better able to return to the apostles' question in Acts 1:6: "Lord, is this the time when you will restore the kingdom to Israel?" For Luke, it was the obvious question for them to ask. Jesus had told them only forty days earlier at the Last Supper that they would rule over the restored kingdom of Israel: "I confer on you, just as my Father has conferred on me, *a kingdom,* so that you may eat and drink at my table in *my kingdom,* and you will sit on thrones judging *the twelve tribes of Israel*" (Luke 22:29–30 [emphasis mine]). Nonetheless, at that moment, they still failed to understand (see Luke 22:49–

51). Luke had already mentioned the apostles' misunderstanding of Jesus on several earlier occasions (Luke 9:45; 18:31–34). *After his death and resurrection*, though, Jesus appeared to them "during forty days and speaking about the kingdom of God" (Acts 1:3). During these days, he told them, "Everything must be fulfilled that is written about me in the Law of Moses, the Prophets, and the Psalms." He then "opened their minds so they could understand the Scriptures" (Luke 24:44–45). The disciples finally understood that the suffering, death, and resurrection of the Messiah were at the heart of God's plan to restore Israel.

Jesus's response to the apostles' question was that the restoration was imminent but that only God knew when it would be finalized (Acts 1:7–9). The remainder of Acts 1 served as the necessary prelude to the visible arrival of the kingdom on Pentecost. Jesus ascended to the right hand of God to begin his reign (Acts 1:9–11; 2:34; 5:31–32), after which Peter led the disciples to choose a twelfth apostle so they will be ready to lead "the twelve tribes of Israel" (Luke 22:28–30; Acts 1:15–26). When Pentecost comes a few days later, Luke emphasizes that fifteen nations across the world are gathered (Acts 2:9–11). The Holy Spirit is poured out on the disciples, which Peter says is a sign that the "last days" have begun, the time when God was to fulfill his promises to Israel (Acts 2:15–20). Peter preaches that Jesus is the Messiah, that the Jewish listeners must repent, that they will be forgiven, and that they will receive the gift of the Holy Spirit. In response, a remnant of Israel (3,000) accepts that Jesus is the Messiah, and the restoration of Israel—the ἐκκλησία (the renewed assembly of Israel)—begins. The restored kingdom of Israel is inaugurated.

The preceding survey of the prophetic eschatological promises and their fulfillment in Luke-Acts demonstrates that the early church shared most of the traditional Jewish expectations about the messianic age. However, the church had several distinctive convictions that were rejected by most Jews. Although few in number, these beliefs were at the heart of the church's faith. The most important dealt with 1) the time at which the kingdom would arrive, 2) the nature and role of the Messiah, and 3) the circumstances under which gentiles would join Israel.

STAGES OF THE KINGDOM

Did the events on Pentecost mean that the kingdom had arrived? As almost all NT interpreters have agreed, there was a sense in which the kingdom of God had "already" come and another sense in which the kingdom had "not yet" arrived. When Jesus himself spoke about the timing of the coming kingdom, he most often talked about the future in which *all* of God's promises would be fulfilled. For example, his favorite picture of the kingdom was the future messianic banquet. In Luke 13:28–29, Jesus says, "There will be weeping there, and gnashing of teeth, when you see Abraham, Isaac, and Jacob and all the prophets [at the feast] in the kingdom of God, but you yourselves thrown out." In this instance, Jesus was referring to the kingdom in its final state (see also Luke 14:15; 16:22–24). Similarly, Jesus referred to the kingdom in its fullness when he blessed the hungry and those who grieve, who "*will* be filled" and "*will* laugh" (Luke 6:21 [emphasis mine]).

At the same time, Jesus's recurrent proclamation was that the kingdom "has come near." At times, he even told his hearers that the kingdom of God had already arrived. He says, "But if I drive out demons by the finger of God, then the kingdom of God *has come upon you*" (Luke 11:20; see also 17:20). Luke thus taught that the ministry of Jesus was the beginning of the kingdom. God sent his Messiah, who was winning battle after battle against the demonic enemies. The kingdom of God began small, but it was growing gradually, like a mustard seed (Luke 13:19).

It was clear, though, that many kingdom prophecies had not been fulfilled. Although the apostles were healing disabled persons and the church was feeding its poor, those blessings reached only a tiny fraction of those who needed them. There was not yet justice for the oppressed. The righteous had not been resurrected. War and poverty were ever-present. The Messiah had not vanquished God's enemies. God had not brought about the new heavens and new earth. The full-blown kingdom that God's people longed for had not yet arrived.

CHRISTOLOGY

Christology according to Jesus and Luke

The second essential distinctive belief of the church—and by far the most controversial—revolved around the characteristics of the Messiah. Christians affirmed the traditional Jewish belief that the Messiah would establish justice, peace, prosperity, and the destruction of God's enemies. However, the early church was convinced that the crucified Jesus Messiah was achieving those goals in a very different way from traditional Jewish thinking. The thought of a crucified Messiah was, as Paul wrote, "a stumbling block to Jews" (1 Cor 1:23). They did not expect the Messiah to act like a prophet, to preach about love for the gentile enemies, or, above all, to die on a Roman cross.

In Luke's Gospel, the apostles shared the traditional Jewish view right up until the time of Jesus's resurrection. However, after his resurrection Jesus spent forty days "opening their eyes to understand the Scriptures" (Luke 24:18–27, 44–48). Jesus was finally able to shift their interpretive lenses.

The Suffering Servant

The most important passages Luke used to substantiate Jesus's unanticipated role are found in Isaiah's "Servant Songs" (Isa 42:1–4; 49:1–6; 50:4–11; and 52:13–53:12). Isaiah wrote about a figure called God's "Servant" who "has borne our infirmities and carried our diseases, … was wounded for our transgressions, crushed for our iniquities; … poured out himself to death and was numbered with the transgressors, … and bore the sin of many and made intercession for the transgressors" (Isa 53:4–6, 10–12). As one might guess, the Jews of Jesus's day did not think that these passages referred to the Messiah.

According to Luke, it was Jesus who first identified himself with the Servant. Jesus's words to the apostles about his rejection, suffering, and death alluded to Isa 53 (Luke 9:21–22; 18:34), and Jesus told his disciples that he was the suffering figure in Isa 53:12, who "was numbered with the transgressors" (Luke 22:37). Paul identified Jesus with the Servant who would bring "light for revelation to the gentiles" (Acts 13:47, citing Isa 42:6). When the Ethiopian asked about the identity of the suffering servant in Isa 53, Philip replied that he was the Messiah Jesus (Acts 8:32–33).

The Son of Man

Jesus also identified himself with another mysterious figure, the "Son of Man" of Daniel 7:10–24. In this passage, the Son of Man comes on the "clouds of heaven" and appears before the "Ancient of Days," seated on his throne in heaven. God gives him "dominion and glory and kingship, that all peoples, nations, and languages should serve him. His dominion is an everlasting dominion" (Dan 7:14). The Son of Man has messianic features, but his coming on the clouds and being in the presence of God are not a part of the traditional Jewish view. According to Luke, Jesus, the heavenly Son of Man, ascended through the clouds to the right hand of God (Acts 1:9–11) and was expected to return to earth on the clouds in order to destroy the enemies of God (Luke 9:26–27; 17:20–24; 19:11–27; 21:25–28).

Citing these and other First Testament passages (for example, Ps 110 in Luke 20:43 and Acts 2:35), Luke teaches that God's plans were more complex than anyone realized. Jesus saw himself as the Messiah, the Son of Man, and the Servant. Though these roles may appear to be incongruent, Jesus knew that suffering and dying were necessary for him to accomplish the primary Messianic task of rescuing Israel and the nations from their bondage to sin and death.

JEWS, THE LAW, AND THE GENTILES

Jewish Christians and the Law

The third major distinctive belief of the early church concerns the role of the Law of Moses in the messianic age. The earliest church, composed only of Jews, maintained a strong allegiance to the Law. Luke describes Zechariah and Elizabeth as "righteous before God, living blamelessly according to all the commandments and regulations of the Lord" (Luke 1:6). He shows Mary and Joseph obeying the Law's requirements after the birth of Jesus (2:22–24, 39). Luke also teaches that Jesus himself kept the Law. Jesus was accused of breaking the Sabbath on several occasions, but Luke explains that he was only rejecting the Pharisees' *interpretation* of the Law (Luke 6:6–11; 13:15–16; 14:5).

Jewish Christians continued to observe the whole Law of Moses, including the laws that signified Jewish ethnicity. After all, they did not cease being Jews when they began following the Messiah. Keeping the Law was one of the primary means by which they honored God. They went to the temple, honored their parents, sacrificed lambs and ate Passover meals, circumcised their baby boys, maintained ritual purity, observed Sabbath, and so on. According to Luke, even Paul, the apostle to the gentiles, kept the whole Law. Luke records Paul fulfilling a Nazarite vow in Acts 18:18. Even twenty-five years after he became a Christian, he went to the Jerusalem temple to assist four men who were offering sacrifices to complete their Nazarite vows. In doing so, Paul demonstrated that he himself kept the Law (Acts 21:20–26).

On the other hand, Luke makes it clear that no one was saved by keeping the Law. In Luke's account of Paul's sermon in Antioch of Pisidia, for example, Paul told his Jewish listeners: "[B]y this Jesus everyone who believes is set free from all those sins from which you could not be freed by the Law of Moses" (Acts 13:38–39). Similarly, at the Jerusalem Council, Peter said, "[W]e believe that we [Jews] will be saved through the grace of the Lord Jesus, just as [gentiles] will" (Acts 15:11). The center of their faith and practice was no longer the Law, but rather Messiah Jesus.

Jews, the Law, and the Gentiles

For centuries, Jews had strongly resisted those who attempted to get them to break the Law of God. For example, Daniel and his three friends refused to eat the Babylonian king's (unclean) food (Dan 1:8–21). Seven Jewish brothers and their mother were brutally put to death by the Seleucids for refusing to eat pork (2 Macc 7). In the first century, Pontius Pilate attempted to bring idolatrous Roman banners into Jerusalem. The Jews protested and were willing to die rather than break the Law of God (Josephus, Ant 18.8.2). In the first decades of the church, Jewish zeal *for* the Law and *against* the ways of gentiles was very strong.

The issue over the Law that arose in the early church concerned the salvation of gentiles. The Christian Jews of the early church knew that God loved all peoples and that many gentiles would turn to God in the eschatological age. However, they assumed that these gentiles would keep Israel's laws. After all, God had given his Law to guide his people in his ways. The early Christians were surprised, therefore, when God led Peter in a different direction (Acts 10–11).

Luke's Account of Church Expansion

In order to show how God was rescuing all humanity, Luke narrated the story of the church's expansion from a small group of Jewish Christians in Jerusalem to a large group of Jewish and gentile Christians throughout the Mediterranean world. Luke carefully traces the new movement geographically and demographically. A brief survey of Luke's narrative makes his intention clear.

Luke first focuses on the apostles and the three thousand Jews who were converted on Pentecost (Acts 1–2), underscoring their joy and peace even in the face of opposition from the Sanhedrin (Acts 3–5). Then, in Acts 6–7, Luke shifts his focus to the "Hellenists," Greek-speaking Jewish believers in Jerusalem.[10] When one of their leaders, Stephen, was stoned by non-Christians, a severe local persecution arose, forcing many Christians to flee Jerusalem.

Philip, another leader of the Hellenists, fled north to Samaria, where he evangelized the Samaritans, the long-time enemies of the Jews (Acts 8:4–25). Luke's point was not simply that the church welcomed those whom they formerly hated but rather that the Samaritans were the first non-Jewish converts. Since they were descendants of the tribes of Ephraim and Manasseh, they were Israelites but not Jews (from the former kingdom of Judah).[11] After the Samaritans were baptized, Peter and John visited them to affirm their inclusion and to grant them the gift of the Holy Spirit. Luke narrated this story in order to demonstrate, as the prophets promised, that Israel and Judah were being reunited.

Luke next tells the story of Philip's conversion of the Ethiopian eunuch. As a eunuch, he could not be fully accepted by Jews (Lev 21:20; Deut 23:1), but Luke nonetheless considered him a proselyte. Luke tells this story to demonstrate that the new age had arrived, in which even eunuchs were fully accepted. Luke had in mind the prophecy of Isaiah: "For thus says the LORD: 'To the eunuchs who keep my Sabbaths, who choose the things that please me and hold fast my covenant, I will give them an everlasting name that shall not be cut off'" (Isa 56:3–5).

The Church's Acceptance of Gentiles

The stories of the Samaritans and the Ethiopian, though surprising, were not terribly controversial in the young church. The great controversy among the early Christians arose only after Peter and then Paul reached out to gentiles.

First-century Jews generally despised the gentile nations for the same reasons the prophets had condemned them centuries before. First, gentiles committed abhorrent sins, including idolatry, sexual offenses, murder, and others. Second, Jews detested the gentile nations who had destroyed their cities and Temple, taken Jews as slaves, and ruthlessly oppressed them for centuries. They wanted God to destroy these enemies, especially the Romans who currently ruled over them.

---

[10] Most Hellenistic Jews in Jerusalem had been raised in the Greek-speaking Diaspora and had moved to Jerusalem at some point. In chapter 2, Luke mentions Jews from many nations who were at that time living in Jerusalem (2:8–11).

[11] Jesus himself had attempted to preach to the Samaritans on one occasion, implying that they were Israelites. The Samaritans refused to welcome him on that occasion (Acts 9:51–56).

Nonetheless, Jews knew that God loved all peoples. They knew the many prophecies about God's future plans for penitent foreigners. Many of them had friends in their synagogues who were proselytes and God-fearers. They anticipated that many gentiles would join them at the time that God restored Israel. However, they expected that the Messiah would first defeat the wicked nations and fully establish the kingdom. Then the gentiles who witnessed God's protection and blessings for Israel would repent and turn to Israel's God.

Peter, like almost all Jews of his day, refused to have close contact with gentiles. Jews would not enter the homes of gentiles, and they certainly would not eat with them. They had to avoid ritual or moral contamination. Therefore, Peter had no plans to evangelize gentiles until God gave him a vision and told him to go to the home of a gentile, a God-fearing Roman centurion named Cornelius (Acts 10).[12] Peter preached to Cornelius and his family, and they soon began to speak in tongues. Therefore, he baptized them but did not demand that they keep the Law. When he returned to Jerusalem, he was criticized by the Jerusalem Christians for eating with gentiles. Peter explained that God had given them the Holy Spirit, just as he had given the Jews on Pentecost. The Jerusalem church leaders then celebrated, saying, "God has given even to the gentiles the repentance that leads to life" (Acts 11:18). Luke told this story twice in Acts 10–11 to underscore that God had led Peter, the primary leader of the church, to set the precedent welcoming gentile believers *as gentiles*. At the time, it appeared that the matter was settled.

For several years, an increasing number of gentiles believed and became Christians. Many of these conversions came about through the efforts of Greek-speaking believers who had fled from persecution in Jerusalem. Some of these believers moved to Antioch of Syria, a large cosmopolitan city far north of Jerusalem. There they established the Antioch church, composed of Jews and gentiles from across the Roman empire (Acts 11:19–30).

In the late 40's, the Antioch church sent Paul and Barnabas to plant churches in Galatia. In each town, they went first to the synagogue (Acts 13:46). When Jews accepted Messiah Jesus, Paul and Barnabas baptized them, and the kingdom of Israel was therefore restored in that place. However, the majority of Jews rejected Jesus, and Paul then preached to gentiles. Luke narrates Paul's words to the Jews, "We had to speak ... to you first. Since you reject it, we now turn to the Gentiles" (Acts 13:46–47; see also Rom 1:16). When Paul and Barnabas returned to Antioch after their trip to Galatia, the church celebrated their success.

The Jewish Christians in Jerusalem also heard the news, and some of them were quite disturbed. For reasons that are not fully clear, Peter's conversion of Cornelius had not settled the gentile issue. The issue became acute when some Jewish believers from

---

[12] A Roman centurion would, in the eyes of Jews, be especially impure because of his regular exposure to the idolatry and sinful ways of the Roman military.

Jerusalem travel to Antioch and told the gentile believers, "Unless you are circumcised, ... you cannot be saved" (Acts 15:1). It made no sense to these Jewish Christians that gentiles were able to follow the Messiah of Israel and to worship the God of Israel without keeping the Law of Israel.

The Jerusalem Council. Paul considered the demands of the visiting Jewish Christians from Jerusalem to be a repudiation of the gospel. As he had taught in the Galatian churches, those who believed in Jesus were "free from all those sins from which you could not be freed by the Law of Moses" (Acts 13:38–39). The Antioch church leaders therefore sent Paul and Barnabas to Jerusalem to meet with the apostles and elders (Acts 15). By this time, James, the brother of Jesus, had become the principal leader of the church, and it was he who chaired the council meeting.

The first to speak were a group of Christian Pharisees. They insisted, "It is necessary for [gentile believers] to be circumcised and ordered to keep the Law of Moses" (Acts 15:5). Peter then responded, reminding them that God had called him to be the first to preach to gentiles and that God had given them the Holy Spirit without requiring circumcision. Peter then told them, "We believe that we [Jews] will be saved through the grace of the Lord Jesus, just as [the gentiles] will" (Acts 15:10–11). Paul and Barnabas then spoke, emphasizing that God had worked signs and wonders to affirm his acceptance of the gentiles.

Finally, James settled the issue by making an argument from Scripture (Amos 9:11–12). James says,

> Brothers, ... listen to me. Simon has described to us how God first intervened to choose a people for his name from the Gentiles. The words of the prophets are in agreement with this, as it is written: 'After this I will return and rebuild David's fallen tent. Its ruins I will rebuild, and I will restore it, that the rest of mankind may seek the Lord, even all the Gentiles who bear my name, says the Lord, who does these things—things known from long ago.' It is my judgment, therefore, that we should not make it difficult for the Gentiles who are turning to God. (Acts 15:17–18)

James quoted the passage from Amos 9 because it spoke directly to the gentile issue. First, it looked forward to the eschatological period when God would "rebuild David's tent." God would restore David's kingdom to Israel *so that* "the rest of mankind may seek the Lord." Second, the passage from Amos demonstrated that gentiles did not need to become Jews to become citizens of God's kingdom. The phrase, "all the gentiles over whom my name has been called," meant that not only the nation of Israel but other nations were also God's people.[13] In other words, the last days had arrived in which

---

[13] James's use of Amos 9 in this passage is complex. For more information on the view taken here, see Richard Bauckham, "James, Peter, and the Gentiles," in *The Missions of James, Peter, and Paul:*

God was fulfilling his original plan—for Israel to be the nation through whom he would bless all nations. The council members agreed with James's stance, and the official position of the early church was established.

The Council's Decree. The council then sent a letter to inform the gentile churches of their decision. The letter also included a decree that instructed gentile believers to follow four rules. They were to "abstain from food polluted by idols, from sexual immorality, from the meat of strangled animals and from blood." These directives reflect laws from Leviticus 17–18, some of which apply to "any foreigner living among [Jews]," not only to the Israelites (Lev 17:8, 10, 12, 13; 18:26).

Scholars disagree about the intent of this decree. One popular view is that Luke understood these rules as *practical guidelines* meant to allow table fellowship between gentile and Jewish Christians. It is more likely, though, that these rules were to be seen as Mosaic laws that apply to gentiles. They were not laws about *ritual* impurity but rather *moral* impurity. The council's decree thus demanded that gentile believers maintain sexual purity and abstain from practices related to idolatry, such as eating meat with the blood in it and meat sacrificed to idols.[14] The gentiles were not to keep the whole Law, but they were to keep these moral laws.

In summary, Luke narrated the account of the Jerusalem Council in order to prove to his readers that the church's acceptance of gentiles *as gentiles* was demanded by Scripture and confirmed by signs and wonders. God did not bless Israel for the purpose of making all people Jewish proselytes. Jews were to remain Jews and gentiles were to remain Greeks, Romans, Egyptians, etc., but all were one people in the one kingdom of God.

CONCLUSIONS

Luke states his purpose for writing Luke-Acts in Luke 1:3–4: "[S]ince I myself have carefully investigated everything from the beginning, I too decided to write an orderly account ... so that you may know the certainty of the things you have been taught."[15] Luke's message gave confidence to Jewish Christians, who may have had doubts about the surprising nature of Jesus's Messiahship or the status of gentile Christians. Luke's message was most important, though, for gentile Christians, the primary readers of his two volumes. To them he gave the assurance that he mentioned in his prologue. The

---

Tensions in Early Christianity, ed. Bruce Chilton and Craig Evans (Leiden: Brill, 2005), 91–142; Richard Bauckham, "James and the Gentiles," in *History, Literature, and Society in the Book of Acts*, ed. Ben Witherington (Cambridge: University Press, 1996), 154–84.

[14] The assumption was that any meat not sacrificed at the tabernacle or temple was offered to an idol (Lev 17:2–8).

[15] Luke "dedicated" Luke-Acts to a man named Theophilus who was probably Luke's patron who paid for Luke's expensive undertaking. His target audience appears to have been gentile Christians, although he knew others would also read it.

"certainty" they needed probably included the historical facts, explanations of Jewish customs, and the like. Perhaps most significant, though, was Luke's emphasis on the status of gentile believers before God. They were fully accepted by the God of Israel, exactly as the prophets had spoken and as many signs and wonders had affirmed.

THOUGHTS FOR THE CONTEMPORARY CHURCH

1. The First Testament has not been abolished. It was the Bible of the early Christians. Christians cannot understand the story of Jesus and the church apart from the First Testament.
2. God did not change his ways with the coming of the Messiah. God is and always has been a God of grace.
3. The Law of Moses has not been "abolished." Keeping the Law of Moses is not necessary for believers now that the Messiah has come, but following the "precepts of the Law" (Rom 8:4) is incumbent on all of God's people.
4. The church is not the replacement for Israel. For Luke, the church is not *new* Israel but rather *renewed* Israel. Christians are "Israelites" theologically, those who follow the Messiah of Israel and worship the God of Israel.
5. In the NT, there are no Christians outside the church. Jesus is not simply our "personal savior to be invited into our hearts." Luke's intent is for all to be members of God's eschatological people in the kingdom of God.
6. The mission of the church (renewed Israel) remains the original mission of ethnic Israel—to bring all of humanity out of their former kingdoms and into the kingdom of God by loving, serving, and teaching them. The call to "believe in Jesus" is not primarily about trusting that Jesus's death forgives sins so that we will be with God after we die. That is important, but it ignores the Jewish and OT origins of the church. To believe in Jesus is to accept and follow him as the Messiah who rules God's kingdom.
7. We should take the language of "the kingdom of God" literally. Throughout history, the idea of a "kingdom" has referred to a group of people living in a land that is ruled by a king. Luke teaches that the final kingdom will include the followers of Jesus who live across the restored earth, ruled by the king of all creation.
8. There is no "right" model of church leadership. The first churches followed Jewish norms, not a God-given pattern. The early church adapted those norms as needed.
9. Luke says nothing about the current state of Israel.

8
Here Is Your King! The Characterization of Jesus in John 18–19

Jesse Robertson[1]

INTRODUCTION

It is widely recognized that the kingship of Jesus is a major theme in John's passion narrative, as the earthly powers attempt to be rid of Jesus once and for all, but in the process, they establish his kingship and proclaim it to all the world.[2] With abundant Johannine irony, the details of the arrest, trials, and crucifixion of "Jesus of Nazareth, the King of the Jews" (John 19:19) provide rich insights into the nature of this king.[3] In ancient narratives and biographies, death accounts were poignant opportunities for showing the essence of a figure. Even modern readers immediately perceive that the accounts of the deaths of Jezebel (2 Kgs 9:30–37) or Herod Agrippa I (Acts 12:20–25) indicate character traits quite different from those implied in the deaths of Abraham (Gen 25:7–10) or Stephen (Acts 7:54–60). Authors and rhetoricians were trained to shape the telling of death narratives with recognizable elements that indicated character traits, and audiences were accustomed to recognizing these cues in the abundant examples found in the literature, theater, and discourse of the era. By acquainting ourselves with the strategies of characterization in Greco-Roman and ancient Jewish narrative, we can see more vividly the principal points about Jesus that finalize John's literary portrait of him. As the Fourth Gospel comes to its climax, the details of the passion narrative profoundly impress the audience with the qualities of this king, including his courage, love, authority, and faithfulness, or, as John would say in sum, his *glory*.

---

[1] My first graduate class in the Gospels was Dr. Allen Black's course in the Gospel of Mark. He opened to me in a new way the exegetical and theological riches of a narrative approach to the text, and much of my academic and teaching effort has followed in this vein. I still tell students what he told us, that the two main themes in all the Gospels are Christology and discipleship.

[2] Richard Bauckham, *Gospel of Glory: Major Themes in Johannine Theology* (Grand Rapids: Baker Academic, 2015), 128; Charles H. Talbert, *Reading John: A Literary and Theological Commentary on the Fourth Gospel and the Johannine Epistles*, rev. ed., SHBC (Macon: Smyth & Helwys, 2005), 252; Marianne Meye Thompson, *John: A Commentary*, NTL (Louisville: Westminster John Knox, 2015), 378–98.

[3] Quotations of the Bible are from the New Revised Standard Version (1989) except where otherwise noted.

DEATH AND CHARACTER IN GRECO-ROMAN RHETORIC

Aristotle observed that words and deeds are the primary ways that character is displayed (*Poet.* 15). Since the Gospels are almost entirely composed of the sayings and actions of Jesus, they effectively constitute narrative Christology.[4] They reveal the character of Christ through what he says and does. In this way, the Gospels are similar to ancient biographies. The prolific biographer Plutarch distinguishes biography from history when he states that he will not exhaustively catalog "all the famous actions of these men" (as a historian might) but instead will select those deeds and sayings that provide "a greater revelation of character" and "the signs of the soul in men" (*Alex.* 1.1–3). The purpose statement in John 20:30–31 has close affiliation with this method of selecting and reporting certain words and deeds to reveal character:

> Now Jesus did many other signs in the presence of his disciples, which are not written in this book. But these are written so that you may come to believe that Jesus is the Messiah, the Son of God, and that through believing you may have life in his name." The words and actions of Jesus are "signs" for John, and they signify the character of Jesus so that the audience may know him, believe in him, and have life in him.

Cicero's instructions for constructing arguments rooted in personal characterization identify the following *loci a persona*:

> We hold the following to be the attributes of persons: name, nature, manner of life, fortune, habit, feeling, interests, purposes, achievements, accidents, speeches made. ... Under fortune one inquires whether the person is a slave or free, rich or poor, a private citizen or an official with authority, and if he is an official, whether he acquired his position justly or unjustly, whether he is successful, famous, or the opposite; what sort of children he has. And if the inquiry is about one no longer alive, *weight must be also given to the nature of his death* (*Inv.* 1.24.34–35, emphasis added).

Cicero is writing in the first century B.C., but a similar list occurs in the *Progymnasmata* of Aelius Theon from the first century A.D.: "origin, nature, training, disposition, age, fortune, morality, action, speech, *(manner of) death, and what followed death*" (78.26–27, emphasis added).[5] This list occurs in his discussion of the composition of

---

[4] Richard A. Burridge, *What Are the Gospels? A Comparison with Graeco-Roman Biography*, 2nd ed. (Grand Rapids: Eerdmans, 2004), 289.

[5] George A. Kennedy, *Progymnasmata: Greek Textbooks of Prose Composition and Rhetoric*, WAW 10 (Atlanta: Society of Biblical Literature, 2003), 28.

narratives in this handbook of "preliminary exercises (προγυμνάσματα)" designed to train students in the rudiments of rhetoric in preparation for advanced studies. The strategies he suggests represent a long tradition, as his frequent use of examples from Homer, Herodotus, and other classical authors makes clear. Theon also indicates three broad categories into which these elements fall in his discussion of encomium (praise of a person): (1) "mind and character"; (2) "the body"; (3) things "external to us" (109.29–31).[6] Quintilian, writing about the composition of encomium in the first century A.D., identifies these same three categories when he says, "The praise of the man himself must be based on mind, body, and external circumstances" (*Inst.* 3.7.12), though he adds that paramount among these are the attributes of the mind.

Regarding external circumstances, it is difficult to produce a delimited list of items that might be included. For our purposes, it is notable that in his list of external goods, Theon includes "a good death" (110.1–8).[7] Similarly, but in more detail, the *Progymnasmata* attributed to Hermogenes of Tarsus offers a few examples of circumstances in death accounts that would be relevant:

> how he died fighting for his country; and if there was anything unusual about it, as in the case of Callimachus, because his corpse remained standing. And you will praise him because of who killed him; for example, that Achilles died at the hand of the god Apollo. (16)[8]

An additional element of characterization is noted by Theon: "It is not without utility also to make mention of those already honored, comparing their deeds to those of the persons being praised" (111.1–3).[9] The explicit or implicit comparison of one person's actions with those of others in similar circumstances also provides material for the ancient author's portrait of the character of his subject.

A four-fold rubric of character indicators emerges for highlighting character traits of Jesus in the passion narrative of John 18–19: (1) evidence of the mind, most often through words and actions, (2) descriptions of the state of the physical body, (3) details of the external circumstances and surroundings, (4) similarities to other well-known figures in similar circumstances. Across a wide range of Greek, Roman, Jewish, and early Christian literature these elements are regularly employed to give final nuance to the character of both heroes and villains.[10] We will apply this rubric to the

---

[6] Kennedy, *Progymnasmata*, 50.

[7] Kennedy, *Progymnasmata*, 50.

[8] Kennedy, *Progymnasmata*, 82.

[9] Kennedy, *Progymnasmata*, 51.

[10] For numerous examples from Greek, Roman, and Jewish literature, see Jesse E. Robertson, *The Death of Judas: The Characterization of Judas Iscariot in Three Early Christian Accounts of His Death*, New Testament Monographs 33 (Sheffield: Sheffield Phoenix Press, 2012), 13–43.

account of Jesus's death in John 18–19 to see more vividly what the early Christian audience would have perceived about the character of Jesus. In other words, we will try to hear John's passion narrative with the ears of the ancient audience to deepen our understanding of Johannine Christology.

THE CHARACTER OF JESUS ACCORDING TO JOHN 18–19

The author of the Fourth Gospel has set the stage for significant revelations about Jesus in the passion narrative by anticipating "this hour." In the first half of the book, Jesus avoided certain courses of action because "his hour had not yet come" (2:4; 7:30; 8:20). After his arrival in Jerusalem for Passover, however, he says, "The hour has come for the Son of Man to be glorified" (12:23). This hour is the reason he has come (12:27), the hour in which he will "depart from this world and go to the Father" (13:1), and the hour in which the Father will be glorified (12:28; 17:1).

John also invites the reader to interpret the details of Jesus's death symbolically by his ironic words in 12:32–33: "'And I, when I am lifted up from the earth, will draw all people to myself.' He said this to indicate the kind of death he was to die." John's emphasis on the glory of Jesus that is about to be revealed in these events indicates that we are on the right track to read them with the ancient rhetorician's eye for revelations of character traits. We will see that these attributes add up to a revelation of the kind of king he is.

In the scene of his arrest in John 18:1–12, the courage of Jesus leads the characterization. As Judas and his armed mob approach Jesus and the disciples, the text says, "Then Jesus, knowing all that was to happen to him, came forward and asked them, 'Whom are you looking for?'" (18:4). If we apply our rubric to this opening scene, the narrator begins with attributes of the mind, noting Jesus's knowledge of what he will suffer, then immediately combines this insight with his bodily action of stepping forward. Bold courage is essential to noble death. The characterization goes further when his enemies step back and fall on the ground after Jesus says, "I am he (ἐγώ εἰμι)" (18:6). In a different context, his statement might simply be self-identification, but the backward fall of his enemies and the frequent use of ἐγώ εἰμι in Johannine contexts where divine attributes are in focus (4:26; 6:20, 35, 41, 48, 51; 8:12, 24, 28, 58; 10:7, 9, 11, 14; 11:25; 13:19; 14:6; 15:1, 5), leaves the audience with the impression that we are not simply witnessing a startled response. Instead, the impression is that they suffered a moment of fearful awe by an encounter with someone majestic, possibly divine.[11]

This quality of majesty is combined, however, with protective love for his disciples. Jesus insists that since the soldiers are looking for him, they should let his disciples go

---

[11] George R. Beasley-Murray, *John*, WBC 36, 2nd ed. (Nashville: Thomas Nelson, 1999), 322–23; Thompson, *John*, 156–60.

(18:8). He is the good shepherd who will lay down his life to protect his sheep (10:11, 15). He is fulfilling his word not to lose any of them (18:9; see also 6:39, 10:28, 17:12). This tender care while under great personal duress will be shown again when he places his mother into the household of the beloved disciple (19:26-27). When Peter draws his sword and strikes Malchus, Jesus's response not only protects Peter and the other disciples from further violence but also emphasizes his deliberate alignment with the divine will: "Am I not to drink the cup that the Father has given me?" (18:11). The qualities that are paramount in this opening section—courage, love for one's people, and alignment with the divine will—are among the top qualities of rulers in ancient Greek, Roman, and Jewish discussions of the nature of the ideal king.[12]

John 18:13–14 tells the transition from the garden to the house of the high priest, and the mention of Annas and Caiaphas provides another opportunity for irony. Characterization occurs not only through what the person says and does, but also through what others say about him and do with him. John 18:14 reminds the audience of Caiaphas's earlier comment to the Jewish leaders, "You know nothing at all! You do not understand that it is better for you to have one man die for the people than to have the whole nation destroyed" (11:49–50). In the subsequent verses, 11:51–52, John added the explanatory comment that these words were endowed with more meaning than Caiaphas intended and signified that Jesus's death would be to the benefit of his own nation, as well as the children of God elsewhere. This reminder reinforces the sense that Jesus is carrying out a divine agenda that the earthly powers do not perceive and that the goal of this agenda is the rescue of his people.

The next section of the Johannine passion narrative, 18:15–27, uses the external circumstances of spatial arrangement to contribute to the enrichment of Jesus's character. The textual unit begins with Simon Peter in the courtyard (vv. 15-18), shifts to the interrogation of Jesus inside the house (vv. 19-24), then returns to the setting of Simon Peter outside (vv. 25-27). Raymond Brown points out that even though Peter's threefold denial is recorded in all four Gospels, only John arranges the denials such that the interrogation of Jesus is framed by them.[13] This juxtaposition contributes to the characterization of Jesus by an implicit contrast with Peter. Both men are surrounded by enemies and are being questioned under threat of violence. Peter's denials of Jesus and lies about his identity reveal his lack of courage and unfaithfulness to his Lord. Jesus, however, neither lies nor defends himself, even though the truth would exonerate him. His purpose is not self-preservation but fulfillment of the Father's plan. Peter's cowardice contrasts with Jesus's courage, and Peter's shame with Jesus's honor.

---

[12] Julien Smith, *Christ the Ideal King: Cultural Context, Rhetorical Strategy, and the Power of the Divine Monarchy in Ephesians*, WUNT 313 (Tübingen: Mohr Siebeck, 2011), 86–89, 170–73.

[13] Raymond E. Brown, *The Death of the Messiah: From Gethsemane to the Grave: A Commentary on the Passion Narratives in the Four Gospels*, 2 vols, ABRL (New York: Doubleday, 1994), 1:412.

The scene inside the house of the high priest (18:19–24) contrasts the mind of Jesus with that of the Jewish authorities. The impotence and injustice of the high priest are depicted by his failure to produce significant evidence for prosecution and having to resort to asking Jesus "about his disciples and about his teaching" (18:19) instead of calling witnesses, which was standard procedure.[14] In stark contrast, Jesus firmly and justly asserts that his teaching has been public and that the proper way to prosecute the case would be to bring those who heard him as witnesses to testify against him. The result is that one of the officers strikes him in the face and says, "Is that how you answer the high priest?" (18:22). Physical actions of the body indicate character, and the officer as representative of the enemies of Jesus indicates that brutality, not reason, drives their choices. Jesus's non-retaliation and logical reply, "If I have spoken wrongly, testify to the wrong. But if I have spoken rightly, why do you strike me?" (18:23), dignifies him as self-controlled and rational, grounded in proper standards of truth and justice.

John 18:28–40 forms another cohesive unit of three settings: the courtyard outside Pilate's residence, where the Jews wait (vv. 28–32); inside the governor's residence, where Pilate and Jesus converse (vv. 33–38a); and back outside again with the Jewish leaders (vv. 38b–40).[15] As the scenes shift, different figures come into play, and their character traits are set in contrast.

Jesus does not speak in vv. 28–32, the first courtyard scene. Instead, the Jewish leaders and Pilate talk about Jesus, and their actions and comments contribute to their own literary portrait as well as his. The high priests and their party refuse to enter Pilate's headquarters because they do not want ritual defilement to prevent them from observing the Passover. Indications of the mind are paramount in characterization, and these actions attribute to them a hypocritical scrupulousness as they insist upon upholding ritual cleanliness while at the same time seeking to kill Jesus without evidence or clear charges: "If this man were not a criminal, we would not have handed him over to you" (18:30). The emptiness of their accusations reinforces the innocence of Jesus. Pilate's response to the Jews, "Take him yourselves and judge him according to your law" (18:31), sets his mind in contrast to theirs and affirms that the Pharisees' motives are unjust. Additionally, their need to involve the Roman power because they "are not permitted to put anyone to death" (18:31) gives the author the opportunity to show evidence again of Jesus prophetic power about "the kind of death he was to die" (18:32). Jesus's innocence and divine foreknowledge are reinforced in this scene.

The interaction between Jesus and Pilate (18:33–38a) is dominated by the theme of kingship. Pilate's first question to Jesus is, "Are you the King of the Jews?" (18:33), and a few verses later, Pilate rephrases the question, "So you are a king?" (18:37). This identity, King of the Jews, will dominate the Romans' references to Jesus for the rest of the passion narrative: "Do you want me to release for you the King of the Jews?"

---

[14] Beasley-Murray, *John*, 324.

[15] Thompson, *John*, 371.

(18:39); "Hail, King of the Jews!" (19:3); "Here is your King!" (19:14); "Shall I crucify your King?" (19:15); and the inscription, "Jesus of Nazareth, the King of the Jews" (19:19). For the Romans' part, the use of this title is mockery. What kind of a king would be rejected by his own people, abandoned by his followers, unable to defend himself, and suffering the shame of crucifixion? The external circumstances of Jesus could not be further from their conception of kingship.

Alan Culpepper observed that readers perceive that ironic statements in the Gospel of John are spoken by unstable figures who misunderstand Jesus, but that the reader who finds the meaning that aligns with the teachings of Jesus discovers stable, profound insights.[16] John often leads the audience into deeper reflection about the identity of Jesus through the deliberative comments of others in the story: Nathanael (1:46), Nicodemus (3:2), the Samaritan woman at the well (4:25), and many others. Pilate's struggle to form a coherent understanding of Jesus based on his interactions with Jesus as well as what others are saying about him is another opportunity for John to correct misunderstandings of his identification as the King of Israel earlier in this Gospel (1:49; 6:15; 12:13–15). Jesus has been silent through most of his trials, and the words he now exchanges with Pilate offer insight into his mind, the most essential element in characterization and also the locus of stable meaning in the Gospel.

"My kingdom is not from this world," Jesus says to Pilate, "If my kingdom were from this world, my followers would be fighting to keep me from being handed over to the Jews. But as it is, my kingdom is not from here" (18:36). The rulers of empires and kingdoms of this world establish their power through conquest and killing, not through surrender and sacrifice.[17] Therefore, Pilate does not seem able to grasp the significance of Jesus's claim that his kingdom is from another world and shallowly says, "So you are a king? (οὐκοῦν βασιλεὺς εἶ σύ)" (18:37 NRSV, NA28). Pilate's reply begins with the adverb οὐκοῦν, which can be used to introduce either a question with an implied affirmative answer ("*So then* you are a king, are you not?") or simply an inferential statement ("*Therefore, accordingly*, you are a king.").[18] Most translators take it as a question (for example, NRSV, HCSB, ESV, NASB1995, CEB, NABRE), and only a few render it as a statement (for example, NIV2011, NET). In either case, the inferential tone of Pilate's retort reflects the uncertainty in his understanding. Whether said with incredulity, sarcasm, or some other dismissive tone, the shallow basis of his words contrasts sharply with the divine truth that Jesus embodies: "You say that I am a king. For this I was born, and for this I came into the world, to testify to the truth. Everyone who belongs to the truth listens to my voice" (18:37). Jesus has urged his enemies not to judge by appearance, but with sound judgment (7:24), and he has

---

[16] R. Alan Culpepper, *Anatomy of the Fourth Gospel: A Study in Literary Design* (Philadelphia: Fortress, 1983), 165–80.

[17] Thompson, *John*, 380.

[18] BDAG, 736.

staked the claim that he not only speaks truth but embodies truth (14:6). When Pilate replies, "What is truth?" (18:38), this exchange produces one of the most profound contrasts possible. The authorities of this world have failed to bring witnesses, evidence, or specific charges against Jesus, and now their fundamental problem becomes clear—they have no definition of truth. In contrast, Jesus consistently grounds all things in the Father's will (13:3), knows what will happen to him (18:4), and proceeds purposefully toward the cross. His mind is grounded in divine truth that provides explanatory power to his self-sacrifice, but that logic is incomprehensible to the powers of this world; it is "not from here."

As Pilate again goes outside to the Jewish leaders (vv. 38b–40), it is evident that he finds no threat in Jesus's claim of kingship as he says, "I find no case against him" (18:38). When the Jews refuse his offer to pardon Jesus, preferring that Barabbas be pardoned, there are implications for all the major characters. The Jewish leaders are less merciful and more unjust than the Roman governor, who does not want to condemn an innocent man. Pilate is revealed to have less power than the people over whom he reigns since he cannot achieve the outcome he desires. Jesus's innocence is solidified in the mind of the audience through Pilate's words about him. With these insights into the minds of the major players, the author has established an important basis for reversing the ignominy of crucifixion.

In the details of the crucifixion in John 19, it is inevitable that the state of Jesus's body would enter more prominently into his characterization. We noted earlier that death accounts often provide especially vivid details which contribute to either honor or shame, depending on the evidence of the state of mind of the victim and the circumstances surrounding the death. If Jesus were a notorious villain, the audience would hear in these events an implicit invective and would be assured that the powers of the universe had dispensed justice. Jesus, however, has been declared innocent, not guilty. His trial is a miscarriage of justice, but he submits to this suffering because it will benefit others. Instead of justice, it is injustice; instead of an ugly, ignoble death, it is a beautiful, noble death.[19] So noble, in fact, that it, above all else, defines the nature of his kingship.

The physical suffering of Jesus erupts in 19:1–3, with the flogging of Jesus, then moves directly to the soldiers' ironic mockery of him as king, crowning him with thorns, draping him with a purple robe, and saluting him with "Hail, King of the Jews." The unbeliever and the believer perceive Jesus's character quite differently. The soldiers represent those who do not know Jesus through his actions and words that are recorded earlier in the Gospel. For them, the painful crown and temporary robe show

---

[19] In Greco-Roman and ancient Jewish literature, accounts of noble deaths are widespread, and the motivations that mark them as noble frequently include courage in the face of terrible suffering, love for one's countrymen, and piety towards deity. For selected examples, see Robertson, *The Death of Judas*, 19–32.

the ridiculousness of his claim to be a king.[20] For the believer, however, the definitions of power and nobility are overturned. He is a shepherd King (John 10:11; see also 2 Sam. 5:2; Ezek. 37:24) who would die for his people, and this scene is his coronation by suffering.

In 19:4–12, Pilate presents the crowned and robed Jesus to the crowd. The reactions of the Jews and the response of Pilate confirm and further enhance the characterization of Jesus thus far. First, the shouts of the chief priests calling for him to be crucified are a request for the highest degree of suffering to be inflicted on Jesus and elevate him to the highest level of persecuted martyrs. Their cries give Pilate yet another opportunity to insist that Jesus's execution is not justified. The subsequent assertion by the Jews that "he ought to die because he has claimed to be the Son of God" (19:7) introduces a new factor for Pilate—that Jesus might be divine—and Pilate "was more afraid than ever" (19:8). His fear and hesitation imply that the words and manner of Jesus which he has witnessed himself would not rule out such a claim. Pilate investigates further by asking Jesus about his provenance but receives no reply. When Pilate asserts that he has the power to release or crucify Jesus, Jesus says Pilate "would have no power over me unless it had been given ... from above" (19:11). This response is consistent with other indicators of the mind of Jesus: he is the agent of the highest authority here, not Pilate. When Pilate attempts to release Jesus but is forced in 19:12 to acquiesce to the political pressure brought by the Jews, it is more evident than ever that Pilate is not the authority figure he thinks he is. Likewise, the chief priests are not the righteous figures they purport to be. Jesus, outwardly mocked and persecuted, inwardly has the qualities of authority and righteousness that his enemies pretend to have.

Jesus's kingship dominates the final sentencing and crucifixion in 19:13–27.[21] Pilate brings Jesus out one last time and says to the people, "Here is your King!" (19:14). When they cry out again for his crucifixion, Pilate maintains this caricature of Jesus and says, "Shall I crucify your King?" (19:15). Pilate unwittingly provides a profound portrait of Jesus. Here is your King, people of God. In him, kingship is redefined to what it always should have been: a king loving his people so much that he will suffer and die to save them. Astonishingly, the chief priests say, "We have no king but the emperor" (19:15), and earthly political power is preferred over the divine logos in the flesh (1:1, 14).

The circumstances of the crucifixion itself in 19:16–27 juxtapose the shame and horror of the scene with the noble magnificence of Jesus. He carries his own cross, the public declaration of condemnation, to the "Place of the Skull," a name that darkens the scene with connotations of death and impurity. "There they crucified him, and with him two others, one on either side, with Jesus between them" (19:18). If Jesus had been

---

[20] Talbert, *Reading John*, 248; Thompson, *John*, 383.

[21] Beasley-Murray, *John*, 361.

guilty of murder or other capital crimes, this scene would be the capstone of his defamation as he dies in guilt and shame along with other criminals. The author, however, suddenly overturns these implications and centers the scene on the royal nobility of Jesus when he tells us in 19:19, "Pilate also had an inscription written and put on the cross. It read, 'Jesus of Nazareth, the King of the Jews.'" The inscription serves as a public proclamation: "Many of the Jews read this inscription, because the place where Jesus was crucified was near the city; and it was written in Hebrew, Latin, and in Greek" (19:20). When the Jewish leaders object to the wording, Pilate refuses to change it. In a Johannine sense, this title is irrevocable. The shameful circumstances are inverted by the magnificence of the king, who endures them for the sake of his people.

John 19:23–24 adds a further nuance by interpreting the soldiers' division of Jesus's clothing as fulfillment of Ps 22:18. This lament describes the suffering of one who, though devoted to God, is despised and mocked by the populace. Moreover, Psalms being associated with David, and this author being described by his enemies as "the one in whom [the Lord] delights" (Ps 22:8), the persecution that David faced would likely be heard in this quotation as a parallel to the suffering of Jesus.[22] He is not the first king to suffer and endure mocking comments from those who judged merely by appearances rather than righteous judgment. Vindication will come from above. Moreover, verse 18 occurs at the pivot from complaint to praise in Ps 22. In both the psalm and the passion account, divine reversal will soon vindicate God's chosen king. Furthermore, when John identifies this detail or others below as the fulfillment of Scripture, it affirms that Jesus is following God's consummate plan.[23] His path may seem disastrous to those who are uninformed, but for the believer, he is fully engaged in the divine scheme of redemption.

Before Jesus breathes his last, John 19:25–27 contributes to the characterization of Jesus by turning attention to the setting immediately around Jesus. The soldiers and enemies of Jesus are not the only ones present. His mother, other women with her, and "the disciple whom he loved" are also standing near the cross. The crucified Jesus sees them and commends his mother into the care of the beloved disciple. The recounting of this incident recalls the fuller characterization of Jesus in the Fourth Gospel as a whole. He is a loving and beloved member of a family and community of disciples. The love that he has for the entire world, which compels him to die on its behalf (John 3:16), is also a personal, tender love that applies to individuals even as he suffers. The rejected king who submits to death for the sake of his people is also a teacher with devoted disciples and a son who provides for his mother. Here is your king! He

---

[22] Martin Hengel, *The Atonement: The Origins of the Doctrine of the New Testament*, trans. John Bowden (Eugene: Wipf and Stock, 1981), 41; see also Thompson, *John*, 393.

[23] Talbert, *Reading John*, 252.

embodies "grace and truth" (1:14) in his suffering, and he makes the character of the Father known in his supreme act of love (1:18; 14:8–9)—that is his glory![24]

When in 19:28–29 Jesus says, "I am thirsty," causing the soldiers to give him sour wine to drink, John says Scripture is again fulfilled. Psalm 69 appears to be in view, another lament and psalm associated with David. As with Ps 22 above, by identifying Jesus with the fulfillment of this psalm, the author provides the audience with a precedent for interpreting the suffering and dishonor that Jesus is presently under as a temporary situation that is deceptive on the surface and that will be set right when God acts on behalf of his faithful one.

Jesus will not have to wait much longer for the suffering and shame to end and for his honor to begin to be restored. The moment of Jesus's death in John 19:30 is briefly told: "When Jesus had received the wine, he said, 'It is finished.' Then he bowed his head and gave up his spirit." Jesus has often said that he must complete the Father's work. "To complete his work" was like food to him (4:34). He said, "The works that the Father has given me to complete" would testify for him (5:36). He insisted, "We must work the works of him who sent me while it is day; night is coming when no one can work" (9:4). He glorified the Father by finishing what he sent him to do (17:4). If one carries out the will of God, faithfully carrying it through and finishing it with one's final breath, that is the epitome of a good and noble life, according to the Johannine characterization of Jesus.

In 19:31–37, the soldiers are sent to break the legs of the victims to hasten their death, but Jesus's legs are not broken because it is apparent that he is already dead. The blood and water that come out confirm his humanity and the reality of his suffering, as did his thirst. An important element of the characterization of Jesus is his complete humanity, perhaps because some with Docetic tendencies have mischaracterized Jesus on this point.[25] Two more Scriptures are "fulfilled" in these events. First, by his legs not being broken (19:36), he is like the Passover lamb whose bones must not be broken (Exod 12:46), and his early introduction as the "Lamb of God who takes away the sin of the world" (1:29) is fulfilled. Second, the piercing of his side recalls Zech 12:10: "when they look on the one whom they have pierced, they shall mourn for him, as one mourns for an only child, and weep bitterly over him, as one weeps over a firstborn." The one who is pierced is honored by mourning, but the oracle concludes with a still nobler outcome in Zech 13:1: "On that day a fountain shall be opened for the house of David and the inhabitants of Jerusalem, to cleanse them from sin and impurity." What he suffered has made him the rescuing sacrifice and source of cleansing for his people.

The final scene involving Jesus's dead body (19:38–42) is full of love and honor. Joseph of Arimathea, a disciple, receives permission to bury the body, and Nicodemus

---

[24] Bauckham, *Gospel*, 73–74.

[25] Talbert, *Reading John*, 254.

assists him by bringing a hundred pounds of spices. Together, they anoint the body, wrap it in linen cloths, and place it in a new tomb within a garden. In these details, the character of Jesus receives a modicum of respect from Pilate, and devotion from Joseph and Nicodemus. These two in their care for Jesus in his burial and entombment bring to mind the burial of Abraham by Isaac and Ishmael (Gen 25:9) and Isaac by Jacob and Esau (Gen 35:29). To be laid to rest by those who love you is not the mark of an ugly death.

The ultimate vindication of the character of Jesus comes, of course, in the resurrection. We recall that in the *Progymnasmata* of Aelius Theon not only the details of the death, but also "what followed death" (78.26–27)[26] are important topics for illuminating a personality. We only have space here for summary observations, not detailed exposition. First, the resurrection itself is accomplished by the power of God and demonstrates his favorable judgment of Jesus's character. Second, part of the evidence that Jesus is doing the will of the Father is that he frequently fulfills Scripture, and the resurrection is another occasion of fulfillment, as explained in 20:9: "As yet they did not understand the scripture, that he must rise from the dead." Third, even the resurrected Jesus is still concerned for the Father's plan and sends his disciples out to continue that work (20:21–22). These elements portray this king as fulfilling the long plan of God inscribed in Scripture, sending his disciples out to continue this mission, but continuing to help them by his spirit as he reigns on high.

Conclusion

For centuries, biographers, historians, rhetoricians, and other narrators have used similar strategies to present certain character traits of persons in order to address the needs of their audiences. John's passion narrative uses these elements of his literary milieu to overturn the shameful connotations of death by crucifixion and use the horrors of Jesus's suffering and execution to display his glory. Jesus's words and actions reveal a mind focused on devotion to the Father and filled with love for people in need of rescue from sin and death. Because of his innocence and the injustice of his sentence, the shameful abuse of his body by his enemies is overturned to show his nobility. Being crowned with thorns and robed with purple by soldiers constitutes his coronation, and his crucifixion is the moment of the proclamation of his kingship to the world. The cross becomes the symbol of his majestic goodness that draws all people to him. The external circumstances, such as the physical setting, the words of others, and their reactions to him serve as foils that show his quality by contrast with others. Finally, though his death is unique and without exact parallel, the persecution of the righteous, the trials of David, and even the slaughtered Passover lamb provide points of analogy that the author uses to shape the audience's perception of the character of Jesus. These

---

[26] Kennedy, *Progymnasmata*, 28.

rich, complex elements overturn the painful elements of the death of Jesus so that the church reads them not as shameful but as profound reasons to honor him as the king who loves, remains faithful, suffers, dies, and lives again for not only the masses of humanity who are lost, but also for the individual person. That is his glory.

9

An Exegesis of 1 Peter 5:8–9 with an African Reading and Application

Ananias Moses[1]

INTRODUCTION

In a continent (Africa) that has undergone cultural hegemony and repression, suffered from horrific droughts, witchcraft spells, poverty, pandemics, genocides, evil and corrupt governments and institutions, and is still experiencing malignant circumstances, one could probably do a public reading of 1 Pet 5:8–9 to a gathered African Christian audience, and a majority of them would claim to understand the passage without any interpretation. Certainly, socio-economic, political, religious, and cultural backgrounds play a significant role in how individuals and communities read and interpret scriptures. Hence, the African context and worldview shape the way African Christians would read and interpret 1 Pet 5:8–9. The rhetorical style and context of this passage parallel the African storytelling style, context, and worldview. This essay is an exegesis of 1 Pet 5:8–9 with an African reading and application. Keywords and phrases are exegeted, and then an African reading and application are provided.

In 1 Peter, the Apostle Peter writes to Christians in Asia Minor living in an inimical environment and going through persecution because of their faith.[2] Christians are

---

[1] This essay is written in honor of Dr. Allen Black, who was my professor and dean at Harding School of Theology from 2014 to 2018. Dr. Black taught me several courses, including Advanced New Testament Exegesis. This essay is a revision of a term paper that was written and submitted in the Advanced New Testament Exegesis class. I'm blessed to have sat at the feet of Dr. Black and learned from him. His humility and love for God, God's word, and the church blessed my soul. He inspired and challenged me to grow both academically and spiritually. Dr. Black had faith in what God can do in and through the students he taught (space wouldn't allow me to share a story of how he demonstrated this in my life). Before I graduated, I asked Dr. Black to write me a recommendation letter; to this date, I still have the letter; it's a grace to me. There is a Setswana proverb that says, *"dilo makwati di kwatabololwa mo go ba bangwe,"* meaning one learns wisdom and life lessons from others. I'm so grateful for all the love, support, encouragement, and academic and life lessons I received from Dr. Black. Truly, "what an elder person can see while sitting down, a child or young person cannot see even standing on a tree." I'm so thankful to have learned from the vast wisdom and experience of an elder, Dr. Black. Equally, I'm so humbled and honored to be one of the people writing an essay in honor of him. May the goodness and mercy of God continue to be with Dr. Black and his family. God bless.

[2] The author identifies himself at the beginning of the epistle as "Peter, an apostle of Jesus Christ" (1:1). Traditionally, the epistle is also believed to have been written by Simon Peter. The early Church accepted 1 Peter as an authentic and apostolic epistle. Church Fathers (for example, Irenaeus and

facing social ostracism, accusations, and persecution from their opponents. They are seemingly being accused of disobeying authorities (2:13–17), household slaves are charged with being rebellious to their masters (2:18–25), and wives are possibly accused of being insubordinate to their non-Christian husbands (3:1–7). It is without a doubt that Christians are facing various and fiery trials (1:6; 4:12), but the nature and extent of these sufferings and persecutions are unknown. The theme of persecution is the most debated issue in the letter, and no considerable consensus has been reached. There are those who believe that the persecutions are "localized and sporadic hostility consisting of verbal abuse and discrimination."[3] Other scholars are of the view that the sufferings result from both informal and imperial hostility.[4] In this view, Christians are not hunted down by their antagonists and there are not official laws enacted to persecute them; however, Christians are being accused and brought to the courts by their neighbors or fellow citizens. There is an "accusatorial process," and those convicted of crimes could be executed.[5] This is perhaps reflected in 1 Pet 3:14–17, where Christians are urged to be ready to give a defense for their faith and hope in the Lord. Peter writes to encourage them to be steadfast in the Lord and stand in the true grace of God (5:12). They should anticipate sufferings (4:12), rejoice for sharing Christ's sufferings (4:13), and not suffer because of any sinful or criminal activity (4:15). In the midst of sufferings, they should hold fast to the living hope they are called to in Christ (1:3).

Eusebius) attributed it to Peter. Beginning in the nineteenth century, with the development of historical criticism, Peter's authorship has been questioned. Some scholars believe 1 Peter is a pseudepigraphical letter. They doubt if Peter, an uneducated Galilean fisherman (Acts 4:13), could have composed a well-written Greek letter. It was probably written by Silvanus (5:12), an amanuensis for Peter. However, proponents of Peter's authorship argue that Greek was widely spoken in Palestine as a second language, and Peter was a bilingual speaker. See David G. Horrell, *1 Peter* (New York: T&T Clark, 2008), 11–12; D. A. Carson and Douglas J. Moo, *An Introduction to the New Testament* (Grand Rapids: Zondervan, 2005), 641–45; and Karen Jobes, *1 Peter,* BECNT (Grand Rapids: Baker Academic, 2005), 1–22. The consensus among modern commentators is that 1 Peter is written to Gentile Christians (1:14, 18; 4:3) in Asia Minor. παρεπιδήμοις διασπορᾶς (exiles of the Dispersion) is used in a metaphorical way. The letter was probably written in Rome (5:13) between AD 62 and 64 if Peter died during Nero's persecution. Wayne A. Grudem, *The First Epistle of Peter: An Introduction and Commentary* (Grand Rapids: Eerdmans, 1988), 36–37.

[3] Proponents of this view suppose that the persecutions are likely not violent in nature and there are no official laws criminalizing Christian beliefs and practices. For more on the development of the unofficial view, see Travis B. Williams, "Suffering from a Critical Oversight: The Persecutions of I Peter within Modern Scholarship," *CurBR* 10 (2012): 275–92; John H. Elliott, *1 Peter: A New Translation with Introduction and Commentary*, AB 37B (New York: Doubleday, 2000), 794.

[4] Advocates of this position argue that Christianity was "effectively illegal," especially from the time of Nero, who accused Christians of burning the city. Refusal to pay homage to the Roman gods and emperors was the main reason for persecution. And those who refused to do so were a threat to national peace. See Horrell, *1 Peter*, 56–58.

[5] Horrell, *1 Peter*, 57, uses the term "accusatorial process" to point out that Christians were brought to the Roman governors and magistrates by individuals.

Towards the end of the body of the epistle, Peter identifies an opponent for whom Christians should watch out and resist. He strongly commands them:

> ⁸ Be sober-minded; be watchful. Your adversary the devil prowls around like a roaring lion, seeking someone to devour. ⁹ Resist him, firm in your faith, knowing that the same kinds of suffering are being experienced by your brotherhood throughout the world.[6]

> 8. νήψατε, γρηγορήσατε. ὁ ἀντίδικος ὑμῶν διάβολος ὡς λέων ὠρυόμενος περιπατεῖ ζητῶν τινα καταπιεῖν· 9. ᾧ ἀντίστητε στερεοὶ τῇ πίστει εἰδότες τὰ αὐτὰ τῶν παθημάτων τῇ ἐν κόσμῳ ὑμῶν ἀδελφότητι ἐπιτελεῖσθαι.[7]

In this passage, Peter uses a rhetorical strategy of a vivid visual description (ἔκφρασις) to call his readers to be vigilant and firm in their faith.[8] With visual imagery, he appeals to his readers' cognitive and affective senses. He wants them to see and experience this ferocious, roaring beast walking around, readying to have someone as its meal. This graphic description then awakens both the shepherd and the sheep to be watchful and firm in their faith and not panic lest they get devoured. Peter's audience seems to have knowledge about this graphic description (lion imagery), for he does not expound on it.

First Peter 5:8–9 has been a source of encouragement and admonition to communities of faith over the centuries. It was a favorite passage for the early church and became part of their liturgical worship, included in the closing prayer of the church as a way of encouraging one another.[9]

---

[6] Italics mine. All biblical references in this paper are taken from the English Standard Version.

[7] *Novum Testamentum Graece*, Nestle-Aland, 28th ed., ed. Barbara and Kurt Aland et al. (Stuttgart: German Bible Society, 2012).

[8] ἔκφρασις is a way of engaging the "mental visual library through evoking images connected to a web of cultural associations." The readers or listeners see themselves in front of the object being described. It was a common strategy in the ancient Greco-Roman world of literature and rhetoric. Artworks were presented through ἔκφρασις. Some New Testament writers (for example, Paul) use both visual and rhetorical images to communicate and motivate their recipients (1 Cor 15:35–37; 1 Thess 4:13–18; 5:1–11; 2 Tim 2:1–6). David G. Horrell, Arnold Bradley, and Travis B. Williams, "Visuality, Vivid Description, and the Message of 1 Peter: The Significance of the Roaring Lion (1 Peter 5:8)," *JBL* 132 (2013): 697; Duane Frederick Watson and Terrance Callan, *First and Second Peter* (Grand Rapids: Baker Academic, 2012), 120.

[9] U. Holzmeister, 405, in John H. Elliott, *1 Peter*, 860.

EXEGESIS OF 1 PETER 5:8-9 WITH AN AFRICAN READING

Νήψατε γρηγορήσατε *(be sober-minded; be watchful)*

Peter starts v. 8 with two strong aorist active imperative verbs to call his readers to be vigilant.[10] The imperatives highlight the importance of alertness in the face of an unappeasable enemy, the devil. The verb νήψατε (νήφω) is translated as to be sober and is used figuratively to refer to "be free from every form of mental and spiritual drunkenness; free from passion, excess, rashness, and confusion."[11] This verb is also used in 1:13 (νήφοντες) and 4:7 (νήψατε), and both contexts address the need for alertness. γρηγορήσατε (γρηγορέω) is translated as "to watch, be alert, and stay awake."[12] Christians must prepare their minds and spirits for the battle with the devil by being alert. These verbs are also used in the NT in an eschatological context in Matt 24:42–43; 25:13; 26:38–41; Mark 13:34–38; Luke 12:37; and 1 Thess 5:6. Christians are urged to stay awake and be watchful, for they do not know the day and hour when the Lord will come. Peter uses double imperatives to stress his point and capture his readers' attention to pay attention and focus on what he is saying.

The imperatives in v.8 fit very well with the African lifestyle. Africans are known as observant people, especially the older generations. Agricultural activities and weather predictions are more based on observations and experiences than scientific knowledge.[13] Traditional songs, plays, and proverbs have been formulated to accentuate the importance of being watchful in life. An example is a Setswana agricultural proverb that says, *"mosele wa pula o epiwa go sale gale,"* meaning one should be alert and prepare for the rains or any other life situation in advance. Anything that could lead to being unobservant or inattentive (for example, always slumbering) is discouraged. Many African societies lived a nomadic life, which necessitated being vigilant to what was transpiring in their environments. They were quick to discern the good and bad in their environments. When men went to hunt lions and leopards, only those who were vigilant, brave, observant, and skillful were taken. Thus, Peter's command to be watchful resonates well with the African lifestyle. African Christians should utilize this cultural knowledge and God's wisdom to be watchful of the devil and the second coming of Christ.

---

[10] These aorist tenses "carry a sense of forcefulness due to the urgency conveyed by the context." For more on the use of imperatives in 1 Peter, see Greg W. Forbes, *1 Peter* (Nashville: B & H Academic, 2014), 4–7; J. Ramsey Michaels, *1 Peter*, WBC 49 (Waco: Word Books, 1988), 297.

[11] νήψατε (νήφω) also means to be well-balanced and self-controlled. BDAG, 672; Thomas R. Schreiner, *1, 2 Peter, Jude* (Nashville: Broadman & Holman, 2003), 241.

[12] BDAG, 672

[13] John S. Mbiti, *African Religions and Philosophy* (New York: Praeger, 1969), 181.

Ὁ ἀντίδικος ὑμῶν διάβολος *(your adversary the devil)*

It is only in this passage that Peter identifies a single opponent who incites persecution among the Christians. In other passages, the opponents are mentioned in plural terms (for example, Gentiles in 2:12; unjust masters in 2:18; and unbelieving husbands in 3:1). He uses lawsuit language to describe the opponent. The word ἀντίδικος is translated as the one who brings charges in a lawsuit, an accuser or plaintiff.[14] In addition, it can be translated as an enemy or antagonist. The accuser is identified as διάβολος, meaning slanderous or adversary; however, in the New Testament, διάβολος most often functions as a title for the devil.[15] The word devil is a Greek translation of the Hebrew word *satan*, and in the New Testament, it refers to the archenemy of God and children of God.[16] He is the prince, the ruler and god of this world (Luke 10:18; John 12:31; 14:30; 2 Cor 4:4; Eph 2:2; 6:2). The works of the devil include deceiving, slandering, and accusing children of God (Tim 5:14; Rev 12:10). The New Testament seems to be unambiguous about the origin and identity of Satan. It traces Satan back to heaven, where he and his angels (demons) existed before they were expelled. Revelation 12:9, 12 identifies Satan as the great dragon, the ancient serpent, the deceiver of the whole world who is thrown down to the earth together with his angels. Jesus Christ also affirms to have seen the devil falling away from heaven (Luke 10:18).[17]

The identification of διάβολος in this passage is unknown and disputable, just like the nature and extent of persecution. The devil may be identified as an evil supernatural

---

[14] ἀντίδικος is also used in Matt 5:25; Luke 12:58; 18:3. BDAG, 88.

[15] In most New Testament passages, such as Luke 22:3; John 8:44; Acts 5:3; 1 Cor 5:5; 7:5, διάβολος appears with a definite article (ὁ), but Peter chooses to leave out the article. Elliott, *1 Peter*, 853, notes that it is grammatically possible in this passage for the word διάβολος to function as an adjective modifying ἀντίδικος, but in this context, it functions as a "substantive standing in apposition to adversary."

[16] Elliott, *1 Peter*, 855.

[17] Scholars such as Reinhard Feldmeier and Izak Spangenberg are of the view that the concept of Satan or the devil is a later development that does not appear in the Pentateuch, Psalms, and Prophets (with an exception of Zech 3). Therefore, the idea is alien to the Jews. The word *satan* as a noun appears in three books of the Old Testament: Job 1:6–12; 2:1–7; 1 Chron 21:1; and Zech 3:1–2. None of these books portrays the *satan* as an antagonist of YHWH but rather as a heavenly or celestial being. The idea of Satan as an adversary of YHWH was developed during the Second Temple Judaism as an attempt to understand or rationalize the cause of evil and suffering in the universe. The Jews adopted the concept from the Persian dualism of a good and evil god. During this Persian era, many stories about the origin of the devil as an entity opposed to God emerged and were popularized. In the New Testament world, the concept of Satan as an archenemy of God was widely developed and adopted. Anything contrary to Jesus and the gospel is from the devil. To read more, see Reinhard Feldmeier, *The First Letter of Peter: A Commentary on the Greek Text*, trans. by Peter H. Davids (Waco: Baylor University Press, 2008), 246–47; Izak Spangenberg, "A Brief History of Belief in the Devil (950–70 CE)," *Studia Historiae Ecclesiasticae* 39 (2013): 213–30.

power that oppresses God's children. It is likely that Peter's description of the devil in this text is neither about an earthly nor a heavenly courtroom, but "a universal conflict between the devil and the people of God, with the whole world as its arena."[18] The conflict between good and evil has existed since the fall of mankind in the Garden of Eden (Gen 3:15). It will continue to exist until the final cosmic or universal redemption. Peter's readers are to understand their sufferings within the ongoing conflict between good and evil. Furthermore, the devil in this passage may refer to the Judeo-Christian apocalyptic time in which evil increases and the elect face various trials (4:12–14). Elsewhere, Scripture describes the last days as a time characterized by evil, difficulty, and trials (Eph 5:15–16; 2 Tim 3:1–5, 12). Lauri Thuren believes the court trials (1:6–7) are real, and the devil personifies bad external influence that Christians shouldn't emulate. He calls it a "theological official or beast."[19]

Though there is no consensus about the identification of the devil in this passage, there is no doubt that Satan is inflicting pain upon the children of God. His existence and presence cannot be ignored or denied by the recipients of 1 Peter. The devil refers to an enemy of God and God's people; that is, anything or anyone (sociopolitical systems, individuals, and evil spiritual forces) who is against God and his kingdom. It is probable that Christians' persecutions are coming from both the public (individuals) and imperial powers.[20] This view is probably similar to that of the apostle Paul when he says Satan hinders him from reaching out to others (1 Thess 2:18; Rom 15:22). By Satan, Paul perhaps refers to individuals, spiritual evil forces, governments, or religious systems.

Africans view their world, which is both physical (visible) and spiritual (invisible), as a mysterious space that is saturated by both benevolent and malevolent spirits. The devil is seen as the chief malicious spirit, who can masquerade as an angel of light, take the form of an animal, bird, tree, or an abstract thing such as poverty or sickness.[21] Since the devil is a spirit, he is considered to be more powerful than human beings. Africans believe spirits and the spiritual world are greater and more powerful than physical things or beings; hence, they are dreaded.[22] Additionally, spirits are believed to be situated between God and human beings, and what transpires in the world of spirits (the invisible world) manifests in the physical world.[23]

---

[18] Michaels, *1 Peter*, 298.

[19] Lauri Thuren, "1 Peter and the Lion," in *Evil and the Devil*, ed. Ida Frohlich and Erkki Koskenniemi (London: Bloomsbury T&T Clark, 2013), 147

[20] Horrell, *1 Peter*, 56–58.

[21] Kelvin Onongha, "The African Worldview and Belief in the Demonic," *Journal of Adventist Mission Studies* 18 (2023): 41.

[22] Onongha, "The African Worldview and Belief in the Demonic," 41.

[23] Mbiti, *African Religions and Philosophy*, 16.

In an African world, nothing happens that doesn't have a religious meaning or significance. As one African theologian posits, "Africans are notoriously religious; in other words, religion permeates every facet of their existence; therefore, there is hardly any function without religious significance."[24] Consequently, Africans see the horrendous and excruciating situations that they have undergone as the works of the devil and demonic spirits.[25] They believe spirits influence individuals and communities and may even take them hostage. Though this notion might be true, there is a need to balance it with the free will of an individual or community and not make spirits scapegoats for all personal choices and actions.

Ὡς λέων ὠρυόμενος (like a roaring lion)

Peter compares διάβολος to a roaring and hungry lion. He combines lawsuit and zoological language to describe the behavior of Satan. The lion imagery is not new in the Bible (1 Chr 12:8; Jer 50:17; Hos 11:10). Jesus Christ is called the lion of Judah in Rev 5:5. Also, the imagery is used to refer to hostile human adversaries (Pss 7:2; 17:12; Amos 3:4). The comparison of Satan and the lion is unique and only found in this passage. Peter uses a lion metaphor to symbolize the power and aggressiveness of the accuser. It is likely that he is drawing the imagery from the OT, particularly Ps 22:13: "[T]hey open wide their mouths at me, like a ravening and roaring lion." The lion imagery is a depiction of demonic forces operating within societies where Christians live.

There are different schools of thought regarding the meaning of the lion imagery. It is commonly seen as a metaphor for the "Christian believer's human enemies."[26] Christians are ostracized and persecuted by those who are against the Christian faith. This could be individuals and the government. Figuratively, people are said to devour others (Ps 35:25; Isa 49:19; Jer 51:34). The human enemies in Peter want Christians to forsake their faith and thus be devoured. The imagery may also symbolize "satanic powers that are at work in the sociopolitical system of the Roman Empire."[27] The Roman Empire has become an agent of the devil and thus hostile to those who do not conform to its worldly passions and debauchery (4:1–4). The Roman Empire has

---

[24] Mbiti, *African Religions and Philosophy*, 16.

[25] Diseases, deaths, and misfortunes in the universe are thought to be caused by the devil and demons. See Hans Moscicke, "Reconciling the Supernatural Worldviews of the Bible, African Traditional Religion, and African Christianity," *Missionalia* 45 (2017):129; Onongha, "African Worldview," 37.

[26] Most scholars hold this view or interpretation. See Charles Bigg, *A Critical and Exegetical Commentary on the Epistles of St. Peter and St. Jude* (Edinburgh, T&T. Clark, 1902), 192; Elliot, *1 Peter*, 857–59; Michaels, *1 Peter*, 298; Paul J. Achtemeier, *1 Peter: A Commentary on First Peter*, Hermeneia (Minneapolis: Fortress, 1996), 341.

[27] Jobes, *1 Peter*, 313–14.

become an agent of the devil and thus hostile to those who do not conform to its worldly passions and debauchery (4:1–4). As Elliott suggests, the lion imagery serves as a

> potent means for depicting a hostile society as under the sway of the Devil, the arch-enemy of God and God's people and intent on absorbing or annihilating the brotherhood. The image thus labels and demonizes hostile outsiders who attack the Christians for separating from them (4:2–4) and not conforming to their modes of behavior (1:14–17; 4:2–4) as agents of the Devil.[28]

The imagery refers to the prince or commander of evil spirits, who uses individuals, societies, and governments as his agents. Peter is using this metaphor to point out the evils that await the Christian community. He thus encourages them not to panic and be scattered by the threat; instead, they must be alert, firm in their faith, stay within the community of faith, and resist the devil. Their spiritual death may come if they are to forsake Christ and their faith.

The Apostle Peter uses a rhetorical style analogous to the African storytelling or narrative style. Africans are storytelling people. Stories are mediums through which cultural education, religious beliefs, and life existential issues are inculcated in the present generations and passed on to the future. African stories are punctuated with metaphors, personification, and other figures of speech. Animals, trees, birds, and other non-human things are often personified in the stories. Likewise, spirits can embody or transform themselves and take the form of an animal, bird, tree, rock, or anything.[29] Thus, Peter's depiction of διάβολος as a lion is not a strange imagery or concept to Africans. The African Christians would most likely understand the imagery as a figure of speech. Peter is using a metaphor to portray the spiritual powers and tactics of the devil. It is also feasible that as an African, one could read and interpret this passage in a literal sense.[30] There are stories of wild animals such as hippos, elephants, lions, snakes, and leopards that would suddenly appear from nowhere, then wound or kill a person, and miraculously disappear. In such incidents, it is believed that the devil disguised himself in the body of an animal.

---

[28] Elliott, *1 Peter*, 860.

[29] Onongha, "African Worldview," 37.

[30] Boris A. Paschke, "The Roman Ad Bestias Execution as a Possible Historical Background for 1 Peter 5.8," *JSNT* 28 (2006): 489–500, proposes a literal interpretation of the imagery. He argues that there is evidence of *ad bestias* or *damnatio ad bestias* (condemnation to beasts) executions during the life of Peter under Emperor Caligula. The lion imagery thus refers "to the lion that walked around in the arena hungry and—as a consequence of that—roaring (ὠρυόμενος), and literally swallowed its defenseless victims" (498). The first-century CE mosaics show *ad bestias* executions coming from all over the Roman Empire. The provincial victims condemned *ad bestias* in Rome seem to know exactly what is awaiting them. Therefore, the recipients of 1 Peter have no problem understanding the lion imagery.

Peter describes the devil as prowling around like a roaring lion. In an African context, when a lion roars, it is often to announce his presence and intimidate other animals. However, a roaring lion seldom kills; by roaring, he sensitizes other animals to flee or prepare for a fight. It is only those animals that are unalert, slumbering, sick, and confused or in panic that can be devoured by a roaring lion. In other words, a roaring lion will only devour Christians who are not vigilant.

Περιπατεῖ ζητῶν τινα καταπιεῖν (seeking someone to devour)

The devil, as a roaring lion, is described as walking around (περιπατεῖ) seeking someone to devour. This description might be an allusion to Job 2:2, where the *satan* said he has come "from going to and fro on the earth, and from walking up and down on it." τινα καταπιεῖν means someone to swallow, devour, drink down.[31] The aim of the devil is to annihilate Christians. καταπιεῖν is used in relation to the aggressiveness of the hungry lion. In this context, being swallowed by the devil refers to spiritual death, not physical death; that is, renouncing allegiance to Christ and turning to pagan gods as a way of escaping persecution.[32] Christian suffering is inevitable, and they cannot avoid it by forsaking their faith.

In an African world, to live means to interact wisely with both benevolent and malicious spirits. Some malevolent spirits associated with witchcraft are believed to possess the power to kill and devour human beings; hence, they invoke great fear and terrorize many people. Christians are also beleaguered by these evil spirits, especially witchcraft. As a result, some African Christians seek help from diviners and *sangomas* (traditional healers or doctors). Peter's words come as an exhortation and admonition to African Christians who live in fear of witchcraft and practice syncretism. They ought to be steadfast in the Lord, lest they be swallowed. God has given them the Holy Spirit, the helper, who has power over διάβολος and all malicious spirits (Acts 1:8, 2 Tim 1:7). In addition, Christ on the cross disarmed and put to shame all the demonic rulers and authorities (Col 2:15). Therefore, in Christ, African Christians shouldn't fear; the devil and his demons are defeated.

Ὧι ἀντίστητε (resist)

In addition to being alert, Christians are encouraged to resist the devil by being steadfast in their faith and finding solace in the knowledge that they are not alone in such adversity. The word ἀντίστητε means "to resist, oppose, to set oneself

---

[31] David C. Abernathy, *An Exegetical Summary of 1 Peter* (Dallas: Summer Institute of Linguistics, 1998), 183; Greg W. Forbes, *1 Peter,* Exegetical Guide to the Greek New Testament (Nashville: B & H Academic, 2014), 177.

[32] Michaels, *1 Peter*, 299.

against."[33] Resistance is needed to realize God's victory over the powers of darkness. Peter's readers should not be spiritually paralyzed by fear of the devil. God has not given them a spirit of fear but of power, love, and self-discipline (2 Tim 1:7). They should actively resist the devil and stand against all his wiles.

Life circumstances have compelled and taught African Christians to develop cultural and spiritual resilience. They have seen and experienced the works of the devil in their lives. So, they can rely on God's grace and use their experience, knowledge, and spirituality to resist the devil and his schemes. This would be a testimony of God's saving power and faithfulness even in times of adversity.

Στερεοὶ τῇ πίστει *(firm in faith)*

This phrase can be interpreted as "an instrument; the devil is resisted by means of steadfast faith."[34] The idea of being steadfast in faith is not in reference to holding fast to certain doctrines, but it refers to their faith and trust in God. They have to be solid in their Christian life despite their sufferings. Additionally, they have to be convicted and trust that their God will surely intervene and rescue them. The peace of God will ultimately crush διάβολος under their feet (Rom 16:20a). They should know and remember that they are not alone in their suffering.

Africans are acquainted with suffering. The description of life as an enigma, meaningless, or vapor, by the Teacher in the book of Ecclesiastes, reverberates deeply in many African life stories. Life under the sun seems to be filled with chaotic waters and storms that never cease. Suffering is often associated with evil spiritual forces, witchcraft, curses from ancestors or Mother Earth, or chastisement from God. This means spiritual forces and deities are involved in the well-being of individuals and communities. When an individual or a community experiences severe suffering, the quest is to know who is causing the suffering more than why there is suffering.[35] In other words, there is always a cause for everything that happens.

In 1 Pet 5:8–9, Peter addresses both the "who and why" of Christian's sufferings. He further encourages the Christian community to understand their sufferings in the greater scheme of Christ's redemptive works. Just as Christ suffered, they, too, will be persecuted. Nevertheless, they should rejoice in sharing Christ's sufferings (4:13) and emulate his attitude and spirit (2:20–21). Additionally, Christians have to know that there is a divine purpose to their sufferings. Their faith is refined and strengthened, and there is a great reward for the faithful when Christ is revealed (1:6–10). Peter's theology of suffering aids African Christians to have hope now and in the

---

[33] BDAG, 80.

[34] Peter H. Davids, *The First Epistle of Peter* (Grand Rapids: Eerdmans, 1990), 191.

[35] Kelvin Onongha, "Suffering, Salvation, and the Sovereignty of God: Towards a Theology of Suffering," *Journal of Adventist Mission Studies* 9 (2013): 127.

future. God knows what they have been through and are facing, and he has not abandoned them in times of adversity, for he does not hide his face from the afflicted nor despise their afflictions. Their lives in God will not end in sorrow or death but rather in victory, newness, and continuity of every good thing. There is a living hope because of the resurrection of Jesus (1:3).

Ἐν κόσμῳ (throughout the world)

This phrase may refer to the world as an enmity to God (John 8:23; 8:15–19; 1 John 2:15–16) or as an inhabited earth—geographical space (Mark 4:8; John 9:5; 17:11; 1 Cor 14:10). However, it is commonly understood to be used in a geographical sense.[36] Believers throughout the Greco-Roman world are experiencing the same kind of suffering. Consequently, Peter's appeal to the general brotherhood is to encourage them "by setting their experiences in Asia Minor in the perspective of the experiences of the worldwide Church."[37] Peter's audience should find comfort and hope in knowing that they are never alone, and solidarity in times of persecution should strengthen them to remain solid in faith. Persecution throughout the Roman world should not insinuate a general official persecution, for the Book of Acts and Paul's letters do not mention worldwide official persecution.[38]

The word ἀδελφότητι refers to a community of faith whose members love one another and consider themselves a family of God.[39] This community of faith prays and encourages one another to be faithful to God and their faith even to the point of death. Brotherhood does not only refer to those in close proximity but to everyone worldwide who professes the same faith. Peter's recipients can find solace in the brotherhood.

The concept of a community lies at the heart of African societies. Africans are communal by nature; that is, life, identity, purpose, spirituality, and cultural values are defined by the community. Just like God, who works and exists in community as the God the Father, Son, and Holy Spirit, Africans believe people are created to live and work as a community. The essence of a community is encapsulated in the African *botho or ubuntu* spirit, which says, "*Umuntu Ngumuntu Ngabantu*," meaning a person is a person through other people, or as John Mbiti captures it, "I am because we are; and since we are, therefore I am."[40] This African spirit is about establishing and

---

[36] Michaels, *1 Peter*, 301; Elliot, *1 Peter*, 863; Donald Senior and Daniel J. Harrington, *1 Peter: Jude and Second Peter* (Collegeville: Liturgical Press, 2003), 148.

[37] J. N. D. Kelly, *A Commentary on the Epistles of Peter and of Jude* (London: A. & C. Black, 1969), 212.

[38] Allen Black and Mark C. Black, *1 & 2 Peter*, The College Press NIV Commentary (Joplin: College Press, 1998), 135.

[39] ὑμῶν ἀδελφότητ may be interpreted as dative of agency: the same kind of sufferings are being experienced by the brotherhood. Achtemeier, *1 Peter*, 342.

[40] Mbiti, *African Religions and Philosophy*, 141.

celebrating the common humanity and oneness. One's humanity is affirmed when he or she acknowledges that of others. When one's humanity is degraded, the whole community is affected. Additionally, the *ubuntu* spirit promotes godly virtues for all humanity. The blessing of communal life includes security, accountability, and amity for all the members. People become each other's keepers. Peter's call for solidarity and solace in the community reiterates the African communal spirit and worldview. Much is achieved as a community rather than as individuals. As an African proverb says, "[T]o reach far, don't travel alone; travel with others." A Christian community is indispensable in nurturing faith and defeating the devil. Those who desert the community of faith become a meal for the devil. African Christians should employ this communal spirit as a catalyst for faithfulness to God and their faith even in the midst of sufferings.

The African community consists of the living, the living dead (ancestors), and those yet to be born.[41] The living dead, who continue to live in the invisible (spiritual) world, are in closer proximity to God than the living; hence, they are asked to mediate on behalf of the living.[42] The ancestors are believed to be benevolent, yet they are capable of cursing or inflicting pain on individuals and communities if taboos and traditions are defiled. Though Africans generally claim they do not worship ancestors, reverencing and soliciting help from them can be a window for demonic deceptions and manipulation. Demonic spirits may disguise themselves as ancestral spirits. Besides, God vehemently admonishes his children not to put their hope, faith, or trust in the dead (Deut 18:9–14; Eccl 9:5–6).

CONCLUSION

Peter uses a rhetorical strategy of a vivid visual description (ἔκφρασις) to strongly encourage his readers, who are facing persecution, to be watchful and steadfast in the Lord and faith. They should resist διάβολος, who is prowling around looking for someone to devour. The rhetorical style and context of 1 Pet 5:8–9 mirror the African storytelling style, context, and worldview. The pericope, therefore, offers comfort and hope to African Christians who are suffering and those whose lives may be invaded and pervaded by fear of the devil and malevolent spirits. They should find solace and refuge in God and the community of faith. If they waver in faith, assimilate to the living standards of non-believers, or solicit help from those who consult the dead or ancestors, they will be devoured.

The passage summons Christians to be vigilant of the devil and his wiles. The devil

---

[41] Onongha, "African Worldview," 38.

[42] The belief in ancestors is prevalent among Africans and even Christians. To read more, see James N. Amanze, *African Traditional Religions and Culture in Botswana* (Gaborone, Botswana: Pula Press, 2005), 67–87.

refers to anyone or anything that is an enemy to God and his people. Christians elsewhere may repudiate the existence and presence of demonic forces and their works in the world; however, in an African world, they are real and undeniable. African Christians have a good understanding of spirits and the spiritual world, which is a blessing but can also be a window for evil spirits' deceptions and manipulations. Demonic spirits may disguise themselves as good spirits; hence, there's a need for spiritual discernment and God's wisdom. Peter's message applies to all Christians in every generation and geographical space. The god of this world is salivating and coming for them with great wrath. Therefore, Christians are to be watchful, unswerving in the Lord, and stand in the true grace of God (5:12).

10
Living as an Exile with an Unbelieving Husband (1 Peter 3:1–7)

John Mark Hicks[1]

Joan was born in New York City and grew up in a home unaffiliated with any faith community. At the age of twenty-three, she met Mohammed, an Iraqi Muslim. They fell in love and married. They subsequently moved to Iraq. Mohammed worked for an international company. They welcomed the birth of two children while living in Iraq.

Through friendships with a few of Mohammed's co-workers and connections with an Iraqi house church, Joan became a disciple of Jesus. She loves her husband and her children, of course, though her commitments and priorities changed. She is a Christian. Mohammed is a Muslim, and she is living in a Muslim culture that is often hostile to Christians.

What does her Christian vocation mean for her relationship with her husband? His faith identifies him as the authority figure in the marriage in a strong patriarchal sense, and the culture is potentially hostile to her following Jesus. There are many similar situations in house churches scattered throughout the Muslim world.

Suppose, however, you were writing a letter to all believers scattered across Iraq. What advice would you offer a Christian woman living in Iraq who was married to a devout Muslim? Should she wear the hijab? Should she obey her husband? Should she divorce him? Should she pressure him to convert? Should she publicly practice her faith though it might dishonor her husband and possibly endanger herself and her family? What counsel would you offer her?

This is analogous to the situation 1 Peter addresses. Christian wives sometimes lived with non-Christian husbands in a harsh, patriarchal, and culturally hostile situation. How does Peter counsel them to live faithfully as disciples of Jesus?

---

[1] This essay honors my good friend and former colleague Dr. Allen Black. Allen taught Greek exegesis at Harding School of Theology for many years, and he used 1 Peter as the playground where students exercised their exegetical muscles. He also published a commentary on 1 Peter (Allen Black and Mark C. Black, *1 & 2 Peter,* College Press NIV Commentary [Joplin: College Press, 1998]). I am grateful for his teaching, ministry, and friendship. This chapter is a revised and updated version of a series of blogs on 1 Peter that appeared at johnmarkhicks.com.

LIVING AS EXILES IN 1 PETER

The letter comes to us as a communication from Peter, who is "in Babylon" (1 Pet 5:13), to Christians ("exiles") scattered throughout what is now western and northern Turkey (1 Pet 1:1).[2] "Babylon" is a cryptic Second Temple way of referring to Rome. The language of "exile" and "Babylon" highlights an important theme in the letter. Christians are a socially dislocated minority within Roman culture. They are aliens or foreigners who have a different way of life than their surrounding culture. They live as refugees in a strange country. Writing from the center of Roman power and wealth, 1 Peter addresses the social location of Christians within the empire. They are homeless.

This is the most significant key for reading 1 Peter. The author addresses his readers as "exiles of the Dispersion" (1 Pet 1:1; or Diaspora). It is a Diaspora letter. This was a prominent feature of exilic and Second Temple Judaism. Some good examples are Jer 29, 2 Macc 1:10–2:18, and Elephantine letters 21 & 30. These documents address Jewish communities displaced from the Jewish homeland. They encourage living well within cultures that do not share their values and are often hostile to their presence.

Peter encourages them to live faithfully in the grace of God (5:12). The letter does this in three major moves. First, he stresses their identity as God's chosen people whom God has loved from the foundation of the world (1:13–2:10). Second, he encourages them to live out their identity despite their difficult circumstances as witnesses to the grace of God in the world (2:11–4:11). Lastly, he commends their suffering for the sake of Christ, which is their greatest witness (4:12–5:11).

These faith communities are described as both chosen and exiled. They are both embraced and rejected. They live an exiled existence as aliens. Though settled in Roman provinces, like Abraham before them, they are "sojourners and aliens" (πάροικος καὶ παρεπίδημος, Gen 23:4, LXX). First Peter 2:11 uses the same phrase: παροίκους καὶ παρεπιδήμοις. Specifically, the term παρεπιδήμοις (foreigners, aliens; see also 1 Pet 1:1) refers to one who is not a citizen, and, consequently, actual citizens view παρεπιδήμοις with suspicion, fear, and often hostility.

They are "resident aliens" (to use the title of a significant modern book as well as *The Epistle to Diognetus* [5:4–5] in the second century).[3] Their relationship with Roman power and culture is distinct. The life of their community contrasts with their surrounding environment, and this creates tension in the communities where they live. So much so that the peaceful existence they desire is threatened by violence, incarceration, and local hostility. They suffer for the sake of Christ.

---

[2] Unless otherwise noted, all quotations from the Bible are taken from the New Revised Standard Version.

[3] Stanley Hauerwas and William H. Willimon, *Resident Aliens: Life in the Christian Colony* (Nashville: Abingdon Press, 1989).

Their alien status is not a contrast between earthly existence and heavenly hope, between present life and eternal life. Rather, it is their social location as a community whose values and interests are out of sync with the surrounding culture. They stick out like a sore thumb. Their neighbors are "surprised" or alarmed that they do not engage in the typical cultural practices (4:4) or participate in the civil religion of the empire like good citizens. They face intense questioning, hostility, and mockery from their culture. They are a marginalized community.

SUBMISSION IN 1 PETER

How do "aliens and exiles" (2:11) live in an empire whose commitments and values are not their own? They are to "conduct [themselves] honorably among the Gentiles, so that, though they malign you as evildoers, they may see your honorable deeds and glorify God when he comes to judge" (2:12). The imperatives of 1 Pet 2:13–17 provide a path for that exilic life.

- Accept the authority of (or submit to)
- Honor everyone
- Love the family of believers
- Fear God
- Honor the emperor

The first verb, "accept," heads a long sentence that runs from verses thirteen to sixteen. The difficulty of accepting or submitting to a hostile empire generates a long sentence to contextualize what Peter means. In other words, to tell a group of marginalized people to accept (or submit to) a generally hostile imperial power needs explanation.

Structure

First Peter 2:13–17 is the first section in a series of four that applies what it means to live as "aliens and exiles" (2:11–12) within imperial culture. The first three address specific concerns. The fourth is more general and does not explicitly use the word "accept" though it is the concluding section 1 Pet 2:11–3:12.

- Residents, accept (submit or defer to) imperial authority (2:13–17).
- Slaves, accept (submit or defer to) the authority of your masters (2:18–25).
- Wives, accept (submit or defer to) the authority of your husband (3:1–7).
- Everyone, accept (submit or defer to) everyone as a community (3:8–12).

Peter utilizes a common genre in ancient ethical texts called the Household Code, which lists the respective duties of people in a Roman household (including extended family, slaves, and workers). However, Peter's interest is not an exhaustive delineation of roles and responsibilities. Rather, he addresses sore points within the Christian community, given their circumstances. How do members of a household (whether state or home) live within that household when the authority figure in the household does not share their faith commitments?

- How do Christians live in a hostile empire?
- How do slaves live with hostile masters?
- How do wives live with unbelieving husbands?
- How do Christians live together as a marginalized community?

In effect, Peter does not offer a timeless set of immutable instructions to be reproduced *verbatim* across the history of Christianity. Rather, he addresses a specific concern—what does it mean for Christians to live in this culture under these conditions? In other words, given the Christian narrative with its commitments and values, how does one relate to hostile authority (empire, masters, unbelieving husbands, marginalization)? The answers might be different under different circumstances, even though similar principles would be employed in analogous situations. Consequently, it is important to pay close attention to Peter's advice for the "exiles" in Roman Anatolia to hear what the message is.

Submission

The leading verb for the main sentence in 1 Pet 2:13–16 is ὑποτάγητε, which is usually rendered submit. Etymologically, the verb suggests "to place under." It is translated in various ways, including to yield, accept the authority of, defer to, assume responsibility under another, subordinate, or submit.

Ὑποτάγητε, then, has a wide semantic range from absolute obedience to an imposed authority to willing deferential yielding to another. The former is often an external authority, while the latter is voluntary submission for the sake of some greater purpose or interest. Its meaning, then, is shaped by both its literary context and the historical situation.

Alan Padgett suggests 1 Peter operates in a social context that calls for "a *one-sided* application of the ethic of servant leadership" present in the Gospels and Paul.[4] The external demands and expectations of empire, masters, and unbelieving husbands entail a deferential, accepting, and submissive attitude so that their good lives might receive a hearing and ultimately bring glory to God (3:11, 13, 16–17). Otherwise, overt resistance to these authorities would engender violence and subvert the gospel's mission. Nevertheless, though the term counsels against overt revolt, it does not preclude

---

[4] Alan G. Padgett, *As Christ Submits to the Church: A Biblical Understanding of Leadership* (Grand Rapids: Baker Academic, 2011), 86 (italics original).

subversive, peaceful resistance. In other words, given the situation, live within the established order. A marginalized community can neither change the reality nor materially affect the situation. Consequently, it accepts what it cannot change and seeks to "do good" for the sake of the gospel.

This involves submission and obedience, that is, living as obedient people under a regulated order. This obedience, of course, is not absolute as if the well-being of the empire and its cultural values overrule their commitment to Jesus the Messiah. Rather, they submit "for the Lord's sake" (2:13). They submit for the sake of God's mission rather than out of commitment to the empire, its culture, or its values.

RESIDENTS SUBMIT TO THE EMPEROR (1 PET 2:13–17)

Peter commands submission, literally, to "every human creation." This refers to human institutions rooted in governmental or imperial authority identified as "emperor" (βασιλεῖ) or his "governors" (ἡγεμόσιν). Governments are human creations; they are socio-political constructs. More specifically, the emperor is not God (despite whatever the emperor might claim), and his institutions are not cloaked in divine authority. They are human (ἀνθρωπίνῃ κτίσει), and the Christian's allegiance does not lie with human institutions. Whether constructed by autocratic (like Caesar) or democratic power (social contract theory), they are human. Given social realities, Christians "accept" this situation and live peaceably within it.

God intends these human institutions to praise those who "do good" and punish those who "do evil," but government is not committed to God's intent when faithful Christians are imprisoned, harshly criticized, and treated as criminals (4:15–16). Whatever their design in God's good creation (to restrain evil and promote good), Peter's readers do not have such assurances from Roman authorities. Nevertheless, Peter counsels his readers to submit, "do good" within the Empire and avoid, as much as possible, any governmental action that is designed to punish those who "do evil." They are to live within the order imposed by imperial authority.

This submission, however, is not resignation or acquiescence. Rather, it is a positive witness within the culture. This is displayed by "doing good" (ἀγαθοποιῶν), which has the potential effect of silencing the ignorant (those who pursue folly). This positive approach to cultural engagement offers a public witness in the presence of those who are invested in a different way of life than the wisdom God offers. Foolish does not mean idiotic or stupid but reflects Hebrew wisdom literature where the fool chooses a path that leads to death in contrast to the wise person who chooses a path that leads to life. This is a moral rather than an intellectual characterization.

Why submit? Believers submit to potentially silence the critics, but also to publicly witness to their freedom. They submit because they are free, which is quite paradoxical. Grammatically, the imperative "submit" from verse 13 supplies the verb in verse 16 (which lacks a main verb) so that it reads: "Submit (or, accept) as free people and not as those who use freedom as a covering for evil." Christians, though slaves of God, are free from governmental authority. They submit to governmental authority as a witness to what is good and right rather than using that freedom to hide in the darkness of evil. Yet, they cannot be coerced into evil by governments since their allegiance is to God rather than the state. God has freed them from such obligations. Christians are free of imperial authority (not obligated by imperial authority), but they submit to it for the sake of God's mission in the world. They accept it to further God's witness and goodness in the world. They do not seek chaos, and neither do they seek power (in the context of 1 Peter). Rather, they only desire to "do good."

SLAVES SUBMIT TO THEIR MASTERS (1 PET 2:18–25)

Even "slaves" in the empire are "free." They are "free" because they are bound to no authority other than God (see also 2:16). They submit as "slaves" within the empire because they fear (worship or revere) God. This is the mystery of exilic life for the sake of gospel within an oppressive empire. It may be pictured something like this:

> *free* from worldly authority,
> > but *enslaved* to God, and
> > > therefore, *submissive* within worldly structures
> > > > for the sake of the *gospel*.

This submission is not absolute. It is limited by Christian profession, and it is circumstantial. Slaves, generally, could do little to change their situation. This *submission is missional*, that is, for the sake of God's mission, given the circumstances in which people find themselves within human authority structures (empire, slaves, married to unconverted spouses).

Slavery was often harsh in the Roman world, including beatings, sexual abuse, and restricted freedoms.[5] Yet, slaves are to submit to both "kind" and "harsh" masters, and they submit (accept their place in the order) because they have no other legal or peaceful recourse in the situation. Violent revolt is not an option, and while some could pursue peaceful, legal options (for example, purchasing one's own freedom), those were few and limited. Consequently, unless one embraced violence, there was little choice other than to submit until such time they could secure freedom.

The question, then, becomes, how do we submit? Peter's answer is something like peaceful resistance or subversive conformity. Perhaps we might even say, "kill 'em with kindness."

Peter's specific address to slaves is a subversive act. Slaves are addressed as responsible human beings who must decide how to act in their enslaved condition and

---

[5] S. Scott Bartchy, "Slavery in the Greco-Roman World and the New Testament," *ABD* 6:65–73.

how they will relate to their owners. When Peter calls slaves to submit, he addresses them as people with dignity and choice.

> This is the substance of Peter's counsel for slaves:
> *Situation*: unjust, harsh, painful suffering, including beatings
> *Response*: they endure such treatment
> *Behavior*: they are called to do good rather than evil
> *Motivation*: they fear God and are conscious of God
> *Result*: grace from God
> *Rationale*: following Jesus

Peter has no allusions. Slavery is dangerous and often harsh, though not always (some masters were gentle and kind). In fact, the term "harsh" (σκολιοῖς) literally means bent or crooked. It connotes cruelty or inhumanity. This treatment might include beatings (2:20), just as Jesus of Nazareth endured.

Their submission means they willingly (given their circumstances) endure such treatment. They persevere under pressure and hardship. They are empowered to do this because they "fear" God, and they are aware of God's presence in their lives. While some think the word "fear" refers to their masters (a respect for masters), every other use of "fear" in 1 Peter is directed toward God, including the contrast between "fearing God" and "honoring the emperor" in 1 Pet 2:17. "Fear" is Peter's word for a submissive, reverent, trusting orientation toward God. Slaves live out their faith through the awe-inspiring presence of God rather than out of a terrifying fear of their masters. Their subversive submission is motivated by their trust in God rather than the lash of their masters.

Slaves are called to subversive behavior, that is, to do good. They are neither to wrong their masters nor do them any evil. Rather, they embody goodness and kindness. In this way, they overcome evil by doing good. This is a subversive lifestyle against the unjust human system in which they find themselves. As righteous sufferers, as mistreated innocents, they bear witness to justice and goodness by their godly lives. This is itself a path to liberation, even if they cannot find legal or nonviolent means to secure their freedom. It is a leaven that will, eventually, leaven the whole lump. Peter calls them to peaceful resistance or subversive conformity following the model of Jesus the Messiah (2:21–25).

Even if they cannot eventually secure their freedom, God's grace is present. Peter twice uses the term χάρις in 1 Pet 2:19–20. Grace is divine favor or gift, which is both present and future. Slaves, suffering unjustly, will experience God's grace through godliness in the present, but they will also experience a future grace in the resurrection when their salvation is fully revealed (1:3–12).

WIVES SUBMIT TO UNBELIEVING HUSBANDS (1 PET 3:1–6)

"In the same way" (ὁμοίως) heads the Greek sentence and connects Peter's advice to wives with the same ethic as his directives to slaves and imperial residents. This places 1 Pet 3:1–6 in the framework of 1 Pet 2:12–13, that is, how to live as aliens and exiles among the nations so that the gospel has a witness.[6]

Revolt was not an option in the empire for residents, slaves, or wives. Violence was not an option for followers of Jesus. What they could do was to "do good" and subvert the dominant culture by living exemplary, kind, and gentle lives without returning evil for evil. Since, generally, they had no legal recourse, Christian imperial residents, slaves, and wives suffered abuse. Typically, they could not escape their circumstances. Instead, they suffered, following the model of Jesus.

Because Peter addresses key stress points for Christians living in a hostile environment, several "Household Code" elements are missing. He does not address parents, children, or masters, and husbands only get a brief word. Primarily, he addresses groups who are living under stresses generated by their powerlessness before an external authority within the culture.

The Social Circumstance of Wives with Unbelieving Husbands

Within Roman culture, the general expectation was something like this: the household (including wives, children, slaves, and even employees) would follow the religion of the household's authority figure. The *paterfamilias* set the boundaries of acceptable faith and religion. When a wife converted to Christianity, for example, outside of her husband's permission or authority, this generated an unacceptable and/or tension-filled circumstance.

As Karen Jobes notes, Romans generally believed it violated good order if a wife "adopted a religion other than her own husband's," and the adoption of Christianity also involved conflict with the husband's allegiance to the state where Caesar is Lord.[7] Further, her association with other Christians in their community would probably violate standards of propriety where, as Plutarch advised (writing about 90–100 CE), a wife should have no friends independent of her husband and worship no gods but those of her husband.[8]

Given this situation, what kind of submission does Peter intend? On the one hand, it parallels submission to the empire and masters. Given the cultural circumstances, wives with unbelieving husbands must locate themselves appropriately within the

---

[6] See James Thompson, "The Submission of Wives in 1 Peter," in *Essays on Women in Earliest Christianity, Volume I*, ed. Carroll D. Osburn (Joplin: College Press, 1993), 377–92.

[7] Karen Jobes, *1 Peter*, BECNT (Grand Rapids: Baker Academic, 2005), 204.

[8] Plutarch, *Moralia: Advice to Bride and Groom*, 19; see David L. Balch, *Let Wives Be Submissive: The Domestic Code in 1 Peter* (Chico: Scholars Press, 1981), 99–100, for details and other examples.

cultural order. They submit to functioning within the prevailing order. This is not an endorsement of the prevailing order any more than submitting to the emperor endorses imperial government or submitting to masters endorses slavery. Instead, it is a pragmatic, but missional, response within the system that dominates them so that believers might bear witness to the gospel within that culture.

Yet, they subvert the prevailing order by how they live. By their lifestyle or "conduct" (ἀναστροφῆς, 3:1–2; see also 1:15, 18; 2:12), they will subvert the dominant order within a Roman household. Indeed, their lives might even win their husbands to Jesus, even without words. They might Christianize the household order.

Peter's exhortation is not absolute. Just as with the empire and slaves, so with wives, Peter locates believers in their social situation. They submit for the sake of God's mission, but they also live in such a way as to subvert the prevailing cultural expectations. In no way, then, does this legitimize male abuse or demand husbands force their wives into submission. Wives voluntarily submit for the sake of the gospel, but they do so in a way that subverts the prevailing cultural order. Peter's call for wives to live in such a way to win their husbands to faith is itself a rather significant contravention of cultural expectations. Generally, such encouragement would have been regarded as subversive of good order.

In a different cultural setting, such as in the United States, women have more legal options and resources. They are not forced to submit to abuse when they have peaceful and legal means to avoid such. Submission in 1 Peter does not legitimize abuse, and neither does it demand women remain in abusive situations when they have other options.

What does Peter expect unbelieving husbands to see (observe, or notice in a supervisory manner) in their Christian wives? He identifies two characteristics: (1) purity (ἁγνὴν) and (2) fear (φόβῳ). A godly wife's lifestyle is characterized by these two particulars. Several render "fear" as respectful as if this is respect for husbands. However, φόβον in 1 Peter is directed toward God (1:17; 2:17–18; 3:2, 14, 16). It is reverential piety, a trusting disposition awed by God's majesty. It is the path of wisdom in Hebrew literature. In other words, when a wife is both devout (fully surrendered to God) and pure (loyal to her husband, both emotionally and sexually), this kind of life has the potential to win the heart of an unbelieving husband.

Peter Calls Wives to Inner Beauty Rather than Outward Show

Peter contrasts the inner life and outer appearance. This is typical among Greco-Roman moralists as well as within Scripture (see also Isa 3:18–26; Rev 17:4; see also 1 Tim 2:9–10). Gold, braided hair, and expensive clothing reflect one kind of precious commodity, whereas a "gentle and quiet spirit" (πραέως καὶ ἡσυχίου πνεύματος) is another. (It is a spirit expected of all believers; see also 1 Pet 3:16–17; see also Matt 5:5 for πραεῖς and 1 Tim 2:2 for ἡσύχιον.) The former reflects ego, status, and power, while the latter has a "lasting beauty" valued by God (1 Pet 3:4). The former assumes choices wealthy women enjoyed (unavailable to poor and enslaved women), while the latter assumes a pious devotion.

Some read this as an absolute prohibition. Peter does use an imperative: "do not adorn yourselves outwardly" with braided hair, gold jewelry, or (expensive) clothes. However, we should not absolutize what is relative to the situation addressed. These were symbols of wealth, power, and status in the Roman world. If they symbolize something else in another culture (gold wedding rings in Western culture or braided hair in African cultures), then to apply the imperative without adjustment to the cultural situation does not match Peter's intent. Just as this prohibition is relative to its cultural context, so also submission is best seen as relative to the societal order in which early Christians found themselves.

Like other moralists in his day, Peter invokes examples from an honored past. Peter appeals to "holy women" who hoped in God. Hope is an important feature since the women Peter addressed were subject to terrifying challenges (see the end of verse 6). God is our hope when injustice abounds, and we have no resources to change the situation. Sarah, the wife of the father of faith, is Peter's specific example. She is the mother of women who live in fearful and uncertain systems or orders. Sarah fits the circumstances of the women Peter is addressing.

Some suggest that Sarah's example roots wifely submission to husbands in an imperative grounded in the divine order (though there is no allusion to any such order in the text, especially any sort of supposed order of creation). Sarah, according to 1 Peter 3:6, called Abraham "Lord" (κύριον). Interestingly, Sarah never addresses Abraham as "Lord" in the Hebrew Scriptures. She does so in literature elsewhere (*Testament of Abraham*, 6).[9] Rather, Sarah refers to Abraham as "Lord" (κύριός) in Gen 18:12 (LXX), but she does not address him with that term. It is descriptive rather than a vocative. It may even be, in context, a form of sarcasm.

The reason for calling attention to Sarah's use of the word "lord" is to underscore Sarah's obedience to Abraham (ὑπήκουσεν). She models obedience in submission to her husband. 1 Peter's call for submission—to imperial authority, masters, and unbelieving husbands—includes obedience. In contrast, Paul does not use the word "obey" in the context of marriage but only about children and slaves (Eph 6:1, 5; Col 3:20, 22). The kind of submission Peter is describing is one that willingly accepts an external authority, places oneself under it, and obeys it for the sake of the gospel. It is not an endorsement of that authority or that all wives must obey their husbands. In fact, the situation of wifely obedience in 1 Pet 3:6 is a fearful circumstance (φοβούμεναι).

---

[9] See the examples in Peter H. David, "A Silent Witness in Marriage," in *Discovering Biblical Equality: Complementarity without Hierarchy*, ed. Ronald W. Pierce and Rebecca Merrill Groothuis (Downers Grove: InterVarsity Academic, 2005), 224–38.

This is the point of the analogy. Where did Sarah obey Abraham in circumstances where fear might have been a natural response? Two occasions are rather obvious.[10] Sarah obeyed Abraham when he gave Sarah to two different rulers (Gen 12:11–20; 20:6–9). He claimed she was his sister instead of his wife to preserve his own life. Those must have been frightening moments for Sarah. Yet, she obeyed, and she did it to save Abraham's life. She had a missional rationale.

Sarah's obedience reflected her willingness to save her husband's life even as Abraham failed to trust God in the situation. One can imagine Sarah, living as an alien and stranger in Egypt, was terrified by her circumstances, and this is exactly the sort of situation in which wives of unbelieving husbands found themselves. Though unbelieving husbands might abuse their wives or demean them due to their powerlessness, Peter calls them to accept their situation and, more particularly, obey their husbands. Sarah is their model.

Sarah's example is not an absolute legitimation of a husband's authority over a wife. Instead, it recognizes submission as a Christlike response, given certain circumstances. Just as Sarah submitted to Abraham, even when it was a fearful thing to do, so wives with unbelieving husbands should do what is right despite their fears. In other words, these wives should obey their husbands because it is the right thing to do. They are to "do good" despite their fears, and they are called to act without fear because they are "doing good." In this, they follow not only Sarah's example but Jesus's as well.

Like imperial residents and slaves, wives are called to a submissive or deferential lifestyle where they accept their position within the prevailing cultural order for the sake of the gospel. Peter's instructions are not absolute, timeless, or transcendent injunctions. Quite the opposite, they are pragmatic instructions for godly people living in a hostile environment of hierarchical authority. His words are rooted in key theological values: inner beauty, the example of Jesus, and a missional motive.

HUSBANDS ARE CALLED TO MUTUALITY

The primary burden of 1 Pet 3:1–7 addresses wives, and only a single verse addresses husbands (in contrast to Paul, who addresses wives in three verses but husbands in seven [Eph 5:22–32]). The relative space given to each identifies Peter's focus. Peter recognized the relationship of wives to unbelieving husbands as a significant issue among "aliens and exiles" in Roman culture. Peter focuses on the potentially explosive situation of marginalized women in marriage relationships, but he does not ignore the responsibility of Christian husbands in relation to their own wives. Indeed, he reorients the cultural dominance of the husband toward mutuality within the relationship.

---

[10] See Michal Beth Dinkler, "Sarah's Submission: Peter's Analogy in 1 Peter 3:5–6," *Priscilla Papers* 21.3 (2007), available at https://www.cbeinternational.org/resource/sarahs-submission/.

The cultural perception of a husband's authority created the opportunity for spousal abuse, and few in that culture would have questioned it. The husband, as the stronger sex (both physically and culturally), had the power to dominate and rule his wife.

Peter's language, in its own way, subverts those dominant cultural perceptions.

- Live in the house *with* (συνοικοῦντες) your wife in an understanding way.
- Show her honor as an heir *with* (συγκληρονόμοις) you in the kingdom of God.

Peter calls for shared life or life together. Two verbs describe Peter's point. The first is "live with" (συνοικοῦντες), which is derived from the combination of "with" (σὺν) and "house" (οἶκός). In other words, live in the same house with your wife, and treat her with honor as a "weaker" member. The description of women as "weaker" probably reflects ancient perceptions. Karen Jobes, for example, cites Xenophon (*Oeconomicus*, 7.23–28), who argued that men are stronger and more courageous.[11] These attitudes are embedded in cultural expectations, stereotypes, and traditions.

Peter's specific point, however, is not to put down women by identifying them as weaker. In fact, he may mean it in a way that deserves scare quotes, as if he is using it in a stereotypical way. Despite the denotations accompanying the word "weaker" within the culture, husbands should treat their wives "according to knowledge," that is, according to what is true, real, and known within the Christian worldview. Marginalized, "weaker," women should not be patronized as weaker, inferior humans. Instead, they should be treated according to the values of Christian ethics ("knowledge," new life through new birth) so they are no longer regarded as "weaker" (inferior) and no longer marginalized in these relationships.

The second verb ("show") means to apportion or to give. In other words, husbands are to honor their wives. This kind of honor is significant. It entails a with-ness or shared reality because they are fellow heirs (συγκληρονόμοις) of the kingdom of God. They are co-heirs. This kind of honor underscores their togetherness.

It appears Peter intentionally uses language to stress the shared life of husband and wife, that is, there is a with-ness in their relationship.[12] Living with (*syn*) each other, they honor each other as co-heirs (σὺν). Rather than dominating his wife or exercising authority over her, he shares life with his wife. This shared life, honor, and inheritance reflect mutuality. It transcends the expectations of Roman culture. Indeed, it subverts it.

---

[11] Jobes, *1 Peter*, 209.

[12] See Abeneazer G. Urga, "The Exhortation to the Husbands and Its Significance in the Conversation About the Household Codes: 1 Peter 3:7," *Priscilla Papers* 38.4 (2024), available at https://www.cbeinternational.org/resource/the-exhortation-to-the-husbands-and-its-significance-in-the-conversation-about-the-household-codes-1-peter-37/.

CONCLUSION

In many ways, Joan lives in similar fearful circumstances. Like the first readers of 1 Peter, she is exposed to potential abuse, marginalization, and even violence. Her cultural situation, given her Christian commitments and practices, is precarious.

How might we counsel her? I imagine some egalitarians might suggest an aggressive stance that rebels against patriarchy and actively seeks to overthrow it (though, perhaps, applied with some appropriate wisdom). I imagine some traditional complementarians might suggest full compliance with patriarchy as a matter of God's intended order rooted in creation. Peter, addressing an analogous situation, does not adopt either of those options. On the contrary, he adopts a missional strategy that provides opportunity for witness and doing good. He neither endorses nor promotes complementarianism or egalitarianism. He advises a path of peaceful engagement for the sake of God's mission to transform the situation.

Perhaps, appropriating Peter's counsel, we might say to Joan, whether the adviser is egalitarian (mutualist) or complementarian, something like this:

> *Dear Joan,*
>
> *I honor your commitment to Jesus, and I am so grateful you have found inner peace because of God's grace and mercy.*
>
> *As a disciple of Jesus, you live in a terrifying circumstance. At the same time, your greatest desire is to love your husband and children well in a way faithful to our Lord Jesus Christ. You know the example Jesus has set for us in enduring hardship for the sake of others.*
>
> *This calling means you accept the authority of your husband, live peacefully within the cultural boundaries of your community (including wearing the hijab), and obey your husband according to the order under which you live. You must live peacefully within Islamic culture if it does not violate your commitment to Jesus. This may mean you will endure some abuse. However, if you find legal and peaceful ways to escape such, you are free to pursue those options.*
>
> *Remember Sarah, Abraham's faithful wife, respected and obeyed her husband under fearful circumstances. You would do well to follow her example, given your situation.*
>
> *Most of all, practice a gentle and peaceable presence without embracing the symbols of power and wealth where you live. By so doing, perhaps, you might win your husband to the Lord, even without a word.*
>
> *Grace and peace, dear sister.*

11
Adornment in Context: Illuminating the Passages on Womanhood in 1 Timothy

Anessa Westbrook[1]

INTRODUCTION

The meaning of passages about adornment and childbearing has left churches puzzled, with church leaders unsure how to teach them and women uncertain how to implement them. Should women use head coverings? What types of jewelry and attire are women allowed to wear? How are women saved through childbearing? Unfortunately, the question about childbearing has even led to a spiritual crisis in some of the women with whom I have worked. This chapter will focus on creating a better understanding of 1 Tim 2, its cultural background, and the challenges faced by the church in Ephesus. A comparative look at 1 Pet 3:1–7 will also help provide clarity and guidance on how to approach these passages.

BACKGROUND

Next only to Rome, Ephesus was the most important city that Paul visited on his missionary journeys. It was strategically located along river, land, and sea routes, providing an important connection between the East and the West. Not only did it become the capital city of the Roman province of Asia, but it was heavily populated and wealthy.[2] The rapidly growing city's population at the time of early Christianity is estimated at 250,000.[3] In Acts 19, Ephesus's 25,000-person theatre is referenced, a good indicator of its size and the quality of its public facilities. Because of the linking of the east-west trade routes, multiple cultures created a confluence of Greek, Roman, and local beliefs. While there is no evidence of women filling senior municipal offices during the first

---

[1] This essay is in honor of Dr. Allen Black. Dr. Black opened my eyes into the realities faced by women in the first century, and the complexity of the questions that the early church faced on their behalf.

[2] Sharon Hodgin Gritz, *Paul, Women Teachers, and the Mother Goddess at Ephesus: A Study of 1 Timothy 2:9–15 in Light of the Religious and Cultural Milieu of the First Century* (Lanham: University Press of America, 1991), 12–13.

[3] Richard E. Oster, Jr., "Ephesus," in *The Oxford Companion to the Bible*, ed. Bruce M. Metzger and Michael D. Coogan (New York: Oxford University Press, 1993), 189.

century, there were positions open to younger girls, and women had access to public offices for the first time during the first century.[4] Josephus also noted that there was a significant Jewish population there.[5] Paul had special focus on this important city, spending two years lecturing there in the hall of Tyrannus (Acts 19).

Ephesus was known for the goddess Artemis, also known as Diana. Her temple, called the *Artemision*, dwarfed the Parthenon in Athens at about four times its size.[6] This temple is considered one of the seven wonders of the ancient world.[7] Artemis was held in high honor above other gods, thus referenced in Acts 19:27. The second–century Pausanias explained her renown by saying that a building had been built for her of "vast size" and the respect for the Ephesians, as well as the goddess herself, contributed to it.[8] Her reputation remained strong without significant decline during the period of 50–150 CE, a trend which continued into the second century. Artemis "was well known throughout the world for her goodness and for the success she had brought to Ephesus."[9]

The Temple of Artemis was a place where wealth was deposited, and it controlled huge financial estates, gave out loans, and provided employment.[10] The mother goddess Artemis was a chaste goddess with no sexual acts associated with her or the Temple.[11] This allowed married women to be able to worship the goddess with a clear conscience, appealing to her for safety in childbearing. However, Sharon Gritz suggests that the Ephesian version did not maintain the chastity of this goddess, which would have created a socially accepted understanding of sexual immorality, which the early church would have had to counteract.[12] In addition, other mystery cults in the ancient Near East utilized priestesses and shrine prostitutes.[13] With Ephesus being a link from the east to the west, these influences surely would have been felt there as well.

There were also two other local beliefs that affected the religious scene. The first belief was the emphasis on magic and incantations. Ephesus attracted Jewish exorcists

---

[4] S. M. Baugh, "A Foreign World, Ephesus in the First Century," in *Women in the Church: An Interpretation and Application of 1 Timothy 2:9–15*, 3rd ed., ed. Andrea J. Kostenberger and Thomas R. Schreiner (Wheaton: Crossway, 2016), 32, 50.

[5] Oster, "Ephesus," 189.

[6] Michael J. Gorman, *Apostle of the Crucified Lord* (Grand Rapids: Eerdmans, 2017), 577.

[7] Oster, "Ephesus," 189.

[8] Pausanias, *Description of Greece*, 4.31.8.

[9] Rick Strelan, *Paul, Artemis, and the Jews in Ephesus* (New York: de Gruyter, 2014), 81.

[10] Strelan, *Paul, Artemis, and the Jews in Ephesus*, 76–77.

[11] Strelan, *Paul, Artemis, and the Jews in Ephesus*, 72–73.

[12] Gritz, *Paul, Women Teachers, and the Mother Goddess at Ephesus*, 38.

[13] Gritz, *Paul, Women Teachers, and the Mother Goddess at Ephesus*, 35.

and magic, as can be seen in Acts 19:11–20, when the seven sons of Sceva, a Jewish high priest, attempted to drive out an evil spirit. After the evil spirit refused them because they only answered to Jesus and Paul, the city was so affected that they burned scrolls valued at 50,000 days' wages. Second, Artemis worship was influenced by the legacy of the Amazons. These were warrior women who reversed gender roles and raised children on their own. Their connection to Ephesus is well established through literature and art for centuries.[14] Pliny reported the influence of this culture on the temple, which featured Amazon women.[15]

Citing the strong examples of powerful women influencing the city, Edgar Stubbersfield says, "Ephesus was a city where women could at least dream of freedom from male domination."[16] While there would have been a range of attitudes towards women, the women would have also benefited from the gradual changes occurring in the Greco-Roman world, which provided some improved liberation and esteem for women.[17] The presence of Artemis and the Amazon women, both examples who were single and independent, would have certainly been on Paul's mind as he wrote 1 Timothy.

FALSE TEACHING

Proto-Gnosticism was another ideology Paul would have had to deal with. This was a speculative religious belief set in a framework of philosophy, astrology, and mythology that later combined with Christianity. There is evidence of an early form of Gnosticism developing in Ephesus, which would have been present around the time Paul was writing.[18] Scholars dispute if this heresy existed in its full-blown form during the first century, referring to what was present at the time there as proto-Gnosticism.[19] This heresy was developed enough by the time that John wrote his Gospel in Ephesus that he was refuting an early proponent, Cerinthus. Polycarp told the story of John going into a bathhouse in Ephesus and perceiving that the false teacher Cerinthus was within it, so he rushed out without bathing in case the bathhouse should fall down upon the false

---

[14] Sandra L. Glahn, *Nobody's Mother: Artemis of the Ephesians in Antiquity and the New Testament* (Downers Grove: InterVarsity Press, 2023), 40–43.

[15] Pliny, *Natural History*, 34.19.52.

[16] Edgar Stubbersfield, *Women in Ministry: Paul's Advice to Timothy in Its Historical Setting* (Eugene: Wipf & Stock, 2022), 4.

[17] Gritz, *Paul, Women Teachers, and the Mother Goddess at Ephesus*, 15.

[18] Rudolph Bultmann, "γινώσκω," *TDNT*, 1.692–93.

[19] Clinton E. Arnold, *Ephesians*, Zondervan Exegetical Commentary on the New Testament, (Grand Rapids: Zondervan, 2010), 9.

teacher.[20] This account gives us some insight into the angst and influence that this false teaching held in Ephesus.

The false teaching could be summarized as a blend of Christianity, Hellenistic Judaism, and Gnosticism. First Timothy 6:20 refers to "godless chatter" and "opposing ideas of what is falsely called knowledge." This seems similar to what was happening in 1 Corinthians and Colossians, with some who considered themselves more spiritual and who seemed infatuated with knowledge. In Col 2:3–4, wisdom and knowledge are referenced, and Paul says he is teaching them "so that no one may deceive you by fine-sounding arguments." Besides discouraging marriage (1 Tim 4:3), proto–Gnosticism's low view of the body probably led some to question the bodily resurrection of Christ (2 Tim 2:18).

Paul's Challenge to Artemis

While Luke will name specific deities, Paul never names them but alludes to them in ambiguous ways, perhaps only to affirm the one true God by name. Michael Immendörfer believes that Paul demonstrates the importance of Artemis in Ephesus by paraphrasing her so clearly that the readers would know the goddess to which he is referring. He not only uses terminology referencing her but compares her to Christ in order to show the superiority of the Savior.[21] For example, Artemis's main titles were "first throne," "queen," "lord," "savior," "god," and "manifest." Paul used these titles when describing Christ in 1 Timothy, using four of them in the first chapter. This shows Paul's recognition of the goddess's influence and his effort to show the superiority of Christ.[22] This set Paul up to challenge the goddess from the very beginning of 1 Timothy without naming her directly. This is a similar move to what Paul did in Athens in his speech to the Areopagus in Acts 17:22–31. In this speech, he quotes and makes references to the writings of Zeus. By borrowing words and phrases from writings about him, Paul challenged Zeus by comparing writings about him to statements showing the superiority of Yahweh. For example, in Acts 17:27, he used the phrase "though he is not far from any one of us."[23] This referenced the belief that Zeus, who lived approximately 150 miles away on Mount Olympus, seemed far from his people.

---

[20] Irenaeus, *Against Heresies*, 3.11.1 and 3.3.4.

[21] Glahn, *Nobody's Mother*, 113.

[22] Glahn, *Nobody's Mother*, 6.

[23] F. F. Bruce, *The Book of the Acts*, rev. ed. (Grand Rapids: Eerdmans, 1988), 334–40.

CONTEXTUALIZATION

Readers often feel confused when Paul gives drastically different advice from book to book. However, it is important to consider the role of the letters and their context. All four Gospels are focused on telling the Good News of Jesus Christ. Acts covers the history of the early church, but the letters are written to specific groups of people to address specific issues. While some issues may be similar between churches, many congregations had unique struggles that required different guidance and advice. For example, Corinth and Ephesus both have robust systems of pagan worship; however, the specific challenges to the churches are different, so we should expect to see them handled differently.

This is one example of the advice that Paul gave to the women of Ephesus, which was opposite of what he gave to the women of Corinth, who were facing pressure and persecution along with the rest of the church. To the Corinthian women, he urged them to consider remaining unmarried. In 1 Cor 7:8, he advised, "Now to the unmarried and the widows I say: It is good for them to stay unmarried, as I do."[24] However, in Ephesus, young widows were encouraged to marry and bear children in 1 Tim 5:14. To them, Paul advised, "I counsel younger widows to marry, to have children, to manage their homes and to give the enemy no opportunity for slander." Why the sudden change in tone?

The goddess Artemis's promotion of chastity led to a high view of celibacy that was pervasive in the local culture. Rick Strelan writes about Achilles Tatius's novel, saying, "[O]ne of the main points of the story is to demonstrate how those devoted to Artemis—both male and female—will find her a protectress and will retain their virginity despite immense pressures to do otherwise."[25] This emphasis on celibacy, combined with the strong female example of Artemis and the Amazon women, would have impacted womens' ideas surrounding marriage.

Gnosticism had a low view of the body. Childbearing would have been a giving into the role of the body, and some gnostic teachers encouraged women to give up their feminine roles.[26] Additionally, Gnosticism also had prohibitions on marriage, and with Ephesus being a site for its early development, this would have also been on Paul's mind. Paul encouraged pushback against this pagan cultural influence by encouraging young widows to marry and bear children (1 Tim 5:14). Therefore, the advice for the

---

[24] All quotes from the Bible are taken from the New International Version, 2011 version.

[25] Strelan, *Paul, Artemis, and the Jews in Ephesus*, 73.

[26] Richard Clark Kroeger and Catherine Clark Kroeger, *I Suffer Not a Woman: Rethinking 1 Timothy 2:11–15 in Light of Ancient Evidence* (Grand Rapids: Baker, 1992), 176.

young widows to get married would have been counteracting outside religious influences.

Paul's approach is similar to what we see Jesus do in the Gospels. A couple of examples of Jesus pushing back against the prevailing culture can be found in Matt 9. Here, Jesus pushed back against pressure to not eat with sinners or to make his disciples fast.[27] In chapter 10, he challenged the cultural concept of the "retribution principle," which promoted the idea that the wicked would suffer and the righteous would prosper. Given this principle, the rich young ruler in Matt 10:17–31 would have been an example of righteousness, his answers to Jesus of how he had kept the law since he was a boy accentuating that perception. However, Jesus challenged the very characteristic others would have seen as a blessing from God: the rich young ruler's wealth. Jesus challenged him to give it up, and when he would not, Jesus commented on how hard it was for the rich to enter into the kingdom of heaven. Jesus challenged the prevailing cultural understanding of what blessing from God looked like, giving hope to the majority of the early Christians who were poor that they could also experience God's blessing.

PAUL'S HANDLING OF INFLUENCES ON NEW CONVERTS

When someone is baptized, previous experiences and beliefs do not wash away in the water but instead can be carried with them into their new faith. One of the major tasks of the early church was to monitor and rid itself of outside influences that were constantly attempting to creep in. In Roman areas, the churches were largely made up of converts from other pagan religions who were used to operating and worshiping in specific ways that were counter to what was practiced in the early church.

Women converting from the cult of Artemis would have carried expectations of their role with them. Women were able to serve as high priestesses in Asia. While scholars such as S. M. Baugh believed these women were leaning on their husbands' reputation, there are many inscriptions that do not name a male relative or patron.[28] With this in the background, when women were coming from a religion in which they could be actively involved it might have been difficult for them to accept restrictions upon roles they had already filled.[29] Stubbersfield points out that men who converted from Judaism were also unlikely to want to accept changes to the subordinate position

---

[27] See also Mark 2:15–22 and Luke 5:29–39.

[28] Linda L. Belleville, "Exegetical Fallacies in Interpreting 1 Timothy 2:11–15," *Priscilla Papers* 17.3 (2003): 7.

[29] Stubbersfield, *Women in Ministry*, 25.

that they were accustomed to women holding.[30] These two competing expectations would certainly create an environment that would require careful navigation by Paul.

As Paul worked with churches in Gentile areas whose pagan setting had cultural and religious impact, he worked to rid them of outside influences such as idolatry, immorality, classism, and external pressure on households. For example, in 1 Corinthians, Paul addressed a whole host of issues that had crept into the church. In Gal 2:11–13, Paul confronted Peter because of his distancing himself from the Gentile Christians as a Jew, a change in practice seemingly because of peer pressure from James. In 1 Cor 11:3–6, Christian men who had formerly worshipped in pagan religions imported the practice of wearing a head covering into the church, the use of which indicated socioeconomic status, something that was incompatible with the Christian community.[31] In 1 Tim 5:13, the issue of false teaching was certainly a concern, with young widows going from house to house spreading false teaching.[32] As in other cities, counteracting other religious practices would have been at the forefront of Paul's mind in Ephesus.

Adornment

After addressing false teaching, Paul addressed another issue that had crept into the church: adornment. Strelan writes, "Ephesian women had a reputation for wealth, beauty, and virtue."[33] The emphasis on adornment probably entered into the church from two different sources: emphasis on adornment from the local practices of the cult of Artemis and typical Roman adornment practices, which also marked women socially. The Ephesians might have been especially focused on adornment because of the tradition of adorning the statue of Artemis. In many festivals, a feature was to wash, oil, crown, and dress Artemis.[34] Therefore, the topic of adornment would likely have been an important aspect of their local culture.

Paul addressed modesty in 1 Tim 2:9, specifically encouraging women not to adorn themselves with "elaborate hairstyles or gold or pearls or expensive clothes." We see a similar list in 1 Pet 3:3, which states, "Your beauty should not come from outward adornment, such as elaborate hairstyles and the wearing of gold jewelry or fine clothes." The character of a woman was reflected in what she wore. For the Romans,

---

[30] Stubbersfield, *Women in Ministry*, 25.

[31] Although not written by Paul, James 2:1–9 explores a scenario where a wealthy man is given preferable seating, further indication of the push to rid the church of socioeconomic indicators.

[32] The phrase "house to house" is also used to describe church gatherings in Jerusalem in Acts 2:46 and Acts 5:42. It is also found in 2 Tim 3:6.

[33] Strelan, *Paul, Artemis, and the Jews in Ephesus*, 119.

[34] Strelan, *Paul, Artemis, and the Jews in Ephesus*, 74.

clothing "accurately reflected the birth, wealth, moral character, social standing and the personal influence of a person."[35] A woman's adornment not only displayed who she was but whose she was.[36] Purple, gems, and gold specifically could indicate a woman's own financial base, status, or influence. The use of these indicated a desire to be seen as different from the lower classes, marking her social position.[37] Beauty and adornment were immediately visible ways for a woman to put herself forward in society, to create a social space for herself, and to construct herself as an individual."[38] Kelly Olson says, "[B]eauty, cosmetics, and fashion were ways for a woman to create visibility and personal space for herself, to enjoy other's attention and admiration, and to wield power and influence over those around her."[39] Roman women could own and pass down property. Jewelry was durable wealth for a woman since it would not wear out.[40] Pliny stated that a pearl, for instance, could be passed to an heir or offered up for public sale.[41]

Adornment, however, was also viewed negatively since it changed a woman's natural appearance, could be linked to unchastity, and was wasteful in both time and resources.[42] "Elaborate hairstyles, especially those of the second and third centuries CE required an excess of leisure and slave labor, and thus marked the woman so adorned as being of (or wishing to belong to) the elite class."[43] Women were encouraged to be unadorned. Plautus believed that a woman who wore purple was overdressed. Cicero believed that women were more beautiful when unadorned.[44]

While modesty was certainly a virtue that the Greco-Roman culture valued, Paul's naming of elaborate hairstyles, gold, pearls, and expensive clothing does not seem to relate to physical modesty as they were unattainable to the average woman without leisure time or economic means. These specific items would have indicated that a woman belonged to the ruling or upper class—an indication of rank that was incompatible with the Christians' ideals of everyone standing equal before Christ (Gal 3:28). Paul's advice to the Ephesian women might have been to challenge their socio-

---

[35] Kelly Olson, *Dress and the Roman Woman: Self–Presentation and Society* (New York: Routledge, 2008), 98, 113.

[36] Glahn, *Nobody's Mother*, 123.

[37] Olson, *Dress and the Roman Woman*, 115.

[38] Olson, *Dress and the Roman Woman*, 111.

[39] Olson, *Dress and the Roman Woman*, 108.

[40] Olson, *Dress and the Roman Woman*, 98.

[41] Pliny, *Natural History*, 9.124.

[42] Olson, *Dress and the Roman Woman*, 80.

[43] Olson, *Dress and the Roman Woman*, 114.

[44] Olson, *Dress and the Roman Woman*, 91–92.

economic status. The focus on adornment ran counter to this goal as it marked people in a certain way.

THE NEW ROMAN WIFE

Around 44 BC, a new type of wife appeared among the upper class in Rome. Wealthy women pushed back against acceptance of their husband's extramarital liaisons to develop their own. These women had the right to divorce and even claim back their dowries, lessening their personal risk through their actions.[45] This practice became so widespread that in CE 9, Augustus became so concerned with the falling birthrate and deterioration of the family that he issued legislation on marriage, remarriage, and divorce.[46] He went so far as to make legislative distinctions between a modest wife, an adulteress, and a prostitute.[47] Bruce W. Winter says, "It is sometimes overlooked that the Christian movement was not the only one that sought to represent its view of marriage against an antithetical image in society."[48] Paul was not alone in his concerns. Poets, philosophers, and historians expressed concern about these developments surrounding the role of women.[49] Addressing issues with broad influence, in addition to those of local concern, would have certainly been within Paul's prerogative. This may have led him to discuss the importance of childbearing.

SAVED THROUGH CHILDBEARING

In 1 Tim 2:15, Paul further emphasized his encouragement for women to marry and bear children by saying that they will be "saved through childbearing."[50] This statement has created a lot of guilt and confusion among women who either cannot have children or who are not married. From a practical standpoint, if Paul was saying that women could not be saved without physically birthing a child, this excludes men, children, and women who cannot have children. As Christopher R. Hutson says, "[T]o imagine that a woman will be saved to eternal life by means of bearing children requires tortuous logic indeed."[51] This would not make sense, and a literal understanding also goes

---

[45] Bruce W. Winter, "The 'New Roman Wife' and 1 Timothy 2:9–15: The Search for a *Sitz im Leben*," *TynBul* 51.2 (2000): 287.

[46] Winter, "The New Roman Wife," 291.

[47] Thomas A. J. McGinn, *Prostitution, Sexuality, and the Law in Ancient Rome* (Oxford: Oxford University Press, 1998), 154.

[48] Winter, "The New Roman Wife," 294.

[49] Winter, "The New Roman Wife," 288–90.

[50] Glahn, *Nobody's Mother,* 118.

[51] Christopher R. Hutson, *First and Second Timothy and Titus* (Grand Rapids: Baker Academic, 2019), 79.

against the core of the Gospel message itself since Jesus never alluded to any salvation other than that which was granted by God and marked by repentance, belief, and baptism.

There also would have certainly been local concerns that Paul would need to address. Artemis was the goddess of midwifery, and Paul referenced this to highlight that Jesus was the one who saves, thus the use of the word σῴζω. By using this specific terminology, Paul was showing the superiority of Yahweh to Artemis. Women who had converted from Artemis worship certainly would have been nervous approaching childbirth without being able to appeal to the goddess for safe delivery. Artemis was known as the patron of women in childbirth.[52] This may explain Paul's use of the term "saved." While Paul did not generally use the term σῴζω, his use here is interesting, especially as it also shows up in several places in 1 and 2 Timothy. This seems to be a reference to teachings about Artemis, which appears to be a move to show the superiority of Yahweh over Artemis, including in the area of childbearing and reassurance about God being with women during childbirth.

There has been a robust discussion among scholars about what the term σῴζω could mean. Suggestions have ranged from the physical to the spiritual. Given the issues with women's role in society, it could have been an encouragement for women to uphold the typical feminine roles. George W. Knight III suggests another understanding, writing that "it refers to spiritual salvation through the birth of the Messiah."[53] He believes that this view has been rejected by some without giving it adequate reflection. He proposes that this also explains Paul's reference to the fall. Sin entered into the world through Adam and Eve, and it was only through the Messiah that one can be saved from it. Paul took this one step further to call for restraint and discretion when it comes not only to role but also to how one presents herself to her community.[54] Rabbinic tradition has written about the connection between women who do not follow the commandments and death in childbirth. This connection is reminiscent of the retribution principle, encouraging virtuous women who are following the commands of God by saying that God will protect them in childbearing.[55]

---

[52] Richard E. Oster, Jr., "Artemis of the Ephesians," in *The Oxford Companion to the Bible*, ed. Bruce M. Metzger and Michael D. Coogan (New York: Oxford University Press, 1993), 60.

[53] George W. Knight, III, *The Pastoral Epistles: A Commentary on the Greek Text* (Grand Rapids: Eerdmans, 1992), 146.

[54] Knight, *The Pastoral Epistles*, 146–48.

[55] Hutson, *First and Second Timothy and Titus*, 79.

PAUL'S USE OF JEWISH EXAMPLES

First Timothy 2:11 indicated a problem that had arisen in the church. Paul instructed women to learn in quietness and full submission. Paul followed this by asking the women not to engage in the same type of disputes and anger that had been present among the men but rather to learn in a modest way marked by quietness and submission. Winter believes that the limitation of this statement particularly to wives may reflect Roman law, which does call for regulated behavior patterns.[56]

He then appears to follow this with an example taken from the Jewish concepts of primogeniture, citing Adam to show that men were the firstborn. First Timothy 2 seems to reflect the account in Gen 2, creating a literary connection.[57] One surprising statement in 1 Tim 2:14 is that Adam was not deceived. A. E. Harvey has suggested that this may be pushing back on the local teachings about the superiority of women over men by holding up Adam as the one who did not sin.[58] This is a rather odd example to use here, given that the main influences in Ephesus were pagan, and it begs the question whether Paul is drawing upon the Genesis story in response to a competing interpretation of false teaching. The basic argument for the superiority of the first created, the priority of creation, is offered in 1 Tim 2:13. This is widely accepted in both Jewish and Greek sources.[59] However, Linda Belleville notes that the "first–then" language points to a temporal sequence of events and ideas rather than ontological or functional priority. She points to 1 Thess 4:16–17, where the dead will rise first, then those who are alive will join Christ in the air. Here, the dead do not have an advantage over being raised first. Here, the "first-then" argument does not hold true; neither does it in 1 Tim 2.[60] Paul may have made this reference as an argument against the Ephesian origin story, which viewed Artemis as firstborn. Within the cult of Artemis, "the female was exalted and considered superior to the male."[61] He then compared her origin story to that of Jewish Scripture to show that God is superior to Artemis. "The apostle corrects a false story with a true one. He is using a narrative to counter a competing narrative."[62]

---

[56] Bruce W. Winter, *Roman Wives, Roman Widows* (Grand Rapids: Eerdmans, 2003), 3.

[57] Philip H. Towner, "1–2 Timothy and Titus," in *Commentary on the New Testament Use of the Old Testament*, ed. G. K. Beale and D. A. Carson (Grand Rapids: Baker Academic, 2007), 894.

[58] A. E. Harvey, *A Companion to the New Testament*, 2nd ed. (New York: Cambridge University Press, 2004), 664.

[59] Towner, "1–2 Timothy and Titus," 895.

[60] Belleville, "Exegetical Fallacies," 8.

[61] Belleville, "Exegetical Fallacies," 7.

[62] Glahn, *Nobody's Mother*, 133.

If the new Christians were importing this practice, and the Ephesian women were presenting themselves as superior to men, then this might help explain Paul's statements in 1 Tim 2:13–14.[63] First Tim 2:8 indicates that there is strife in the teaching, asking men to "[lift] up holy hands without anger or disputing." There was a false content to some of the teaching, and from 1 Tim 2:12 we know that some of the women were involved with it. I. Howard Marshall suggests the following:

> In the context it seems most likely that through their being 'deceived' there was a false content to their teaching and that this element included some kind of emancipatory tendency, especially by wealthy women (cf. 2.9f), expressed in what was a socially unacceptable way in that time and culture. There may have well been a misreading of material in Genesis as part of the speculative use of 'myths and genealogies' practiced by the writer's opponents, further, the tendency to abstain from certain foods and from marriage on the part of the opposition must have included a rejection of sexual relations and the bearing of children.[64]

He goes on to suggest that because of the women's previous experiences, they might have viewed teaching as necessary, but in this case, Paul reminded them that fulfilling their role as women was what was necessary. If the false teaching also discouraged women from motherhood, then this would be especially important for Paul to refute. This places these verses in the same category as others which refute references to false teaching.[65]

The Greek word γυνή, which is used for both woman and wife, is deeply dependent upon context. However, 1 Tim 2:15 gives an indication of which population Paul was referring to in this section, as only wives would be bearing children. This makes more sense than a blanket prohibition since Paul commands older women to teach younger women in Titus 2:3–5. In 1 Cor 11, Paul also referenced women prophesying. It appears that the women in Ephesus had abused their authority in the way they were teaching, but this opens the door to the probability that Paul was not prohibiting women from teaching in all situations in 1 Timothy. Paul had the difficult task of addressing a variety of challenges in different cultural and church settings. To take one of his statements and make it universal makes his writings contradict one another.

---

[63] Belleville, "Exegetical Fallacies," 8.

[64] I. Howard Marshall, *A Critical and Exegetical Commentary on The Pastoral Epistles* (New York: T&T Clark, 2003), 441.

[65] Marshall, *The Pastoral Epistles*, 441

While it is impossible to ascertain why Paul chose to use a Jewish example, perhaps it is because Jesus was the Messiah first to the Jews that Paul chose to utilize Jewish examples. However, it could simply be that Paul's use of his Jewish lens as being the "Hebrew of Hebrews" (Phil 3:5) that caused his selection of this example.

CONCLUSION

The instructions to women in 1 Tim 2 have created confusion and additional questions, and teachers and preachers alike have found teaching on these passages challenging. Part of the issue has been our tendency to read the text without taking into account the complex cultural milieu that affected the Ephesian church. When this chapter is being studied and taught, efforts need to be taken to understand the complexities of it. Hutson says when we are going to teach about the role of women in 1 Tim 2:11–12, "we have a burden to explain the logic of 2:13–15."[66] When cultural background is considered, verses and phrases that are hard to comprehend come into sharper focus. As with any of Paul's letters, we need to take time to understand the setting in order to understand the teaching. Without their context, we run the risk of drawing conclusions that are not true to the original meaning of the text. While this is necessary with any section of Scripture, when it comes to handling the "tricky passages" scattered among the various church situations Paul was trying to address, it is even more vital.

---

[66] Hutson, *First and Second Timothy and Titus*, 80.

12
Justification by Faith (and Works)?

Barry Blackburn[1]

INTRODUCTION

A primary cause of the Protestant Reformation was a dispute over the Catholic doctrine of justification by faith and works (spelled out at the Council of Trent [1545–1563]). The magisterial reformers (primarily Martin Luther and John Calvin) insisted that the Holy Scriptures (especially Romans and Galatians) taught that justification is conditioned only on faith in Christ. Therefore, it is interesting that the Stone-Campbell reformers followed Alexander Campbell, a former Presbyterian, in holding a position similar to that of the Catholic Church. Were the Stone-Campbell reformers correct in their rejection of justification by faith alone, the doctrine regarded by many Protestants as "the doctrine upon which the church stands or falls" (Luther)? This article aims to answer this question with a "yes," at least with respect to our acceptance before God on the Day of Judgment. Inclusion in the consummated Kingdom of God will be conditioned on faith and works.

SETTING THE STAGE: JUSTIFICATION IN PROTESTANT AND CATHOLIC THEOLOGY

Martin Luther (1483–1546) discovered relief for his tortured conscience and his fear of being damned on Judgment Day in Paul's teaching that believers are justified by faith as opposed to the works of the law (for example, Rom 3:28), a doctrine which he described as "justification by faith alone." Luther exalted this teaching as the doctrine upon which the church stands or falls.[2]

According to Luther and other magisterial Protestant reformers,[3] especially John Calvin (1509–1564), this doctrine provides believers the absolute assurance of right standing before God *throughout* the Christian life and, most importantly, *at the Day of*

---

[1] I met Allen Black in the summer of 1974, as we were about to embark on our studies at (as it was called then) Harding Graduate School of Religion. We hit it off immediately and bonded even more as we studied under Professors Carroll Osburn and Jack Lewis, among others. Those three years were the beginning of a lifelong and rare friendship of encouragement and camaraderie. His love for the church has inspired me and his scholarship has guided me. I hope that the following article will honor his desire to follow the One who is the Way, the Truth, and the Life.

[2] Martin Luther, *Luthers Werke: Kritische Gesamtausgabe [Schriften]* (73 vols.; Weimar: H. Böhlau, 1883–2009), 40/3: 352.

[3] I stress *magisterial* reformers because "justification by faith alone" was rejected by the Anabaptist tradition (Timothy George, *Theology of the Reformers* [Nashville: Broadman, 1988], 269).

Judgment. According to the reformers, faith, given to the believer by God in such a way that it cannot be resisted, would naturally show itself in obedience to God's commands, including works of mercy. A favorite Reformation slogan is "Faith alone saves, but the faith that saves is not alone."[4] Be that as it may, the reformers sharply distinguished between "faith" (mental assent to the Gospel and trust in the God of Jesus Christ) and "works" (acts of obedience to God's will). "Works" are fruit and evidence of "faith," but only the latter, it is claimed, is the *condition* of our right standing with God. This manner of understanding the relationship between believers and God, so claimed the Reformers, enables believers to have absolute confidence in their right standing before God in the present *and in the future*.

This doctrine placed the magisterial Protestant reformers at loggerheads with the Roman Catholic Church, which taught that the faith of Christians would have to be accompanied by works in order for them to remain in a state of grace during their lifetimes and be ushered into Heaven on Judgment Day. This Catholic teaching on the saving role of good works received its classic expression in the "Decree concerning Justification" formulated during the sixth session of the Council of Trent (January 13, 1547), which was the Catholic Church's response to the Protestant Reformation.[5]

Catholics agreed with the reformers that at the outset of the Christian life, justification is pure gift.[6] Justification must be preceded by faith and repentance, and it becomes a reality in baptism, but no actions prior to and including repentance and baptism merit the righteous state given us when we are justified by God. As the fathers of Trent say:

> We are therefore said to be justified freely, because that none of those things which precede justification—whether faith or works—merit the grace itself of justification. For, if it be a grace, it is not now by works, otherwise, as the same Apostle says, grace is no more grace.[7]

---

[4] For a possible origin of this slogan, see John Calvin's response to Canon 11 of the Sixth Session of Trent in his *Acts of the Council of Trent with the Antidote*, 1547 (https://www.monergism.com/thethreshold/sdg/calvin_trentantidote.html): "I wish the reader to understand that as often as we mention Faith alone in this question, we are not thinking of a dead faith, which worketh not by love, but holding faith to be the only cause of justification (Gal 5:6; Rom 3:22). It is therefore faith alone which justifies, and yet the faith which justifies is not alone: just as it is the heat alone of the sun which warms the earth, and yet in the sun it is not alone, because it is constantly conjoined with light."

[5] An English translation of the "Decree Concerning Justification" can be easily accessed at https://www.papalencyclicals.net/councils/trent/sixth-session.htm. This article will not address the role of faith and works in Eastern Orthodoxy, but limits itself to a theological controversy that emerged in Western Christianity.

[6] However, it should be noted that while Catholics believe that the Holy Spirit gives a person the freedom to accept the gift of faith, adherents of the magisterial reformers believe that God gives faith to elect sinners in such a way that refusal is impossible.

[7] Chapter 8 of the "Decree Concerning Justification."

Thus, faith, repentance, and baptism are necessary conditions of justification, but they do not merit it.

However, so says Trent, after our initial justification, after being forgiven and filled with Holy Spirit who transforms us, and having become inwardly righteous and not righteous in name only, we must apply ourselves to the keeping of God's commandments, including works of mercy, to remain in the divine favor. Thus, the fathers of Trent describe the ideal for newly justified Christians in this way:

> Having, therefore, been thus justified, and made the friends and domestics of God, advancing from virtue to virtue, they are renewed, as the Apostle says, day by day; that is, by mortifying the members of their own flesh, and by presenting them as instruments of justice unto sanctification, they, through the observance of the commandments of God and of the Church, faith co-operating with good works, increase in that justice which they have received through the grace of Christ.[8]

Thus, after Christians have received their initial justification, for the remainder of the Christian life, including the Last Judgment, the affirmation of James (2:24) holds true: "You see that a person is justified by works and not by faith alone."[9]

This Protestant-Catholic debate is complicated by the fact that the two sides understand "justification" somewhat differently.[10] For Catholics, justification is a *process* that begins when we freely accept the faith in Christ and the love of God that he offers us. Then, throughout the remainder of our lives, God makes us more and more righteous (= just) as we freely cooperate with the indwelling Holy Spirit who makes us more

---

[8] Chapter 10 of the "Decree Concerning Justification."

[9] All biblical quotations are taken from the NRSV. For a Protestant evaluation of Trent's affirmation of justification that is more favorable than many Protestants would allow, see Matthew W. Bates, *Salvation by Allegiance Alone* (Grand Rapids: Baker Academic, 2017), 184–88. In this book and in his more popular *Gospel Allegiance* (Grand Rapids: Brazos Press, 2019), he critiques the typical Protestant doctrine of justification by faith alone, offering "salvation by allegiance alone" as a mediating position between Trent and the magisterial Reformers.

[10] In 1999 the Catholic Church's Pontifical Council for Promoting Christian Unity and the Lutheran World Federation produced a "Joint Declaration on the Doctrine of Justification," which can be viewed at http://www.christianunity.va/content/unitacristiani/en/dialoghi/sezione-occidentale/luterani/dialogo/documenti-di-dialogo/1999-dichiarazione-congiunta-sulla-dottrina-della-giustificazion/en.html. This document contains statements on justification that were accepted by both Catholic and Lutheran participants. For example, "Together we confess: By grace alone, in faith in Christ's saving work and not because of any merit on our part, we are accepted by God and receive the Holy Spirit, who renews our hearts while equipping and calling us to good works" (3.15). Nevertheless, in my opinion this document does not resolve the conflict between Protestants and Catholics as to the role of good works in the final divine verdict on Judgment Day.

holy as we prove obedient to the will of God, grow in the Christian virtues, and show ourselves to be productive in works of mercy and charity.

For Protestants who follow closely the magisterial Reformers, justification is not a process but a divine declaration issued at the outset of the Christian life. According to these Protestants, in response to the faith in Christ that God plants in our hearts, God declares all our sins forgiven and thus acknowledges that we are in a right standing with him. Since this gift of faith is permanent, so that no true believer, as one of the elect, will ever commit apostasy, believers will continue to enjoy right standing with God throughout their lives. On the Day of Judgment, the right standing with God, which believers have enjoyed ever since the declaration of justification, will be confirmed by God in the sight of all.

Catholics and Protestants also disagree with regard to the content of the gift that God offers through the Gospel. Catholics believe that justification is initially accomplished when we receive not only faith but also love for God. Thus, for Catholics, God not only issues a legal decision according to which we are released from the guilt of our sins and placed in a right relationship with him but simultaneously makes us righteous inwardly, for from the very outset of the Christian life we love God, hardly the description of someone who is righteous in name only. For most Protestants, justification is logically prior to sanctification and is based only on faith.

JUSTIFICATION IN THE STONE-CAMPBELL MOVEMENT

Now that we have laid out the Catholic and Protestant conflicting positions on the role of faith and works in the scheme of salvation, we move forward by several centuries to the Stone-Campbell Movement of the 19th century. To get a reading of this movement's approach to the role of faith and works in salvation, I will engage the work of Alexander Campbell, who dominated this movement to a degree that Barton Stone did not.[11]

Alexander Campbell addressed the role of faith and works in justification several times in the journals that he edited, *The Christian Baptist* (1823–1830) and *The Millennial Harbinger* (1830–1870), as well as in his book on *Christian Baptism*.[12] Campbell consistently rejected the Protestant slogan, "justification by faith alone," and argued that there was no contradiction between Paul's denunciation of justification by

---

[11] Barton W. Stone wrote much less on "justification" than did Alexander Campbell. In "Justification," *Christian Messenger* 13 (1843): 9–12, Stone contemplates "justification" as the act by which God forgives sinners and welcomes them into the sphere of salvation. Stone argues that justification occurs "without the deeds of the law [of Moses] in whole or in part" (9), but when sinners obey "the law of Christ, or the gospel" by doing what "the faith or the gospel requires, viz: to believe, to repent, to confess the Lord, and to be baptized into him" (10). In this article Stone does not engage with the teaching of James 2. At any rate, he rejects the teaching that "we are justified by faith alone."

[12] Alexander Campbell, *Christian Baptism with Its Antecedents and Consequents* (1851; repr., Nashville: Gospel Advocate, 1951).

the works of the Law and James's insistence that justification comes not by faith alone but through faith *and* works. In 1827, he cut the knot by maintaining that Paul addressed the justification of those outside of Christ, while James was speaking of the justification of *Christians* during their lives, but especially at the end: "Without faith it is impossible for a sinner to please God, and without works it is impossible for any to be justified in the day when every man shall be rewarded according to his works."[13] Succinctly put, "Sinners are justified by faith, and christians [sic] by works."[14] In this context, Campbell appealed to the judgment scene of Matt 25, where admission to the Kingdom of God is conditioned on acts of mercy.

Later, Campbell modified his earlier interpretation of James by maintaining that what James says about justification by faith and works applies *not only* to the justification of "professors," that is, Christians, at the Last Judgment, *but also* to the initial justification of sinners at the time of conversion. James, he points out, speaks "of a *man*, and not of a *professor* only: for ... he says, 'You see that by works a *man* is justified, and not by faith alone.'"[15] Campbell thus continued to denounce "justification by faith alone" but focused his attention on justification as the initial *pardon* received by sinners when they submit to baptism. In several passages, Campbell points out that the Bible identifies multiple "causes" of justification: faith, God's grace, baptism, Christ's blood, by the name of the Lord Jesus Christ and the Spirit of God, by Christ, by knowledge, and by works (defining works as "the concurrent or concomitant cause").[16] In this scenario, baptism, the crowning act of conversion when forgiveness is bestowed, is "*faith perfected*."[17] The allusion to Jas 2:22 (KJV) is unmistakable ("Seest thou how

---

[13] Alexander Campbell, "'To 'Paulinus.'—Letter III," *The Christian Baptist* 4 (1827): 216.

[14] Campbell, "'To 'Paulinus.'—Letter III," 215.

[15] In 1891, B. W. Johnson, a prominent member of the Disciples of Christ, student of Alexander Campbell, and editor of *The Evangelist* and *The Christian-Evangelist*, published his highly influential *The People's New Testament with Explanatory Notes* in two volumes. For many decades thereafter his notes functioned as an unofficial guide to the interpretation of the NT among the heirs of the Stone-Campbell movement: Disciples of Christ, Christian Churches/Churches of Christ, and a cappella Churches of Christ. In his comments on Jas 2:14-26, Johnson claimed that the apparent contradiction between James and Paul was due to the erroneous teaching that each was combatting. Paul was affirming that works (obedience to the laws of Moses?) without faith (in Christ) would not justify, while James was opposing those who argued that faith alone, without works, would result in justification. "Neither teaches that either faith alone, or works alone will justify." In this brief discussion, Johnson does not define "faith" or "works," nor does he explain "justification" or distinguish between one's initial justification or justification on the Day of Judgment. It is enough for him to emphasize that faith alone is worthless. This clearly places Johnson in Campbell's tradition: "Justification by faith alone" is to be soundly rejected.

[16] "Review of Archippus—No. III," *The Millennial Harbinger* (1831): 268; "Faith Alone," *The Millennial Harbinger* (1840): 492-93; "Justification," *The Millennial Harbinger* (1851): 320; *Christian Baptism*, 225.

[17] *Christian Baptism*, 229.

faith wrought with his [Abraham] works, and by works was faith made perfect"). In Campbell's mind, baptism was not a work of the Law (and thus ineffectual for justification according to Paul) but a "work of faith."[18] Campbell's reasoning, therefore, resulted in a new way of squaring Paul and James: Paul was speaking of "works of the Law" while the "works" of James were (1) "works of faith," baptism in particular, with respect to sinners seeking divine pardon and (2) obedience to God's commands generally with respect to Christians appearing before God on Judgment Day.

Campbell's rejection of "justification by faith alone," whether speaking about the initial justification of sinners or the final justification of believers on the Day of Judgment, has had a profound effect on the denominations sprung from his (and his colleagues') labor. In this regard, the theology of the Stone-Campbell churches has more closely resembled the decisions of Trent than the magisterial Reformers.

THE BIBLICAL CASE FOR JUSTIFICATION BY FAITH AND WORKS ON THE DAY OF JUDGMENT

Now I turn to the burden and body of this article: to demonstrate that the Bible teaches that the divine verdict on Judgment Day will be conditioned on our faith *and* its manifestation in our works. In other words, our faith and works are conditions of our ultimate salvation. In Roman Catholic theology, our good works will "merit" God's favorable verdict on us on Judgment Day.[19] In this essay, however, I will leave this claim to the side and argue only that our good works will constitute a "condition" for receiving the crown of righteousness on the last day.

Throughout the NT, the salvation of humans is depicted as a process. There is a *beginning* when we entrust ourselves to God in the faith that culminates in baptism, in which God confers forgiveness and the gift of the Holy Spirit. There is a *middle*, the living of the Christian life in this "present evil age" (Gal 1:4), during which the Spirit of God transforms us from one degree of glory to another, and an *end* when the Lord raises us from the dead, conforming us completely to the perfect humanity of Jesus and judges us fit to inherit his eternal kingdom.

Of these three "moments," I wish to now focus on the *end*, specifically the Last Judgment. From the time of the providential rise of belief in bodily resurrection in Judaism, there has accompanied it a belief in a Final Judgment conducted by God. Perhaps the earliest attestation of resurrection followed by an implied judgment in Jewish literature appears in Dan 12:2: "Many of those who sleep in the dust of the earth shall awake, some to everlasting life, and some to shame and everlasting contempt." The

---

[18] *Christian Baptism,* 229. Earlier ("'To 'Paulinus.'—Letter III," *Christian Baptist* 4 [1827]: 214–15) Campbell distinguished between "good works," whose end was to help other people, and "acts of devotion," such as prayers, praises, baptism, and the Lord's Supper. It would seem that Campbell's "acts of faith" were more or less the same as these "acts of devotion."

[19] Chapter 16 of the "Decree Concerning Justification."

authors of the New Testament writings accept this (Pharisaic) Jewish conjunction of resurrection and final judgment, with one very significant alteration: The LORD will judge the world through Jesus the Messiah.[20]

In multiple passages in the NT, we are told that at this Last Judgment, "everyone will be repaid for what has been done." This represents an eschatological extension of the OT principle that the LORD "will repay all according to their deeds."[21] Here are most of the relevant NT passages, listed in canonical order:

> For the Son of Man is to come with his angels in the glory of his Father, and then he will repay everyone for what has been done (Matt 16:27).

> Do not be astonished at this; for the hour is coming when all who are in their graves will hear his [Jesus's] voice and will come out—those who have done good, to the resurrection of life, and those who have done evil, to the resurrection of condemnation (John 5:28–29).

> For he [God] will repay according to each one's deeds: to those who by patiently doing good seek for glory and honor and immortality, he will give eternal life; while for those who are self-seeking and who obey not the truth by wickedness, there will be wrath and fury. There will be anguish and distress for everyone who does evil ... but glory and honor and peace for everyone who does good (Rom 2:6–10).

> For all of us must appear before the judgment seat of Christ, so that each may receive recompense for what has been done in the body, whether good or evil (2 Cor 5:10).

> If you invoke as Father the one who judges all people impartially according to their deeds, live in reverent fear during the time of your exile (1 Pet 1:17).

> And all the churches will know that I [Jesus] am the one who searches minds and hearts, and I will give to each of you as your works deserve (Rev 2:23).[22]

> See, I am coming soon; my reward is with me, to repay according to everyone's work (Rev 22:12).

---

[20] For example, John 5:19–23.

[21] Prov 24:12; see also Ps 62:12 and Jer 17:10.

[22] Similarly, 18:6; 20:12–13; 22:12.

The teaching of the foregoing verses is graphically exemplified by Jesus's prophetic depiction of the Last Judgment in Matt 25:31–46. Here, the criterion of judgment is participation in deeds of mercy: feeding the hungry, providing drink to the thirsty, welcoming the stranger, clothing the naked, caring for the sick, and visiting the prisoners. By this criterion, the nations are divided into sheep and goats, with the former invited into the Kingdom and the latter expelled into eternal punishment.[23]

In light of the foregoing texts, it would seem impossible to deny that the works of Christians will be a criterion of the Final Judgment. These "works" appear to encompass obedience to the commands of Jesus, including especially deeds of mercy. Thus, righteous Christian behavior in its broadest sense appears to be a condition of entering into the Kingdom prepared from the foundation of the world.

This notion of eternal life as being conditioned on Christian "works" is also supported by the many texts in the NT that portray eternal life as a reward or prize for Christian faithfulness to the teachings of Jesus.[24] The following constitute a sampling of texts that explicitly link the reward to Christian action or behavior and not merely faith or trust as a disposition of the soul.

> Blessed are you when people revile you and persecute you ... on my account. Rejoice and be glad, for your reward is great in heaven (Matt 5:11–12).

> But when you give alms, do not let your left hand know what your right hand is doing, so that your alms may be done in secret; and your Father who sees in secret will reward you (Matt 6:3–4).

---

[23] However, there are some who have argued that the judgment depicted in Matt 24:31–45 is not a judgment of *all* human souls, but is either a judgment of *non*-Christians only or perhaps non-Christian gentiles. An advocate of the former, T. W. Manson observed that "the least of these my brothers" (vv. 40, 45) seems to refer to a group separate from the merciful and those who refrained from mercy (*The Teaching of Jesus* [Cambridge: Cambridge University Press, 1935], 249–50). This observation might be coupled with the fact that "brothers" (ἀδελφοί) in Matthew, when not employed to denote biological brothers (1:2, 11; 4:18, 21; 10:2, 21; 12:46, 47; 13:55; 14:3; 17:1; 19:29; 20:24; 22:25) sometimes seems to be synonymous with "fellow believers" (12:48–50; 18:15, 21, 35; 23:8; 28:10). However, compelling arguments that Matt 25 envisions a universal judgment appear in W. D. Davies and Dale Allison, Jr., *The Gospel of Saint Matthew*, 3 vols. ICC (London: Bloomsbury, 1988-97), 3:429.

[24] See Robert N. Wilkin, "Christians will be Judged by their Works at the *Rewards* Judgment but *not* at the *Final* Judgment," in *Four Views on the Role of Works at the Final Judgment*, ed. Alan P. Stanley (Grand Rapids: Zondervan, 2013), 25–50, for a wholly unconvincing argument that the reward/s promised to those who persevere in faith is/are distinct from the enjoyment of eternal life. In fact, he denies that people who at *any time* in their lives have believed in Christ will even appear at the Last Judgment since their eternal salvation was secured the instant they believed in Christ even if they fail to persevere.

> [W]hoever gives even a cup of cold water to one of these little ones in the name of a disciple—truly I tell you, none of these will lose their reward (Matt 10:42).
>
> But love your enemies, do good, and lend, expecting nothing in return. Your reward will be great, and you will be children of the Most High; for he is kind to the ungrateful and the wicked (Luke 6:35).
>
> Whatever your task, put yourselves into it, as done for the Lord and not for your masters, since you know that from the Lord you will receive the inheritance as your reward (Col 3:23–24).
>
> I have fought the good fight, I have finished the race, I have kept the faith. From now on there is reserved for me the crown of righteousness (2 Tim 4:8).
>
> Be on your guard, so that you do not lose what we have worked for, but may receive a full reward (2 John 8).

Given the survey of biblical teaching provided above, why then would there be objection to claiming that a positive verdict by God on the Day of Judgment will be based not only on faith but also works?[25] Why not apply the words of James ("You see that a person is justified by works and not by faith alone" [2:24]) to the verdict of the Last Judgment?[26] There are three major objections made by heirs of the magisterial Reformation to which we now turn and test.

THE FIRST OBJECTION

First, the magisterial Reformers and their successors have argued that Paul, especially in Romans and Galatians, teaches that our justification before God, from regeneration until Judgment Day, is conditioned only on our faith, a subjective disposition of the soul, namely trust in Christ, that can be distinguished from any acts of obedience, pious observances, and works of mercy.

Take, for example, Rom 4:1–5:

> What then are we to say was gained by Abraham, our ancestor according to the

---

[25] See also Bates, *Allegiance*, 107–10.

[26] While James's prooftexts on justification by works pertain to moments during the lifetime of the righteous (Abraham, when he offered Isaac on the altar [2:23], and Rahab, when she saved the Israelite spies [2:25]), his section on Faith Without Works (2:14–26) is prefaced and followed by references to the Last Judgment (2:12–13; 3:1). This strongly suggests that James would have understood his principle of "justification by works and faith" as operative at the Last Judgment.

flesh? ²For if Abraham was justified by works, he has something to boast about, but not before God. ³For what does the scripture say? "Abraham believed God, and it was reckoned to him as righteousness." ⁴Now to one who works, wages are not reckoned as a gift but as something due. ⁵But to one who does not work but trusts him who justifies the ungodly, such faith is reckoned as righteousness.

Along the same lines, consider Rom 3:27–28:

Then what becomes of boasting? It is excluded. Through what kind of law? That of works? No, rather through the law of faith. ²⁸For we hold that a person is justified by faith apart from works prescribed by the law.

Famously, in Luther's translation of the New Testament into German, he added the word *allein,* "only" after "faith" in 3:28, thus precipitating the most famous slogan of the Reformation: "justification by faith alone."[27]

It is well known that while a monk, Luther's conscience had been tortured by the fear of damnation for his sins and his failure to fulfill the commands of God. His conscience became a demon, continuing to berate him for his many failures to live up to the justice=righteousness of God. He felt liberated when he came to the momentous conclusion that "the righteousness of God" in texts such as Rom 1:17 refers not to God's own righteousness, which Luther could never attain, but to God's gift of a righteous status granted to all who entrust themselves to Jesus in faith. For Luther, this righteousness is granted to those who believe rather than those who try to establish their own righteousness by obedience to the will of God. Thus, Luther pitted "righteousness by faith" against "righteousness by works."

On the basis of select texts, especially Rom 4:1–5, Luther, Calvin, and other Reformers saw Paul as drawing a strong contrast between "doing" (obedience to commands) and "believing"/"trusting." They inflated "*doing the works of the law*" into "obeying God's commandments (whether those of the Law of Moses or those issued by Jesus and his apostles). Thus, the Reformers argued that God places into a right relationship with him those who believe that God handed Jesus over to death for our trespasses and raised him for our justification (Rom 4:24) rather than those who attempt to earn justification by obeying the commands of God. This argument proceeded on the assumption that the Jews of Paul's day believed that they could merit inclusion in God's covenant community in the present and coming Kingdom by obeying the commands of God's law. One can, therefore, understand why, for the Reformers, there could be no other condition besides faith for experiencing the saving favor of God. Justification by faith *alone*!

---

[27] *Die Bibel* (Stuttgart: Deutsche Bibelgesellschaft, 1984).

The position of the magisterial Reformers on the doctrine of "justification by faith" remained secure for well over three hundred years, but the second half of the twentieth century witnessed major challenges and calls for modification.[28] On the one hand, the research into second Temple Jewish sources embodied in E. P. Sanders's *Paul and Palestinian Judaism* (1983) seriously called into question the Christian (especially Protestant) assumption that the Judaism of Paul's day was a *legalistic* religion. According to Sanders, Jewish sources make it clear that membership in Israel was not "earned" but was based on God's gracious election of Israel as his covenant people. A Jew did not merit membership among the covenant people but was born (and circumcised) into it. Once one belonged to the covenant people, with all its privileges, it was necessary to observe the obligations (laws) of the covenant to remain within its boundaries and to inherit the Kingdom to be established at the end time.[29]

The other major flaw of the traditional Protestant doctrine of justification, admirably demonstrated by Krister Stehdahl, James Dunn, and N. T. Wright, was its failure to reckon with the concrete historical-theological context in which Paul spoke of "justification by faith" in Romans and Galatians.[30] In both letters, it is obvious that Paul was adamant that all believers in Christ, Gentile as well as Jew, were heirs of the covenant that God made with Abraham, a covenant that promised that the Gentiles would ultimately be blessed by Abraham's "seed," whom Paul identified as Christ (Gal. 3:16). After the appearance of Messiah Jesus, membership in the covenant renewed by him would by faith and baptism into him, not by Jewish ethnicity or adherence to the laws of Moses that maintained the separation of Jews from Gentiles, especially circumcision, and the laws regarding Sabbath, ritual purity, and food. Particularly in Galatians (see also Acts 15), it is easy to see that some Jewish Christians were trying to convince the Galatian Gentiles that they needed to submit to circumcision and other Mosaic laws in order to be legitimate members of the messianic congregation that Jesus had established. Such aggressive proselyting is not evidenced in Romans, but throughout this long letter, the theological relationship between Jews and Gentiles is a major concern.

Now, it is in *this* context that Paul insisted that justification (which for Paul included forgiveness, reception of the Holy Spirit, and membership in the church) came not by performing the works of the Law but by adherence to/faith in Jesus Christ. In other

---

[28] For a similar account of the following history of NT scholarship, see Bates, *Allegiance*, 112–14.

[29] Notice the similar position espoused by Alexander Campbell in 1827: "[F]aith is accounted to a man for righteousness, by the mere favor of God. But the continued enjoyment of such a state is by the same favor made to depend on our behavior" ("Paulinus," 215).

[30] Krister Stendahl, "The Apostle Paul and the Introspective Conscience of the West," *HTR* 56 (1963): 199–215; James D. G. Dunn, *The Theology of Paul the Apostle* (Grand Rapids: Eerdmans, 1998), 334–89; N. T. Wright, *Paul and the Faithfulness of God*, Christian Origins and the Question of God, vol. 4 (Minneapolis: Fortress Press, 2013), 912–1042; N. T. Wright, *Justification: God's Plan & Paul's Vision* (Downers Grove: InterVarsity Academic, 2009).

words, Gentile believers (*qua* Gentiles) stood on equal footing with their Jewish sisters and brothers. There could be no possible theological unity between Jews and Gentiles were it otherwise.

For Paul, the justification that was experienced by Jews and Gentiles as soon as they put their faith in Jesus the Messiah was not received on the condition of prior good works but on faith. But this initial declaration of justification at the outset of the Christian life was, as Wright has argued, an anticipation of the "final" justification to be pronounced at the Last Judgment when all "appear before the judgment seat of Christ" and are recompensed "for what has been done in the body, whether good or evil" (2 Cor 5:10).[31] This is precisely the final justification discussed by Paul in Rom 2:1–16, which will occur when "God, through Jesus Christ, will judge the secret thoughts of all" (2:16).[32] In that judgment, as in 2 Cor 5:10, God will "repay each according to each one's deeds," bestowing eternal life on those "who by patiently doing good seek for glory and honor and immortality" (2:6–7), that is to say, on everyone who "does good" (2:10). This final judgment will be based, in the words of James (3:22), not on faith in contrast to works, but on faith "perfected by works."[33]

As we saw above, Paul's anticipation of a final justification according to works is also attested by Jesus (according to the Gospels), the author of 2 Timothy, the author of 1 Peter, and John the Prophet. It would seem impossible to deny that the NT uniformly understands that all, including Christians, will be judged according to their works on the Day of Judgment when Jesus returns. But if this is so, then the final judgment of believers will not be "by faith alone," but by faith *and* the manner in which believers live their lives.

THE SECOND OBJECTION

Many Protestant theologians would say that if our ultimate justification is conditioned not only, of course, on faith but also by works, then the door is opened for Christians to attribute their final justification, at least partially, to their own efforts. This then could

---

[31] This initial and final justification is also evidenced in Rom 5:9: "Much more surely then, now that we have been justified by his blood, will we be saved through him from the wrath of God." "Being saved from the wrath of God" is tantamount to receiving a positive verdict on the Day of Judgment, when the "final" justification is pronounced (see also Rom 2:5 and 1 Thess 1:10). Since the Greek word for "justification" is normally used in the setting of a trial in a law court to denote a positive outcome, one can scarcely object to the language of a "final justification" since our appearance before God upon resurrection is envisioned as "the Day of Judgment."

[32] For this interpretation of Rom 2:1–16 see, for example, Wright, *Paul*, 1088–89, and John M. G. Barclay, *Paul & the Power of Grace* (Grand Rapids: Eerdmans, 2020), 78–82.

[33] The author of 2 Tim 4:8 hoped to receive "the crown of righteousness" that the Lord would award on the Day of Judgment to all who love him. See also Col 3:23–24, where the author of Colossians encouraged Christian slaves to do their work "as to the Lord," knowing that they would receive the inheritance as their reward.

lead Christians to boast about themselves, an unseemly behavior which Paul, in particular, forbids (Rom 3:27; 4:2; 1 Cor 1:26–31; Gal 6:14; Phil 3:3; see also Eph 2:8–9).

Of course, it is true that some Christians may boast in their obedience to the commands of Christ, just as some may boast in their faith. The NT, however, excludes any grounds for boasting, whether with regard to faith or faithful Christian living. That the believer's initial response of faith to the word of the gospel is a gift is attested by Rom 12:3; 1 Thess 1:4–5; Eph 2:8–10;[34] and Acts 16:14.[35]

However, the Lord who gifts believers with their initial faith in the gospel also empowers them to obey the commands of Jesus, including the performance of acts of mercy. Believers are, of course, personally present in their actions but cannot boast about them, for it is God through the Spirit of Christ that inspires and enables them to obey and perform good works. The following Pauline texts are classics in that regard:

> For through the law I died to the law, so that I might live to God. I have been crucified with Christ; and it is no longer I who live, but it is Christ in me. And the life I now live in the flesh I live by faith in the Son of God (Gal 2:19–20a).

> Therefore, my beloved, just as you have always obeyed me ... work out your own salvation with fear and trembling; for it is God who is at work in you, enabling you both to will and to work for his good pleasure (Phil 2:12–13).

It is not incorrect to see in such passages a cooperation, a synergism, between God and his people, but it is by no means one that is symmetrical. Percentages of activity cannot be assigned to God and to the believer. This is not a zero sum game where God and the believer are in competition, as it were. Rather, the activity of the believer is completely *enveloped* in the working of God so that human boasting would be completely unjustified.[36] Wright, in particular, has emphasized the role of the Holy Spirit as the agent of transformation of the behavior of believers: "[I]t is by the energy of the Spirit, working in those who belong to the Messiah, that the new paradox comes about in which the Christian really does exercise free moral will and effort but at the same time ascribes

---

[34] The "gift" in this verse does not exclusively refer to "faith" (πίστις), for "this" (τοῦτο) and "faith" do not match in gender. Rather the "gift of God" would seem to refer to the whole complex of v. 8a, that is, being saved by grace through faith.

[35] That the person in question must choose to accept God's gift does not in any way affect faith's character as a gift. The Holy Spirit instills faith in the heart, but not without a person's willing acceptance.

[36] Barclay, *Paul*, 140: "Nor does Paul play off divine against human agency, as if the effect of grace is to *replace* the human actor with the action of the Spirit. To be sure, the believer's agency is now energized by, and enveloped within, the agency of the Spirit/Christ, but it would be misleading to deploy here a generalized contrast between passive and active, grace and work."

this free activity to the Spirit."[37] The righteous living of the believer is "the fruit of the Spirit" (Gal 5:22–23). It is this asymmetrical work of the Spirit that means that a "final justification" "according to works" provides no legitimate grounds of boasting for those who receive a positive verdict on the last day.

THE THIRD OBJECTION

Many Protestant Christians believe that the doctrine of justification by faith alone gives them certainty that they will be judged favorably by Christ at the Last Judgment, for it makes their final salvation dependent, not on their obedience or works of mercy, but only on their faith in what God has done for them in Christ—a faith that they are confident they possess.

Against this background, the NT texts that speak of the Final Judgment "according to works" seem to pose a potential threat to a Christian's confidence. How will believers know whether they have been obedient enough? How will they know whether they have engaged in enough good works? I can know whether I have the subjective experience of faith, but how can I know whether my works will pass the test?

One response to this dilemma is to concede that works will be examined at the Last Judgment, not as the "ground for final salvation," but as necessary evidence of genuine trust in Christ and his saving work.[38] However, this will not solve the threat posed to Christian assurance, for one can always doubt whether one's life has demonstrated the genuine faith that alone secures salvation. Moreover, if works are necessary evidence of the faith that will issue forth in final justification, then it would seem confusing at best to claim allegiance to a doctrine of "justification by faith alone" when works are clearly *necessary* as evidence of faith and, therefore, a condition of a positive verdict at the Last Judgment.

It is frequently observed that "justification by faith alone" fails to deliver certainty of salvation at the Last Judgment because no one can know with certainty that one's faith will endure until the end. That being the case, absolute certainty of one's eternal destiny is only possible because "justification by faith alone" is married to an Augustinian/Lutheran/Calvinist theology of election, according to which God alone accomplishes our ultimate salvation by unconditionally choosing us for salvation from before the foundation of the world, giving us faith, and causing us to persevere in faith and good works until death. This monergistic understanding of God's working in the elect rules out the possibility of apostasy and appears to provide for certainty, of course, but fails to do justice to the NT texts that (1) speak of a Final Judgment according to works,

---

[37] N. T. Wright, *Justification* (Downers Grove: InterVarsity Academic, 2009), 236.

[38] The thesis of Thomas R. Schreiner, "Justification apart from and by Works: At the Final Judgment Works will *Confirm* Justification," in *Four Views on The Role of Works at the Final Judgment*, ed. Alan P. Stanley (Grand Rapids: Zondervan, 2013), 71–98.

(2) acknowledge actual apostasy or warn believers against such a possibility,[39] as well as those texts that (3) speak of the real agency of believers as they approach glorification in Heaven.

Moreover, even this monergistic theology does not actually provide for certainty of salvation, for there is room for doubt about the authenticity of one's faith. After all, everyone is familiar with people who experience what they interpret as faith in Christ and who appear to have faith in the eyes of others, who yet later clearly renounce their faith either in words or in behavior. How does one know with certainty that one's faith is a genuine one that will persevere? At this point, some Christians begin to look for evidences of true faith in their lives, a venture that may provide confidence but can hardly provide certainty.

In light of the totality of scriptural teaching, it is preferable to acknowledge that at conversion believers are justified by faith, that is, apart from any action or disposition of the heart that would provide any merit. But once forgiven and endowed with the Holy Spirit, Christians are expected to cooperate actively with God as he works within us to transform our minds so that we serve the world in love. By that process, the Lord sanctifies us, day by day, transforming us into the image of his Son. Then at the end of human history as we know it, God will judge us "according to faith and works" or by faith "perfected by works." Those judged faithful will be ushered into God's consummated kingdom.

This understanding of the salvific process does not allow for certainty, apart from a special revelation from God, that we will inherit the bliss of Heaven. It is one thing to have confidence, quite another to possess certainty. Witness the reserve of Paul regarding the Last Judgment:

> [W]ith me it is a very small thing that I should be judged by you [Corinthian Christians] or any human court. I do not even judge myself. I am not aware of anything against myself, but I am not thereby acquitted ($\delta\epsilon\delta\iota\kappa\alpha\iota\omega\mu\alpha\iota$, elsewhere translated as "justified"). It is the Lord who judges me. Therefore do not pronounce judgment before the time, before the Lord comes, who will bring to light the things now hidden in darkness and will disclose the purposes of the heart. Then each one will receive commendation from God (1 Cor 4:3–5).

It is true, of course, that Paul is discussing the evaluation of "stewards" of the gospel, such as himself and Apollos, but it is difficult to see how the principles he adduces here would not apply to the Final Judgment of all souls.

---

[39] Actual: Matt 24:10–13; Gal 5:4; 1 Tim 1:19–20; 4:1–3; 2 Tim 4:3; 2 Pet 2:17–22; Possible: Matt 13:20–21//Mark 4:16–17//Luke 8:13; John 15:6; 1 Cor 1:12; 2 Tim 2:12; Heb 3:12; 6:1–6; 10:25–31; 2 Pet 3:9; Rev 2:20–22.

Notwithstanding this eschatological reserve, Paul and others in the NT reveal a confident hope in their ultimate inclusion in the future Kingdom. Classic are Paul's words in 2 Tim 4:7-8: "I have fought the good fight, I have finished the race, I have kept the faith. From now on there is reserved for me the crown of righteousness, which the Lord, the righteous judge, will give me on that day, and not only to me but to all who have longed for his appearing." The apostle also bolsters the confidence of believers in Rome with his words in Rom 5:9–10:

> But God proves his love for us in that while we still were sinners Christ died for us. *Much more surely then* [my emphasis], now that we have been justified by his blood, will we be saved [note the future tense] through him from the wrath of God. For if while we were enemies, we were reconciled to God through the death of his Son, *much more surely then* [my emphasis], having been reconciled, will we be saved by his life.

Another classic of Christian confidence is found in 1 John 5:13: "I write these things to you who believe in the name of the Son of God, so that you may know that you have eternal life."[40]

If the God and Father of Jesus Christ is like the father of the prodigal son,[41] if he is like the owner of the vineyard who graciously pays the same wage to the one-hour worker that he pays to those who labored the whole day,[42] if he is the shepherd who wills that not "one of these little ones should be lost,"[43] if he is the one who rewards even the person who offers a cold drink of water to one of his disciples,[44] if he is like Jesus who opens the gates of paradise to a penitent bandit,[45] if he is like Jesus who forgave Peter for denying him with an oath,[46] then disciples who have followed Jesus may hope that their Master will mercifully forgive their failures and reward their feeble efforts out of all proportion to their inherent worth.[47] Thus, in light of the foregoing,

---

[40] This verse might be used to support that view, held by many of the Reformers, that believers on the basis of faith alone can have *certainty* that they are in a state of grace at any given time and thus have *certainty* of their future inclusion in the population of Heaven, but *only* if it can be proven that in this verse οἶδα means "to know with certainty." However, this Greek verb has a considerable lexical range, and its use two verses later, in 1 John 5:15, does not support the notion of "certain knowledge" over against "confidence."

[41] Luke 15:11–32.

[42] Matt 20:1–16.

[43] Matt 18:14.

[44] Mark 9:41.

[45] Luke 23:43.

[46] John 21:15–19.

[47] For another effort to boost Christian confidence in final salvation, see Bates, *Allegiance*, 124–26.

belief that Christians will be judged according to their faith-revealing works on the Day of Judgment need not rob disciples of their joyful hope.

CONCLUSION

The Reformed Baptist scholar Thomas Schreiner has robustly argued that "Paul, like James, believes that works are necessary at the final judgment."[48] In other words, Schreiner affirms that the NT "demonstrates that good works are necessary for eschatological salvation."[49] This is precisely the argument of this present article. But if this is true, then I would argue that talk of "justification by faith alone" is potentially misleading unless one carefully distinguishes between an initial justification at the beginning of the Christian life and a final justification at the Last Judgment. Talk of "justification by faith alone" seems to suggest that faith is the only condition for a positive outcome on the Day of Judgment, especially as "justification" and "salvation" are often conflated.

Despite these pitfalls, Schreiner attempts to salvage "justification by faith alone" by making a distinction between works as a "condition" of eschatological salvation versus faith as the "basis" for such.[50] Thus, he concludes that while faith is the basis of salvation (understood comprehensively), works are "the necessary fruit or consequence of being a new creation."

But surely this places the emphasis on the human response to the work of God in Christ rather than upon the Christ event itself along with the work of the Spirit in enabling us to come to faith. The *basis* of our salvation surely lies in the work of the Father, through the Son, and in the Spirit. Our *response* to this work is completely asymmetrical. It is more theologically sound, in my opinion, to regard both faith and works as closely intertwined *means* by which we *appropriate* the saving work of God by divine help. This becomes clearer when we remember that the object of God's saving work is not simply to forgive human sin, but to conform us to the perfect humanity of Jesus. This object by definition, will not and cannot be achieved apart from our obedience to God and our increasing fellowship with the divine Persons of the Trinity until at last we are perfected in the Resurrection of the Dead.

Finally, if good works are a condition for our ultimate salvation, then those of us who are children of the Stone-Campbell Movement may be grateful that our forefathers balked at "justification by faith alone" as they felt their way toward an understanding of justification that is accountable to the whole NT canon and to the Christian tradition preceding the Reformation.

---

[48] Schreiner, "Justification," 98.

[49] Schreiner, "Justification," 92.

[50] Schreiner, "Justification," 97–98, cannot find this linguistic distinction in the NT, but believes that it is suggested by Eph 2:8–9 and Jas 2:14–26.

13
"As Long as the Heavens are Above the Earth": Children in Deuteronomy

Harold Shank

> And you shall teach them [the words of Moses] to your *children*, talking of them when you are sitting in your house, and when you are walking by the way, and when you lie down, and when you rise. And you shall write them upon the doorposts of your house and upon your gates, that your days and the days of your *children* may be multiplied in the land which the LORD swore to your fathers to give them, as long as the heavens are above the earth (Deut 11:19–21).[1]

Childhood lasts only a short time, but Deuteronomy promises a way for children to have their "days … multiplied" so they can enjoy life "as long as the heavens are above the earth" (Deut 11:21). This "long life" or "good life" refrain appears twenty times in Deuteronomy.[2] Deuteronomy 32:47 summarizes this vision of the future: "For it [passing on the teaching of Moses] is no trifle for you; but it is your life, and thereby you shall live long in the land…." The hope of a long life for the Israelites included settling in a land with many resources (8:7–10), having children (4:25), and living in a prosperous community where justice prevailed (16:20). They would live where the financially troubled found support (15:1–11), where leaders organized the community for the benefit of all (16:18–17:19), where crops flourished (28:4–14), where worship united (16:11, 14; 31:10–13), and where outsiders were welcomed (10:18–19).

This ongoing life, which included children, might be summarized by the term *prosperity*, a significant theme of Deuteronomy, reflected in italics in the following passages: "And the LORD will make you abound in *prosperity*, in the fruit of your body, and in the fruit of your cattle, and in the fruit of your ground, within the land which the LORD swore to your fathers to give you" (Deut 28:11) and "Therefore be careful to do the words of this covenant, that you may *prosper* in all that you do" (Deut 29:9). The

---

[1] All scripture citations are from the *Revised Standard Version* (1962). I have italicized all references to children for the purposes of this essay.

[2] Repetition is a key element in Deuteronomy. The concepts of the good life, keeping the commandments, fathers, blessing, gift of land, etc. appear regularly. See a complete analysis of these refrains in the introduction to Harold Shank, *Deuteronomy* (Searcy: Resource Publications, in press). The good life or long life refrain appears in Deut 4:1, 9, 40; 5:16, 33; 6:2; 8:1, 3; 11:9, 21; 16:3, 20; 19:13; 25:15; 30:6, 16, 19, 20; 32:47. The refrain includes the recurring phrases "all the days of your life," "that you may live," "that it may go well with you," and "live long."

repeated use of "you" in these two passages included the children. The commands of Deuteronomy are God's "best practices" for a well-lived life of prosperity.

This essay explores two potential ways Deuteronomy connects children with prosperity. I have focused on these two because they have implications for contemporary thinking about children which I will discuss at the end. First, Deuteronomy grounds the children's future prosperity in their teachability, their innate spirituality, and children's ability to understand and reflect on their own faith history. Second, the vulnerability of children, which appears frequently in Deuteronomy, is countered by the connection between obedience and prosperity. Initially, this essay will summarize the status of studies focused on children, define what we mean by children, point out how children fit within the context of Deuteronomy, and explore the multi-generational context claimed by Deuteronomy itself, all within a maximalist OT perspective.

This piece is dedicated to Allen Black, who carefully centered his life not only on his students but on his church and especially on his family. Having raised our children together, by being in each other's homes and vacationing together, and having a friendship which spanned almost forty years, I watched up close as this teacher went well beyond the classroom and fulfilled Deuteronomy's lofty dream of preparing children for a prosperous life.

STUDIES ON CHILDREN

Biblical scholars have increasingly been paying attention to the status of children in the Bible. Patrick Miller notes that Deuteronomy "gives prominent attention to children and especially to what and how they are taught."[3] Julie Parker goes beyond Deuteronomy and says, "Children are integral to the literature of the Hebrew Bible."[4] The work of Miller and Parker is part of a larger move in biblical studies to view passages from a child's perspective. Amy Allen describes the move in this way, "Child-centered, or childist, interpretation seeks to learn equally from both the children and the adults in the biblical texts by paying attention to the presence and experience of all the characters in the story, even the children who are too frequently forgotten or assumed to be adults."[5] Much biblical interpretation has been done by adult, white males. In the past several decades, women and people of color have expanded our understanding by allowing us to see the Bible through their eyes. More recently, some have taken a childist approach, seeking to see the same material from a child's point of view.

---

[3] Patrick Miller, "That the Children May Know: Children in Deuteronomy," in *The Child in the Bible,* ed. Marcia J. Bunge (Grand Rapids: Eerdmans, 2008), 45.

[4] Julie Parker. *Valuable and Vulnerable: Children in the Hebrew Bible* (Providence: Brown Judaic Studies, 2013), 1.

[5] Strategies for reading this way include asking how a child might see this passage or where might children be in this story, and paying attention to the place and role of children in the biblical world. Amy Allen, *The Gifts They Bring* (Louisville: Westminster John Knox, 2023), 7.

THE NATURE OF DEUTERONOMY

This essay on children is based on the story as it unfolds in the book of Deuteronomy.[6] As it stands, the book claims to be three sermons of Moses delivered at the end of the wilderness period on the plains of Moab on the eve of the conquest of Canaan. The first speech (Deut 1:1–4:43) includes a rehearsal of ten recent events in the later years of the wilderness and exhortation to keep the Horeb (Sinai) covenant. The second sermon (4:44–28:68) presents the covenant made at Moab on the eve of the conquest. Moses begins the third speech (29:1–34:12) by calling "all Israel" (29:2) to affirm this covenant. Moses then identifies the participants in the covenant-making ceremony,

> "You stand this day all of you before the LORD your God; the heads of your tribes, your elders, and your officers, all the men of Israel, your *little ones*, your wives, and the sojourner who is in your camp, both he who hews your wood and he who draws your water, that you may enter into the sworn covenant of the LORD your God…. Nor is it with you only that I make this sworn covenant, but with him *who is not here with us* this day as well as with him who stands here with us this day before the LORD our God" (Deut 29:10–12,14, 15).

Moses addresses both "little ones" and those "not here with us this day"[7] in the covenant-making process. Later in the third speech, Moses tells the people to read the law every seven years at the Feast of Booths. On those occasions, the audience was to include "the men and the women and *children* and the alien who is in your town" (Deut 31:12). "All Israel" (29:1, 2) gathered to affirm the covenant included the children, an admittance which raises the question of how Israel might have defined what it meant to be a child.

DEFINITIONS OF CHILDREN

The Hebrew Bible uses a variety of terms for children, which have been described in numerous places.[8] Deuteronomy 1:39 refers to the "*little ones*" (טף; *taph*) which it then defines as those who do not know right from wrong. Marriage was a major dividing

---

[6] The various critical proposals about the development of Deuteronomy are often rehearsed. See Duane Christensen, *Deuteronomy 1:1–21:9,* rev. ed. (Nashville: Thomas Nelson, 2001), lxviii–lxx. This essay takes the final canonical form of Deuteronomy as its starting point.

[7] The line "not here with us this day" refers to future generations, not to absentees. Jeffrey Tigay, *The JPS Torah Commentary Deuteronomy* (Philadelphia: Jewish Publication Society, 1996), 278.

[8] See the presentations and sources in Parker, *Valuable and Vulnerable,* 41-76; Miller, "That the Children May Know," 47–48; and Marcia J. Bunge, "Introduction," in *The Child in the Bible,* ed. Marcia J. Bunge (Grand Rapids: Eerdmans, 2008), xiv–xxvi.

line between children and adults.⁹ The various terms for children also refer to those without moral discretion on one hand and the future generation on the other hand.¹⁰ Additionally, Num 14:29 and 32:11 point to those under the age of twenty as children. We can conclude that the concept of children was somewhat fluid. Although Deuteronomy describes children in a wide variety of ways,¹¹ several significant trends appear. Children were recipients of teaching (6:1–8), participants in the festivals (16:11, 14), part of the covenant-making ceremony (29:11,12), and eventually inheritors of the land (11:21). Children were even permitted to ask challenging questions (6:20). Thus, children were participants in a community which had a multi-generational focus.

The first hearers of Deuteronomy tended to be young. Jeffrey Tigay suggests that one-third of those listening to Moses had been children at Sinai forty years before. Those under the age of twenty at Sinai were now in their forties or fifties. The other two-thirds of those in Moses's audience, according to Tigay, were born in the wilderness and were under forty, some of them children.¹²

Deuteronomy, with its focus on children and generations, calls the people to make decisions that allow the whole community, including the future generations, to prosper. The hopeful future prosperity of children rested on several assumptions about their children.

TEACHABILITY, INNATE SPIRITUALITY, AND THE REFLECTIVE ABILITY OF CHILDREN

Deuteronomy regularly assumes children are teachable. Moses says, "Only give heed to yourself and keep your soul diligently, so that you do not forget the things which

---

⁹ Parker, *Valuable and Vulnerable*, 55.

¹⁰ Miller, "That the Children May Know," 47, 48.

¹¹ The following descriptions of children appear in Deuteronomy: children are descendants of patriarchs (1:8), carried by a father (1:28), offspring of those inheriting the land (1:31), offspring of other nations (2:90), unaware of good or evil (1:39), killed in the cities of Sihon and Og (2:34, 3:6), dependents of Israelite soldiers (3:19), ones taught (4:10), future generations (4:25), suffering for the sins of adults (5:9), resting on Sabbath (5:14), fearing God (6:2), asking questions (6:20), forbidden to marry people in the land (7:3), disciplined by a father (8:5), do not know (11:2), inheriting the land (11:21), joining in community joy (12:12), participants in family meals (12:18), will flourish (12:28), idol worshippers (13:6), festival attendees (16:11, 14), offspring of priests (18:5), burned in fire (18:10), prisoners of war (20:14), firstborn (21:16), stubborn and rebellious (21:18), marriage partners (22:16), banned from assembly (23:8), not to die for sins of fathers or vice versa (24:16), children in same family (25:5), victims of sexual abuse (27:22), taken from parents (28:32), victims of cannibalism (28:54-57), participants in covenant making (29:11,12), witnesses of aftermath of apostasy (29:22), recipients of God's revelation (29:29), returning to God (30:2), listening to the law being read (31:12), witnesses (31:21), children of God (32:19), called to obey (32:46), and not acknowledged by brothers (33:9).

¹² Tigay, *Deuteronomy*, 46. Other passages contributing the potential age of Moses's audience Num 1:45–46; 26:1–4, 51; Josh 4:13.

your eyes have seen and they do not depart from your heart all the days of your life; but make them known to your *children* and your *children's children*" (Deut 4:9). Moses continues, "so that they may learn to fear me all the days that they live upon the earth, and that they may teach their *children* so" (4:10). Deut 6 opens with the same concern,

> "Now this is the commandment, the statutes and the ordinances which the LORD your God commanded me to teach you, that you may do them in the land to which you are going over, to possess it; that you may fear the LORD your God, you and your *son* and your *son's son*, by keeping all his statutes and his commandments, which I command you, all the days of your life; and that your days may be prolonged" (Deut 6:1, 2).

"Commandment," "statutes," and "ordinances" refer to the content of what Moses taught for the benefit of three generations, "you and your *children* and your *children's children*." The core of that teaching is to love God (Deut 6:4, 5), which Jesus would later call the "great commandment" (Matt 22:36–38; Mark 12:28–34; see also Luke 10:25–28). Then Moses goes further:

> "And these words which I command you this day shall be upon your heart; and you shall teach them diligently to your *children*, and shall talk of them when you sit in your house, and when you walk by the way, and when you lie down, and when you rise. And you shall bind them as a sign upon your hand, and they shall be as frontlets between your eyes. And you shall write them on the doorposts of your house and on your gates" (Deut 6:6–9).

Moses makes abundant use of merism, in which several items are used to mean the whole. Just as the "commandment, the statutes, and the ordinances" of 6:1 served as merism, meaning "all the content God assigned," so the instruction to teach when they "talk," "sit," "walk," "lie down," and "rise" means "all the time" or "at every opportunity." They were to teach by the "house," "way," "doorposts," and "gates," which means "to teach everywhere possible." When they taught, they were to use their "hand" and "eyes," that is, use all the daily routines that demonstrate God's commands.

This passage calls for the children to learn both by hearing and reading. The adults instruct the young verbally. The parents/adults also were to write teachings down ("write them on your doorposts") so the children could read them. They were to teach diligently (שנן, *shanan*). *Shanan* has the sense of sharpening, repeating, or reciting.[13] Children did not just hear and read, but they were also sharpened by repetition and

---

[13] David Firth, "Passing on the Faith in Deuteronomy," in *Interpreting Deuteronomy: Issues and Approaches*, ed. David G. Firth and Philip S. Johnston (Downers Grove: InterVarsity Academic, 2012), 171.

remembered what they were taught. Deuteronomy operates on the assumption that children were teachable—and not just teachable, but capable of understanding the spiritual.

The teaching of children rested on the expectation that children can appreciate the divine and the spiritual. In the third sermon, Moses issues this challenge:

> "Assemble the people, men, women, and *little ones*, and the sojourner within your towns, that they may hear and learn to fear the LORD your God, and be careful to do all the words of this law, and that their *children*, who have not known it, may hear and learn to fear the LORD your God, as long as you live in the land which you are going over the Jordan to possess" (Deut 31:12–13).

That the children could "hear and learn" reflects the teachability assumed in Deut 4, 6, but now the assumption includes learning "to fear" and "to do" spiritual disciplines. Calls to "fear the LORD" and to "do all the words" appear regularly in Deuteronomy (for example, 5:29), but in this climatic statement in Deut 31, Moses calls on the "*little ones*" and the "*children*" to "hear and learn to fear the LORD" and "to do all the words." Miller writes,

> If the fear of the Lord—that is, reverence, obedience, and worship of God who has saved and cared for us—is the aim of human existence, as it surely is for those who live by and with the Holy Scriptures, then that fear is something to be learned and developed from the earliest days onward.[14]

Deuteronomy assumes children have spiritual capacity. Not only can children learn to do domestic chores and participate in the family economy, but children benefit from spiritual teaching and can learn to fear God and do as He says. Contemporary voices affirm this same point. Holly Allen notes, "Children have an innate, God-bestowed spirituality that is their greatest source of resilience."[15] Deuteronomy builds on the supposition that children can appreciate the divine.

Closely associated with the teachability and innate spirituality of children is that children can absorb and reflect on what they are taught, including their faith history. Only one child speaks in Deuteronomy, and that child is unnamed. In Deut 6:20, Moses says, "When your *son* asks you in time to come, 'What is the meaning of the testimonies and the statutes and the ordinances which the LORD our God has commanded you?'" The boy's question provides significant insight into what the community of Israel thought about children. They allowed children to ask questions, even inquiries that focused on and questioned the foundation of the teaching curriculum. They believed

---

[14] Miller, "That the Children May Know," 62.

[15] Holly Allen, *Forming Resilient Children: The Role of Spiritual Formation for Healthy Development* (Downers Grove: InterVarsity Academic, 2021), 13.

children would have these kinds of spiritual questions, so they assumed the children could think about and reflect on what they learned. Deuteronomy presumes children would want to know what was behind the laws they were taught and why they should keep them. In a book filled with the words of God conveyed by Moses, children have a voice, and they have a question about faith.

Deuteronomy 16 calls for the community to gather for worship, teaching, and fellowship. Children are included (16:11, 14) in the gatherings. Deuteronomy held that children needed to be at times of worship, teaching, and fellowship, and that they had the capacity to benefit from such activity. It is striking that the list of attendees includes the orphaned (16:11, 14). Children who lacked a parent were expected to join the community and were thought to benefit from such experiences. Even vulnerable, at-risk children could benefit from the spiritual life of the community.[16]

Furthermore, the teaching of children in Deuteronomy also assumes the children could understand and reflect on their inherited faith story. Moses addressed this issue in Deut 4:9–10:

> "Only take heed, and keep your soul diligently, lest you forget the things which your eyes have seen, and lest they depart from your heart all the days of your life; make them known to your *children* and your *children's children*—how on the day that you stood before the LORD your God at Horeb, the LORD said to me, 'Gather the people to me, that I may let them hear my words, so that they may learn to fear me all the days that they live upon the earth, and that they may teach their *children* so.'"

Because the youngest children were not at Horeb, the community needed to let them know about what happened at Horeb so it could become part of their faith story.

The ratification of the covenant at Moab, which includes the children (29:11), begins with a historical review (29:2–9). Moses says, "You have seen all that the LORD did before your eyes" (29:2), but in reality the children who were listening (29:10, 11) had not seen those marvelous events. In a similar way, when the boy raises his question in Deut 6:20, the answer to why they had all the testimonies, statutes, and ordinances is a history lesson. It begins, "We were Pharaoh's slaves in Egypt" (6:21), but even though the boy asking the question was not a slave in Egypt, such stories (which the book assumes the children can internalize) were the stories of their faith. Children could learn the history of their faith as part of the formula for the prosperity of children.

---

[16] Another at-risk child appears in Deut 21, a child who is "stubborn and rebellious" who "will not obey the voice of his father or the voice of his mother" (21:18). The circumstances of this uncooperative child appear as an exceptional case which assumes that most children are less stubborn and less rebellious and more often obey their parents. The case of the rebellious son suggests that all children are teachable, but some significantly less so.

The important theme in Deuteronomy of teaching children in order to ensure their future prosperity builds on children being teachable and moldable individuals, having an innate ability to appreciate the divine, and having the skill to reflect on what they are taught and absorb the history of their faith. Yet not all children experienced the prosperity promised in Deuteronomy.

PROTECTION FOR VULNERABLE CHILDREN

The children who participated in the faith-centered events of the Israelite community recorded in Deuteronomy heard talk about matters that were potentially disturbing, which raises the question of how Deuteronomy intended for children to prosper in light of these vulnerabilities.

Moses left no doubt that some children were vulnerable. Moses told of the victories over Sihon and Og, saying, "We captured all his cities at that time and utterly destroyed every city, men, women, and *children*; we left none remaining" (2:33; 3:6). The death of children during the victorious Transjordan campaign was not simply a matter of inadvertent civilian casualties as part of the destructiveness of war, but rather the intentional killing of children for theological reasons.[17] The innocent and vulnerable children of these nations died in the God-ordered punishment. The vulnerability of children also appears in other places in Deuteronomy, some of them central to the book.

The second of the Ten Commandments raises the issue of the vulnerability of children. God said,

> "You shall not make for yourself a graven image, or any likeness of anything that is in heaven above, or that is on the earth beneath, or that is in the water under the earth; you shall not bow down to them or serve them; for I the LORD your God am a jealous God, visiting the iniquity of the fathers upon the *children* to the third and fourth generation of those who hate me, but showing steadfast love to thousands of those who love me and keep my commandments" (Deut 5:8–10).

Now the threat against children moves from the children of Israel's unrepentant enemies to the children of idol worshippers in Israel. While there are several interpretations of the meaning of "visiting the iniquity of the fathers on the *children*," the issue here is

---

[17] The death of these children raises the oft-addressed issue of the justice of God which is beyond the scope of this essay. In short, God used Israel to punish these nations for their unrepentant sins. God called for the removal of those peoples who had polluted God's land. See Lev. 18:24, 25; Deut 9:5. Charlie Trimm, *The Destruction of the Canaanites* (Grand Rapids: Eerdmans, 2022), treats the issue at length.

that the children listening to the unfolding of Deuteronomy would have again sensed their vulnerability.[18]

When Moses told the story of the failed invasion from the south (Deut 1:19–46), many of those in the audience, now adults, would likely have recalled their own childhood. When the generation before them had refused to take the land, God punished that "evil generation" (Deut 1:35) by letting them die in the wilderness. However, their children grew up in the desert during the wilderness period. They lived in tents, not houses. They were constantly searching for water, not drawing from wells. They ate manna and quail every day rather than the diet of a settled people. They never had a house, harvested a vineyard, cultivated a field, gone to market, or visited a city. Their childhood was sand, tents, sheep, and a life of vulnerability.

The children listening to Moses also heard him speak about God's protection in the wilderness. Deuteronomy 8:1–4 and 29:5 celebrate how God watched over Israel during the wilderness. When Moses claimed, "Your clothing did not wear out upon you" (8:4), the children might have exclaimed, "You can't say that."[19] They likely wore "hand-me-downs" from their older siblings. Perhaps the durability of clothing applied only to the adults since the development of children over those decades would have called for clothing that accommodated their growth.[20] When Moses talked about moving into a land with cities, "houses full of good things," cisterns, vineyards, and olive trees (6:10, 11), the children born and reared in the wilderness would have had no experience with such luxury. The wilderness experience of the children would have confirmed their vulnerability.

Several other passages in Deuteronomy alerted the listening children to their vulnerability. Children could be executed (13:6ff; 21:18ff), although not for the sins of their parents (24:16). The Song of Moses referred to the destruction of children (32:25). The curses on those who failed to keep the covenant are disturbing to child and adult alike. Children will enjoy the blessing of the obedient (28:4, 11), but if among the disobedient families, they would be cursed (28:18), separated from their parents (28:32), taken into captivity (28:41; see also 4:25–26), and potentially eaten by their cannibalistic parents (28:53–57).

---

[18] Harold Shank, "The Decalogue and Justice for Children: The Value and Vulnerability of Children," *Journal of Christian Studies* 2.1 (2023): 63–77.

[19] I include this possible exclamation which Allen Black once used in a similar way at an elders-staff retreat.

[20] It is not clear whether this passage meant that the children wore the same clothes as they grew or outgrew the smaller apparel or that it was a sign of God's ample provision in a time of scarcity. See Tigay, *Deuteronomy*, 276. Some suggest the children's clothes grew with them. Yonatan Neril and Leo Dee, *Eco Bible: An Ecological Commentary on Leviticus, Numbers, and Deuteronomy* (Jerusalem: Interfaith Center for Sustainable Development, 2021), 144.

Clearly, the children in the audience hearing or reading parts of Deuteronomy would have realized their vulnerability. The children who sensed their exposure to harm in Deuteronomy would also have learned about God's plan for a place of safety, protection, and security, which would offer them prosperity. Children are always vulnerable, but Deuteronomy proposed an alternative community in at least three ways.

First, Deuteronomy clearly called for a just society. Leaders were told, "Justice, and only justice, you shall follow" (Deut 16:20). Instructions about how to address poverty (14:28–29), financial crises of the poor (15:1–11), economic slavery (15:12–18), fair courts (25:17–18), and hunger (24:19–22) explain how a community of faith responds to the inequities and misfortunes of life. These instructions offered protection for children, including the orphan.

Second, Deuteronomy explains that the stipulations, ordinances, and commandments of the book are the means to a long life of prosperity. When people live by faith and follow God's appointed "best practices," the result is life. "Life" appears in Deuteronomy in the context of prosperity, security, and happiness (Deut 30:15, 19, 20; 32:39; 32:47). The book of Deuteronomy additionally reflects on living for God. Deuteronomy describes the ideal human community as one focused on love for and obedience to a compassionate God. One of the greatest descriptions of this kind of deity appears in Deut 10:17–19:

> "For the LORD your God is God of gods and Lord of lords, the great, the mighty, and the terrible God, who is not partial and takes no bribe. He executes justice for the *fatherless* and the widow, and loves the sojourner, giving him food and clothing. Love the sojourner therefore; for you were sojourners in the land of Egypt."

The LORD was above all other authorities but also concerned with the most vulnerable. After all, He rescued Israel from Egyptian slavery. The Israelite God was not the possession of the affluent and powerful, but rather, in this description, He is the God of the oppressed and vulnerable. The vulnerable child had and has a protective ally at the highest level.

Third, Deuteronomy is built around grace. The book repeatedly cites the grace of God in electing Israel (1:8; 7:6), delivering the people from Egypt (for example, 1:27), protecting them in the wilderness (8:1–20), providing them the law (5:6–21), and giving them the land (for example, 1:8).[21] Israel did nothing to benefit from all these gifts. Yet, at the same time, Deuteronomy calls for the people to obey the commandments of God.[22] The concern to distinguish between grace and works so prevalent in the NT

---

[21] The gift of land refrain in Deuteronomy is one of the most oft-repeated concepts in the book.

[22] The obedience refrain appears over 130 times in Deuteronomy. Deuteronomy 27:10 is a typical case.

exists already in Deuteronomy. Just as people in NT times misunderstood the relationship of grace and law, the same potential exists in reading Deuteronomy. The laws, commandments, ordinances, and statutes provide the foundation for a prosperous life rather than being a set of legalistic demands from a capricious God. God, who for the first time in Scripture is called "father" (32:6, see also 4:31), cares about His children just as most parents do. Just as Jesus offers grace and then calls for discipleship, so Deuteronomy offers the grace of the Exodus, land and law, and calls for obedience.

The children in Deuteronomy, like our own children, were aware of their vulnerability, but they would also learn that their community was structured to be a place of safety and protection. Moreover, their God had provided them with instructions on how to avoid many of life's threats and directed them to the way of living in prosperity under the watchfulness of a great God. These children would learn that the commandments came in the context of grace, that based on what they had been given, they should live in ways that led to prosperity.

IMPLICATIONS FOR CONTEMPORARY CHILDREN

Viewing the ancient book of Deuteronomy from a childist perspective suggests several implications for contemporary faith communities. The perceptions that children should be "out of sight, out of mind" or "children are better seen than heard" continue to operate in our own day. Church is often seen as an adult affair, with children relegated to a place where they will not disturb the adults. Deuteronomy keeps children in sight and in mind, allows them to be seen and heard, and includes them in the spiritual community. Viewing children as part of the house of faith, as people who are teachable, with spiritual appetites, and who can reflect on matters of faith should be adopted and practiced by contemporary faith communities.

Considerable attention has been given to issues about our environment, ecology, and care for the earth. Such concerns are certainly part of the Hebrew Bible and can be found in Deuteronomy.[23] However, Deuteronomy gives more emphasis to the character of the children who will live in the environment than to the care of the environment in which they will live. With church attendance in the first quarter of the twenty-first century decreasing, especially among children, society must be concerned with teaching the children about God's "best practices." Parents would do well to be aware of their role in teaching their own children. Allen Black strikes me as a worthy model. He not only prospered in his own life of teaching and ministry, but he led his family and others around him to the same exemplary life. Leaders of the faith communities in contemporary society should be concerned about not only what their own children are learning, but about what unchurched children are learning or not learning. Moses included

---

[23] Neril and Dee, *Eco Bible*, 126, 141–44, 151, 164–69, 171, 180, 186, 190.

children in the audience for spiritual instruction. Contemporary society increasingly excludes them.

Finally, the vulnerability of children so evident in Deuteronomy continues to be a significant contemporary issue.[24] Some might suggest we jettison the entire book of Deuteronomy as a representative of a barbaric period of history, but the vulnerability of children is still with us. The faith community may be one of the most significant voices in our distracted and adult-centered culture to call attention to the plight of children both at home and abroad. Today's faith community should not only sing songs inspired by the language "God of gods and Lord of lords" in Deut 10:17, but we should pay attention to the vulnerable in the rest of the verse in Deut 10 to remind the faith community of its obligation to be concerned about the same things our God is concerned about. The faith community should advocate for the orphan, widow, and sojourner among us, especially as their vulnerability increases in our own time. My own work with Network 1:27 partners with nearly fifty ministries nationwide that serve these vulnerable children.[25]

In the distant past, Deuteronomy expected children could prosper because they were capable of spiritual learning and discernment. Long ago, Deuteronomy addressed the vulnerability of children by laying out a plan for prosperity that included safety and protection. Childhood, then and now, does not last long, but Deuteronomy presented a way for children to prosper as long as the heavens are above the earth.

---

[24] The significant dangers children face globally in the contemporary world are described in Rosalind Tan, Nativity Petallar, and Lucy Hefford, *God's Heart for Children* (Carlisle: Langham Global Library, 2022) while the hazards encountered by American children appear in Nicholas Kristof and Sheryl Wudunn, *Tightrope: Americans Reaching for Hope* (New York: Alfred A. Knopf, 2020). Nearly 14,000 of the world's children under the age of five died every day in 2020 due to malnutrition and health complications. UNICEF, "Under-five mortality" (December 2021) at data.unicef.org/topic/child-survival/under-five-mortality/.

[25] network127.org.

14
Genesis 1 as Pedagogy

Nathan Bills[1]

Every year across the globe, a new batch of students begin their studies at Christian institutions of higher education. The vast majority of students who choose a Christian school will very likely be required to take at least one class that introduces and engages Christian Scripture. At my institution, Heritage Christian University (HCU) of Ghana, every new student enrolls in a survey of the Old Testament as a requirement in the university's core curriculum. This survey course is introductory on more than one level. Not only do students freshly encounter the rigor and rigmarole that comes with tertiary education in general; it is also for many their entrée into academic learning as an explicitly *Christian* enterprise.

How should the qualifier "Christian" affect the experience of students enrolled in an institution of higher education? It is a good question that is necessarily addressed from a variety of angles and with plenty of literature available from the way *Christian* higher education has in fact materialized in various forms and time periods.[2] One angle of analysis surely relevant to this question is pedagogy—the method and practice of teaching. To pose the question from a pedagogical angle: what difference with regard to classroom instruction will a student encounter in Christian education? Or, to render the question from the perspective of the instructor: how does a teacher's Christian

---

[1] I offer this essay in honor and admiration of my professor Dr. Allen Black. Although Dr. Black did not teach Old Testament, he consistently attuned his students to the ways the authors of the New Testament worked out of their Holy Scriptures to witness to God in Christ. It was always apparent that Dr. Black genuinely cared about his students and his work, epitomizing for those within his orbit the sacred vocation of a scholar-pastor. I remain deeply grateful for the hours he reserved for me in his office to debate scholarship, share struggle, and pray for the kingdom to come in our lives.

[2] Perry L. Glanzer, Theodore F. Cockle, and Jessica Martin, *Christian Higher Education: An Empirical Guide* (Abilene: Abilene Christian University Press, 2023), analyzes and evaluates how a range of North American Christian universities embody (or don't!) their confessional identities. See a survey of scholarship on the issue in both David I. Smith, Joonyong Um, and Claudia D. Beversluis, "The Scholarship of Teaching and Learning in a Christian Context," *Christian Higher Education* 13 (2014): 74–87; and Allan Harkness, "Exploring the Interface between Christian Faith and Education: An Annotated List of Current Journals," *Journal of Education and Christian Belief* 17 (2013): 99–114. For an assessment from the Catholic perspective, see James L. Heft, *The Future of Catholic Higher Education: An Open Circle* (Oxford: Oxford University Press, 2021). More broadly, see George M. Marsden, *The Soul of the America University Revisited: From Protestant Establishment to Postsecular* (Oxford: Oxford University Press, 2021), and Todd C. Ream and Perry L. Glanzer, *The Idea of a Christian College: A Reexamination for Today's University* (Eugene: Cascade, 2013).

commitments affect the way s/he goes about her/his course instruction? What effect does an educator's faith have on the material presented, the interaction elicited, and the work assigned? In essence, what does it mean to teach *Christianly*?

One might think the question about the difference Christian faith makes to teaching receives routine reflection in scholarship on Christian education, but David I. Smith, in his book *On Christian Teaching*, asserts that it is not so.[3] Smith argues that disquisitions on Christian teaching typically tackle epistemology, history, content, or the teacher's role, virtue, or spirituality—all of which undoubtedly impinge on the vocation of teaching. Nonetheless, consideration of how faith informs the *actual practice of teaching*, that is, the instruction and learning experience in the classroom, is noticeably sparse. "Christian" and "teaching" label two separate entities, according to Smith, rather than one thick interrelationship. In the context of education, the designation "Christian" describes normative ideas, allegiances, and passions; "teaching" identifies a repertoire of practices, techniques, and philosophies. When it comes to scholarship on how faith shapes teaching, Smith asserts the former too often informs the latter only at the level of broad and theologically shallow generalizations.

Smith's *On Christian Teaching* makes the case for how faith might inhabit pedagogy.[4] I say faith "inhabiting" pedagogy deliberately because Smith urges teachers to reimagine their teaching as a hospitable act of faith-oriented *homemaking* rather than in the more conventional terms of method, strategy, or technique. The metaphorical redescription of pedagogy as homemaking has much resonance with the more widespread metaphor of hospitality in teaching literature.[5] Homemaking, though, trains the

---

[3] David I. Smith, *On Christian Teaching: Practicing Faith in the Classroom* (Grand Rapids: Eerdmans, 2018). His final chapter (161–76) "The State of Christian Scholarship" details the following claims through a survey of the literature. See also David I. Smith and James K. A. Smith, "Introduction: Practices, Faith, and Pedagogy," in *Teaching and Christian Practices: Reshaping Faith and Learning*, ed. David I. Smith and James K. A. Smith (Grand Rapids: Eerdmans, 2011). Since Smith's publication, one work stands out for its attempt to survey various ways Christian teachers' faith animates their teaching and other responsibilities: Perry L. Glanzer and Nathan F. Alleman, *The Outrageous Idea of Christian Teaching* (Oxford: Oxford University Press, 2019). Unfortunately, Smith's latest monograph *Everyday Christian Teaching: A Guide to Practicing Faith in the Classroom* (Grand Rapids: Eerdmans, 2025), arrived too late in the process of publication to integrate into the discussion here.

[4] Although I have described "Christian teaching" in the previous paragraph as a "thick interrelationship" between the two words, Smith's concern in *On Christian Teaching* is entirely with the one-way influence of faith upon practice. It is a notable limitation of an otherwise excellent treatment.

[5] For a survey, see SOH Hui Leng Davina, *The Motif of Hospitality in Theological Education: A Critical Appraisal with Implications for Application in Theological Education*, ICETE Series (Carlisle, UK: Langham Global Library, 2016), 9–148; Liselotte Van Ooteghem, "What Do We Mean by Hospitality in Education?" *Social Sciences and Education Research Review* 9 (2022): 17–32.

attention directly on the concrete practices of the classroom.[6] It invites teachers to consider what kind of experiential abode they "build" with their patterns of instruction and interaction, with their design of syllabi and space, with their decisions about time and trajectories, rules and rhythms. In this regard, the *manner* in which one teaches, that is, the home one welcomes students into, itself carries and contributes to the *meaning* of what is learned in the classroom. And, Smith argues, the *how* of Christian teaching as homemaking attends to *how well* the practices constituting the home (that is, the classroom) are congruent with the wider invitation of Christian education, namely, to learn how to inhabit the world according to the story of Scripture. Thus, a goal of Christian teaching should be to configure the pedagogical experience—whatever the subject—so that it is consistent with, contributes to, and ultimately even helps to cultivate the kind of habitation corresponding to the kingdom of God in Jesus Christ.

As an illustration of his argument, Smith walks the reader through a detailed, nine-minute sequence of his own teaching on the first day of a semester course on the German language.[7] He explores how his choice of the learning activity (both its content and presentation), the arrangement of space in the classroom, the use of time, and his interaction with the students all work together to shape an emerging pedagogical "home." Smith's decision to present the *first* day of a class is not superfluous. Research indicates that the first day(s) of class matters for many reasons, not the least of which is that it is a particularly impressionable time in the student's experience of the course. Course beginnings are more effective when they intentionally set the tone for the habits of mind that will characterize the class as well as model the kinds of relational interaction welcomed in the class.[8] Hence, the first few meetings are a disproportionately fertile time for teachers. In this time and space, teachers set up the frame and assemble (some of) the furniture, as it were, of the kind of pedagogical habitation s/he wishes to construct *for* and *with* the students throughout the semester.

I find Smith's metaphor of homemaking—especially as it relates to the beginning of class—an accommodating entrée into Christian pedagogy, not least because it resonates well with Scripture's own logic of presentation. It is here that Walter Brueg-

---

[6] Smith, *On Christian Teaching*, 18–19, points out that before "pedagogy" came to mean a method of teaching after the 17th century, the *paedogogium* specified the house in which students dwelled and learned together.

[7] Smith, *On Christian Teaching*, ch. 2, entitled "The Whole Nine Minutes."

[8] See, for example, Barbara A. Iannarelli, Mary Ellen Bardsley, and Chandra J. Foote, "Here's Your Syllabus, See You Next Week: A Review of the First Day Practices of Outstanding Professors," *Journal of Effective Teaching* 10 (2010): 29–41; Preeti G. Samudra, Inah Min, Kai S. Cortina, and Kevin F. Miller, "No Second Chance to Make a First Impression: The 'Thin Slice' Effect on Instructor Ratings and Learning Outcomes in Higher Education," *Journal of Educational Measurement* 53 (2016): 313–31; Stephanie deLuse, "First Impressions: Using a Flexible First Day Activity to Enhance Student Learning and Classroom Management," *International Journal of Teaching and Learning in Higher Education* 30 (2018): 308–21.

gemann's reflections on the educational agenda housed in the canon of Scripture can bolster the point. In his *Creative Word: Canon as a Model for Biblical Education*, he avers that the very shape and shaping of Israel's Scriptures into the tripartite division of Torah, Prophets, and Writings offer a pedagogical paradigm.[9] Each of the three divisions represents a disparate mode and deposit of knowledge that together inform the task of education.

I mention Brueggemann's stimulating thesis in order to extrapolate from it in ways Brueggemann himself does not consider, namely, to suggest that the way the canon of Scripture itself *begins* offers wisdom for the facilitation of learning. I propose we can build on the assumption that the design of the canon is instructive for the pedagogical process (following Brueggemann) in order to ask what pedagogical guidance Scripture's own opening might yield for the actual teaching and learning of Scripture (following Smith). To state what I am arguing toward as a more succinct and specific question: how might Gen 1 guide me to teach Gen 1 in my first-year survey course on the Old Testament?[10]

Though Gen 1–11 is often designated as a "prologue" and set off from the rest of Genesis, there is still much scholarly wrestling to be done in coming to terms with the theological and hermeneutical import of what it might mean to read this literary unit as an entrance into the canon of Christian Scripture.[11] For example, it might seem self-evident that one start with the Gen 1 at the beginning of a basic course on the Old

---

[9] Walter Brueggemann, *The Creative Word: Canon as a Model for Biblical Education*, 2nd ed. (Philadelphia: Fortress Press, 2015). An educational agenda is central to Israel's faith and vision. Early on in Israel's grand narrative YHWH ties this agenda directly to Abraham's election and promise: "For I have elected him so that he will direct his children and his posterity to keep the way of YHWH by doing justice and righteousness in order that YHWH will bring upon Abraham what he has promised" (Gen 18:18). Later pivotal texts in Exodus, Deuteronomy, and Joshua paint a picture of how that educational agenda is to be routinize and ritualized in Israel's life, such that it is not too far off to describe Israel as a "nation of educators" (Jonathan Sacks, *Covenant and Conversation. Exodus: The Book of Redemption* [New Milford: Maggid Books, 2010], 78).

[10] At the risk of stating the obvious, I also contend that whatever this thought experiment yields will inform the practice of teaching that is wider than the subject of Scripture, beyond the first day of class, and (mutatis mutandis) to virtual modalities.

[11] Along these lines and from a variety of perspectives, see R. Norman Whybray, *Introduction to the Pentateuch* (Grand Rapids: Eerdmans, 1995), 35–40; Terence E. Fretheim, *God and World in the Old Testament: A Relational Theology of Creation* (Nashville: Abingdon, 2005); Mark S. Smith, *The Priestly Vision of Genesis 1* (Minneapolis: Fortress, 2010), 117–38; Richard S. Briggs, "Humans in the Image of God and Other Things Genesis Does Not Make Clear," *Journal of Theological Interpretation* 4 (2010): 111–26; Iain Provan, *Seriously Dangerous Religion: What the Old Testament Really Says and Why it Matters* (Waco: Baylor University Press, 2014), 1-20; Andreas Schüle, *Der Prolog der hebräischen Bibel: Der literar- und theologiegeschichliche Diskurs der Urgeschichte [Genesis 1–11]*, 2nd ed., AThANT 86 (Zürich: Theologischer Verlag, 2017).

Testament.¹² However, much of twentieth-century biblical scholarship tended to downplay the primeval history (Gen 1–11) as a particularly judicious starting point for introducing the Old Testament (notwithstanding addressing standard, prefatory content).¹³ I begin my first day of class with Genesis 1, and that decision owes something to the more recent emphasis in scholarship on narrative and canonical approaches (on display, for example, in Brueggemann's *The Creative Word*). To put it somewhat simplistically, Scripture begins here and so should I, which is to say that I consider the canonical arrangement as theologically important for learning to think *with* the text and not just *about* the text.¹⁴

Now, granted we take the introductory function of Gen 1–11 for the entire Bible, commensurate with its opening canonical placement, what could we learn if we look for *pedagogical* implications of regarding Gen 1 as such? To come at the question more imaginatively, what might we discover if we envision Gen 1 as the Master Teacher's "opening day of class"—a moment that is a particularly impressionable time for those encountering this text? The proposal that I offer as a generative experiment is that we imagine God in Gen 1 in the initial stages of pedagogical "homemaking" (à la Smith). From this viewpoint, Gen 1 pictures God at work setting up the frame and assembling the furniture for the kind of pedagogical dwelling into which the divine Tutor welcomes the human students. What might this homemaking God teach us about the art of homemaking (that is, teaching)?

---

¹² One could begin well by addressing more traditional questions of prolegomena that helpfully orient students to Scripture— for example, what comprises Scripture? who wrote it? when was it written? etc. These types of questions are necessary to tackle, but in my general introduction I choose to save any direct comment on these matters in the first session by devoting a later class period to some of them and allowing others to bubble up in discussion along the way.

¹³ This is a conclusion owed to the modernist belief that the "real story" starts with "real history." So, for example, consider Bernhard Anderson's *Understanding the Old Testament* (now in its fifth edition), a standard survey text of the last half of the twentieth century. The first chapter focuses on the formative event of the exodus—the primeval history does not take center stage until the fifth chapter. Gerhard von Rad, a giant among 20th century Old Testament theologians, rather (in)famously devalued the theological importance of creation in his influential essay "The Theological Problem of the O.T. Doctrine of Creation," trans. E. W. T. Dicken, in *Creation in the Old Testament*, ed. Bernhard W. Anderson; IRT 6 (Philadelphia: Fortress, 1984), 53–64. At one point in the essay von Rad describes the placement of Gen 1 at the beginning of the Bible as "circumstance" that unfortunately makes it appear more important to the faith of Israel than it actually was (54). See further Walter Brueggemann, "The Loss and Recovery of Creation in Old Testament Theology," *ThTo* 53 (1996): 177–90.

¹⁴ I borrow here language from Rabbi Abraham Heschel as relayed by Albert C. Outler, "Toward a Postliberal Hermeneutics," *ThTo* 42 (1985): 290: "It has seemed puzzling to me how greatly attached to the Bible you seem to be and yet how much like pagans you handle it. The great challenge to those of us who wish to take the Bible seriously is to let it teach us its own essential categories; and then for us to think *with* them, instead of just *about* them."

The metaphorical framing of Gen 1 as homemaking for the first day of class serves well the intent to listen for what the text might disclose about pedagogy. And yet, this framing also correlates with the metaphorical register Gen 1 itself draws on to recount the first week of creation. Genesis construes the primordial creation week in language and imagery that imaginatively draws from, inter alia, ancient Near Eastern temple building accounts.[15] Talk of divine rest, image-bearing, and the prominence of patterns of sevens are just a few of the more explicit cues that signal the creation narrative evokes and invokes cultic-liturgical symbolism. The theological upshot of such description conveys that in creation, God constructs the "heavens and the earth" as a cosmic sanctuary. God "temples" his creation by establishing his abode ("the heavens"), interlocking and overlapping with humanity's abode ("the earth"). Through the process of creating this "heaven and earth" habitat, God comes to reside in his cosmic temple in order to rule over his creation with and through the human vice-regents.[16] Creation, in a word, is God's archetypical act of sacred homemaking. Thus, interpreting the beginning of the canon as analogous to the project of classroom homemaking holds great promise for pedagogical reflection precisely because of the text's own imaginative, homologous vision.

If Gen 1's promise for pedagogical reflection unfolds in metaphorically reimagining creation as God's homemaking for class, then it follows to ask how—or even if—God's homemaking is a project that teachers can and should emulate. I would contend that God's creation of humankind "in the image of God" (1:26–27) anticipates this question. Much can be (and has been) said about the *imago dei*, but I want here to draw out in brief only two points germane to this discussion.[17] First, here—and in my opening

---

[15] Some of the definitive articles in this regard are collected in L. Michael Morales, ed. *Cult and Cosmos: Tilting Toward a Temple-Centered Theology*, Biblical Tools and Studies 18 (Leuven: Peeters, 2014). See also the collection and synthesis of Richard Davidson, "Earth's First Sanctuary: Genesis 1–3 and Parallel Creation Accounts," *AUSS* 53 (2015): 65–89. A more popular treatment is provided by John H. Walton, *The Lost World of Genesis One: Ancient Cosmology and the Origins of Debate* (Downers Grove: InterVarsity Academic, 2009), esp. 77–85. A short, accessible, and worthy presentation of this theme is The Bible Project's video entitled "Temple," which can be located on youtube.com or at https://bibleproject.com/videos/temple/.

[16] Isaiah 66:1–2 makes the connection between creation and temple building explicit: "Thus says Yhwh: Heaven is my throne, and earth is my footstool. Where is the house that you will build me? And where is the place of my rest? All this was made by my hand, and thus it all came into being, declares Yhwh."

[17] The history of interpretation on the "image of God" in Gen 1:26–27 (and beyond) is voluminous. See most recently Ronald Hendel, *Genesis 1–11: A New Translation with Introduction and Commentary*, AYB 1A (New Haven: Yale University Press, 2024), XXX; John Day, *From Creation to Abraham: Further Studies in Genesis 1–11* (London: T&T Clark, 2022), 21–41; Kumiko Takeuchi, "Interpretations of Genesis 1,26-27: A Case of 'The Emperor's New Clothes'?" *SJOT* (2025): 1–24. My own interpretation owes much to J. Richard Middleton, *The Liberating Image: The Imago Dei in Genesis 1* (Grand Rapids: Baker, 2005), though I am in sympathy with the critiques offered by Richard

class on Gen 1—I propose that the *imago dei* implies in the narration of Genesis that humans reflect God, and this reflection is primarily (though not exclusively) focused in Gen 1 on the representational task of exercising dignified empowerment as divine emissaries. God sets humanity apart as image bearers, blessing them in their representational role, so that they rule, proliferate, fill, and subdue (1:26–28). Humans thereby serve as extensions of God's own power and presence in the world, filling the world. The *imago dei*, therefore, assumes humans can and should emulate God in their inhabitation. God the homemaker, in fact, summons and equips them to participate with God in the ongoing, creative "home-flourishing" of creation. It is the primordial purpose and sacred delight of every human to live into this creational status whatever their vocational station.

Second, whatever interpretations or implications, related or otherwise, that one further deduces about how humanity manifests the *imago dei*, they must all reckon ultimately with the fact that the designation is derivative of God's character and activity. That is, to ask how humanity reflects the image in Gen 1 inescapably leads to examining in what manner God is imaged in Gen 1—how does Gen 1 portray God? A good start to answer the question surely comes by discerning God's character through God's actions in Gen 1. In Smith's vocabulary, by creating, God is making "choices about how time and space are used, what interactions will take place, what rules and rhythms will govern them, what will be offered as nourishment and used to build shared imagination, and what patterns will be laid out for [creatures] to move among."[18] God's homemaking activity reveals the *kind* of God at work in creating.[19] And, I suggest, Gen 1's depiction of the kind of God at work—the ethos of God—is where the pedagogical promise of Gen 1 finds its surest, analogical footing. In other words, the principal manner in which humans can and should imitate God is by reflecting the divine, ethical disposition discovered in the display of God's creative words and deeds. In stating this conclusion, I reveal what I settle on as the overriding theme of my first day of class in my introduction to the Old Testament course, namely, *to explore with my students what kind of God Gen 1 imagines*.

My proposal, of course, beckons for further exegetical elaboration on the characteristics of God on display in the divine homemaking act that is Gen 1. So, too, it remains to explore how such characteristics find concrete expression in actual pedagogical contexts. Unfortunately, the limitations of this essay mean an earnest exploration must await another time. I only gesture here toward my belief that the text brims with

---

S. Briggs, "Humans in the Image of God and Other Things Genesis Does Not Make Clear," *Journal of Theological Interpretation* 4 (2010): 111–26.

[18] Smith, *On Christian Teaching*, loc. 264, in describing what he means by a pedagogy characterized by "homemaking" rather than a methodology or technique.

[19] See especially Michael J. Chan and Brent A. Strawn, eds., *What Kind of God? Collected Essays of Terence Fretheim*, Siphrut 14 (Winona Lake: Eisenbrauns, 2015), esp. 25–39, 87–97, 195–205.

theology that is ripe with pedagogical ramifications. I will briefly give one example as a model of the kind of reflection I am commending, but let me first set the context of my opening day of class. About midway through the class, I ask for volunteers to read aloud for the class Gen 1:1–2:4. I prime the whole group to listen to the reading with this question in mind: how does Gen 1 depict or "picture" God? I encourage them to pay attention to how God is portrayed by the narrative as if encountering this narrative construal for the first time. I give the example of their inevitable formation of impressions of me and this class—which they have encountered for the first time—as an apt analogy for what I am asking them to do with the text. After the reading, I invite the class to name with their surrounding colleagues three or four characteristics that describe the God rendered in the passage. I advise them that they must be able to explain their characteristics with specifics from the text.

One of the first characteristics students usually identify is God's commanding power. It is not difficult, of course, to make the case for divine power from Gen 1. But what is often underappreciated by my students is how God's practice of power reveals an authority that creates room for other participants. God invites significant contribution to, responsibility for, even ruling within the shared, creational abode from a variety of created beings (for example, 1:11–12, 16, 22, 24, 28). God's authority delegates authority. How might God's sharing of power find a place in my teaching as I teach Gen 1 in my (first day of) class? A few practices come immediately to mind. In my Ghanaian context, where the "sage on the stage" pedagogical model dominates (and is often experienced dominatingly), I express delegated authority by initiating involvement from students ("let us...") with well-prepared, open-ended questions and sufficient space for productive dialogue. If the space allows, I could summon students to position their chairs or desks toward one another even as I maintain my role to weave in and out to listen in on—and perhaps nonchalantly to prompt—their exchange of views. Having the students actually move chairs and tables draws them into the creative act of building community. I engage student contributions with affirming responses, being deliberate to model positive, fruitful dialogue. Moreover, I could choose to pose this very question to the students as a way of naming (think Gen 2!) a relational repertoire of practices to shape our collective learning experience of thinking with Scripture instead of just about it.[20]

Along similar lines, we could ponder other divine characteristics emerging from the divine design in Gen 1, such as variety ("according to their kinds"), beauty ("it is good!"), generous allocation ("I have given you every"), subduing the chaos ("fill and rule"), rhythmic rest ("God rested"), and sacred affirmation ("God blessed"). These primordial themes and more are charged with potential when refracted through the lens

---

[20] Beyond the first day of class, we might imagine a power-delegating model of education that includes the co-creation of the course syllabus by faculty and students or giving students the opportunity for input in assessment questions or procedures.

of divine pedagogy, analogously contextualized to classroom practice. Indeed, God's own sevenfold evaluation throughout the creation week (1:4, 10, 12, 18, 21, 25, 31) offers warrant for the regular appraisal of our classroom homemaking in this angle of reference.

In sum, I believe for the teacher to create his or her pedagogy "in appropriate correspondence" derived from God's activity is itself an application welcomed by the text's own theological vision. Genesis 1, I suggest, holds great promise for expanding our educational habitus when we pay attention to God's own homemaking within the text. Meditating on the divine character revealed in creation could allow the primordial "pedagogical" beginning to inform our ongoing pedagogical practice—especially the beginning of class. It seems appropriate to conclude this essay, offered in tribute to our teacher Dr. Allen Black, with an observation from the Jewish tradition of the significance of teachers whose craft reflects the Divine Teacher.

> Study and teaching, in this tradition, are holy acts; and the teacher of divine wisdom is a revered personality. The rabbinic teacher represents God both symbolically, by imitating Divine behavior, and pedagogically, by leading students to understand and embrace divine teachings. ... This is why the rabbis taught that if you must choose between saving your teacher or your parent, save your teacher first, for your parent 'brings you into this world, but your teacher introduces you to the world to come' (Mishnah, Bava Metzia 3: 11).[21]

---

[21] Hanan A. Alexander, "God as Teacher: Jewish Reflections on a Theology of Pedagogy," *Journal of Beliefs and Values* 22 (2001): 6

15
The Imagery of Níkē (Victory), Animal Sacrifice, and Incense Offering on an Ephesian Altar:
An Ephesian Altar with Two Níkai at Sacrifice

Richard E. Oster, Jr. [1]

The monument discussed here is a marble altar (65 x 87 x 40 cm)[2] that dates from the mid-first century AD (Photo 1), and its imagery focuses upon two winged humanoids called Níkai.[3]

Photo 1, Richard E. Oster, Jr. Used by Permission.

---

[1] In my forty-six years of teaching at Harding School of Theology (Fall 1978–Spring 2024), I have served under four University Presidents, about half a dozen Deans, with every librarian that HST has ever had, and with a variety of scholars on the Bible faculty at Harding School of Theology. Yet, I cannot think of a greater blessing I received while teaching at Harding School of Theology than to have had Allen Black as a dear friend and colleague during most of this time. Allen Black was a marvelous sounding board for some of my ideas and approaches to Scripture, and on occasion he kept me out of trouble. Allen has been a confidant for me personally, and I am forever thankful for that. Allen is truly a beloved friend and brother in Christ. It is a joy to contribute to this volume of essays. It is a small way to honor and thank him for decades of work together and fellowship at Harding School of Theology. Dr. Black did a great job introducing students to the many facets and bumps in the road of exegesis, both of the Greek and English texts of the New Testament. *Ad multos annos*.

[2] Dr. Georg Plattner, Director, Collection of Greek and Roman Antiquities/Ephesos Museum kindly provided me with this information, email dated 02.07.2025.

[3] Johannes Scherf, "Nike, I. Mythology," BNP 9:754–55; Balbina Bäbler, "Nike, II. Iconography," BNP 9:755–56; Johannes Scherf, "Victoria," BNP 15:399–400. See also Tonio Hölscher and Victoria Romana, *Archäologische Untersuchungen zur Geschichte und Wesenart der römischen Siegesgöttin von den Anfängen bis zum Ende des 3. Jhs. n. Chr.* (Mainz: Philipp von Zabern, 1967); Annette Brosend and

Long before and geographically beyond the setting of this Ephesian altar, elements of Níkē's visual language were already ubiquitous. In the far eastern parts of the former Seleucid Empire, for example, iconic presence is known at the Hellenistic archaeological site of Al-Khanoum (see also Al-Khanoum plaque) in central-eastern Afghanistan, north of the Hindu Kush mountain range.[4] Níkai were also known in Western Greek colonies from an earlier era. "Victories" is the simple gloss for the Greek term Níkai, proclaiming victory and success in diverse visual ways, for example, military warfare, athletic competition of gladiators, civil litigation, civic accomplishments, and religious rewards.[5] Those prominently displayed two-winged beings on the Ephesian altar represent heavenly beings.[6] As in the case of Hermes, these wings on a Níkē were intended to connote travel, and rapid travel at that, as a Níkē carried out the will of deities toward humans and likewise brought petitions to the appropriate deities. Within artistic variety reflecting a multiplicity of historical settings, cultures, timeframes, aesthetic perspectives, and space available to an artist's medium, to name a few, Níkai are visible on ancient coins, in statuary art, on cult statues, on numerous vase paintings, frescoes, miniature arts, architecture, and mosaics. Níkē is also well known in classical literature and epigraphy.

On this Ephesian monument, these Níkai are leading two animals to sacrifice, and one of the Níkē is carrying a censer for the offering of incense. Depictions of Níkai from the Greek, Hellenistic, and Roman worlds are preserved among the various corpora of ancient artifacts, for example, coins, vases, statuary, friezes, frescoes, weaponry, mosaics, epigraphic artwork, lamps, and jewelry, to name some of the most obvious corpora.

This artifact is an altar discovered at the site of ancient Ephesus. The altar is currently housed in the Ephesos Museum in Vienna, Austria rather than in the Ephesus

---

Martin Kemkes, *Victoria der römische Sieg und seine göttlichen Garanten* (Oppenheim: Nünnerich-Asmus, 2023).

[4] At the Early Kushan period (1–2 centuries AD) Greek language and symbols were still in use in the iconography of coinage. Razieh Taasob, "Development of Greek Religious Iconography in Early Kushan Coinage: Adaptation, Integration and Transformation," *Studia Hercynia* 27.1 (2023): 178–88.

[5] Richard E. Oster, Jr. *Seven Congregations in a Roman Crucible: A Commentary on Revelation 1–3* (Eugene: Wipf & Stock, 2013), 108–12. Tonio Hölscher, *Visual Power in Ancient Greece and Rome. Between Art and Social Reality*, Sather Classical Lectures 73 (Berkeley: University of California Press, 2018), 6, says, "For a long time, studies of human culture were primarily oriented toward script and literature: mostly scholarly disciplines from history to theology and law, are traditionally based on written sources. Yet, in the realm of active politics, the significance of visuality was realized much earlier." The use of visual materials, iconography, is slowly coming into New Testament Studies.

[6] While the wings on the Níkai are seemingly canonical, many of the other iconographic facets that depict victory, for example, the wreath, Palm frond, and a globe of the earth, were sometimes variable. To be sure, there was adaptation in the visual depictions of Níkē throughout the Mediterranean, yet these were seemingly not for the goals of iconotropy.

Archaeological Museum in Selçuk, Turkey, situated about 2 kilometers from the archaeological site of ancient Ephesus.[7] Unfortunately, archaeologists did not discover this altar in situ. When discovered, this artifact served as a column base in the Arcadiane section of Ephesus, along the lengthy colonnaded road stretching between the Ephesian theater and the ancient harbor.[8] The reuse of this altar during the early Byzantine period precludes our knowing its original setting, whether, for example, it was used in a domestic setting, in a small cultic setting, or even serving as a pietistic offering by a devotee in a larger temple of the first century. Notwithstanding the fact that the details of this altar's original location are forever lost (and that is a consequential loss), religious convictions and spiritual aspirations of those who worshipped at it during the early Roman Empire are not lost without a trace. This altar is devoid of written words but contains pregnant imagery that is helpful for New Testament students in their appreciation of Hellenistic-Roman religious artifacts such as this. This early Roman altar is not unique as a bearer of important images, but rather is part of a vast largely unpublished corpus[9] of such artifacts that reveal the quality and quantity of ancient iconography. By means of this artifact's visual vocabulary and expressions, New Testament scholarship can better understand and appreciate iconographic investigations and methodology and thereby improve one's understanding of this sacred artifact made of stone.

Since it could be easily overlooked by some, it is noteworthy that the iconography on this artifact corresponds to the purpose of the monument on which it is found. Specifically, the spiritual ambience conjured up by imagery of a lively worship scene has heightened significance when utilized on an artifact originally designed for worship. This pattern of correspondence between iconography and the purpose of the artifact upon which it is found is not unique to this Ephesian monument. One of the numerous other examples includes imagery of the afterlife (for example, the door to the underworld; Hermes waiting to escort the dead into Hades) carved onto sarcophagi, or another, the imagery of the god of wine depicted on various drinking vessels used in Dionysiac banquets. The few iconographic elements of this particular Ephesian altar were prosaic for the inhabitants of Ephesus. The presence of divine winged beings in a cultic setting, depictions of large and uncooperative animals being led to slaughter,[10]

---

[7] Wolfgang Oberleitner, *Funde aus Ephesos und Samothrake* (Vienna: Ueberreuter, 1978).

[8] This road was 528 meters long and originated sometime in the early Roman period. Its final form and name came during the reign of Emperor Arcadius (AD 395–408). See Peter Scherrer, *Ephesus: The New Guide,* trans. Lionel Bier and George M. Luxon, rev. ed. (Istanbul: Ege, 2000), 172.

[9] To my knowledge the *Lexicon Iconographicum Mythologiae Classicae (=LIMC)* Artemis Verlag is the best representative collection.

[10] Showing a restive animal being led to sacrifice is a standard iconographic theme, see Parthenon Frieze, North Frieze, Slab II, 4–5.

and a cultic instrument for burning incense[11] that would waft aromas upwards to the gods were all part and parcel of a liturgical setting.

Any representative Hellenistic-Roman person within eyesight of this altar or worshipping in its presence would have a nearly instinctive recognition of iconographic elements. This person's "nearly instinctive" familiarity with cultic scenes and the separate elements of the altar's iconography would result from this person's unending exposure to the graven gods of antiquity. The typical family of Ephesus was decidedly polytheistic and worshipped a multitude of carved deities that were associated with frequently occurring rituals and public processions. From childhood, Ephesian babies were swaddled in the garments of polytheistic prayers, hymns, rituals, colors, religious themes on the facades of temples and many public buildings, aromas associated with worship, and artifacts of worship, both domestic[12] and public.

Unlike their ancient counterparts, it is a very different experience when modern Western visitors tour museum galleries of classical antiquities. For these modern tourists, the iconographic details and spiritual meaning of this sacrificial tableau are rarely comprehended, much less appreciated. One can be sure, however, that in the era of the early Roman Empire, the religious imagery of this Ephesian monument was transparent even to the most uneducated person, even to individuals laden with disease and physical limitations, and even to those who survived from the scraps (both literal and metaphoric) of the few wealthy who led opulent and luxurious lives in Hellenistic-Roman urban centers like Ephesus. When this lapidary and other craftsmen produced this wordless monument, they thereby encouraged convictions, devotion, and hopes about the sacred task of the Níkai who, anthropomorphically speaking, offered up sacrifices from the worshippers to the gods and goddesses and likewise carried hopes and gratitude to them in the celestial regions. They also brought down to the various devotees a myriad of sought-after blessings.[13]

THE NEXUS OF METAPHYSICS AND LITURGY

Most of the women and men of the Hellenistic and early Roman period, whether

---

[11] A fundamental idea associated with incense is that if the aroma pleases humans, then it also pleases the gods. This liturgical process was pleasing to the olfactory senses of both gods (anthropomorphically) and humans, relishing in the fragrances of wood, leaves, bark, resins or crushed grains. E. Simon and H. Sarian, "Rauchopfer (2.c)," *ThesCRA* 1:255.

[12] Marcus T. Cicero, a prominent Roman citizen assassinated during the final decades of the Roman Republic, wrote, "What is more sacred, what more inviolably hedged about by every kind of sanctity, than the home of every individual citizen? Within its circle are his altars, his hearths, his household gods, his religion, his observances, his ritual; it is a sanctuary" (*Fragmentary Speeches*, 41).

[13] Hölscher, *Visual Power*, 252, says that "the primary purpose of images was not to give unambiguous information about unknown topics but to provide visual evidence of (pre)given beings and events, of myth of past and present time, in order that the community of 'users' could socially live with them."

Jewish, those belonging to Jesus the Anointed, or those who revered many deities (usually with images), believed that the whole truth about their gods and goddesses included thoughts about terrestrial, celestial, and subterranean religious realities. Within these cosmological thoughts embraced by various devotees, the Níkai played a vibrant role in performing/reflecting the terrestrial worship within the celestial realms. Into the presence of one or more deities, the Níkai bring the religious facts and truths of sacrificed animals and aromatic incense. Assuming the petitioned goddess or god was pleased with the life of the worshipper and the cultic purity of the sacrifice, he would then grant the wishes of the petitioner.[14]

To better appreciate this nexus of metaphysics and liturgy and the subsequent traffic between heaven and the earth, one should ruminate on the fact that the sky surely hung low in the cosmology of the typical Ephesian. Coincidentally, there are two literary sources from the first century AD that reflect the conviction that heavenly beings visited terrestrial realms from their empyrean homes.

Pagan worshippers held a firm belief in the transcendent nature of their gods and goddesses, many residing at Mount Olympus.[15] Nevertheless, they also believed in the immanence of their deities. When Luke represents an episode of healing (Acts 14:8–20), the two Christian apostles Barnabas and Paul (Acts 14:4, 14) were mistaken for the deities Zeus and Hermes, demonstrating in the eyes of pagans that "gods have come down to us in human form" (οἱ θεοὶ ὁμοιωθέντες ἀνθρώποις κατέβησαν πρὸς ἡμᾶς, Acts 14:11).[16] Another ancient voice addressing this issue speaks in one of the few Latin novels preserved, viz., the Satyricon. Its author Gaius Petronius wrote about the city of Rome at a time generally contemporary with the Apostle Paul's Letter to the Romans. In the Satyricon, a character reportedly says (with only a little hyperbole), "Indeed the gods walk abroad so commonly in our streets that it is easier to meet a god than a man."[17]

In the midst of this aspect of Graeco-Roman theology regarding transcendence on the one hand and immanence on the other, the divine Níkai served a crucial role by giving assurance to worshippers about the success of their offerings to those in the transcendent world.

---

[14] Simon Pulleyn, *Prayer in Greek Religion*, OCM (Oxford: Clarendon, 1997).

[15] Johannes Scherf, "Olympus, II. Myths," BNP 10:115. Hölscher, *Visual Power*, 209, rightly reminds modern, Western readers that, "The themes of Greek and Roman works of art go far beyond the world of human life: a large part of ancient art represents gods and goddesses, heroes and events of myth and fantastic monsters, like Centaurs, Griffins and Sphinxes. Often, the spheres of human and superhuman beings are even intertwined in the same scene or composition."

[16] Craig S. Keener, *Acts: An Exegetical Commentary* (Grand Rapids: Baker Academic, 2013), 2:2148–49.

[17] Petronius, *Satyricon*, 17. Vtique nostra regio tam praesentibus plena est numinibus, ut facilius possis deum quam hominem invenire.

In the Olympian realms of worship, Níkai would give assurance of success in the sacrifices and the numerous votive requests. After all, approaching the gods and goddesses on Mt. Olympus for the purpose of securing petitions was no facile undertaking. There should be no doubt that it was some earthly priest or his assistant who physically struggled to control and then to slaughter a possibly restive bull or ram (like the rams on this Ephesian monument), but the artist sometimes carved the imagery of Níkai rather than human officiants on this Ephesian altar. In so doing, the lapidary, or the one who chose him, chose to leave *terra firma* and move to the celestial realms. When he carved two Níkai leading those animals and bearing a censer with aromatic sacrifices, he ignited the religious imagination and broadened the metaphysical landscape of the worshipping believers.[18] It seems highly doubtful that worshipers would have been equally enraptured by worshipping while contemplating a human priest and victimarius carved upon an altar in comparison with worshipping in the presence of winged Níkai who had been in the celestial presence of, *inter alia*, Zeus, Athena, Isis, or Dionysus.

Under the guise of a dialogue between Socrates and Diotima (imaginary woman, priestess, prophetess, tutor of Socrates in the Symposium), Plato expresses an important view about the role of invisible intermediaries moving between a workaday, visible, terrestrial world and a supernal, transcendent, and largely invisible world where sacrifices speak in metaphysical overtones. This scene presented by Plato corresponds in some measure to the role manifested by the Níkai when offerings were made. Plato wrote (Symp. 202e–203a) from the perspective that there were οἱ δαίμονες [divinities] who were responsible for communicating and for bringing blessings between the supernal and the terrestrial worlds:

> "for everything concerned with spirits (γὰρ πᾶν τὸ δαιμόνιον) lies between god and mortal."
> "What function does it have?" I asked.
> "To interpret and communicate the affairs of men to the gods and from the gods to men, the petitions and sacrifices of the former [the humans], and of the latter [the gods] the commands and favors returned for the sacrifices, and, being in the middle of both, it fills the gap between them, so that the whole is bound together into one (ὥστε τὸ πᾶν αὐτὸ αὑτῷ συνδεδέσθαι). Through this also

---

[18] Pertinent to a worshipper's encounter with the divine in the form of Níkē is this description of the encounter of the worshipper with deities. "By contrast, in ritual-centered viewing, the grounds for a direct relationship have been prepared. The viewer enters a sacred space, a special place set apart from ordinary life, in which the god dwells. In this liminal site, the viewer enters the god's world and likewise the deity intrudes directly into the viewer's world in a highly ritualized context. ... Viewing the sacred is a process of divesting the spectator of all the social and discursive elements which distinguish his or her subjectivity from that of the god into whose space the viewer will come," Jas Elsner, "Between Mimeses and Divine Power, Visuality in the Greco-Roman," *Roman Eyes, Visuality and Subjectivity in Art and Text* (Princeton: Princeton University Press, 2007), 23–24.

all divination proceeds, the skill of priests and those engaged in sacrifice and ritual and incantations and the whole of prophecy and magic. God does not mix with humanity, but by this means all exchange and communication from the gods to humans takes place both when they are awake and when asleep."[19]

Regarding this liturgical setting of Níkai on the Ephesian altar, it is very instructive and to the point that the two most important temples in the ancient classical world, namely the Temple of Zeus (in Olympia) and the Temple of Ἀθηνᾶ Παρθένος (in Athens), contained statues of Níkai, and they were configured strategically and prominently with the worshipper in mind. Specifically, Níkai were placed in the outstretched right hand of the respective deities Zeus and Athena. The significance of this fact should not be minimized. The famous classical Greek sculptor Phidias designed both of these colossal cult statues.[20] From this important location in the right hand of the god Zeus or the goddess Athena, Níkē gave assurance of successful vows, offerings, and prayers to Zeus or Athena and also assurance to those receiving blessings and requests made to the deities. It is clear that Phidias did not intend for the Níkai to be worshipped alongside Zeus and Athena, but to stand in the palms of their hands, always prepared to answer their beck and call.

CULT STATUE OF ZEUS AT OLYMPIA

Sadly, the temple of Zeus in Olympia and its world-famous cult statue of Zeus met their final doom in the ravages of the post-classical world, caused by earthquakes and Christian jihadism against pagan monuments and artifacts. Coins, gems, and literary testimony[21] concur, however, that Níkē was an essential part of the cult statue of Zeus at Olympia (Photo 2). These sources make clear the integral presence of Níkē at the right hand of Zeus.[22]

---

[19] Plato, *Lysis, Symposium, Phaedra*, 246–47.
[20] Richard Neudecker, "Phidias," BNP 11:3–6.
[21] Gisela M. A. Richter, *The Sculpture and Sculptors of the Greeks*, 4th ed. (New Haven: Yale University Press, 1970), 171–74.
[22] See "*Níkē* und Zeus," *LIMC* 6.2 (1992): 202–6.

Photo 2: Realistic anonymous drawing of Zeus statue in temple at Olympia. The numismatic image of Zeus at Olympia is from a coin of Tarsus used kindly by permission of Classical Numismatic Group, Inc., http://www.cngcoins.com.

CULT STATUE OF ATHENA IN THE PARTHENON

The observation of archaeologist and art historian Gisela M. A. Richter in the twentieth century that one's "imagination has to work hard to reconstruct from these faint reflections the vision of the great temple statue about forty feet high (with its base), which the worshiper beheld when he entered the cella of the Parthenon"[23] is fortunately no longer true. In the late twentieth century, the State of Tennessee (USA), in conjunction with the Tennessee Centennial Exposition, constructed in the state capital of Nashville a replica of the Greek Parthenon found in Athens, but without a replica of the cult statue. Later, employing the numerous ancient literary sources, ancient statues of Athena Parthenos (Photo 3), and numismatic testimony, this Nashville Parthenon received a replica of the cult statue of the goddess Athena Parthenos in the late 20th century (May 20, 1990); the gilding of the cult image occurred in the early years of the 21st century (2002). Scholars, professors, and tourists can now behold with approximate accuracy what Gisela M. A. Richter could only imagine, and now one sees what "the worshiper beheld when he entered the cella of the Parthenon." It is clear that Níkē, located in Athena's right hand, served an important role in the success of the sacrifices and petitions presented by those who piously gave prayers and offerings to this Athenian goddess.

---

[23] Richter, *The Sculpture and Sculptors of the Greeks*, 170.

*Photo 3: Richard E. Oster, Jr.
Used by Permission.*

Temple of Athena Níkē

Although certainly not as famous as the two above-mentioned temples, there is a third temple that affords helpful insights for this investigation, namely the Temple of Athena Níkē (Ναός Αθηνάς Νίκης) situated on the Acropolis in Athens. Adjacent to the Propylaea on the Acropolis stood a smaller temple dedicated to the goddess Athena Níkē. It was originally constructed for the worship of the goddess Athena, who protected the city and provided victory in times of war. Of significance for this study is the frieze of the Temple of Athena Níkē and the parapet around the temple. One slab from this frieze shows Níkē controlling a restive animal by placing her foot on a rock, while another slab contains a frieze showing two Níkai leading a bull bucking combatively with its two front legs in the air. Another Níkē on the parapet of the temple is the famous "Níkē adjusting her sandal." The earlier statements of interpretation by Maria Brouskari are helpful in understanding Níkē participation in the sacrificial activities of worshippers at the temple of Athena Níkē. She observes about the "Níkē adjusting her sandal":

> Swift-winged Níkai quickly come and go, clad in swirling garments. They lead animals to the altar or arrange trophies or offer something to the goddess who

is herself present. ... This relief of a Níkē mounting a stair originally stood above the right side of the stairway by means of which people approaching the Propylaia could enter the precinct of Athena Níkē. Thus worshipers at the temple of Athena Níkē were accompanied up the steps by Níkē.[24]

I conclude from all of the above evidence, principally iconographic,[25] that the ubiquitous Níkai were depicted in temples and often upon countless altars and minted in numismatic iconography in order to visualize the Níkai assistance with offerings and sacrifices of various kinds. It was a moment when unsuspecting animals became victims at worship and altars became religious abattoirs. Libations were poured and incense was burnt to various gods and goddesses, and this provided assurance of the efficaciousness of these offerings.

OFFERING OF INCENSE

The final piece of significant iconography on this Ephesian altar pertains to the incense offered in a censer. This container is generally known by the term thymiatērion (θυμιατήριον). A censer is depicted on the Ephesian monument in the left hand of the second Níkē[26] and was held vertically. Thymiatēria came in all shapes and dimensions.[27] In Athens, one can see a censer carved on the Parthenon Frieze, carried upright by the leading figure (Photo 4).[28]

---

[24] Maria S. Brouskari, *Acropolis Museum: A Descriptive Catalogue*, (Athens: Commercial Bank of Greece, 1974), 157, 162.

[25] An attendant discipline is "iconology" often associated with, among others, Erwin Panofsky. Its nuances are very important at times, but not in this study of Níkai. See Jan Bialostocki, "Iconography and Iconology," *Encyclopedia of World Art* (London: McGraw-Hill, 1963), 7:769–85.

[26] BDAG, s.v. defines this word "as a place or vessel for the burning of incense," 461, or a container to transport incense. This term is employed in Heb 9:4, but Rev 8:3–4 uses the term λιβανωτός (generally meaning incense but in Revelation the place of the incense). Besides *thymiatērion* being one of the standard terms used by classical authors for incense burner (Tonio Hölscher, "Rauchopfer," *ThesCRA*, 5:212–24), it also has that meaning in the LXX at 2 Chron 26:19, Ezek 8:11 and 4 Macc 7:11.

[27] Cristiana Zaccagnino, *Il Thymiaterion nel Mondo Greco* (Rome: L'Erma di Bretschneider, 1998).

[28] Slab 8, no. 57, East Frieze of Parthenon. See Ian Jenkins, *The Parthenon Frieze* (London: British Museum Press, 1994), 82.

Photo 4: Richard E. Oster, Jr. Used by Permission.

On our Ephesian monument, Níkē is employing an easily portable model of a thymiatērion. In the collection of the J. Paul Getty Museum, one can see a well-preserved marble example of a thymiatērion similar in design and appearance to the one depicted on our Ephesian altar.[29] The museum label helpfully states:

This thymiaterion is composed of three parts: a stemmed foot, a deep receptacle, and a lid. The deep bowl, which would have held a large amount of costly incense, rests on the spreading tray-like top of the tall foot. ... Traces of red paint remain on the foot and lid suggesting that the thymiaterion was originally brightly painted. A yellowish, shiny, resin-like staining on the interior of the lid indicates that this incense burner was actually used and not just a display piece.

As noted earlier, the important connection of Níkē with incense offerings is demonstrated here with the iconography of thymiatērion. She provided assistance and assurance with the burnt sacrifice of incense just as she had done also with animal life or liquid offerings. The liquids coming from the slaughter of animals flowed downward and were ritually collected. The liquid of the libations naturally flowed downward when they were poured upon the altar. The scent and aroma from the censer, however, naturally rose upward in the direction of the supernal dwellings of the gods and goddesses.

Any particular artifact might illuminate the understanding of Níkē in antiquity, but the following two artifacts (from the Berlin Museum) are examples of artifacts that

---

[29] http://www.getty.edu/art/collection/objects/32131/unknown-maker-thymiaterion-and-lid-greek-south-italian-or-sicilian-4th-century-bc/. Accessed Feb. 08, 2025.

shine light brightly.[30] The two bull slaying scenes in Photo 5 draw the worshipper not only toward the world of liturgy but actually place them into the metaphysical world while they worship. These Níkai are not only leading animals to an event sacrifice as on the Ephesian altar, but they are themselves, knives in hand, drawing the blood of the cultic sacrifices in the presence of the Olympian deities.

Photo 5: Richard E. Oster, Jr. Used by Permission.

The scene of the two Níkai slitting the throats of these sacrificial animals was sculpted into the altar in order to depict the supernal/metaphysical realities which on earth were performed by one of the human victimarii, that is to say, professional attendants who physically stun the large animals with a mallet or beetle and then kill it by slitting its throat and collecting the warm, fresh blood. To be clear, no one saw or expected to see Níkai appearing as they flew down from the heavenly realms, arriving at a site for sacrifice, in order to slit the throat of sacrificial animals, to pour libations, or to offer incense. Literal Níkai never belonged to this mortal world; they are at home in the world of the immortals. Accordingly, it is not the terrestrial setting that those Níkai depict, but rather, they depict a supernal, divine, and invisible reality of what human eyes could never see, but desired to know, viz., that the gods were benevolently interested in them, were pleased with their lives and religious ceremonies, and would reward them accordingly. We moderns, unlike those living as contemporaries of the ancient altars, prefer to perform an autopsy of a dead monument, dissecting its artistic and archaeological corpus and classifying what was discovered. The ancients knew naturally that these were stone Níkai, but those who believed rested their worship and hope on a metaphysical reality that these pointed to and which invited them to participate in.

---

[30] Hölscher, *Visual Power*, 326–27, Fig. 159, "Frieze with Victories slaughtering a bull," in the Forum of Trajan. Similar iconography is seen at Benevento, Italy on the impressive Arch of Trajan, AD 114, on its bas-relief panels.

As is true in most religions, the devotees of gods and goddesses worshipped with the expectation of benefit and reward for their devotion and pious offering of sacrifices.[31] Human participants were enwrapped with thoughts and emotions pertaining to their own lives and circumstances.[32] A Roman duumvir would have concerns and petitions distinct from those of a farm slave. A farmer struggling with the success of his crops would have concerns distinct from a person with disabilities. One can only imagine the plethora of petitions and concerns expressed by those who sought the aid of the Olympians. Those experiencing political instability, domestic chaos, threats from curses and malevolent magic, romantic interests, judicial prayers seeking justice against an opponent,[33] and economic uncertainties, they all might seek the victory that came from the Olympians by the efforts of the Níkai. The artistic incorporation of the Níkai on various media, established and affirmed the presence of a divine/supernatural umbilical cord that came from the Olympian world. Worshippers were nurtured, and the pain and concerns of those manacled to workaday troubles and needs had deities upon whom they could call: Angst, mortality of one's children,[34] fecundity of livestock, domestic malnutrition, sporadic uncertainty of grain deliveries from North Africa, incursions from border areas in Armenia and Britain, personal health, and so many more stemming from the general experiences of life.[35]

Moreover, the visual message of the winged Victory gave assurances to the Ephesian worshippers about the rewards of such cultic activity. This reality of assurance was not impacted by one's gender, legal status, social standing, or economic resources. The sights, sounds, tastes, tactility, and aromas of worship could be and were experienced in public celebrations as well as in domestic and cultic festivals. In addition, cultic scenes with similar images were minted on ancient coins, even on small denominations. Numismatic iconography reinforced the knowledge of deities, animal sacrifice, and incense, all of which were shared by most of the population. The rudiments of pagan mythology and the liturgical expressions of this mythology were widely embraced

---

[31] Pulleyn, *Prayer in Greek Religion*.

[32] Alexandra Sofroniew, *Household Gods: Private Devotion in Ancient Greece and Rome* (Los Angeles: The J. Paul Getty Museum, 2015), 3, says, "The ancients conceived of their relationship with the gods as based upon reciprocity."

[33] Chrysi Kotsifou, "Prayers and Petitions for Justice. Despair and the 'Crossing of Boundaries' between Religion and Law," *Tyche: Contributions to Ancient History, Papyrology, and Epigraphy* 31 (2016): 167–200. https://doi.org/10.15661/tyche.2016.031.11. Accessed Feb. 8, 2025.

[34] Sofroniew, *Household Gods*, 73, says, "Both human and agricultural fertility was of huge concern in the ancient world and the reason behind countless prayers."

[35] Sofroniew, *Household Gods*, 2–3, says, "Indeed, every part of the ancient world was touched by the divine. The traditional pantheon of deities oversaw all aspects of human affairs, from marriage to childbirth to illness and death, as well as success in athletic competitions and in law-courts. ... In the bustling polytheistic environment, religious behavior was embedded in daily life. Few actions and activities could have been regarded as purely secular."

whether by those who lived in rather unbearable insulae or in covetable "terrace houses" in Ephesus, replete with costly and numerous accoutrements, with mythic scenes shown in its boldly colored frescoes and the delicate mosaics of its homes.[36]

It seems reasonable to explore the question, perhaps an admittedly anachronistic question, of how iconography was employed to express to the Graeco-Roman soul the concerted effort and symbiotic relationship between humans who petition deities through Níkai and the joint effort of the gods and Níkai to reciprocate. There are scores of examples in the Classical world of the symbiotic effort between Níkai and devout petitioners who seek confidence of victory in their undertaking, be it sexual or military prowess.

Classical athletic competition was an obvious way to demonstrate human effort and exertion, celebrated in chiseled physiques and athletes depicted in mano a mano activities.[37] Of course, the success of these competitors, characterized by hard work and disciplined training, was often celebrated visually by portraying the assurance of victory attributed to Níkē. Notwithstanding the general celebration of human effort, these represent iconographically divine/heavenly contributions that were decisive in the competitor's success at a sporting event.[38]

There is a famous example of declaring both verbally and iconographically a certainty and an assurance of military victory, a victory that was inextricably associated with Níkē. Turning from a personal athletic example to a national demonstration of a symbiotic effort, one should consider famous Roman suppressions in foreign lands of those opposed to its hegemony. These rigorous military encounters would include months and sometimes years of protracted and strenuous human fighting based upon the best Roman war strategies and machines. Not the only example, but one of the best, is the Roman defeat of the Jews in the First Jewish-Roman War of AD 66–70. This brutal, costly, and protracted military response is well documented through accounts that depict Roman struggles in achieving their victory against the Jews (Josephus, *Jewish War*, especially books 5 and 6). On land and sea, there were casualties beyond numbering, and there were both intermittent victories and defeats for the Romans. The iconography of the well-trained victors and their conquest dared not be remiss toward Níkē and her symbiotic role in the final Roman victory. The well-known Arch of Titus,

---

[36] For the various media used in the visual world of antiquity, see Milette Gaifman, "Visual Evidence," in *The Oxford Handbook of Ancient Greek Religion*, ed. Esther Eidinow and Julia Kindt (Oxford: Oxford Academic, 2015), 51–66. For the well-known "terrace houses," ranging from the early Roman to the Byzantine era, see Scherrer, *Ephesus: The New Guide*, 100–13.

[37] Detailed listing with sources, "*Níkē* und Athleten," *LIMC* 6.2 (1992): 315–33.

[38] For numismatic examples, see National Archaeological Museum, Numismatic Museum, *Myth and Coinage, Representations, Symbolisms and Interpretations from Greek Mythology* (Athens: Alpha Bank, 2011), 172–77.

"erected by Domitian in honor of his brother Titus after his death in 81,"[39] was one of only two Arches of Titus known in Rome. Fragments of a no longer standing Arch of Titus, situated at the Circus Maximus, were unearthed in the early 21st century. Originally both arches provided a significant architectural testimony to the Roman triumph over the Jewish rebels which resulted in the destruction of Jerusalem and the razing of the Jewish temple.[40]

Many tourists to Rome quickly visit the famous Arch of Titus situated near the Roman Forum, but unfortunately primarily to see the Menorah and other Jewish iconography on part of one panel. Naturally, the Romans believed the Jewish symbols were also important, but for the Roman conquerors, they only served as indications of a defeated people, a humiliated religion, and a destroyed nation. One of the two major panels inside the Arch of Titus depicts Titus riding majestically in a quadriga, celebrating the defeat of the Jews (Photo 6). In the quadriga, standing next to the conquering Roman general Titus, a winged Nikē bestows upon Titus a victory wreath.

Photo 6: Richard E. Oster, Jr. Used by Permission.

---

[39] Diana E. E. Kleiner, *Roman Sculpture*, Yale Publications in the History of Art (London: Yale University Press, 1992), 183.

[40] Kleiner, *Roman Sculpture*, 183–91.

Besides Níkē in Titus's quadriga, four additional Níkai are prominently displayed on the Arch of Titus, each of them in one of the four large spandrels of the arch. This prominent iconography of Níkē and Roman soldiers that covers the Arch of Titus demonstrates well the collaboration of human and divine effort in celestial victory and success. Diana Kleiner observed, "What is of special interest is that the protagonists of the scene are both human and divine, and the triumph panel of the Arch of Titus is the first monumental state relief in which the two coexist (there are earlier numismatic examples)."[41]

Another well-known artistic celebration of Roman's crushing of the Jewish anarchy in the Holy Land is the Judaea Capta series of Roman coins. These particular coins iconographically display a Níkē on the Reverse (Photo 7).

Photo 7: Used with the kind permission of the Classical Numismatic Group, Inc. https://www.cngcoins.com.

Visually the imagery proclaims the defeat of the Jews through the depiction of a personified Judaea sitting on the ground, employing the posture and gestures of a vanquished, humiliated, and mourning individual. To his left is a winged, victorious Níkē, proclaiming with a victorious posture and with one foot resting on a military helmet that Rome dominated with divine protection and assurance. The visible Palm branches

---

[41] Kleiner, *Roman Sculpture,* 188. The visual accounts and celebrations of this triumph are evident in Roman numismatic artifacts, viz., the visually diverse *Judaea Capta* coinage, and is often associated with the power of Níkē.

are also associated with Níkē's credentials of invincibility. The verbal testimony around the coin affirms the victory of the Emperor.[42]

Having Níkē on our Ephesian altar is not merely artistic convention. Rather, this is a visual way to depict the divine guarantee of a victorious outcome of human effort at worship when it is accompanied by heavenly superintendence. This modest Ephesian altar participates, in my judgment, in the same iconographic pattern of assurance that is seen on the far more famous Arch of Titus where Níkē guaranteed the hard-fought Roman victory over the Jews. To be sure, one event is personal piety and the other is imperial conquest and protection of Rome's Eastern front, but they both presuppose the role of the Níkai in guaranteeing the outcome of divinely supported human effort.

Concluding Thoughts

The audiences for whom the New Testament was written, were not hermetically sealed from all the atmosphere breathed by their close or distant relatives, by their fellow-slaves, by their fellow-followers of Christ whose livelihood was in the construction business, building structures adorned with idolatrous images or mythological frescoes. There were fellow-believers whose impoverishment led by necessity to work in cleaning pagan temples or in the menial task of picking up morsels of food from pagan dining halls, or by the entrepreneur in their fellowship who labored in the commercial agora by the harbor.

I will conclude with examples of two other facets of victory and success associated with Níkē and that are found in the Gospels, among other places, of the New Testament. Two exemplars of attributes held in common with Níkē and New Testament texts are wreaths (often mistranslated and misunderstood as a modern crown) and palm fronds. It is fitting to conclude this essay with observations about two Graeco-Roman-Jewish artifacts mentioned in the Gospels, since the dedicatee of this celebratory volume, Dr. Allen Black, has given the many decades of his life to the teaching of the Four Gospels, *Ad maiorem Dei gloriam*, and serving seminary students as an advocate for the Gospels and their relevance for the life and mission of God's people.

Wreaths

The image of a wreath (στέφανος; Photo 08)[43] is regularly pictured with Níkē and also appears in the New Testament, typically associated with either royal lineage/assoc-

---

[42] Josephus, *The Jewish War* 7.132–55, contains the narration of the triumphal procession in Rome. He also mentions statues of *Victoria* in the procession leading the Jewish captives and their great wealth to Rome.

[43] Photo in the Kunsthistorisches Museum Vienna. Two layered early Roman cameos, depicting an eagle as Roman power, assisted by Roman *Victoria* (=Greek Níkē). Photo is copyrighted by Richard E. Oster, Jr.

iation with royalty (sarcastic at crucifixion, Matt 27:29; Mark 15:17; John 19:2, 5; Heb 2:7, 9; Rev 4:4, 10; 6:2; 9:7; 12:1; 14:14) or a reward, an honor, or a prize for an accomplishment (1 Cor 9:25; Phil 4:1; 1 Thess 2:19; 2 Tim 2:5; 4:8; Jas 1:12; 1 Pet 5:4; Rev 2:10; 3:11).

Photo 8: Richard Oster, Jr. Used by Permission.

In the case of New Testament writers, we see that these authors were not hesitant to use ideas shared with the pagan culture, although they were certainly stripped of idolatrous theology and unacceptable ethics. Apostolic teaching about crowns did not come from men unaware of crowns in the surrounding Graeco-Roman culture, crowns mentioned in inscriptions, papyri, and literature, and displayed predominantly in plastic art as well as in numismatic iconography. The Apostles, moreover, would have planted and nurtured Christian congregations filled with former pagans from the gentile world that only knew about Níkē from the religious atmosphere they constantly breathed.

Palm Frond

When Jesus of Nazareth entered Jerusalem in his "Triumphal Entry," there is no doubt that he was claiming ownership over the Royal Covenant that God had promised to David's heritage (2 Sam 7:11c–17). This "Triumphal Entry" is found in all four Gospels, and two of them, Matt 21:3–5 and John 12:12–16, directly connect Jesus's victorious entry with the Zech 9:9 and the king's victorious rule. The crowds in Jerusalem used palm fronds to herald the coming victory of Jesus as King over God's people. The use of palm fronds to visually proclaim "victory" was a ubiquitous iconographic message in the Mediterranean Basin.

The confluence of the Semitic cry "Hosanna" with the placement of "branches of palm trees" in the presence of Jesus, seated on the royal animal, with the use of terms like "King" and "Son of David," distinctly draws the attention of the modern student to Ps 118:25, when the psalmist writes, "O Lord, we pray, give us success." These palm branches at Jesus's entry bespeak ideas roughly similar to those experienced by pagans who saw Níkē bringing rescue and success, with her attendant palm branches (Photo 9).[44]

Photo 9: Richard E. Oster, Jr. Used by Permission.

In conventional and historic exegesis, all the tools and methodologies presume the primacy of words, a focus on ideas best expressed in words, and conformed to rules of grammar, syntax, and lexicography. In spite of best efforts, exegetical essays can still display myopic exegesis, fallacious exegesis, and the much-dreaded eisegesis. The same types of issues occur in the practice of iconography, the interpretation of images rather than words. The future use of images in the interpretation of the New Testament must avoid the anachronistic use of visual materials, have an awareness of iconotropy, embrace the significance of the social diversity among artisans and their intended audiences, and work with a knowledge of the diversity of meanings for a similar icon. Regarding written art, for example, it is ironic that some lapidaries were illiterate and

---

[44] A well-known monument on display at the site of Ephesus, from the Roman era. This particular monument, like so many, displays more than one visible attribute. The use of the wreath is prominent here.

did, therefore, easily introduce errors into texts.[45] In matters of extant visual art, questions exist whether we have an idealization or a caricatural depiction of a scene or person. A generally well-known example in the plastic arts is the reuse of the Prima Porta statue of Augustus, which depicted him as a youthful military commander and emperor, decades after his youthful appearance had faded. Regarding caricatural depiction, the outward appearance, for example, of Germans and other barbarians in the lower panel of the Gemma Augustea (from Rome, but generally contemporary with the marble Ephesian altar) artifact is certainly pejorative. Stereotypes of ethnicity and gender were at times maintained by the use of color and types of metal, marble, or gems. The exacerbated images of the gestures of their faces, limbs, and body-postures (Photo 10).[46]

Photo 10: Gemma Augustea. Kunsthitorisches Museuem, Vienna Austria.

Naturally, there are also interpretive issues about recapturing the artist's original voice and intention in contrast to a focus on the impact of the art of each observer.

In this essay I have encouraged an appreciation for the value of images in the study of ancient monuments, in particular, a stone altar recovered in Ephesus. In my judgment, with the burgeoning corpus of Graeco-Roman visual materials (for example, coins, plastic arts, and frescoes), the use of iconographic evidence for an enhanced and more accurate knowledge of the meaning of the New Testament is a desideratum.

---

[45] Dirk Booms, *Latin Inscriptions* (Los Angeles: J. Paul Getty Museum, 2016), 99–100.

[46] Gemma Augustea. Photo in public domain. Used from Wiki Media. Artifact is located in the Kunsthistorisches Museum, Vienna, Austria.

Bibliography and Indices

Bibliography

Abernathy, David C. *An Exegetical Summary of 1 Peter*. Dallas: Summer Institute of Linguistics, 1998.

Achtemeier, Paul J. *1 Peter: A Commentary on First Peter*. Hermeneia. Minneapolis: Fortress, 1996.

Addison, Steve. *Acts and the Movement of God: From Jerusalem to the Ends of the Earth*. 100 Movements Publishing, 2023.

Alexander, Hanan A. "God as Teacher: Jewish Reflections on a Theology of Pedagogy." *Journal of Beliefs and Values* 22 (2001): 5–17.

Allen, Amy. *The Gifts They Bring*. Louisville: Westminster John Knox, 2023.

Allen, C. Leonard, and Danny Swick. *Participating in God's Life*. Abilene: ACU Press, 2001.

Allen, Holly. *Forming Resilient Children: The Role of Spiritual Formation for Healthy Development*. Downers Grove: InterVarsity Academic, 2021.

Amanze, James N. *African Traditional Religions and Culture in Botswana*. Gaborone, Botswana: Pula Press, 2005.

Andersen, Francis. *Habakkuk: A New Translation with Introduction and Commentary*. AYB 25. New Haven: Yale University Press, 2001.

The Apostolic Fathers: Greek Texts and English Translations. 3rd ed. Edited and translated by Michael W. Holmes. Grand Rapids: Baker Academic, 2007.

Aristotle. *The Art of Rhetoric*. Translated by John Henry Freese. LCL. Cambridge: Harvard University Press; reprint, 2000.

———. *Nicomachean Ethics*. Translated by H. Rackham. LCL. Harvard University Press; reprint, 2003.

Arnold, Bill T. "The Love-Fear Antinomy in Deuteronomy 5–11." *VT* 61 (2011): 551–69.

———. *Genesis*. New Cambridge Bible Commentary. New York: Cambridge University Press, 2009.

Arnold, Clinton E. *Ephesians*. Zondervan Exegetical Commentary on the New Testament. Grand Rapids: Zondervan, 2010.

Austin, Michel. *The Hellenistic World from Alexander to the Roman Conquest: A Selection of Ancient Sources in Translation*. 2nd ed. Cambridge: Cambridge University Press, 2006.

Bäbler, Balbina. "Nike, II. Iconography." *BNP* 9:755–56.

Balch, David L. *Let Wives Be Submissive: The Domestic Code in 1 Peter*. Chico: Scholars Press, 1981.

Barclay, John M. G. *Paul & the Power of Grace*. Grand Rapids: Eerdmans, 2020.

Barrett, C. K. "Paul Shipwrecked." Pages 51–64 in *Scripture: Meaning and Method: Essays Presented to Anthony Tyrell Hanson for his Seventieth Birthday*. Edited by Barry P. Thompson. North Yorkshire: Hull University Press, 1987.

Bartchy, S. Scott. "Slavery in the Greco-Roman World and the New Testament." *ABD* 6:65–73.

Bates, Matthew. *The Birth of the Trinity*. Oxford: Oxford University Press, 2015.

_____. *Gospel Allegiance*. Grand Rapids: Brazos Press, 2019.

_____. *Salvation by Allegiance Alone: Rethinking Faith, Works, and the Gospel of Jesus the King*. Grand Rapids: Baker Academic, 2017.

Batten, Alicia. "God in the Letter of James: Patron or Benefactor?" *NTS* 50 (2004): 257–72.

Bauckham, Richard. *Gospel of Glory: Major Themes in Johannine Theology*. Grand Rapids: Baker Academic, 2015.

_____. "James and the Gentiles." Pages 154–84 in *History, Literature, and Society in the Book of Acts*. Edited by Ben Witherington. Cambridge: University Press, 1996.

_____. "James, Peter, and the Gentiles." Pages 91–142 in *The Missions of James, Peter, and Paul: Tensions in Early Christianity*. Edited by Bruce Chilton and Craig Evans. Leiden: Brill, 2005.

_____. "The Restoration of Israel in Luke-Acts." Pages 435–87 in *Restoration: Old Testament, Jewish, and Christian Perspectives*. Edited by James Scott. JSJSup 72. Leiden: Brill, 2001.

Bauer, David R. *The Book of Acts as Story: A Narrative-Critical Study*. Grand Rapids: Baker Academic, 2021.

Baugh, S. M. "A Foreign World, Ephesus in the First Century." Pages 25–64 in *Women in the Church: An Interpretation and Application of 1 Timothy 2:9–15*, 3rd ed. Edited by Andrea J. Kostenberger and Thomas R. Schreiner. Wheaton: Crossway, 2016.

Beasley-Murray, George R. *John*. 2nd ed. WBC 36. Nashville: Thomas Nelson, 1999.

Beavis, Mary Ann. *Mark*. Paideia: Commentaries on the New Testament. Grand Rapids: Baker Academic, 2011.

_____. "The Trial before the Sanhedrin (Mark 14:53–65): Reader Response and Greco-Roman Readers." *CBQ* 49 (1987): 581–96.

Beker, J. Christiaan. *Paul the Apostle: The Triumph of God in Life and Thought*. Philadelphia: Fortress, 1980.

Belleville, Linda L. "Exegetical Fallacies in Interpreting 1 Timothy 2:11–15." *Priscilla Papers* 17.3 (2003), available at https://www.cbeinternational.org/resource/ exegetical- fallacies-interpreting-1-timothy-211-15/

Bernier, Jonathan. *Rethinking the Dates of the New Testament: The Evidence for Early Composition*. Grand Rapids: Baker Academic, 2022.

Betz, Hans Dieter. *Galatians: A Commentary on Paul's Letter to the Churches in Galatia*. Hermeneia. Philadelphia: Fortress, 1979.

Bialostocki, Jan. "Iconography and Iconology." *Encyclopedia of World Art* 7:769–85.

The Bible Project. "Temple." https://bibleproject.com/videos/temple/.

Biblia Hebraica Stuttgartensia. Edited by Karl Elliger, Wilhelm Rudolph et al. 4th edition. Stuttgart: Deutsche Bibelgesellschaft, 1997.

Bigg, Charles. *A Critical and Exegetical Commentary on the Epistles of St. Peter and St. Jude*. Edinburgh: T&T. Clark, 1902.

Black, Allen. *Mark*. The College Press NIV Commentary. Joplin: College Press, 1995.

———. "'Your Sons and Your Daughters Will Prophesy...': Pairings of Men and Women in Luke-Acts." Pages 193–206 in *Scripture and Traditions: Essays on Early Judaism and Christianity in Honor of Carl R. Holladay*. Edited by Patrick Gray and Gail R. O'Day. Leiden: Brill, 2008.

Black, Allen, and Mark C. Black. *1 & 2 Peter*. College Press NIV Commentary. Joplin: College Press, 1998.

Black, C. Clifton. *A Three-Dimensional Jesus: An Introduction to the Synoptic Gospels*. Louisville: Westminster John Knox, 2023.

Blümel, Wolfgang. *Die Inschriften von Iasos*. Bonn: R. Habelt, 1985.

Bock, Darrell L. *Luke*. Downers Grove: InterVarsity Press, 1994.

Bond, Helen K. *The First Biography of Jesus: Genre and Meaning in Mark's Gospel*. Grand Rapids: Eerdmans, 2020.

Booms, Dirk. *Latin Inscriptions*. Los Angeles: J. Paul Getty Museum, 2016.

Bovon, François. *A Commentary on the Gospel of Luke 1:1–9:50*. Translated by Christine M. Thomas. Minneapolis: Fortress Press, 2002.

Bridges Johns, Cheryl. *Re-Enchanting the Text: Discovering the Bible as Sacred, Dangerous, and Mysterious*. Grand Rapids: Baker, 2023.

Briggs, Richard S. "Humans in the Image of God and Other Things Genesis Does Not Make Clear." *Journal of Theological Interpretation* 4 (2010): 111–26.

Brosend, Annette, and Martin Kemkes. *Victoria der römische Sieg und seine göttlichen Garanten*. Oppenheim: Nünnerich-Asmus, 2023.

Brouskari, Maria S. *Acropolis Museum: A Descriptive Catalogue*. Athens: Commercial Bank of Greece, 1974.

Brown, Jeannine K. "Narrative Criticism." *DJG* 619–24.

Brown, Raymond E. *The Death of the Messiah: From Gethsemane to the Grave: A Commentary on the Passion Narratives in the Four Gospels*. 2 vols. ABRL. New York: Doubleday, 1994.

———. *An Introduction to the New Testament*. The Abridged Edition. New Haven: Yale University Press, 2016.

Bruce, F. F. *The Book of the Acts*. Rev. ed. Grand Rapids: Eerdmans, 1988.

_____. *The Epistle to the Galatians: A Commentary on the Greek Text*. NIGTC. Grand Rapids: Eerdmans, 1982.

Brueggemann, Walter. *The Creative Word: Canon as a Model for Biblical Education*. 2nd ed. Philadelphia: Fortress Press, 2015.

_____. "The Loss and Recovery of Creation in Old Testament Theology." *ThTo* 53 (1996): 177–90.

Bunge, Marcia J. "Introduction." Pages xiv–xxvi in *The Child in the Bible*. Edited by Marcia J. Bunge. Grand Rapids: Eerdmans, 2008.

Burnett, D. Clint. *Christ's Enthronement at God's Right Hand and Its Greco-Roman Cultural Context*. BZNW 242. Berlin: de Gruyter, 2021.

_____. "Eschatological Prophet of Restoration: Luke's Theological Portrait of John the Baptist in Luke 3:1–6." *Neot* 47 (2013): 1–24.

_____. *Studying the New Testament Through Inscriptions: An Introduction*. Peabody: Hendrickson, 2020.

Burridge, Richard A. *What Are the Gospels? A Comparison with Graeco-Roman Biography*. 2nd ed. Grand Rapids: Eerdmans, 2004.

Calvin, John. *Acts of the Council of Trent with the Antidote*. 1547. https://www.monergism.com/thethreshold/sdg/calvin_trentantidote.html

Campbell, Alexander. *Christian Baptism with Its Antecedents and Consequents*. 1851; repr., Nashville: Gospel Advocate, 1951.

_____. "Faith Alone," *The Millennial Harbinger* (1840): 491–93.

_____. "Justification," *The Millennial Harbinger* (1851): 318–25.

_____. "'To Paulinus.'—Letter III," *The Christian Baptist* 4 (1827): 213–17.

_____. "Review of Archippus—No. III," *The Millennial Harbinger* (1831): 266–69.

Camery-Hoggart, Jerry. *Irony in Mark's Gospel: Text and Subtext*. SNTSMS 72. Cambridge: Cambridge University Press, 1991.

Carey, Holly J. *Women Who Do: Female Disciples in the Gospels*. Grand Rapids: Eerdmans, 2023.

Carson, D. A., and Douglas J. Moo. *An Introduction to the New Testament*. Grand Rapids: Zondervan, 2005.

Carter, Warren. "Aquatic Display: Navigating the Roman Imperial World in Acts 27." *NTS* 62 (2016): 79–96.

Chan, Michael J., and Brent A. Strawn, eds. *What Kind of God? Collected Essays of Terence Fretheim*. Siphrut 14. Winona Lake: Eisenbrauns, 2015.

Chance, J. Bradley. *Acts*. SHBC. Macon: Smyth and Helwys, 2007.

Chilton, Bruce, and Edwin Yamauchi. "Synagogues." *DNTB* 1145–53.

Christensen, Duane. *Deuteronomy 1:1–21:9*. Rev. ed. Nashville: Thomas Nelson, 2001.

Cicero. *Fragmentary Speeches*. Edited and Translated by Jane W. Crawford and Andrew R. Dyck. LCL. Cambridge: Harvard University Press, 2024.

_____. Translated by H. Grose Hodge. 30 vols. LCL. Cambridge: Harvard University Press, 1913–2010.
Clark Kroeger, Richard, and Catherine Clark Kroeger. *I Suffer Not a Woman: Rethinking 1 Timothy 2:11–15 in Light of Ancient Evidence*. Grand Rapids: Baker, 1992.
Cohick, Lynn H. *Women in the World of the Earliest Christians: Illuminating Ancient Ways of Life*. Grand Rapids: Baker Academic, 2009.
Collins, John J. *Daniel: A Commentary on the Book of Daniel*. Hermeneia. Minneapolis: Fortress, 1993.
_____. *The Scepter and the Star*. New York: Doubleday, 1995.
Conzelmann, Hans. *1 Corinthians: A Commentary on the First Epistle to the Corinthians*. Edited by George W. MacRae. Translated by James W. Leitch. Hermeneia. Philadelphia: Fortress, 1975.
_____. *Acts of the Apostles: A Commentary on the Acts of the Apostles*. Translated by James Limburg, A. Thomas Kraabel, and Donald H. Juel. Hermeneia. Philadelphia: Fortress, 1987.
Cranfield, C. E. B. *The Epistle to the Romans*. ICC. 2 vols. Edinburgh: T&T Clark, 1975.
Crook, Z. A. "Fictive-Friendship and the Fourth Gospel." *HvTSt* 67 (2011): 1–7.
Cukrowski, Kenneth L. "Paul as Odysseus: An Exegetical Note on Luke's Depiction of Paul in Acts 27:1–28:10." *ResQ* 55 (2013): 24–34.
Culpepper, R. Alan. *Anatomy of the Fourth Gospel: A Study in Literary Design*. Philadelphia: Fortress, 1983.
_____. *Matthew: A Commentary*. NTL. Louisville: Westminster John Knox, 2021.
Dale, Moyra. "Dismantling Socio-Sacred Hierarchy: Gender and Gentiles in Luke-Acts." *Priscilla Papers* 31, no. 2 (2017): 19–23.
D'Angelo, Mary Rose. "(Re)Presentations of Women in the Gospel of Matthew and Luke-Acts." Pages 171–196 in *Women & Christian Origins*. Edited by Ross Shepard Kraemer and Mary Rose D'Angelo. New York: Oxford University Press, 1999.
Danker, Frederick W. *Benefactor: Epigraphic Study of a Graeco-Roman and New Testament Semantic Field*. St. Louis: Clayton Publishing House, 1982.
_____. *Jesus and the New Age: According to St. Luke*. St. Louis: Clayton Publishing House, 1980.
Davids, Peter H. *The First Epistle of Peter*. Grand Rapids: Eerdmans, 1990.
_____. "A Silent Witness in Marriage." Pages 224–38 in *Discovering Biblical Equality: Complementarity without Hierarchy*. Edited by Ronald W. Pierce and Rebecca Merrill Groothuis. Downers Grove: InterVarsity Academic, 2005.
Davidson, Richard. "Earth's First Sanctuary: Genesis 1–3 and Parallel Creation Accounts." *AUSS* 53 (2015): 65–89.

Davies, Jamie. *The Apocalyptic Paul: Retrospect and Prospect*. Eugene: Cascade, 2022.

Davies, W. D., and Dale Allison, Jr. *The Gospel of Saint Matthew*. 3 vols. ICC. London: Bloomsbury, 1988–97.

Davina, SOH Hui Leng. *The Motif of Hospitality in Theological Education: A Critical Appraisal with Implications for Application in Theological Education*. ICETE Series. Carlisle, UK: Langham Global Library, 2016.

Day, John. *From Creation to Abraham: Further Studies in Genesis 1–11*. London: T&T Clark, 2022.

The Dead Sea Scrolls: Study Edition. 2 vols. Edited by Florentino García Martínez and Eibert J.C. Tigchelaar. Grand Rapids: Eerdmans, 1997–1998.

de Boer, Martinus C. *Paul, Theologian of God's Apocalypse*. Eugene: Cascade, 2020.

Decker, Rodney J. *Mark 1–8: A Handbook on the Greek Text*. Waco: Baylor University Press, 2014.

"Decree Concerning Justification." Council of Trent. https://www.papalencyclicals.net/councils/trent/sixth-session.htm

deLuse, Stephanie. "First Impressions: Using a Flexible First Day Activity to Enhance Student Learning and Classroom Management." *International Journal of Teaching and Learning in Higher Education* 30 (2018): 308–21.

Dempsey, Carol J. "Love: The Fulfillment of the Law and the Prophets." Pages 67–82 in *Biblical Ethics: Tensions Between Justice and Mercy, Law and Love*. Edited by Markus Zehnder and Peter Wick. Gorgias Biblical Studies 70. Piscataway: Gorgias, 2019.

deSilva, David Arthur. *An Introduction to the New Testament: Contexts, Methods & Ministry Formation*. 2nd ed. Downers Grove: InterVarsity Press, 2018.

_____. *Honor, Patronage, Kinship & Purity: Unlocking New Testament Culture*. 2nd ed. Downers Grove: InterVarsity Press, 2022.

Die Bibel. Stuttgart: Deutsche Bibelgesellschaft, 1984.

Dinkler, Michal Beth. "Sarah's Submission: Peter's Analogy in 1 Peter 3:5–6." *Priscilla Papers* 21.3 (2007), available at https://www.cbeinternational.org/resource/sarahs-submission/.

Dodd, C. H. *The Apostolic Preaching*. London: Harper & Brothers, 1954.

Donahue, John R., and Daniel J. Harrington. *The Gospel of Mark*. SP 2. Collegeville: Liturgical Press, 2002.

Dunn, James D. G. *Baptism in the Holy Spirit: A Re-examination of the New Testament Teaching on the Gift of the Spirit in Relation to Pentecostalism Today*. 2nd ed. London: SCM, 2010.

_____. *The Epistle to the Galatians*. BNTC. Peabody: Hendrickson, 1993.

_____. "If Paul Could Believe both in Justification by Faith and Judgment according to Works, Why Should that be a Problem for Us." Pages 119–41 in *Four*

Views on the Role of Works at the Final Judgment. Edited by Alan P. Stanley. Grand Rapids: Zondervan, 2013.

_____. *The Theology of Paul the Apostle*. Grand Rapids: Eerdmans, 1998.

Edwards, James R. "Markan Sandwiches: The Significance of Interpolations in Markan Narratives." *NovT* 31.3 (1989): 193–216.

Elliott, John H. *1 Peter: A New Translation with Introduction and Commentary*. AB 37B. New York: Doubleday, 2000.

Elsner, Jas. "Between Mimeses and Divine Power, Visuality in the Greco-Roman." Pages 1–26 in *Roman Eyes, Visuality and Subjectivity in Art and Text*. Princeton: Princeton University Press, 2007.

Embudo, Lora Angeline B. "Women Vis-À-Vis Prophecy in Luke-Acts 2." *Asian Journal of Pentecostal Studies* 20 (2017): 131–46.

Eusebius. *Ecclesiastical History*. 2 vols. Translated by Kirsopp Lake. LCL. Cambridge: Harvard University, 1926.

Fedler, Kyle D. *Exploring Christian Ethics: Biblical Foundations for Morality*. Louisville: Westminster John Knox, 2006.

Fee, Gordon D. *The First Epistle to the Corinthians*. Rev. ed. NICNT. Grand Rapids: Eerdmans, 2014.

Feldmeier, Reinhard. *The First Letter of Peter: A Commentary on the Greek Text*. Translated by Peter H. Davids. Waco: Baylor University Press, 2008.

Feldmeier, Reinhard, and Hermann Spieckermann. *The God of the Living: A Biblical Theology*. Waco: Baylor University Press, 2011.

Ferguson, Everett. *Backgrounds of Early Christianity*. 3rd ed. Grand Rapids: Eerdmans, 2003.

Fiorenza, Elisabeth Schüssler. *In Memory of Her: A Feminist Theological Reconstruction of Christian Origins*. New York: Crossroad Publishing, 1987.

Firth, David. "Passing on the Faith in Deuteronomy." Pages 157–176 in *Interpreting Deuteronomy: Issues and Approaches*. Edited by David G. Firth and Philip S. Johnston. Downers Grove: InterVarsity Academic, 2012.

Fitzmyer, Joseph A. *The Acts of the Apostles: A New Translation with Introduction and Commentary*. AB 31. New York: Doubleday, 1998.

_____. *To Advance the Gospel: New Testament Studies*. 2nd ed. Grand Rapids: Eerdmans, 1998.

_____. *First Corinthians: A New Translation with Introduction and Commentary*, AYB 32 (New Haven: Yale University Press, 2008),

_____. *Romans: A New Translation with Introduction and Commentary*. AB 33. New York: Doubleday, 1993.

Forbes, Greg W. *1 Peter*. Exegetical Guide to the Greek New Testament. Nashville: B & H Academic, 2014.

France, R. T. *The Gospel of* Matthew. NICOT. Grand Rapids: Eerdmans, 2007.

Fretheim, Terence E. *God and World in the Old Testament: A Relational Theology of Creation*. Nashville: Abingdon, 2005

Fuller, Michael E. *The Restoration of Israel: Israel's Re-gathering and the Fate of the Nations in Early Jewish Literature and Luke-Acts*. BZNW 138. Berlin: de Gruyter, 2006.

Gaifman, Milette. "Visual Evidence." Pages 51–66 in *The Oxford Handbook of Ancient Greek Religion*. Edited by Esther Eidinow and Julia Kindt. Oxford: Oxford Academic, 2015.

Gardner, Gregg. "Jewish Leadership and Hellenistic Civic Benefaction in the Second Century B.C.E." *JBL* 126 (2007): 327–43.

Gaventa, Beverly. *Our Mother Saint Paul*. Louisville: Westminster John Knox, 2007.

Geldenhuys, Norval. *Commentary on the Gospel of Luke*. NICNT. Grand Rapids: Eerdmans, 1988.

George, Timothy. *Theology of the Reformers*. Nashville: Broadman, 1988.

Glahn, Sandra L. *Nobody's Mother: Artemis of the Ephesians in Antiquity and the New Testament*. Downers Grove: InterVarsity Press, 2023.

Glanzer, Perry L., and Nathan F. Alleman. *The Outrageous Idea of Christian Teaching*. Oxford: Oxford University Press, 2019.

Glanzer, Perry L., Theodore F. Cockle, and Jessica Martin. *Christian Higher Education: An Empirical Guide*. Abilene: ACU Press, 2023.

Goldingay, John. *Genesis*. Baker Commentary on the Old Testament. Grand Rapids: Baker Academic, 2020.

Gonzalez, Justo L. *A History of Christian Thought in One Volume*. Nashville: Abingdon, 2014.

Goodacre, Mark. *The Case Against Q: Studies in Markan Priority and the Synoptic Problem*. Harrisburg: Trinity Press International, 2002.

Goodrich, John K., Jason Maston, and Ben Blackwell, eds. *Paul and the Apocalyptic Imagination*. Minneapolis: Fortress, 2016.

Gorman, Michael J. *Apostle of the Crucified Lord*. Grand Rapids: Eerdmans, 2017.

Gritz, Sharon Hodgin. *Paul, Women Teachers, and the Mother Goddess at Ephesus: A Study of 1 Timothy 2:9–15 in Light of the Religious and Cultural Milieu of the First Century*. Lanham: University Press of America, 1991.

Grudem, Wayne A. *The First Epistle of Peter: An Introduction and Commentary*. Grand Rapids: Eerdmans, 1988.

Gundry, Robert H. *Matthew*. Grand Rapids: Eerdmans, 1994.

Gurtner, Daniel M. "Jesus as Teacher of Israel's Scriptures in His Judaic Context." Pages 32–48 in *Jesus as Teacher in the Gospel of Matthew*. Edited by Charles L. Quarles and Charles Nathan Ridlehoover. London: Bloomsbury/T&T Clark, 2023.

Guthrie, Donald. *New Testament Introduction*. 3rd rev. ed. Downers Grove: InterVarsity Press, 1970.

Haenchen, Ernst. *The Acts of the Apostles: A Commentary*. Translated by Bernard Noble and Gerald Shinn. Philadelphia: Westminster, 1971.
Harkness, Allan. "Exploring the Interface between Christian Faith and Education: An Annotated List of Current Journals." *Journal of Education and Christian Belief* 17 (2013): 99–114.
Harrington, Bobby, Carl Williamson, and Alicia Williamson. *Trust and Follow Jesus: Conversations to Fuel Discipleship*. 2nd ed. Nashville: Renew.org, 2023.
Harvey, A. E. *A Companion to the New Testament*, 2nd ed. New York: Cambridge University Press, 2004.
Hauerwas, Stanley, and William H. Willimon. *Resident Aliens: Life in the Christian Colony*. Nashville: Abingdon, 1989.
Hays, Richard B. *Echoes of Scripture in the Gospels*. Waco: Baylor University Press, 2016.
———. *Echoes of Scripture in the Letters of Paul*. New Haven: Yale University Press, 1989.
Heiser, Michael S. *Unseen Realm: Recovering the Supernatural Worldview of the Bible*. Bellingham: Lexham, 2015.
Hendel, Ronald. *Genesis 1–11: A New Translation with Introduction and Commentary*. AYB 1A. New Haven: Yale University Press, 2024.
Hendrix, Holland. "Benefactor/Patron Networks in the Urban Environment: Evidence from Thessalonica." *Semeia* 56 (1991): 39–58.
Hengel, Martin. *The Atonement: The Origins of the Doctrine of the New Testament*. Translated by John Bowden. Eugene: Wipf and Stock, 1981.
———. *The Four Gospels and the One Gospel of Jesus Christ: An Investigation of the Collection and Origin of the Canonical Gospels*. Translated by John Bowden. Harrisburg: Trinity Press International, 2000.
Hicks, John Mark. "Breaking Bread in Luke-Acts V: Acts 27." *John Mark Hicks* (blog). March 26, 2009. https://johnmarkhicks.com/2009/03/26/breaking-bread-in-luke-acts-v-acts-27/.
Holladay, Carl R. *Acts: A Commentary*. NTL. Louisville: Westminster John Knox, 2016.
———. *A Critical Introduction to the New Testament, Volume 1*. Nashville: Abingdon, 2005.
Hölscher, Tonio. "Rauchopfer." *Thesaurus Cultus et Rituum Antiquorum* 5:212–24. Los Angeles: J. Paul Getty Museum, 2006.
———. *Visual Power in Ancient Greece and Rome. Between Art and Social Reality*. Sather Classical Lectures 73. Berkeley: University of California Press, 2018.
Hölscher, Tonio, and Victoria Romana. *Archäologische Untersuchungen zur Geschichte und Wesenart der römischen Siegesgöttin von den Anfängen bis zum Ende des 3. Jhs. n. Chr.* Mainz: Philipp von Zabern, 1967.

Horrell, David G. *1 Peter*. New York: T&T Clark, 2008.

Horrell, David G., Arnold Bradley, and Travis B. Williams, "Visuality, Vivid Description, and the Message of 1 Peter: The Significance of the Roaring Lion (1 Peter 5:8)." *JBL* 132 (2013): 697–716.

Hurtado, Larry W. "Lord." *DPL* 560–69.

Hutson, Christopher R. *First and Second Timothy and Titus*. Grand Rapids: Baker Academic, 2019.

Iannarelli, Barbara A., Mary Ellen Bardsley, and Chandra J. Foote. "Here's Your Syllabus, See You Next Week: A Review of the First Day Practices of Outstanding Professors." *Journal of Effective Teaching* 10 (2010): 29–41.

Irenaeus. "Against Heresies." In *Ante-Nicene Fathers,* Vol. 1. Edited by A. Roberts, et al. Oak Harbor: Logos Research Systems, 1997.

Jenkins, Ian. *The Parthenon Frieze*. London: British Museum Press, 1994.

Jennings, Willie James. *Acts*. Belief: A Theological Commentary on the Bible. Louisville: Westminster John Knox, 2017.

Jervell, Jacob. *Luke and the People of God: A New Look at Luke-Acts*. Minneapolis: Augsburg, 1972.

———. *The Theology of the Acts of the Apostles*. Cambridge: University Press, 1996.

———. *The Unknown Paul: Essays on Luke-Acts and Early Christian History*. Minneapolis: Augsburg, 1984.

Jewett, Robert. *Romans: A Commentary*. Hermeneia. Minneapolis: Fortress, 2006.

Jipp, Joshua W. *Divine Visitations and Hospitality to Strangers in Luke-Acts: An Interpretation of the Malta Episode in Acts 28:1–10*. NovTSup 153. Leiden: Brill, 2013.

———. *Reading the Gospels as Christian Scripture: A Literary, Canonical, and Theological Introduction*. Grand Rapids: Baker Academic, 2024.

Jobes, Karen. *1 Peter*. BECNT. Grand Rapids: Baker Academic, 2005.

Johnson, B. W. *The People's New Testament with Explanatory Notes*. 2 vols. 1891; repr., Delight, AR: Gospel Light Publishing Co., n.d.

Johnson, Luke Timothy. *The Acts of the Apostles*. SP. Collegeville: Liturgical, 1992.

———. *The First and Second Letters to Timothy: A New Translation with Introduction and Commentary*. AYB 35A. New Haven: Yale University Press, 2001.

———. *The Gospel of Luke*. SP. Collegeville: The Liturgical Press, 1991.

Josephus. Translated by Henry St. J. Thackeray et al. 10 vols. LCL. Cambridge: Harvard University Press, 1926–1965.

Joubert, Stephan J. "One Form of Social Exchange or Two? 'Euergetism,' Patronage, and Testament Studies." *BTB* 31 (2001): 17–25.

———. *Paul as Benefactor: Reciprocity, Strategy and Theological Reflection in Paul's Collection*. Tübingen: Mohr Siebeck, 2000.

Karris, Robert J. "Women and Discipleship in Luke." *CBQ* 56 (1994): 1–20.

Kee, Min Suc. "The Heavenly Council and its Type-scene." *JSOT* 31 (2007): 259–73.

Keener, Craig S. *Acts: An Exegetical Commentary*. 4 vols. Grand Rapids: Baker Academic, 2012–2015.
_____. *Acts*. New Cambridge Bible Commentary. Cambridge: Cambridge University Press, 2020.
_____. *The Gospel of Matthew: A Socio-Rhetorical Commentary*. Grand Rapids: Eerdmans, 2009.
_____. *The Historical Jesus of the Gospels*. Grand Rapids: Eerdmans, 2009.
_____. *The IVP Bible Background Commentary: New Testament*. 2nd ed. Downers Grove: InterVarsity Press, 2014.
_____. *Miracles: The Credibility of the New Testament Accounts*. 2 vols. Grand Rapids: Baker Academic, 2011.
Kelly, J. N. D. *A Commentary on the Epistles of Peter and of Jude*. London: A. & C. Black, 1969.
Kennedy, George A. P*rogymnasmata: Greek Textbooks of Prose Composition and Rhetoric*, WAW 10. Atlanta: Society of Biblical Literature, 2003.
Kern, Otto. *Die Inschriften von Magnesia am Maeander*. Berlin: de Gruyter, 1967.
Kleiner, Diana E. E. *Roman Sculpture*. Yale Publications in the History of Art. London: Yale University Press, 1992.
Knight, George W., III. *The Pastoral Epistles: A Commentary on the Greek Text*. Grand Rapids: Eerdmans, 1992.
Koperski, Veronica. "Luke 10,38–42 and Acts 6,1–7: Women and Discipleship in the Literary Context of Luke-Acts." Pages 517–44 in *The Unity of Luke-Acts*. Edited by J. Verheyden. Leuven: Leuven University Press, 1999.
Kotsifou, Chrysi. "Prayers and Petitions for Justice. Despair and the 'Crossing of Boundaries' between Religion and Law." *Tyche: Contributions to Ancient History, Papyrology, and Epigraphy* 31 (2016): 167–200. https://doi.org/10.15661/ tyche.2016.031.11. Accessed Feb. 8, 2025.
Kristof, Nicholas, and Sheryl Wudunn. *Tightrope: Americans Reaching for Hope*. New York: Alfred A. Knopf, 2020.
Lapsley, Jacqueline E. "Feeling Our Way: Love for God in Deuteronomy." *CBQ* 65 (2003): 350–69.
Larkin, William J., Jr. *Acts*. Downers Grove: InterVarsity Press, 1995.
Levenson, Jon D. *The Love of God: Divine Gift, Human Gratitude, and Mutual Faithfulness in Judaism*. Princeton: Princeton University Press, 2015.
Levine, Amy-Jill, and Ben Witherington III. *The Gospel of Luke*. Cambridge: Cambridge University Press, 2018.
Levine, Lee. *The Ancient Synagogue: The First Thousand Years*. 2nd ed. New Haven: Yale University Press, 2005.
Lifshitz, B. *Donateurs et Fondateurs dans les Synagogues Juives*. Paris: J. Gabalda, 1967.

Lim, Timothy H. *Earliest Commentary on the Prophecy of Habakkuk*. Oxford: Oxford University Press, 2020.

Longenecker, Richard N. "The Acts of the Apostles." Pages 207–573 in vol. 9 of *The Expositor's Bible Commentary*. 12 vols. Edited by Frank E. Gaebelein and J. D. Douglas. Grand Rapids: Zondervan, 1981.

_____. *The Epistle to the Romans*. NIGTC. Grand Rapids: Eerdmans, 2016.

_____. *New Wine into Fresh Wineskins: Contextualizing the Early Christian Confessions*. Peabody: Hendrickson, 1999.

Lull, David J. "The Servant-Benefactor as a Model of Greatness (Luke 22:24–30)." *NovT* 28 (1986): 289–305.

Lukacs, John. *A Student's Guide to the Study of History*. Wilmington: ISI Books, 2000.

Luther, Martin. "The Distinction Between the Law and the Gospel." Translated by Willard L. Bruce. *Concordia* (1992): 153–63.

_____. *Luthers Werke: Kritische Gesamtausgabe [Schriften]*. 73 vols. Weimar: H. Böhlau, 1883–2009.

Lynch, Matthew. *The Flood and the Fury: Old Testament Violence and the Shalom of God*. Downers Grove: InterVarsity Academic, 2023.

Manson, T. W. *The Teaching of Jesus*. Cambridge: Cambridge University Press, 1935.

Marcus, Joel. "Crucifixion as Parodic Exaltation." *JBL* 125.1 (2006): 73–87.

_____. *Mark 1–8: A New Translation with Introduction and Commentary*. AB. New York: Doubleday, 2000.

Marsden, George M. *The Soul of the America University Revisited: From Protestant Establishment to Postsecular*. Oxford: Oxford University Press, 2021.

Marshall, I. Howard. *A Critical and Exegetical Commentary on The Pastoral Epistles*. New York: T&T Clark, 2003.

_____. *The Gospel of Luke: A Commentary on the Greek Text*. NIGTC. Grand Rapids: Eerdmans, 1978.

Martyn, J. Louis. *Galatians: A New Translation with Introduction and Commentary*. AYB 33. New Haven: Yale University Press, 1997.

_____. *Theological Issues in the Letters of Paul*. Nashville: Abingdon, 1997.

McGinn, Thomas A. J. *Prostitution, Sexuality, and the Law in Ancient Rome*. Oxford: Oxford University Press, 1998.

Mbiti, John S. *African Religions and Philosophy*. New York: Praeger, 1969.

Menéndez Antuña, Luis. "Male-Bonding, Female Vanishing: Representing Gendered Authority in Luke 23:26–24:53." *Early Christianity* 4 (2013): 490–506.

Metzger, Bruce M. *A Textual Commentary on the Greek New Testament: A Companion Volume to the United Bible Societies' Greek New Testament*. 3rd ed. London: United Bible Societies, 1975.

Michaels, J. Ramsey. *1 Peter*. WBC 49. Waco: Word Books, 1988.

Middleton, J. Richard. *The Liberating Image: The Imago Dei in Genesis 1*. Grand Rapids: Baker, 2005.

Miller, Amanda C. "Cut from the Same Cloth: A Study of Female Patrons in Luke-Acts and the Roman Empire." *Review & Expositor* 114 (2017): 203–10.

Miller, Patrick. "That the Children May Know: Children in Deuteronomy." Pages 45-62 in *The Child in the Bible*. Edited by Marcia J. Bunge. Grand Rapids: Eerdmans, 2008.

Moberly, Walter. *Old Testament Theology: Reading the Hebrew Bible as Christian Scripture*. Grand Rapids: Baker, 2015.

Moessner, David P. *Jesus and the Heritage of Israel: Luke's Narrative Claim upon Israel's Legacy*. Vol. 1 of *Luke the Interpreter of Israel*. LNTS 452. Harrisburg: Trinity Press International, 1999.

Moloney, Francis J. *The Gospel of Mark: A Commentary*. Peabody: Hendrickson, 2002.

Moo, Douglas J. *A Theology of Paul and His Letters*. Grand Rapids: Zondervan, 2018.

Morales, L. Michael, ed. *Cult and Cosmos: Tilting Toward a Temple-Centered Theology*, Biblical Tools and Studies 18. Leuven: Peeters, 2014.

Moran, William L. "The Ancient Near Eastern Background of the Love of God in Deuteronomy." *CBQ* 25 (1963): 77–87.

Morris, Leon. *The Gospel According to St. Luke: An Introduction and Commentary*. Grand Rapids: Eerdmans, 1974.

Moscicke, Hans. "Reconciling the Supernatural Worldviews of the Bible, African Traditional Religion, and African Christianity." *Missionalia* 45 (2017): 127–43.

Moxnes, Halvor. "Patron-Client Relations and the New Community in Luke-Acts." Pages 241–69 in *The Social World of Luke-Acts: Models for Interpretation*. Edited by Jerome H. Neyrey. Peabody: Hendrickson, 1991.

Muecke, D. C. *The Compass of Irony*. London: Methuen, 1969.

National Archaeological Museum, Numismatic Museum. *Myth and Coinage, Representations, Symbolisms and Interpretations from Greek Mythology*. Athens: Alpha Bank, 2011.

Neril, Yonatan, and Leo Dee. *Eco Bible: An Ecological Commentary on Leviticus, Numbers, and Deuteronomy*. Jerusalem: Interfaith Center for Sustainable Development, 2021.

Neudecker, Richard. "Phidias." BNP 11:3–6.

Nolland, John. *Luke 1:1–9:20*. WBC 35A. Dallas: Word Books, 1989.

Novenson, Matthew V. *Christ among the Messiahs: Christ Language in Paul and Messiah Language in Ancient Judaism*. Oxford: Oxford University Press, 2012.

_____. *The Grammar of Messianism: An Ancient Jewish Political Idiom and Its Users*. Oxford: Oxford University Press, 2017.

Novum Testamentum Graece. Edited by Barbara and Kurt Aland et al. Nestle-Aland, 28th ed. Stuttgart: German Bible Society, 2012.

Nussbaum, Martha C. *Political Emotions: Why Love Matters for Justice*. Cambridge: Belknap, 2013.

_____. *Upheavals of Thought: The Intelligence of Emotions*. Cambridge: Cambridge University Press, 2003.

Oberleitner, Wolfgang. *Funde aus Ephesos und Samothrake*. Vienna: Ueberreuter, 1978.

Oliver, Isaac W. *Luke's Jewish Eschatology: The Restoration of Israel in Luke-Acts*. Oxford: Oxford University Press, 2021.

Olson, Kelly. *Dress and the Roman Woman: Self-Presentation and Society*. New York: Routledge, 2008.

Onongha, Kelvin. "The African Worldview and Belief in the Demonic." *Journal of Adventist Mission Studies* 18 (2023): 36–45.

_____. "Suffering, Salvation, and the Sovereignty of God: Towards a Theology of Suffering." *Journal of Adventist Mission Studies* 9 (2013): 126–36.

Oster, Richard E., Jr. "Artemis of the Ephesians." Pages 60–61 in *The Oxford Companion to the Bible*. Edited by Bruce M. Metzger and Michael D. Coogan. New York: Oxford University Press, 1993.

_____. "Ephesus." Page 189 in *The Oxford Companion to the Bible*. Edited by Bruce M. Metzger and Michael D. Coogan. New York: Oxford University Press, 1993.

_____. *Seven Congregations in a Roman Crucible: A Commentary on Revelation 1–3*. Eugene: Wipf & Stock, 2013.

Outler, Albert C. "Toward a Postliberal Hermeneutics." *ThTo* 42 (1985): 281–91.

Padgett, Alan G. *As Christ Submits to the Church: A Biblical Understanding of Leadership*. Grand Rapids: Baker Academic, 2011.

Paschke, Boris A. "The Roman Ad *Bestias* Execution as a Possible Historical Background for 1 Peter 5.8." *JSNT* 28 (2006): 489–500.

Parker, Julie. *Valuable and Vulnerable: Children in the Hebrew Bible*. Providence: Brown Judaic Studies, 2013.

Paulsen, Judith. *A New and Ancient Evangelism: Rediscovering the Ways God Calls and Sends*. Grand Rapids: Baker Academic, 2024.

Pausanias. *Description of Greece*. Translated by W. H. S. Jones, H. A. Ormerod, et al. 5 vols. LCL. Cambridge: Harvard University Press, 1918–1935.

Perkins, Pheme. *Introduction to the Synoptic Gospels*. Grand Rapids: Eerdmans, 2007.

Pervo, Richard I. *Acts: A Commentary*. Hermeneia. Minneapolis: Fortress, 2009.

Petronius. *Satyricon*. Translated by Michael Heseltine. LCL. Cambridge: Harvard

University Press, 1961.

Philsy, Sr. "Diakonia of Women in the New Testament." *The Indian Journal of Theology* 32 (1983): 110–18.

Plato. *Lysis, Symposium, Phaedra*. Edited and translated by Chris Emlyn-Jones and William Preddy. LCL. Cambridge: Harvard University Press, 2022.

Pliny. *Natural History*. Translated by W. H. S. Jones. 10 vols. LCL. Cambridge: Harvard University Press, 1938–1963.

Plutarch. *Moralia*. Translated by Harold Cherniss, William Helmbold, et al. LCL. Cambridge: Harvard University Press, 1927.

_____. *Parallel Lives*. Translated by Bernadotte Perrin. 11 vols. LCL. Cambridge: Harvard University Press, 1914–1926.

Poirier, John C., and Jeffrey Peterson. *Marcan Priority Without Q: Explorations in the Farrer Hypothesis*. LNTS 455. London: Bloomsbury, 2015.

The Pontifical Council for Promoting Christian Unity and the Lutheran World Federation. "Joint Declaration on the Doctrine of Justification." 1999. http://www.christianunity.va/content/unitacristiani/en/dialoghi/sezione-occidentale/luterani/dialogo/documenti-di-dialogo/1999-dichiarazione-congiunta-sulla-dottrina-della-giustificazion/en.html.

Pope-Levison, Priscilla. *Models of Evangelism*. Grand Rapids: Baker Academic, 2020.

Porter, Stanley E. *Paul in Acts*. Library of Pauline Studies. Peabody: Hendrickson, 2001.

Porter, Stanley E., and Gregory P. Fewster, eds. *Paul and Pseudepigraphy*. Pauline Studies 8. Leiden: Brill, 2013.

Powell, Mark Allan. *Introducing the New Testament: A Historical, Literary, and Theological Survey*. 2nd ed. Grand Rapids: Baker Academic, 2018.

_____. *Matthew*. IBC. Louisville: Westminster John Knox, 2023.

Praeder, Susan Marie. "Acts 27:1–28:16: Sea Voyages in Ancient Literature and the Theology of Luke-Acts." *CBQ* 46 (1984): 683–706.

Provan, Iain. *Seriously Dangerous Religion: What the Old Testament Really Says and Why it Matters*. Waco: Baylor University Press, 2014.

Pulleyn, Simon. *Prayer in Greek Religion*. OCM. Oxford: Clarendon, 1997.

Putman, Jim, and Bobby Harrington. *DiscipleShift: Five Steps That Help Your Church to Make Disciples Who Make Disciples*. Grand Rapids: Zondervan, 2013.

Rajak, Tessa. *The Jewish Dialogue with Greece and Rome: Studies in Cultural and Social Interaction*. Leiden: Brill, 2000.

Rajak, Tessa, and David Noy. "Archisynagogoi: Office, Title and Social Status in the Greco-Jewish Synagogue." *JRS* 83 (1993): 75–93.

Rapske, Brian M. "Acts, Travel, and Shipwreck." Pages 1–47 in *The Book of Acts in* its *Graeco-Roman Setting*. Vol. 2 of *The Book of Acts in Its First Century Setting*. Edited by David W. J. Gill and Conrad Gempf. Grand Rapids: Eerdmans, 1994.

Ream, Todd C., and Perry L. Glanzer. *The Idea of a Christian College: A Reexamination for Today's University*. Eugene: Cascade, 2013.

Reid, Barbara E. *Choosing the Better Part? Women in the Gospel of Luke*. Collegeville: Liturgical Press, 1996.

———. "The Gospel of Luke: Friend or Foe of Women Proclaimers of the Word?" *CBQ* 78 (2016): 1–23.

Reid, Barbara E., and Shelly Matthews. *Luke 1–9*. Collegeville: Liturgical Press, 2021.

Resseguie, James L. *Narrative Criticism of the New Testament: An Introduction*. Grand Rapids: Baker Academic, 2005.

Rhoads, David, Joanna Dewey, and Donald Michie. *Mark as Story: An Introduction to the Narrative of a Gospel*. 2nd ed. Minneapolis: Fortress, 1999.

Richards, E. Randolph. *Paul and First-Century Letter Writing: Secretaries, Composition and Collection*. Downers Grove: InterVaristy, 2004.

Richter, Gisela M. A. *The Sculpture and Sculptors of the Greeks*. 4th ed. New Haven: Yale University Press, 1970.

Richter Reimer, Ivoni. *Women in the Acts of the Apostles: A Feminist Liberation Perspective*. Minneapolis: Fortress Press, 1995.

Roberts, J. J. M. *Nahum, Habakkuk, and Zephaniah: A Commentary*. NTL. Louisville: Westminster John Knox, 1991.

Robertson, Jesse E. *The Death of Judas: The Characterization of Judas Iscariot in Three Early Christian Accounts of His Death*. New Testament Monographs 33. Sheffield: Sheffield Phoenix Press, 2012.

Robinson, John A. T. *Redating the New Testament*. Philadelphia: Westminster, 1976.

Rowe, C. Kavin "Biblical Pressure and Trinitarian Hermeneutics." *Pro Ecclesia* 9 (2002): 295–312.

Rudolph, David, and Joel Willitts, eds. *Introduction to Messianic Judaism: Its Ecclesial Context and Biblical Foundations*. Grand Rapids: Zondervan, 2013.

Runesson, Anders. *The Origin of the Synagogue: A Socio–Historical Study*. Schweden: Almqvist & Wilksell, 2001.

Sacks, Jonathan. *Covenant and Conversation. Exodus: The Book of Redemption*. New Milford: Maggid Books, 2010.

Samudra, Preeti G., Inah Min, Kai S. Cortina, and Kevin F. Miller. "No Second Chance to Make a First Impression: The 'Thin Slice' Effect on Instructor Ratings and Learning Outcomes in Higher Education." *Journal of Educational Measurement* 53 (2016): 313–31.

Schaberg, Jane. "Luke." Pages 363–80 in *Women's Bible Commentary*. Edited by Carol A. Newsom and Sharon H. Ringe. Expanded ed. Louisville: Westminster John Knox, 1998.

Scheffler, Eben. "Caring for the Needy in the Acts of the Apostles." *Neot* (2016): 131–65.

Scherf, Johannes. "Nike, I. Mythology." BNP 9:754–55.

_____. "Olympus, II. Myths." BNP 10:115.

_____. "Victoria." BNP 15:399–400.

Scherrer, Peter. *Ephesus: The New Guide*. Translated by Lionel Bier and George M. Luxon. Rev. ed. Istanbul: Ege, 2000.

Schnabel, Eckhard J. *Acts*. Zondervan Exegetical Commentary on the New Testament. Grand Rapids: Zondervan, 2012.

_____. "Fads and Common Sense: Reading Acts in the First Century and Reading Acts Today." *JETS* 54 (2011): 251–78.

Schreiner, Patrick. *Acts*. Christian Standard Commentary. Nashville: Holman Reference, 2021.

Schreiner, Thomas R. *1, 2 Peter, Jude*. New American Commentary. Nashville: Broadman & Holman, 2003.

_____. "Justification apart from and by Works: At the Final Judgment Works will *Confirm* Justification." Pages 25–50 in *Four Views on the Role of Works at the Final Judgment*. Edited by Alan P. Stanley. Grand Rapids: Zondervan, 2013.

Schüle, Andreas. *Der Prolog der hebräischen Bibel: Der literar- und theologiegeschichtliche Diskurs der Urgeschichte [Genesis 1-11]*. 2nd ed. AThANT 86. Zürich: Theologischer Verlag, 2017.

Seim, Turid Karlsen. *The Double Message*. Nashville: Abingdon Press, 1994.

Seitz, Christopher R. *The Elder Testament: Canon, Theology, Trinity*. Waco: Baylor University Press, 2018.

_____. "The Trinity in the Old Testament." Pages 28–40 in *The Oxford Handbook on the Trinity*. Edited by Gilles Emery and Matthew Levering. Oxford: Oxford University Press, 2011.

Seneca. *Moral Essays, Volume III: De Beneficiis*. Translated by John W. Basore. LCL. Cambridge: Harvard University Press, 1935.

Senior, Donald, and Daniel J. Harrington. *1 Peter: Jude and Second Peter*. Collegeville: Liturgical Press, 2003.

Septuaginta. Rev. ed. Edited by Alfred Rahlfs and Robert Hanhart. Stuttgart: Deutsche Bibelgesellschaft, 2006.

Shank, Harold. "The Decalogue and Justice for Children: The Value and Vulnerability of Children." *Journal of Christian Studies* 2.1 (2023): 63–77.

_____. *Deuteronomy*. Searcy: Resource Publications, in press.

Shepherd, Tom. "The Narrative Function of Markan Intercalation." *NTS* 41.4 (1995): 522–40.

Simon, E., and H. Sarian. "Rauchopfer (2.c)." *Thesaurus Cultus et Rituum Antiquorum* 1:255. Los Angeles: J. Paul Getty Museum, 2004.

Smith, David I. *Everyday Christian Teaching: A Guide to Practicing Faith in the Classroom*. Grand Rapids: Eerdmans, 2025.

———. *On Christian Teaching: Practicing Faith in the Classroom*. Grand Rapids: Eerdmans, 2018.

Smith, David I., and James K. A. Smith. "Introduction: Practices, Faith, and Pedagogy." Pages 1–23 in *Teaching and Christian Practices: Reshaping Faith and Learning*. Edited by David I. Smith and James K. A. Smith. Grand Rapids: Eerdmans, 2011.

Smith, David I., Joonyong Um, and Claudia D. Beversluis. "The Scholarship of Teaching and Learning in a Christian Context." *Christian Higher Education* 13 (2014): 74–87.

Smith, James K. A. *You Are What You Love: The Spiritual Power of Habit*. Grand Rapids: Brazos, 2016.

Smith, Julien. *Christ the Ideal King: Cultural Context, Rhetorical Strategy, and the Power of the Divine Monarchy in Ephesians*. WUNT 313. Tübingen: Mohr Siebeck, 2011.

Smith, Mark S. *The Priestly Vision of Genesis 1*. Minneapolis: Fortress, 2010.

Sofroniew, Aledandra. *Household Gods: Private Devotion in Ancient Greece and Rome*. Los Angeles: The J. Paul Getty Museum, 2015.

Sommer, Benjamin D. *The Bodies of God and the World of Ancient Israel*. Cambridge: Cambridge University Press, 2010.

Spangenberg, Izak. "A Brief History of Belief in the Devil (950–70 CE)." *Studia Historiae Ecclesiasticae* 39 (2013): 213–30.

Spencer, F. Scott. *Salty Wives, Spirited Mothers, and Savvy Widows: Capable Women of Purpose and Persistence in Luke's Gospel*. Grand Rapids: Eerdmans, 2012.

Stein, Robert H. *Luke*. Nashville: Broadman Press, 1992.

———. *Mark*. BECNT. Grand Rapids: Baker Academic, 2008.

Stendahl, Krister. "The Apostle Paul and the Introspective Conscience of the West," *HTR* 56 (1963): 199–215.

Stone, Barton W. "Justification." *Christian Messenger* 13 (1843): 9–12.

Strawn, Brent A. "And These Three are One: A Trinitarian Critique of Christological Approaches to the Old Testament." Pages 167–188 in *The Incomparable God: Readings in Biblical Theology*. Edited by Collin Cornell and M. Justin Walker. Grand Rapids: Eerdmans, 2023.

Strelan, Rick. *Paul, Artemis, and the Jews in Ephesus*. New York: de Gruyter, 2014.

Stubbersfield, Edgar. *Women in Ministry: Paul's Advice to Timothy in Its Historical Setting*. Eugene: Wipf & Stock, 2022.

Stuhlmacher, Peter. "The Pauline Gospel." Pages 149–72 in *The Gospel and the Gospels*. Edited by Peter Stuhlmacher. Grand Rapids: Eerdmans, 1991.

Supplementum Epigraphicum Graecum. Leiden: A. W. Sijthoff, 1923–.

Taasob, Razieh. "Development of Greek Religious Iconography in Early Kushan Coinage: Adaptation, Integration and Transformation." *Studia Hercynia* 27.1 (2023): 178–88.

Takeuchi, Kumiko. "Interpretations of Genesis 1,26-27: A Case of 'The Emperor's New Clothes'?" *SJOT* (2025): 1–24.

Talbert, Charles H. *Literary Patterns, Theological Themes, and the Genre of Luke-Acts*. SBLMS. Missoula: Scholars, 1974.

———. *Reading John: A Literary and Theological Commentary on the Fourth Gospel and the Johannine Epistles*. New York: Crossroad, 1992.

Talbert, Charles H., and J. H. Hayes. "A Theology of Sea Storms in Acts." Pages 267–83 in *Luke's Narrative Claim upon Israel's Legacy*. Vol. 1 of *Jesus and the Heritage of Israel*. Edited by David Moessner. Harrisburg: Trinity Press International, 1999.

Tan, Rosalind, Nativity Petallar, and Lucy Hefford. *God's Heart for Children*. Carlisle: Langham Global Library, 2022.

Tannehill, Robert C. *The Acts of the Apostles*. Vol. 2 in *The Narrative Unity of Luke-Acts: A Literary Interpretation*. Minneapolis: Fortress, 1990.

Thompson, James. "The Submission of Wives in 1 Peter." Pages 377–92 in *Essays on Women in Earliest Christianity, Volume I*. Edited by Carroll D. Osburn. Joplin: College Press, 1993.

Thompson, Marianne Meye. *John: A Commentary*. NTL. Louisville: Westminster John Knox, 2015.

Thucydides. *History of the Peloponnesian War*. Translated by C. F. Smith. LCL. Cambridge: Harvard University, 1910.

Thuren, Lauri. "1 Peter and the Lion." Pages 142–55 in *Evil and the Devil*. Edited by Ida Frohlich and Erkki Koskenniemi. London: Bloomsbury T&T Clark, 2013.

Tigay, Jeffrey. *Deuteronomy*. The JPS Torah Commentary. Philadelphia: Jewish Publication Society, 1996.

Towner, Philip H. "1–2 Timothy and Titus." Pages 891–918 in *Commentary on the New Testament Use of the Old Testament*. Edited by G. K. Beale and D. A. Carson. Grand Rapids: Baker Academic, 2007.

Trimm, Charlie. *The Destruction of the Canaanites*. Grand Rapids: Eerdmans, 2022.

Troftgruben, Troy M. "Slow Sailing in Acts: Suspense in the Final Sea Journey (Acts 27:1–28:15)." *JBL* 136 (2017): 949–68.

Tucker, Paavo N. "Why Love Matters for Justice: Political Emotions Between Narrative and Law in the Holiness Code." Pages 83–104 in *Biblical Ethics:*

Tensions Between Justice and Mercy, Law and Love. Edited by Markus Zehnder and Peter Wick. Gorgias Biblical Studies 70. Piscataway: Gorgias, 2019.

Urga, Abeneazer G. "The Exhortation to the Husbands and Its Significance in the Conversation About the Household Codes: 1 Peter 3:7." *Priscilla Papers* 38.4 (2024), available at https://www.cbeinternational.org/resource/the-exhortation-to-the-husbands-and-its-significance-in-the-conversation-about-the-household-codes-1-peter-37/.

van der Toorn, Karel. *Scribal Culture and the Making of the Hebrew Bible*. Cambridge: Harvard University, 2007.

Van Ooteghem, Liselotte. "What Do We Mean by Hospitality in Education?" *Social Sciences and Education Research Review* 9 (2022): 17–32.

von Rad, Gerhard. "The Theological Problem of the O.T. Doctrine of Creation." Translated E. W. T. Dicken. Pages 53–64 in *Creation in the Old Testament*. Edited by Bernhard W. Anderson. IRT 6. Philadelphia: Fortress, 1984.

Vaughan, Joy L. *Phenomenal Phenomena: Biblical and Multicultural Accounts of Spirits and Exorcism*. Waco: Baylor University Press, 2023.

Veyne, Paul. *Bread and Circuses: Historical Sociology and Political Pluralism*. New York: Penguin Press, 1990.

Via, E. Jane. "Women, the Discipleship of Service, and the Early Christian Ritual Meal in the Gospel of Luke." *Saint Luke's Journal of Theology* 29 (1985): 37–60.

von Harnack, Adolf. *Constitution & Law of the Church in the First Two Centuries*. Edited by H. D. A. Major. Translated by F. L. Pogson. New York: Williams & Norgate, 1910.

Wall, Robert W. "The Acts of the Apostles: Introduction, Commentary, and Reflections." Pages 3–368 in Vol. 4 of *NIB*. 12 vols. Nashville: Abingdon, 2002.

Walton, John H. *The Lost World of Genesis One: Ancient Cosmology and the Origins of Debate*. Downers Grove: InterVarsity Academic, 2009.

Wankel, Hermann, et al. *Die Inschriften von Ephesos*. Inschriften griechischer Städte aus Kleinasien I 11.1–17.4. Bonn: Rudolf Habelt, 1979–1984.

Watson, Duane Frederick, and Terrance Callan. *First and Second Peter*. Grand Rapids: Baker Academic, 2012.

Weinfeld, Moshe. "The Loyalty Oath in the Ancient Near East." *UF* 8 (1976): 379–414.

Whiston, William, trans. *The Works of Josephus*. Peabody: Hendrickson, 1987.

Whybray, R. Norman. *Introduction to the Pentateuch*. Grand Rapids: Eerdmans, 1995.

Williams, Travis B. "Suffering from a Critical Oversight: The Persecutions of I Peter within Modern Scholarship." *CurBR* 10 (2012): 275–92.

Wilkin, Robert N. "Christians Will be Judged according to their Works at the Rewards Judgment, but not at the Final Judgment." Pages 71–98 in *Four Views on the Role of Works at the Final Judgment*. Edited by Alan P. Stanley. Grand Rapids: Zondervan, 2013.

Winter, Bruce W. "The 'New Roman Wife' and 1 Timothy 2:9–15: The Search for a *Sitz im Leben*." *TynBul* 51.2 (2000): 285–94.

_____. *Roman Wives, Roman Widows*. Grand Rapids: Eerdmans, 2003.

Witherington, Ben. *The Acts of the Apostles: A Socio-Rhetorical Commentary*. Grand Rapids: Eerdmans, 1998.

_____. *Women in the Earliest Churches*. SNTSMS 59. New York: Cambridge University Press, 1988.

_____. *Women in the Ministry of Jesus: A Study of Jesus' Attitudes to Women and Their Roles as Reflected in His Earthly Life*. SNTSMS 51. New York: Cambridge University Press, 1984.

Witherington, Ben, and Ann Witherington. *Women and the Genesis of Christianity*. New York: Cambridge University Press, 1990.

Wolter, Michael. *Paul: An Outline of His Theology*. Translated by Robert L. Brawley. Waco: Baylor University, 2015.

Wright, N. T. *Acts for Everyone: Part 2, Chapters 13–28*. London: SPCK, 2008.

_____. *Jesus and the Victory of God*. Vol. 2 of *Christian Origins and the Question of God*. Minneapolis: Fortress, 1996.

_____. *Justification: God's Plan & Paul's Vision*. Downers Grove: InterVarsity Academic, 2009.

_____. *The New Testament and the People of God*. Vol. 1 of *Christian Origins and the Question of God*. Minneapolis: Fortress, 1992.

_____. *Paul and the Faithfulness of God*. Christian Origins and the Question of God, vol. 4. Minneapolis: Fortress Press, 2013.

Wright, N. T., and J. Christiaan Beker. *Paul: Narrative or Apocalyptic*. Minneapolis: Fortress, 2023.

Yarbro Collins, Adela. *Mark: A Commentary*. Edited by Harold W. Attridge. Hermeneia. Minneapolis: Fortress, 2007.

Yarbro Collins, Adela, and John J. Collins. *King and Messiah as Son of God: Divine, Human, and Angelic Messianic Figures in Biblical and Related Literature*. Grand Rapids: Eerdmans, 2008.

Yonge, C.D., trans. *The Works of Philo*. Peabody: Hendrickson, 1993.

Zaccagnino, Cristiana. *Il Thymiaterion nel Mondo Greco*. Rome: L'Erma di Bretschneider, 1998.

Author Index

Abernathy, C. David, 129, 225

Achtemeier, Paul J., 127, 131, 225

Addison, Steve, 62, 225

Alexander, Hanan A., 225

Alleman, Nathan F., 194, 232

Allen, Amy, 182, 225

Allen, C. Leonard, 45, 225

Allen, Holly, 186, 225

Amanze, James N., 132, 225

Andersen, Francis, 23, 225

Aristotle, 67, 68, 71, 108, 225

Arnold, Bill T., 37, 47, 225

Arnold, Clinton E., 151, 225

Austin, Michel, 70, 225

Bäbler, Balbina, 203, 225

Balch, David L., 142, 225

Barclay, John M. G., 174, 175, 225

Bardsley, Mary Ellen, 195, 234

Barrett, C. K., 85, 226

Bartchy, S. Scott., 140, 226

Bates, Matthew, 38, 50, 165, 171, 173, 178, 226

Batten, Alicia, 75, 226

Bauckham, Richard, 89, 103, 104, 107, 117, 226

Bauer, David R., x, 83, 88, 226

Baugh, S. M., 150, 154, 226

Beasley-Murray, George R., 110, 112, 115, 226

Beavis, Mary Ann., 31, 32, 34, 39, 226

Beker, J. Christiaan., 226

Belleville, Linda L., 154, 159, 160, 226

Bernier, Jonathan, 10, 226

Betz, Hans Dieter, 16, 227

Beversluis, Claudia D., 193, 242

Bialostocki, Jan, 212, 227

Bigg, Charles, 127, 227

Black, Allen, i, iii, iv, x, 1, 3, 5, 6, 9, 27, 32, 33, 39, 41, 53, 54, 55, 56, 57, 58, 65, 79, 107, 121, 131, 135, 149, 163, 182, 189, 191, 193, 201, 203, 219, 227

Black, C. Clifton, 29, 31, 131, 227, 235

Black, Mark, ix, 2, 6, 89, 131, 135, 227

Blümel, Wolfgang, 227

Bock, Darrell L., 65, 74, 76, 227

Bond, Helen K., 31, 32, 37, 38, 227

Booms, Dirk, 222, 227

Bovon, François, 76, 227

Bradley, Arnold, 123, 234

Bridges Johns, Cheryl, 227

Briggs, Richard S., 196, 199, 227

Brosend, Annette, 203, 227

Brouskari, Maria S., 211, 212, 227

Brown, Jeannine K., x, 31, 227

Brown, Raymond E., 10, 12, 111, 182, 227, 238

Bruce, F. F., 16, 152, 227

Brueggemann, Walter, 196, 197, 228

Bunge, Marcia J., 182, 183, 228

Burnett, D. Clint., ix, 5, 9, 19, 22, 228

Burridge, Richard A., 108, 228

Calvin, John, 46, 163, 164, 172, 228

Camery-Hoggart, Jerry, 27, 228

Campbell, Alexander, 6, 163, 166, 167, 168, 173, 179, 228

Carey, Holly J., 60, 61, 228

Carson, D. A., 12, 122, 159, 228, 243

Carter, Warren, 80, 84, 228

Chan, Michael J., 199, 228

Chance, J. Bradley, 84, 85, 87, 195, 228, 240

Chilton, Bruce, 91, 104, 226, 228

Christensen, Duane, 183, 228

Cicero, 108, 156, 206, 228

Clark Kroeger, Catherine, 153, 229

Clark Kroeger, Richard, 153, 229

Cockle, Theodore F., 193, 232

Cohick, Lynn H., 229

Collins, John J., 20, 23, 94, 229, 245

Conzelmann, Hans, 12, 18, 229

Cortina, Kai S., 195, 240

Cranfield, C. E. B., 15, 229

Crook, Z. A., 75, 229

Cukrowski, Kenneth L., 80, 229

Culpepper, R. Alan., 33, 113, 229

D'Angelo, Mary Rose, 53, 229

Dale, Moyra, 46, 58, 59, 170, 229, 230

Danker, Frederick W., x, 65, 66, 69, 70, 76, 229

Davids, Peter H., 125, 130, 229, 231

Davidson, Richard, 198, 229

Davies, Jamie, 16, 230

Davies, W. D., 43, 44, 45, 46, 48, 50, 170, 230

Davina, SOH Hui Leng, 194, 230

Day, John, 198, 230

de Boer, Martinus C., 16, 230

Decker, Rodney J., 34, 230

Dee, Leo, 189, 191, 237

deLuse, Stephanie, 195, 230

Dempsey, Carol J., 49, 230

deSilva, David Arthur, 33, 39, 230

Dinkler, Michal Beth, 145, 230

Dodd, C. H., 11, 12, 13, 230

Donahue, John R., 36, 37, 38, 39, 230

Dunn, James D. G., 16, 89, 173, 230

Edwards, James R., 31, 231

Elliott, John H., 122, 123, 125, 128, 231

Elsner, Jas, 208, 231

Embudo, Lora Angeline B., 53, 56, 57, 231

Eusebius, 13, 122, 231

Fedler, Kyle D., 63, 231

Fee, Gordon D., 18, 231

Feldmeier, Reinhard, 45, 125, 231

Ferguson, Everett, 29, 42, 231

Author Index

Fewster, Gregory P., 12, 239

Fiorenza, Elisabeth Schüssler, 55, 231

Firth, David, 185, 231

Fitzmyer, Joseph A., 11, 13, 15, 20, 231

Foote, Chandra J., 195, 234

Forbes, Greg W., 124, 129, 231

France, R. T., 33, 49, 231

Fretheim, Terence E., 196, 232

Fuller, Michael E., 89, 232

Gaifman, Milette, 216, 232

Gardner, Gregg, 71, 232

Gaventa, Beverly, 16, 232

Geldenhuys, Norval, 76, 232

George, Timothy, 163, 232

Glahn, Sandra L., 151, 152, 156, 157, 159, 232

Glanzer, Perry L., 193, 194, 232, 240

Goldingay, John, 37, 232

Gonzalez, Justo L., 10, 232

Goodacre, Mark, 33, 232

Goodrich, John K., 16, 232

Gorman, Michael J., 13, 150, 232

Gritz, Sharon Hodgin, 149, 150, 151, 232

Grudem, Wayne A., 122, 232

Gundry, Robert H., 45, 232

Gurtner, Daniel M., 41, 232

Guthrie, Donald, 30, 232

Haenchen, Ernst, 82, 83, 233

Harkness, Allan, 193, 233

Harrington, Bobby, 60, 233, 239

Harrington, Daniel J., 36, 37, 38, 39, 131, 230, 233, 241

Harvey, A. E., 159, 233

Hauerwas, Stanley, 136, 233

Hayes, J. H., 79, 243

Hays, Richard B., 28, 30, 233

Hefford, Lucy, 192, 243

Heiser, Michael S., 50, 233

Hendel, Ronald, 198, 233

Hendrix, Holland, 66, 75, 233

Hengel, Martin, 11, 116, 233

Hicks, John Mark, ix, 6, 85, 135, 233

Holladay, Carl R., 5, 54, 73, 79, 227, 233

Hölscher, Tonio, 203, 204, 206, 207, 212, 214, 233

Horrell, David G., 122, 123, 126, 234

Hurtado, Larry W., 22, 234

Hutson, Christopher R., 157, 158, 161, 234

Iannarelli, Barbara A., 195, 234

Irenaeus, 121, 152, 234

Jenkins, Ian, 212, 234

Jennings, Willie James, 81, 83, 87, 234

Jervell, Jacob, 56, 57, 89, 234

Jessica Martin, Jessica, 193, 232

Jewett, Robert, 15, 234

Jipp, Joshua W., 31, 80, 82, 84, 234

Jobes, Karen, 122, 127, 142, 146, 234

Johnson, B. W., 167, 234

Johnson, Luke Timothy, 12, 76, 79, 80, 85, 86, 88, 167, 234

Josephus, 71, 100, 150, 216, 219, 234, 244

Joubert, Stephan J., 66, 67, 68, 69, 234

Karris, Robert J., 58, 63, 234

Kee, Min Suc, 50, 234

Keener, Craig S., 33, 34, 35, 38, 43, 50, 80, 81, 82, 83, 84, 86, 87, 88, 89, 207, 235

Kelly, J. N. D., 131, 235

Kemkes, Martin, 204, 227

Kennedy, George A., 108, 109, 118, 235

Kern, Otto, 235

Kleiner, Diana E. E., 217, 218, 235

Knight, George W., 158, 235

Koperski, Veronica, 56, 58, 235

Kotsifou, Chrysi, 215, 235

Kristof, Nicholas, 192, 235

Lapsley, Jacqueline E., 47, 235

Larkin, William J., Jr., 235

Levenson, Jon D., 48, 235

Levine, Amy-Jill, 74, 76, 235

Levine, Lee, 91, 235

Lifshitz, B., 71, 235

Lim, Timothy H., 23, 236

Longenecker, Richard N., 15, 83, 236

Lukacs, John, 10, 236

Lull, David J., 73, 236

Luther, Martin, 19, 20, 50, 51, 163, 172, 236

Lynch, Matthew, 49, 236

Manson, T. W., 170, 236

Marcus, Joel, 29, 31, 32, 206, 236

Marsden, George M., 193, 236

Marshall, I. Howard, 36, 65, 76, 78, 160, 236

Martyn, J. Louis, 16, 236

Matthews, Shelly, 65, 74, 76, 240

Mbiti, John S., 124, 126, 127, 131, 236

McConville, J. Gordon, iv

McGinn, Thomas A. J., 157, 236

Menéndez Antuña, Luis, 58, 59, 236

Metzger, Bruce M., 29, 149, 158, 236, 238

Michaels, J. Ramsey, 124, 126, 127, 129, 131, 236

Michie, Donald, 30, 240

Middleton, J. Richard, 198, 237

Miller, Amanda C., 237

Miller, Kevin F., 195, 240

Miller, Patrick, 182, 237

Min, Inah, 195, 240

Moberly, Walter, 49, 237

Moessner, David P., 89, 237

Moloney, Francis J., 31, 34, 237

Moo, Douglas J., 12, 22, 122, 228, 237

Morales, L. Michael, 198, 237

Moran, William L., 47, 237

Morris, Leon, 65, 74, 237

Moscicke, Hans, 127, 237

Moxnes, Halvor, 75, 76, 237

Muecke, D. C., 28, 237
Neril, Yonatan, 189, 191, 237
Neudecker, Richard, 209, 237
Nolland, John, 60, 74, 78, 237
Novenson, Matthew V., 17, 22, 237
Noy, David, 71, 239
Nussbaum, Martha C., 47, 238
Oberleitner, Wolfgang, 205, 238
Oliver, Isaac W., 89, 238
Olson, Kelly, 156, 238
Onongha, Kelvin, 126, 127, 128, 130, 132, 238
Oster, Richard E., Jr., ix, 6, 149, 150, 158, 203, 204, 219, 238
Outler, Albert C., 197, 238
Padgett, Alan G., 138, 238
Parker, Judith, 182, 183, 184, 238
Paschke, Boris A., 128, 238
Paulsen, Judith, 62, 238
Pausanias, 150, 238
Perkins, Pheme, 32, 238
Pervo, Richard I., 80, 86, 238
Petallar, Nativity, 192, 243
Philsy, Sr., 58, 239
Plato, 208, 209, 239
Pliny, 151, 156, 239
Plutarch, 108, 142, 239
Poirier, John C., 33, 239
Pope-Levison, Priscilla, 62, 239
Porter, Stanley E., x, 12, 83, 239

Powell, Mark Allan, 10, 12, 42, 43, 44, 49, 239
Praeder, Susan Marie, 80, 83, 84, 85, 239
Provan, Iain, 196, 239
Pulleyn, Simon, 207, 215, 239
Putman, Jim, 60, 239
Rajak, Tessa, 67, 69, 70, 71, 72, 74, 239
Rapske, Brian M., 80, 82, 239
Ream, Todd C., 193, 240
Reid, Barbara E., 22, 55, 56, 57, 58, 65, 74, 76, 240
Resseguie, James L., 28, 29, 240
Rhoads, David, 30, 240
Richards, E. Randolph, 12, 240
Richter Reimer, Ivoni, 55, 240
Richter, Gisela M. A., 209, 210, 240
Roberts, J. J. M., 240
Robertson, Jesse E., ix, 6, 107, 109, 114, 240
Robinson, John A., 10, 240
Romana, Victoria, 203, 233
Rowe, C. Kavin, 51
Rudolph, David, 89, 240
Runesson, Anders, 91, 240
Sacks, Jonathan, 196, 240
Samudra, Preeti G., 195, 240
Sarian, H., 206, 242
Schaberg, Jane, 53, 55, 56, 241
Scheffler, Eben, 57, 241
Scherf, Johannes, 203, 207, 241

Scherrer, Peter, 205, 216, 241

Schnabel, Eckhard J., 80, 83, 84, 85, 241

Schreiner, Patrick, 79, 81, 179, 241

Schreiner, Thomas R., 81, 124, 150, 176, 179, 226, 241

Schüle, Andreas, 196, 241

Seim, Turid Karlsen, 54, 56, 57, 241

Seitz, Christopher R., 50, 51, 241

Seneca, 66, 69, 241

Senior, Donald, 131, 241

Shank, Harold, ix, 6, 181, 189, 241

Shepherd, Tom, 31, 242

Simon, E., 206, 242

Smith, David I., 12, 193, 194, 195, 196, 197, 199, 242, 243

Smith, James K. A., 49, 194, 242

Smith, Julien, 111, 242

Smith, Mark S., 242

Sofroniew, Aledandra, 215, 242

Sommer, Benjamin D., 51, 242

Spangenberg, Izak, 125, 242

Spencer, F. Scott, 58, 59, 242

Spieckermann, Hermann, 45, 231

Stein, Robert H., 31, 32, 33, 34, 61, 65, 76, 242

Stendahl, Krister, 173, 242

Stone, Barton W., 6, 163, 166, 167, 168, 179, 242

Strawn, Brent A., 51, 199, 228, 242

Strelan, Rick, 150, 153, 155, 242

Stubbersfield, Edgar, 151, 154, 155, 242

Stuhlmacher, Peter, 13, 243

Swick, Danny, 45, 225

Taasob, Razieh, 204, 243

Takeuchi, Kumiko, 198, 243

Talbert, Charles H., 79, 80, 81, 88, 107, 115, 116, 117, 243

Tan, Rosalind, 192, 243

Tannehill, Robert C., 82, 84, 86, 243

Thompson, James, 142, 243

Thompson, Marianne Meye, 85, 107, 110, 112, 113, 115, 116, 226, 243

Thucydides, 11, 12, 243

Tigay, Jeffrey, 183, 184, 189, 243

Towner, Philip H., 159, 243

Trimm, Charlie, 188, 243

Troftgruben, Troy M., 87, 243

Tucker, Paavo N., 41, 48, 243

Um, Joonyong, 193, 242

Urga, Abeneazer G., 146, 244

van der Toorn, Karel, 12, 244

Van Ooteghem, Liselotte, 194, 244

Vaughan, Joy L., 35, 244

Veyne, Paul, 67, 68, 69, 244

Via, E. Jane, 58, 244

von Harnack, Adolf, 13, 20, 244

Von Rad, Gerhard, 197, 244

Wall, Robert W., 86, 244

Walton, John H., 198, 244

Wankel, Hermann, 244

Watson, Duane Frederick, 123, 244

Weinfeld, Moshe, 47, 244

Whybray, R. Norman, 196, 244

Wilkin, Robert N., 170, 245

Williams, Travis B., 122, 123, 234, 244

Williamson, Alicia, ix, 53, 60, 233

Williamson, Carl, ix, 5, 53, 60, 233

Willimon, William H., 136, 233

Willitts, Joel, 89, 240

Winter, Bruce W., 157, 159, 245

Witherington, Ann, 59, 245

Witherington, Ben, 56, 58, 59, 74, 76, 104, 226, 235, 245

Wolter, Michael, 13, 245

Wright, N. T., 22, 30, 86, 89, 173, 174, 175, 176, 245

Wudunn, Sheryl, 192, 235

Yamauchi, Edwin, 91, 228

Yarbro Collins, Adela, 20, 33, 35, 36, 245

Zaccagnino, Cristiana, 212, 245

Subject Index

Abraham, 20, 44, 45, 51, 54, 57, 94, 97, 107, 118, 136, 144, 145, 147, 168, 171–3, 196, 198, 230

Apocalyptic, 5, 9, 14, 16, 23–5, 30, 33, 126

Apostle, 2, 9, 11-19, 21, 24, 25, 55-7, 59, 60, 79, 82, 83, 86, 89, 96, 97, 100, 122, 126, 159, 178, 220, 229, 231, 233, 234, 236, 240, 241, 243–5

Baptism, 17–9, 30, 91–3, 158, 164, 165, 167, 168, 173

Benefaction, 5, 59, 66–77

Caesar, 42, 43, 82, 139, 142

Children, 4, 6, 43, 47, 63, 108, 111, 117, 121, 125, 126, 132, 135, 142, 144, 147, 151, 153, 157, 160, 171, 179, 181–92, 196, 215

Christ, ix, 2, 3, 5, 6, 11, 17, 19, 22, 23, 29, 30, 35, 49, 51, 58, 61, 62, 79, 88, 90, 93, 108, 111, 122, 123, 125, 127–30, 136, 138, 143, 147, 152, 153, 156, 159, 163–7, 169–71, 173–9, 193, 195, 203, 219, 228, 233, 238, 242

Church , 2, 3, 5, 6, 9, 13, 15, 21, 34, 39, 52–9, 61, 62, 89, 90, 92–105, 119, 121, 123, 135, 149, 150, 153, 154, 155, 159, 161, 163, 174, 182, 191

Ekklesia, 90, 92

Cross, 28, 98, 114, 116, 118, 129

Crucifixion, 6, 29, 30, 60, 81, 107, 113–15, 118, 220

David, 6, 14, 17, 21, 22, 49, 50, 89, 94, 103, 116, 117, 119, 193, 220, 221

Dead Sea Scrolls, 21–4, 230

Death, 5, 10, 12, 17, 19, 20, 28–30, 32, 37–40, 45, 75, 81, 93, 97, 99, 100, 105, 107–12, 114, 116–9, 128, 129, 131, 139, 158, 172, 176, 178, 188, 215, 217

Demon, 32, 35, 98, 127, 129, 132, 133, 172

Devil, see *Satan*

Diaspora, 91, 101, 122, 136

Disciple, 1, 5, 10, 12, 29, 36–8, 40–2, 44, 48, 54–6, 58, 59, 60–3, 76, 87, 89, 92, 93, 97, 99, 108, 110–2, 116–8, 135, 136, 147, 154, 171, 178, 179

Discipleship, 5, 39, 40, 53, 55, 60, 62, 63, 107, 191

Elders, 66, 74, 75–8, 88, 92, 93, 103, 183, 189

Elijah, 45, 94

Emperor, see *Caesar*

Ephesus, 6, 149–53, 155, 159, 160, 204–6, 216, 221, 222, 226, 232, 238, 241, 243

Ephesian, 6, 88, 150, 155, 157, 159, 160, 161, 203–9, 212–5, 219, 222

Eschatology, 6, 9, 14, 19, 20, 24, 25, 35, 44, 45, 56, 90, 93, 94, 96, 97, 100, 103, 105, 124, 169, 178, 179

Eucharist/Last Supper, 85, 93, 96

Faith, 3–6, 11, 15, 17, 20, 25, 36–8, 40, 49, 65, 66, 76, 77, 78, 84, 85, 88,

Subject Index

89, 91, 97, 100, 121–3, 127–32, 135, 136, 138, 141–4, 154, 163–8, 170–9, 182, 186–92, 194, 196, 197

Faithfulness, see *faith*

Family, 2, 33, 34, 94, 190

Father, 48, 51, 63, 96, 110–2, 114, 117, 118, 131, 169, 170, 178, 179

Forgiveness, 39, 76, 93, 95, 167, 168, 174, 178, 179

Gentile, 24, 76, 92, 94, 98, 100–5, 220

Glory, 6, 68, 70, 99, 107, 110, 117–9, 138, 168, 169, 174

Gospel, 5, 9–26, 29, 53–7, 60–3, 79, 81, 87, 88, 91, 103, 125, 138–40, 142–5, 166, 175, 177

Gospels, x, 2–4, 9–13, 18, 28–32, 38, 45, 46, 48, 60, 107, 108, 111, 138, 153, 154, 174, 219, 220, 227, 228, 233–5, 239, 243

Herodians, 41, 42, 49

Holy Spirit, 14–6, 18, 19, 22, 24, 26, 34, 50–2, 56, 57, 62, 79, 81, 82, 87–9, 93, 95–7, 101–3, 129, 131, 164–8, 174–7, 179, 230

Household, 61, 111, 122, 137, 138, 142, 143, 146, 206, 244

House, 229

Husbands, 122, 125, 135, 138, 142–6, 154, 244

Irony, 5, 28–31, 34–6, 39, 107, 110, 111, 113, 114, 221

Isaac, 44, 45, 51, 97, 118, 171

Israel, 1, 5, 6, 9, 14–6, 20–3, 25, 26, 30, 39, 41, 42, 44, 47–9, 51, 57, 65, 78–90, 93–7, 99–105, 113, 173, 183, 187–90, 196, 197, 226, 232, 237, 238, 242, 243

Jacob, 44, 45, 51, 97, 118

Jerusalem, 32, 39, 42, 43, 53, 62, 79, 81–83, 88, 91, 92, 94, 95, 100–4, 110, 117, 155, 189, 217, 220, 221, 225, 238

Jesus, x, 5, 6, 9–11, 14–24, 26, 28–46, 48–63, 65, 72–9, 81–90, 92–105, 107–19, 122, 125, 127, 131, 135, 136, 139, 141–3, 145, 147, 151, 153, 154, 158, 161, 164, 167–70, 172–5, 178, 179, 185, 191, 195, 207, 220, 221, 226, 227, 229, 232, 233, 235–7, 243, 245

Jewish, see *Second Temple Judaism*

Judaism, see *Second Temple Judaism*

Judgment, 30, 82, 96, 103, 114, 116, 118, 167, 169, 170, 174, 177, 179, 219, 222

Judge, 95, 112, 114, 137, 169, 174, 177, 178

Kingdom of God, 5, 21, 30, 33, 38, 43–5, 53, 55–7, 60–5, 72, 73, 75–9, 84, 88–90, 94–8, 101–5, 113, 126, 146, 154, 168, 177, 193, 195

Law, 6, 32, 43, 46, 48, 49, 91, 100, 104, 112, 122, 154, 159, 163, 166, 167, 172–5, 183, 184, 186, 187, 190, 191, 204, 215

Lord, 15, 16, 18–20, 22–4, 27, 28, 36, 39, 41–4, 46–8, 50, 51, 79, 83, 85, 89, 93, 94, 96, 99–101, 103, 112, 116, 122–4, 129, 132, 133, 139, 142, 144, 147, 150, 166–9, 171, 174, 175, 177, 178, 181, 183, 185–8, 190, 192, 221, 232, 234

Love, 1, 3, 39, 43, 46–9, 63, 68, 74, 76, 77, 89, 96, 98, 107, 111, 114, 116–8, 121, 130, 131, 135, 147, 163–6, 171, 174, 177, 178, 185, 188, 190

Messiah, 5, 6, 9, 10, 14–27, 29, 30, 38, 40, 49, 50–2, 57, 89, 90, 92–100, 102, 103, 105, 108, 111, 139, 141, 158, 161, 169, 173, 174, 176, 227, 238, 246

Ministry, 4–6, 9, 10, 29, 30, 33, 34, 38, 39, 44, 53–5, 57, 58, 61–3, 98, 135, 191

Moses, 22, 44, 45, 49, 91, 94, 97, 99, 100, 103, 105, 166, 167, 172, 173, 181, 183–9, 192

Obedience, 15, 24, 25, 47, 48, 138, 139, 144, 145, 164, 167, 168, 170, 171, 172, 175, 176, 179, 182, 186, 190, 191

Pentecost, 5, 56, 90, 93, 95, 97, 101, 102

Peter, 2, 6, 18, 31, 32, 37–40, 54, 93–7, 100–3, 111, 112, 121–33, 135–47, 155, 174, 178, 225–7, 229–35, 237, 241–3, 245

Pharisees, 32, 35, 41, 42, 46, 49, 72, 100, 103, 112

Pilate, 29, 100, 112–6, 118

Poor, The, 58, 72, 73, 77, 96, 190

Prophecy, 4, 21–3, 54–8, 82, 88, 95, 98, 101, 102, 209, 227

Prophet, 21, 23, 48, 49, 94, 96–8, 125, 196, 230

Reformation, 20, 163, 164, 171, 172, 180

Resurrection, 5, 10, 14, 15, 17–20, 22, 30, 35, 39, 43–5, 60, 61, 81, 96–8, 118, 131, 141, 152, 168, 169, 174

Rhetoric, 6, 33, 37, 46, 47, 55, 56, 62, 109, 121, 123, 128, 132

Rome, 1, 15, 39, 43, 67, 79, 81–3, 87, 88, 96, 122, 128, 136, 149, 157, 178, 204, 207, 212, 215, 217–9, 222, 234, 236, 240, 242, 246

Sadducees, 41–4, 46, 49

Salvation, 6, 16, 19, 25, 26, 28, 29, 33, 37, 40, 48, 56, 76, 78, 81, 83–8, 95, 96, 100, 103, 115, 141, 145, 149, 157, 158, 165, 166, 168, 170, 171, 174–9, 186, 197, 201

Satan, 33–6, 125, 126, 127

Saul/Paul, x, 5, 6, 9, 12–26, 28, 56, 57, 61, 62, 67–9, 79–89, 92, 93, 96, 98–103, 123, 126, 131, 138, 144, 145, 149–61, 163, 167, 168, 171–5, 177–9, 207, 225, 226, 229–37, 239, 240, 242–4

Scripture, 3, 5, 9, 10, 14, 15, 17, 20, 23–6, 28, 30, 31, 44, 46, 49, 51, 52, 54, 59, 61, 84, 85, 90–2, 103, 104, 116–8, 126, 143, 159, 161, 191, 193, 195–7, 200, 203, 226, 227, 233, 234, 237

Second Temple Judaism, 21–3, 125, 136

Slavery, 143, 190

Slave, 15, 108, 156, 188, 215

Son, 14–8, 20–2, 25, 26, 29, 51, 54, 57, 99, 108, 110, 115, 131, 169, 175, 177–9, 221, 246

Son of Man, 99, 110, 169

Subject Index

Submission, 6, 24, 137–45, 159, 167, 173, 230

Suffer, 98, 122, 130, 153, 229, 238, 245

Synagogue, 36, 66, 71–4, 91, 92, 102

Teacher, 1–4, 32, 41, 117, 151, 152, 182, 193, 194, 201

Temple, 38, 42, 43, 45, 90, 91, 100, 104, 150, 151, 198, 205, 209–12, 217, 227

Trinity, 5, 10, 11, 33, 49–52, 79, 89, 179, 226, 232, 233, 237, 240, 241, 243

Wives, 6, 122, 135, 138, 142, 143–6, 157, 159, 160, 183, 245

Women, 5, 6, 36–8, 40, 43, 53–63, 71, 76, 77, 113, 116, 135, 143–6, 149, 150, 151, 153–61, 182, 183, 186, 188, 206, 208

Worship, 2, 84, 90–3, 103, 105, 123, 132, 140, 142, 150–53, 158, 181, 186, 187, 205–8, 211, 212, 214, 215, 219

www.ingramcontent.com/pod-product-compliance
Lightning Source LLC
Chambersburg PA
CBHW080836230426
43665CB00021B/2858